MOLLY BROWN
Unraveling the Myth
3rd Edition

T0162248

MOLLY BROWN

Unraveling the Myth

3rd Edition

Kristen Iversen

BOWER HOUSE

DENVER

For Sean and Nathan

BowerHouseBooks.com

Cover design by Margaret McCullough
Cover photos courtesy Denver Public Library, Western History Department

Printed in Canada

Library of Congress Cataloging-in-Publication Data
Iversen, Kristen.
Molly Brown: unraveling the myth / Kristen Iversen: foreword by
Muffet Brown.
p. cm.
Includes bibliographical references and index.
ISBN 978-1-55566-468-8 (paper: alk. paper) 1. Brown, Margaret Tobin,
1867–1932. 2. Titanic (Steamship). 3. Women social reformers—United
States—Biography. 4. Denver
(Colo.)—Biography. I. Title.
CT275.B7656I94 1999
910'.91634—dc21   98-49266

10 9 8 7 6 5 4

Contents

Foreword

Kristen Iversen

NEVER HAS THERE BEEN a more important moment in American history for a story like the one of Margaret Tobin Brown. At a time when many Americans feel that the political, social, and cultural issues Margaret felt so strongly about—workers' rights, women's rights, a fair and just society for all, regardless of race, color, or creed—are experiencing new challenges and threats, it is wise to remind ourselves of her extraordinary voice and vision. And in the era of "fake news," Margaret was one of the first, but certainly not the last, to experience how a story can be twisted and altered to fit the agenda of politics or profit, particularly for strong women with talent and ambition who attempt to enter the political arena. Years before women even had the right to vote, Margaret Tobin Brown ran for office and made her voice known in the face of enormous opposition. She made a lasting impact, both in the United States and abroad. But history and Hollywood have sought to marginalize and erase her accomplishments as well as her profound political and cultural influence. Even her name was changed to fit the (false) story of a saloon girl and society hostess.

In the nearly twenty years since *Molly Brown: Unravelling the Myth* was first published, Molly Brown's place in the world has changed. For one thing, people now know she was never called "Molly"—that name was largely a Hollywood invention—and her real name, Margaret Tobin Brown, is taking its rightful place in history. And her story has righted itself as well. The legend of Molly Brown, which began even before Margaret's death in 1932, gathered color and detail over the years with every retelling, so that by the time I began my research in the 1990s, the myth had been largely accepted as fact. This is no longer the case. The book was warmly received, winning the Colorado Book Award in Biography and the Barbara Sudler Award for Nonfiction, leading to a number of film biographies, notably A & E Biography's *Molly Brown: An American Original,* and more recently *Molly Brown: Biography of a Changing Nation.* The much-loved myth of a high-kicking saloon girl—albeit fun and interesting to audiences—receded as the real story finally emerged. Margaret Tobin Brown was devoted to education, suffragism, feminism, the rights of children, the rights of miners, and social and political change. Now she can be understood and appreciated for who she really was: a progressive woman ahead of her time who believed she could make the world a better place for those less fortunate than herself. One aspect of the myth is true: born into impoverished circumstances, Margaret Tobin Brown truly did "pull herself up by her bootstraps." And then she set her sights on helping others, from Leadville to Denver to New York and beyond. When Margaret was awarded the French Legion of Honor in 1932, it was for a long list of humanitarian and philanthropic activities that spanned two continents and represented decades of work.

The life story of Margaret Tobin Brown, while extraordinary in many ways, is also a quintessential American story and reflects the ways in which America, as a nation, changed dramatically in the post-Civil War era. She is memorialized in two museums—one at her childhood home, the Molly Brown Birthplace and Museum in Hannibal, Missouri, and the other at her home in Denver. But when Historic Denver first purchased Margaret's home on Pennsylvania Avenue in 1971 and began restoration, there was little factual information available about who she actually was. What was "known" about her relied heavily on the hugely popular 1964 film, *The Unsinkable Molly Brown* (starring Debbie Reynolds), which had very little to do with Margaret's real life story. After the publication of this book, the museum began a dramatic effort to evaluate and change the way Margaret's story was told. The first step, funded by the National Endowment for the Humanities, was to bring scholars from around the country to read *Molly Brown: Unraveling the Myth*, consider the national and regional forces that shaped Margaret's life, and then guide the museum in its creation of a new tour script. The museum's sixty-five volunteers were retrained using this new, more historically accurate material, and a number of new educational programs resulted, including exhibits on Margaret's world travels, the Irish community in Colorado, and many others. The most ambitious interpretive project, also funded by the National Endowment for the Humanities, was the creation of a permanent exhibit, a documentary entitled *Molly Brown: Biography of a Changing Nation*, and a series of interactive learning stations to help set the context for the world in which

Margaret Brown lived. Now when visitors come to see the Molly Brown House Museum in Denver, they get a much more accurate sense of who Margaret Tobin Brown was, what she accomplished, and the political and social context of her remarkable life.

For me, one of the most delightful results of writing this book was bringing together many of Margaret Tobin Brown's descendants from around the country. Her great-grandchildren were generous in sharing their family's history and artifacts with me as I was doing my research, and they continue to support the efforts of the Molly Brown House Museum. Today, there is a great deal of information available about Margaret's life. The papers of the Brown family members are available at the Colorado Historical Society. A revival of the 1960 Broadway play, *The Unsinkable Molly Brown* (originally starring Tammy Grimes), opened with revised lyrics that more accurately represent Margaret's life. The Molly Brown House Museum continues to offer teacher-training workshops designed to address how biography can be used as a teaching tool for history teachers around the country—indeed, one of the great pleasures of my life has been receiving letters and emails from young students (particularly girls and young women) working on school projects about Margaret Brown. Thanks to the work of people like Andrea Malcomb, Stephanie McGuire, Leigh Grinstead, Annie Robb Levinksy, and all the historians, scholars, and volunteers involved with the Molly Brown House Museum, Margaret's story continues to find relevance in today's world.

Margaret Tobin Brown would have been thrilled to see that many of the changes she worked for are now generally part of the common fabric of everyday life: women in business and politics, an extensive juvenile court system and treatment facilities, day care centers, family planning and birth control, labor laws that protect workers, and greater race and gender equality in all aspects of American life. These were radical ideas in her lifetime—yet even today, these important and necessary steps face new and ongoing challenges that threaten their very existence. Now, perhaps more than ever, we need individuals with the character, resilience, and forward-thinking actions of Margaret Tobin Brown. What would Margaret be doing if she were alive today? I venture she'd be leading the country. She was a woman who set high standards and set her sights high, and she let few things stand in her way.

Kristen Iversen
Professor, University of Cincinnati
December 2017

Preface

THE LEGEND OF Molly Brown is an old story that has resurfaced once again in director James Cameron's film *Titanic*. The myth, however, has very little to do with the real Margaret Tobin Brown. She was indeed on the *Titanic*, but there most of the similarity ends. The reasons for the dissimilarities are both personal and political. The myth of Margaret as a bawdy, eccentric social outcast began with storyteller-historians such as Gene Fowler and Caroline Bancroft, who freely amplified, exaggerated, and created their own morality plays about what happened to Victorian-era women who didn't follow Victorian rules. Caroline Bancroft turned an article for a romance magazine into a best-selling tourist booklet, *The Unsinkable Mrs. Brown*, and a few years later coauthored *The Unsinkable Molly Brown Cookbook*. Gene Fowler, a wisecracking reporter for the *Denver Post* known for his ability to spice up a good story, dedicated a chapter of his novel *Timberline* to the "Unsinkable." These fantastic stories fed an eager public and played into well-established stereotypes of unconventional women—and no one bothered to check the facts. The legend culminated most spectacularly in the 1960 Broadway play starring Tammy Grimes and the 1964 Metro-Goldwyn-Mayer movie *The Unsinkable Molly Brown*, which launched the career of actress Debbie Reynolds. A few bad novels, lesser films, and made-for-television movies also happened along the way. Although the Brown family attempted from time to time to stem what they perceived to be a string of lies, the story—with its rags-to-riches drama and emphasis on how anyone, with enough gumption, can achieve the American dream—took on a life of its own.

Here in the West, we love our folk legends, and we're loath to give them up. But it's also appropriate to use the word "backlash" when you're talking about a woman who tried to run for both the House of Representatives and the Senate; a woman who traveled all over the world on her own, taking notes and publishing highly opinionated travel articles; a woman who didn't have much need for social convention but recognized enormous need for social change—and set about to effect it. The tawdry myth we have today of a burlesque woman who mustered enough courage to lead the others in her lifeboat in song speaks to her spirit, but it obscures the more interesting and significant aspects of her life. The life of Molly Brown has been turned into a stereotype that denies, and continues to deny, the historical significance of women in the West.

The distinction between myth and reality begins with the name. Margaret Tobin Brown was never called Molly Brown; the name is a Hollywood invention. Margaret was known as Maggie as a child and young woman; after that she was called Margaret or, more formally after her marriage, Mrs. J.J. Brown. Richard Morris, who wrote *The Unsinkable Molly Brown,* chose the name "Molly" because, he said, it was easier to sing. Molly it was, and Molly it's been ever since.

A brief overview of the legend begins with Molly's rescue as a baby from the Mississippi River by none other than Mark Twain. According to Gene Fowler in the fictitious chapter titled "The Unsinkable Mrs. Brown" in *Timberline,* a cyclone occasioned Molly's birth two months before the laws of nature warranted such an event. After the cyclone had destroyed their shanty, her father replaced it with a new one built of "scantlings and tin cans." This "high-spirited, bosomy girl" had very little public school education, and what she had didn't take very well. Molly was always too busy being a tomboy. Despite the fact that she could neither read nor write, she eventually obtained a job as a waitress at the Park Hotel in Hannibal, Missouri. One day young Molly overheard Mark Twain describing his adventures in the wild West, and she immediately decided to go to Leadville, Colorado. Not only was this trip her first time on a train, but she was so poor—according to Caroline Bancroft in the booklet she wrote for Colorado tourists—that she had to carry the food her mother had prepared for her in a cardboard shoebox. Once she arrived in Leadville, she found a job in a local saloon, and one lucky day met an entrepreneurial man named "Leadville Johnny." Depending upon the source, Molly was somewhere between thirteen and seventeen and Johnny, at thirty-seven, was, according to Gene Fowler, "as homely as a hippopotamus—although not so fat—unlettered, open-fisted, and had red hair. He seldom was in funds, but when luck infrequently came his way was foremost among the belly-up-to-the-bar boys. Homely or not, he had a way with the dance-hall girls." Molly overlooked his reputation and married him at the bottom of a mine shaft. At the wedding "buffet," whiskey was the main course.

One day Johnny came home from a long day of prospecting to tell his new wife he had hit his first pay dirt—which, again depending upon the version one reads, was worth upward of $300,000. Johnny went on down to the Saddle Rock Cafe to celebrate. Molly, fearful that their fortune might be lost or stolen, decided to hide the bills in a place where no one would suspect—the potbellied stove. Johnny came home in the early morning hours, a bit under the influence, and decided to warm the cabin by, of course, lighting the stove. Molly screamed and jumped from the bed. She "scorched her fingers on the stove lids. She couldn't find a lifter and used a steel-pronged fork instead. She almost set herself and the cabin on fire. She delved among the burning sticks, but it was too late. Of all places, she had hidden the money in the stove, and now her fortune had gone up the flue; three hundred thousand dollars floating in the Leadville morning sky," Gene Fowler wrote.

Johnny gamely assessed the situation and assured her that he would just go out and find some more. He was true to his word. Fowler wrote, "Fantastic as it may seem, Leadville Johnny went out that very afternoon and located 'The Little Johnny,' one of the greatest producers of gold in Colorado history."

Of course, the most famous part of Molly's legend is her dramatic triumph on the *Titanic,* for which she earned the name "the Unsinkable." She made a splash, so to speak, before the ship even hit the iceberg by "amusing some and terrifying others with pistol-feats, one of which consisted of tossing five oranges or grapefruits over the rail and puncturing each one before it reached the surface of the sea." On that fateful *Titanic* night, according to Fowler, Molly "came from her cabin prepared for battle with the night sea air. She had on extra-heavy woolies, with bloomers bought in Switzerland (her favorite kind), two jersey petticoats, a plaid cashmere dress down to the heels of her English calfskin boots, a sportsman's cap, tied on with a woolen scarf, knotted in toothache style beneath her chin, golf stockings presented by a seventy-year-old admirer, the Duke Charlot of France, a muff of Russian sables, in which she absent-mindedly had left her Colt's automatic pistol—and over these frost-defying garments she wore a sixty-thousand-dollar chinchilla opera cloak!"

Molly refused to enter a lifeboat until all other women and children had been loaded, and even then crew members had to literally throw her into a boat. The people in the lifeboat, however, seemed bent upon their own demise, and Molly resorted to military tactics. Fowler wrote, "Keeping an eye on the rowers, she began removing her clothes. Her chinchilla coat she treated as though it were a blanket worth a few dollars. She used it to cover three small and shivering children. One by one she divested herself of historic woolens. She 'rationed' her garments to the women who were the oldest or the most frail. It was said she presented a fantastic sight in the light of flares, half standing among the terrified passengers, stripped down to her corset, the beloved Swiss bloomers, the Duke of Charlot's golf stockings and her stout shoes." She sang from various operas and told stories to keep the minds of her fellow survivors occupied. "'Some of you people—the guy here with heart trouble that I'm curing with oars—are rich,' she cried. 'I'm rich. What in hell of it? What are your riches or mine doing for us this minute? And you can't wear the Social Register for water wings, can you? Keep rowing, you sons of bitches, or I'll toss you all overboard!'"

Molly Brown returned to Denver society with fame, notoriety, and respect—something that had been held like a carrot in front of her nose ever since she and Johnny had bought their mansion on Pennsylvania Street. After years of poking fun at her poor social graces and high social ambitions, the "Sacred Thirty-six" of Denver high society welcomed her with open arms and a proper luncheon. Molly Brown got what she deserved. She had finally made it.

Unfortunately, however, Johnny decided he'd had enough of high society, including hers, and left for Leadville. Her son and daughter followed suit. As Molly grew old and eccentric, her friends abandoned her. She claimed to have been awarded the French Legion of Honor—an award, Caroline Bancroft sniffed, that had been "bought in a hock shop." Her royal friends were imaginary, her social and political ambitions nothing more than excessive narcissism. Our last image of Molly Brown is of an overdressed, overeducated woman who can speak five languages sitting in a gaudy room, despondent and alone.

And of course, none of this is true.

THROUGH LETTERS, JOURNALS, court records, newspaper articles, family memoirs, and other authentic documentation, I have attempted to accurately reconstruct the life of Margaret Tobin Brown not only to uncover the "real story" but also determine a kind of pattern or order that might suggest why her life was so disguised and diminished. This book opens and closes with Margaret's *Titanic* experience, written in a narrative style, culled with exacting precision from numerous authentic accounts by the survivors themselves—including Margaret's own written account—of exactly what happened that night. Despite all the other accomplishments of Margaret's life, her experience in Lifeboat Six the night of April 14, 1912, was not only a turning point or catalyst for subsequent events in her life but to some degree a nightmare from which she never completely recovered. Subsequent chapters in the book trace her life from its beginnings in Hannibal, Missouri, to her important political work in Denver, Colorado, Newport, Rhode Island, and Europe, and finally her death at the Barbizon Hotel in New York City in 1932.

Gene Fowler called Margaret Brown a "vital Amazon," a woman who, although she could swear like a pit boss, conversed fluently with her two French maids and spoke five European languages—a woman who was born into poverty but pulled herself "up by her bootstraps" to hear the compliments of kings and princes. Truth or fantasy? One fact remains: Margaret Tobin Brown was as unforgettable as she was unsinkable. Nearly seventy years after her death, her story is as relevant as ever.

Acknowledgments

THE RESEARCH FOR this book was extensive and involved the cooperation and hard work of many individuals to whom I am very grateful.
The staff at the Molly Brown House Museum in Denver has been
more than generous, and I owe very special thanks to Director Leigh
Grinstead and Curator Elizabeth Walker. Lyn Spenst, previous curator
of the Molly Brown House Museum for many years, was also very helpful. In Hannibal, Roberta Hagood provided a wealth of information and
photographs pertaining to the Tobin family and early Hannibal history.
I am grateful to Terrell and Vicki Dempsey, who restored Margaret's
childhood home, for their hospitality as well as their research assistance
and Faye Bleigh and the Hannibal Convention and Visitors Bureau,
who made sure I got to Hannibal to see it for myself. I could not have
completed this book without the dedicated work of my research assistants, Jennifer R. Keil in Denver and Katherine Kulpa and Susan Grant
in Newport, Rhode Island, and in New York. Susan Grant's knowledge
and insight into the early feminist movement in Newport was invaluable.
Special thanks to Lynn Cotton of the Archdiocese of Denver; the French
Embassy in Washington, D.C.; the Alliance Française de Denver; and the
Grande Chancellerie de la Legion D'Honneur in Paris. I am grateful to
Sister Lavon at the Mount St. Vincent Home; Vicki Makings, librarian at
the *Denver Post;* and the Colorado School of Mines, particularly Kappa
Sigma Fraternity. Thanks to Margaret Shaw Coe in Cody, Wyoming,
for sharing her childhood stories of Margaret. George Behe, former
vice-president of the *Titanic* Historical Society and author of *Titanic:
Speed, Safety, and Sacrifice,* reviewed the *Titanic* chapters for historical
accuracy. Don Lynch provided the photograph of Lifeboat Six, and
Stanley Lehrer graciously allowed me to use photographs of Margaret's
Egyptian talisman and the medal she presented to the *Carpathia* crew.
I am most grateful to the staff at the Colorado Historical Society,
particularly Stan Oliner and Eric Paddock, for their help with the Lawrence Brown scrapbook and information on the Ludlow massacre. The
Western History Room at the Denver Public Library also helped enormously, particularly with the sections on early Denver society and the
publications of Polly Pry. Thanks to Bernard Lippincott III at the New-

port Historical Society for information on Margaret's life in Newport. I also wish to thank the State Historical Society of Missouri; the Western History Manuscript Collection at the University of Missouri; the Rhode Island Historical Society; the Newport Public Library; the Hannibal Public Library; the New York Public Library; Jessica Johnson at the Flagler Museum in Florida; the Mariners' Museum in Newport News, Virginia; Jennifer Genco at the Breakers Hotel in Palm Beach; and Fanny Kim at the Barbizon Hotel in New York. Bill and Wendy Fendt assisted with research in New York. Edna Fiori provided information on Avoca Lodge in Denver. Thanks to Gwendolyn Ashbaugh for information on her family history in early Denver and her insight into early Denver politics. I am indebted to the Denver Fortnightly Club, a women's literary organization first established in 1881, for its ongoing enthusiasm and support as well as the Rocky Mountain Women's Institute, which has been of great benefit to me and many other women writers and artists in Colorado.

Finally, it was a writer's dream come true to have the cooperation of the Brown and Benziger families during the research of this book. Scrapbooks, letters, photographs, newspaper clippings, family stories—from Hannibal to Newport to Denver to California and Canada, I have been blessed with their enthusiasm and willingness to share their family history. Muffet Laurie Brown, Lance Brown, Helen Benziger McKinney, Heidi Benziger Rautio, Pamela Benziger Feeley, Lynne Davy, Albert and Margaret Frier, Patricia Rey Benziger, Katherine Benziger, Catherine Roach Belgard, Emilie Wilson, and especially Lisa and Scott Vollrath—thank you all. Muffet Laurie Brown has been especially helpful with research and documentation—and rescued me when the airline lost my luggage. Heartfelt thanks to Annie Azzariti of Arts and Entertainment (A&E) cable television (Greystone Productions) for her hard work and enthusiasm in making the first full television biography on the life of Margaret Tobin Brown.

I am grateful to Linda Doyle, Gail Gibson, Craig Keyzer, and Karyn Masters for their help in reading and proofreading the manuscript. Amelia de la Luz Montes—as always—provided sisterly support and unfailing *esprit de corps* for this project as it stretched over several years. My editor, Stephen Topping, could not be more divine, and I thank Connie Oehring for her copyediting work. Mira Perrizo provided not only guidance but herculean patience. Thanks to my family, especially my mother and sisters, who believed in this book from the very beginning. And finally, thanks to my sons, Sean and Nathan, who were with me every step of the way.

A Note on Sources

WHENEVER I TALK about the extraordinary life of Margaret Tobin Brown, the first question I am asked is, "How did the story get so screwed up?"

Anyone who's done any research on "Molly" Brown soon discovers that despite her fame, both now and in the past, almost nothing has been published about her actual life. What does exist is almost wholly myth and fantasy, begun in the 1930s with writers Gene Fowler, a reporter for the *Denver Post* who fictionalized the life of Molly Brown in a chapter of his book *Timberline,* and Caroline Bancroft, a storyteller and historian who wrote a largely fictionalized booklet titled *The Unsinkable Mrs. Brown* for Colorado tourists. Fowler's and Bancroft's stories culminated in the 1964 MGM movie *The Unsinkable Molly Brown,* and nearly everything published or produced about Mrs. Brown since then has been based on this tall tale.

My research originally began in 1991 as part of my Ph.D. dissertation at the University of Denver. I became fascinated with the stories of two Colorado legends, "Baby Doe" Tabor and "Molly" Brown, and the great gap that existed between the myths about these women and the lives they actually led. I found it incredible that despite the fact that each of these women had left behind voluminous material stored in hundreds of files in archives such as those of the Colorado Historical Society—letters, journals, telegrams, photographs, clippings, and more—very few writers or historians had bothered to look at it. Nor had anyone taken the time to interview their descendants, friends, acquaintances, or business associates. Instead, historians, journalists, playwrights, and scriptwriters relied on the Hollywood stereotype— perhaps that approach is not surprising, because those stories are fun. But the damage to women's history with respect to the true stories of prominent women in the West is inestimable. It's no surprise that many people confuse the legends of "Baby Doe" Tabor (whose real name was Elizabeth McCourt Tabor) and "Molly" Brown—the myths, and the stereotypes those myths promote, are very similar.

Margaret Tobin Brown and James Joseph Brown had two children, Helen and Lawrence Brown, and also raised three nieces, Grace, Florence, and Helen Tobin. Their descendants, Margaret Brown's great-grandchildren and great-grandnephews and -nieces, have provided me with extraordinary primary source material that would be any writer's dream. It is our collective hope that these materials will soon be publicly available in a Margaret Tobin Brown Memorial Library.

Some of these sources are already available for scholarly research. Lawrence Brown's scrapbook and many of the family papers are held at the Colorado Historical Society. The Western History Room at the Denver Public Library holds a number of family photographs and newspaper clippings. The Molly Brown House Museum in Denver also holds a large collection of miscellaneous materials.

The family's willingness to allow me access to privately held source material is what truly makes this book the first authentic account of the life of Margaret Tobin Brown. An incredible source has been the scrapbook (actually two scrapbooks, one containing primarily photographs) of Helen Tobin Kosure, Margaret's niece. This scrapbook may actually be a composite of scrapbook pages kept by Helen, Grace, and Florence Tobin and perhaps even Margaret herself. Owned by Scott Vollrath, Helen Tobin Kosure's grandnephew and Grace Tobin Carroll's grandson, and his wife, Lisa, this scrapbook has been the source for countless newspaper articles, letters, and photographs, including the extraordinary photograph of Margaret and her daughter, Helen, in Cairo, perched atop camels, just before Margaret departed to board the *Titanic* at Cherbourg, France.

Another incredible source of primary material was a box filled with the bundled letters and memorabilia of Helen Brown Benziger, which had been kept for decades in the basement of Patricia Benziger, wife of James Benziger, Helen's son. Patricia Benziger was gracious enough to have someone help her carry this box out of the basement (it contained literally hundreds of letters) and ship it to Colorado to her daughter Katherine (great-granddaughter of Margaret Tobin Brown). On numerous occasions, Katherine sat with me late into the night as we combed through letters and telegrams dated roughly from 1905 to 1920, tracing the lives of Margaret and her children and nieces—and sneezing from dust nearly a hundred years old.

Muffet Brown, Lawrence Brown's granddaughter, graciously accompanied me to the Colorado Historical Society to peruse her grandfather's scrapbook with me and ensure that we correctly identified photos, places, and dates. Muffet also shared family letters and memorabilia that had been passed down from her famous great-grandparents.

I was also fortunate to interview Alfred Frier, grandson of Catherine (Katie) Becker, Margaret's half-sister, and his wife, Margaret, in Hannibal, Missouri. Alfred could vividly remember being with Margaret as a young child on several occasions, and his sincerity and humor were a delight.

Roberta Hagood, Hannibal historian, was also invaluable in helping me trace the history of the Tobin family.

Much of the primary research material for this book has obviously not yet been cataloged or archived. For the purposes of the book, I have been as careful and thorough as possible in noting the exact item cited and where it is located. Many of the items in the scrapbooks, particularly in the Helen Tobin Kosure scrapbook, are not fully marked with respect to date, headline, or place of publication. Considering that Margaret traveled extensively, was interviewed often on both continents, and published her own travel essays in the United States and overseas, tracing the sources of these articles has been a challenge.

As a writer, researcher, and historian, the opportunity to work with such a wealth of previously unavailable primary source material has been exciting and enriching. Not only do we now have a fuller understanding of the life of Margaret Tobin Brown, but a broader, more expansive view of the lives of women in the West.

A Bump in the Night

April 14, 1912

ON THE BRIGHT spring morning of Sunday, April 14, 1912, Mrs. James Joseph Brown was walking the deck. The day had dawned clear, the early-morning sun streaming through the promenade decks with just a hint of the icy sea breeze that could send deck chairs scuttling. She had risen early for her walk, part of a daily ritual that sometimes included twenty minutes on the stationary horse or a half-hour of boxing in the gymnasium just down from her cabin on Deck B. Back home in Denver she had a firm leather pouch hanging in the carriage house;[1] boxing, a new trend for women, not only firmed the upper arms and waist but made a corset unnecessary. However, Mr. T.W. McCawley, the gymnastics instructor on board, recommended the mechanical camel for the good it did the liver. She liked Mr. McCawley, with his short, bowed legs, muscled as a mountain climber's, and his trim black mustache. At the age of forty-four she had never felt better, still proud of her firm chin and slender hands but nevertheless a little concerned about her spreading middle. To the dismay of her dinner companions she had given up butter, salt, bread, and sugar and dropped five pounds. Next it was cream, and then coffee altogether, which seemed to help her sleep.[2] Sleep, however, had never been a high priority. She was the sort of person who liked to keep herself busy.

The deck had already been scraped and sanded, and except for two men in sleeveless shirts polishing the brightwork, Margaret was alone. On the heels of a good Saturday night, many first-class passengers wouldn't have retired until after midnight, and few would likely make it to the Divine Service at ten-thirty.[3] She walked briskly, looking out at water smooth as the mirror that lay on the pecan table in her stateroom. If she fixed her eye on a single point on the horizon, it felt almost as if the ship were standing still. Later she would hear a crewman cry that twenty-four of the twenty-nine boilers had been fired; despite the illusion of stillness, the ship was traveling at a high rate of speed.

It was her third day at sea, and she was trying not to worry. In Paris she had received word that her first grandson was ill. The news had caused her to shorten her trip considerably and book the next liner— which, to her great anticipation, had been the maiden voyage of the *Titanic.* But the thought of little Lawrence Jr. lying in his crib fretting with fever, sent a slice of fear through her chest. Her son had taken a job on a ranch in Oregon and left Eileen and the baby with Eileen's mother in Kansas City. Margaret had long anticipated the arrival of a grandchild but had yet to lay eyes on him. A photo of the baby, bright-eyed and wrapped in bunting, was tucked in her satchel. Surely God would see fit to keep this child healthy and earthbound.

She wasn't sorry to leave Paris, and not just because the spring exodus of New York's elite had begun. Like many who could afford to travel, Margaret often ventured to faraway countries in the spring. Summers were spent at her forty-three-room cottage, Mon Etui, in Newport, Rhode Island, but Margaret made a point of visiting family and friends in Denver and Leadville several times a year. With her daughter, Helen, she had spent several weeks traveling, including a treasured few days in Cairo with John Jacob Astor and his new wife, Madeleine, before they all left for Cherbourg. The Astors were enjoying the last few days of a secluded honeymoon away from the vicious sniping of the New York newspapers after Astor's very public divorce and quick remarriage to young Madeleine. Together they walked through the labyrinth of streets and alleyways of an Egyptian bazaar in the very heart of the city, where for fun Margaret sought the counsel of a palm reader. The dark Egyptian man traced the lines in her palm and shook his head forebodingly, muttering, "Water, water, water." In halting English, he spoke of a sinking ship surrounded by bodies. Margaret brushed it off, although she usually enjoyed the game of prophesy; she had often hired fortune-tellers for fun at parties. But this man knew she was an American and naturally would have to cross the water. She wasn't going to give him a single penny more.[4]

Helen was twenty-three, a natural beauty with soft eyes and long, reddish hair. She had been educated at private schools in Europe and at the Sorbonne and enjoyed the attentions of ardent beaus on both sides of the ocean. Her plan to accompany her mother on the *Titanic* had been changed at the last minute when friends in London begged Helen to stay a few weeks longer for the spring social season and Margaret reluctantly conceded. In two more months Helen would come home for the summer, although she would split her time between her mother's home in Newport and her father's hacienda in Taos, New Mexico. The family home on Pennsylvania Street in Denver was no longer a hub of the Denver business or social scenes; tenants and a caretaker now watched over the art, the furniture, and the infamous statuary. Sometimes Margaret mused that the two stone lions guarding their little-worn steps on Pennsylvania Avenue could be J.J. and herself. The legal separation three years ago had eased some of the turmoil in her life, but the thought of him could still make her blood boil. Or her heart ache, depending on her mood.

She was anxious to get back to Denver. Somewhere in the bowels of the ship, tidily packed in sawdust and pine crates, were three crates of models of the ruins of Rome that she was bringing back for the Denver Art Museum.[5] The acquisition was a marvelous coup; her friends in Denver would be thrilled. In her pocket she carried a small Egyptian talisman she had bought for herself as a good-luck charm. Just before she had boarded the tender at Cherbourg, a man had tried to sell her insurance. She had turned him away. One couldn't put a price on antiquity.

She was warm now, despite the cool air, and thought she might dip down to her stateroom to change before the service. She hoped to see Emma Bucknell, her good friend and widow of the founder of Bucknell University, who had also taken the nine-forty transatlantic train from Paris. They had boarded the *Titanic* together at Cherbourg the previous Friday. The ship was late, not arriving until nearly nightfall. Two separate tenders, the *Nomadic* and the *Traffic,* brought them out into the channel, one tug for first-class passengers, the other for additional passengers, mail, and baggage.[6] They waited nearly an hour in the cold, gray mist before the last bags of mail were carried from tender to liner and the shrill whistle warned shore visitors to return. Margaret watched as the gangways were raised and the anchor hove and felt the engines throb to life. All seemed brisk and efficient. "I have a premonition about this ship,"[7] Emma Bucknell said.[8] She stood shivering in the cold, well dressed but rather prim in her pearls, tight curls, and wire-framed glasses. She planned to skip dinner and go straight to her stateroom.

"Nonsense," Margaret said. The Egyptian's words had been forgotten. "You're just anxious to see your family." Emma had four children and several grandchildren eagerly awaiting her return.

"I suppose it's just nerves," Emma replied, and laughed nervously.

She wasn't quite as stout-hearted as Margaret, who enjoyed booking the maiden voyage of a liner whenever possible, but Emma was accustomed to traveling alone. As the second wife of William Bucknell, she had been left with not only loving children but a substantial inheritance at his death. First-class passengers on steamers often recognized each other from social circles in London or New York, and both Mrs. Brown and Mrs. Bucknell had sought out the pleasant company of Dr. Arthur Jackson Brewe, a Philadelphia physician who traveled often but was now eager to return home to his new wife. During the embarkation, he stood solemnly at their side.

"I always feel a little trepidation at the beginning of a journey," Dr. Brewe said. "Not to worry. No other ship in the world is built like this one." They watched the shadowy shore of Cape de la Hogue disappear into the darkness. Since that evening, several days of smooth sailing had proved his point.

ON THAT COLD April night, Margaret's stateroom hummed with warmth. She switched off the small electric heater at the foot of her bed, a decidedly useful benefit of traveling first class. She wasn't sure how anyone managed without one; except for a few brief hours in the afternoon, the sea air was bitter. She was glad she had brought the high-necked fleece nightgown with the long bishop sleeves, even though her daughter had said she looked old-fashioned. Last night she had even slept in her slippers, a pair of satin mules Lawrence had given her last Christmas. Her feet were always cold, a throwback to her Leadville days, she thought. One good frostbite in a pair of solid leather boots and her feet had never completely recovered. Before leaving her cabin she folded the *Atlantic Daily Bulletin* and left it on the bed for close reading later. Each morning before the bugle call, the steward slipped it under her door. Thanks to the new wireless technology and a small on-board printing press, passengers were kept up-to-date on news and stock-market quotations.[9]

When she came back up on deck, a small crowd had gathered in front of the first-class dining saloon. Captain Edward Smith, a stout, white-whiskered man whose every word seemed both paternal and polite, greeted each first-class passenger with a nod. He held his hat in his hand; on each sleeve glistened the four gold rings of his rank. "Mrs.

Brown," he murmured, and dipped his head. She extended a gloved hand. Twice before she had crossed the ocean with Captain Smith, most recently just three months ago on the *Titanic*'s sister ship *Olympic,* when he and she had shared the same dinner table.[10] Many first-class passengers based their travel plans on whether a particular captain or steward was on a certain ship; Margaret, like many of her friends, had been glad to see Captain Smith's familiar white whiskers. She had also recognized one of the stewardesses, a young woman with auburn hair and a brisk Irish accent, who had also been on the *Olympic.*

Once inside she saw that the tables had been removed and the chairs lined up like pews in front of a small podium, with a small cortège of the ship's orchestra seated to the side. Margaret was surprised to see a good show of first-class passengers in the front rows; glancing behind her, she saw passengers from second and third class quietly perched in the back.[11] It wasn't the same as the towering Cathedral of the Immaculate Conception in Denver, which Brown money had helped build, or the quaint Annunciation Church of Leadville, where she and J.J. had been married. But the spirit felt just as strong. Captain Smith tucked a well-worn copy of the company's prayer book, which he preferred to the *Book of Common Prayer,* beneath his arm and closed the doors. An audience of various ranks, classes, and religions meant that he had to tread a fine line between inspiration and indignation; his words would only gently hearten. There had been no daily inspection of the ship, the usual early-morning parade of the captain, the chief officer, the chief engineer, the purser, the chief steward, and the senior surgeon, all dressed in their best. The service would suffice instead.

Just before the captain reached the podium, he fingered a triangle of white paper inside his breast pocket that had been handed to him just as he left the bridge. The tight, cramped handwriting of Harold Bride, a curly-headed twenty-two-year-old from Bromley, Kent, who didn't seem to mind spending long hours bent over an endless stream of static, stated that a wireless had been received from the *Caronia,* an eastbound ship traveling from New York to Liverpool. Smith squinted again at the words: "Bergs, growlers, and field ice." Nothing new, he thought, and tucked it back inside. After a half-hour of general confession and a prayer for those at sea, the congregation concluded with a rousing rendition of "O God Our Help in Ages Past," and the passengers politely filed out into the crisp morning air. Captain Smith went up to the bridge. Margaret Tobin Brown returned to her stateroom. The *Titanic* continued her smooth and effortless speed run to New York, where she was to arrive Tuesday night with as much pomp and glory as when she first pushed off from the dock.

LUNCH AT THE Veranda Cafe was always pleasant, even when one lunched alone. Margaret ordered corned beef, vegetables, and dumplings—not too many dumplings—and gazed out the high bronze windows at the sea, flat and smooth and brilliant in the sun. The illusion of warmth was shattered whenever the door to the deck was opened, however, and few passengers ventured outside. The steward brought a small plate of cheshire and gorgonzola, which she allowed herself, cheese being an occasional indulgence. She planned her afternoon, not unlike yesterday or the day before: a bracing walk on the deck, two hours in the library, a cup of tea and dry toast in her room before dressing for dinner. Her favorite spot to sit and read was just in front of the great bow window at the forward end of the writing room. She loved walking from one end of the ship to the other. The broad corridors, winding companionways, and grand staircase made her feel as if she were in a palace, not on a ship. The White Star Line had given all the first-class passengers a little guidebook to help them find their way around the ship,[12] but she still couldn't quite determine the shortest, most direct route from one end to the other. Much was made of the fact that there were numerous honeymooning couples strolling about, from first class to steerage, her friends John Jacob and Madeleine generating the most gossip. She tried not to think of J.J.

She thought instead of her mother, now dead, who would have relished musing in a deck chair, watching people walk up and down, looking to see who was who and what was what. Tiny as a bantam hen but with enough opinions to fill a newspaper. There were many things she missed about her mother, who could be just as prim as any Victorian matron but wasn't above a pipeful of tobacco when left to her own devices. Ten times a day Margaret could tell her to smoke only in the kitchen, but as soon as she left the house in Denver her mother smoked wherever she pleased. The brocade curtains still held the pungent smell.[13]

She thought of what she might wear to dinner. Just before leaving Paris she and Helen had spent an afternoon browsing in galleries and shops, and she had many new gowns—twenty-five, in fact, not including capes and overcoats, with fourteen matching hats. She was eager to get to New York, where there would be talk of the stock market and the theater and the glory, however short-lived, of being the first passengers on the much-touted *Titanic*. But time was of the essence. She had planned to stay a few nights at her usual room at the Ritz-Carlton before taking the train to Hannibal to visit family, but now her only goal was her grandson.

A dark moment of concern crossed her mind as she thought of the baby. She hadn't heard a word since the telegram in Paris.

AT SIX P.M. Second Officer Charles Herbert Lightoller assumed his watch at the bridge. He was what sailors often called a "hard case."[14] At the ripe age of twenty-six, he had a long list of sea adventures, including a shipwreck, a cyclone, a cargo fire, and a severe bout of malaria.[15] Back in Lancashire, his sister had begged him to consider another career. "Don't you bother about me," he had retorted. "The sea is not wet enough to drown me. I'll never be drowned!"[16] He was proud to be on the *Titanic*, one of many voyages he had made with Captain Smith.

On his way to join Lightoller, Captain Smith passed White Star Line Managing Director J. Bruce Ismay on the promenade deck, where he stood talking to George and Eleanor Widener. As the son of P.A.B. Widener, who served on the board of the bank that had financed the *Titanic*, George Widener shared a congenial relationship with Ismay. Without comment, Captain Smith handed Ismay the brief note from the wireless. Ismay glanced at it, put it in his pocket, and resumed his conversation. Later, on his way down to dinner, Captain Smith saw the three still deep in conversation. He asked for the message back. Ismay retrieved it from his pocket, and before joining the Wideners and a few select guests in the À la Carte Restaurant, Captain Smith took the note up to the bridge, posted it, and entered it into the log. The dinner was in honor of Smith; this was his last voyage on a White Star vessel. After thirty-eight years he was finally ready to retire.

At seven thirty-five, Second Officer Lightoller prepared to go down to his own dinner. He remarked to his colleagues how quickly the temperature had dropped now that the sun had set.

In her stateroom, Margaret finished tying her long brown hair into a tidy coiffure and checked her gown in the mirror. She wore a longer gown, suitable for dinner but not for dancing, although she loved to dance. The dip, the waltz, even the tango. Back in Denver, at the Casanova Room in the Brown Palace Hotel, she might not be the best dancer on the floor, but she laid claim to being the most energetic.[17] She looked forward to joining Dr. Brewe and Emma Bucknell, among others, for a glass of champagne and filet mignon Lili, with just a taste of dessert, which she would justify by another stroll around the deck before retiring. Exercise, excrcise! Mr. McCawley admonished, although privately she felt that an occasional nip of sherry or crème fraîche was good for the character.

Just below, in cabin C-62, John Jacob Astor called to his manservant, Victor Robbins, to brush his suit, a dark blue serge of worsted wool that sometimes scratched at the neck. He usually dined with the wealthier first-class passengers, although he counted many others among his circle of friends. His young wife, Madeleine Force Astor, not yet twenty, hadn't decided whether to go to dinner, given the unstable state of her stomach. It was more than just the motion of the ship, although few people knew that beyond John and herself. The press was an unwelcome intrusion into their happiness; New York newspapers had not yet forgiven John for divorcing his first wife and marrying Madeleine on September 9, 1911. Their lives were filled with eager anticipation, as soon there would be a new heir to the Astor fortune.

Further down in the depths of the ship, the third-class passengers were also preparing for dinner. Herr Muller, the ship's interpreter, was exhausted after a long day of trying to find common ground for communication between so many different languages. Emigrants on board included people from many different countries—Norway, Sweden, Denmark, Russia, Spain, Greece, Italy, Romania—and even a few Chinese traveling to America to work as crewmen on the ship *Anetta*. After they spent a few tense hours eyeing each other with blunt curiosity and distrust, the general mood was one of congeniality and even celebration. For many this was the first time they had ever seen, let alone actually occupied, an ocean liner. The biting air had forced people to come in from the deck; men gathered in the smoking room and two bars, and the women and children filled the noisy general room. The smell of supper filled the air.

Even further below, deep down in the stokehold, the stokers (or "black gang," as they were called) stooped shirtless in front of the deafening furnaces, shoveling coal into the ravenous fires. The air was thick with coal dust, the heat sometimes unbearable, the constant clang of metal doors deafening. Trimmers trundled back and forth with wheelbarrows, dumping each load of coal at the feet of the stokers, who then shoveled it into the furnaces. During a single watch, the *Titanic* would consume close to a hundred tons of coal.[18] The black gang was invisible and anonymous, totaling 177 firemen and 82 trimmers.

High above in the crow's nest, George Symons and Archie Jewel strained their eyes into the darkness. Their job, two hours on, four hours off, was only to look, to report to the bridge the slightest blip on the seascape, whether it be a light, a derelict, a piece of wreckage, even a wisp of smoke.[19] They had been warned to watch particularly for ice. At the beginning of their shift, their eyes burned from the glare on the water, and when they weren't braced against the breeze they felt the wrath of the sun. Now it was cold and dark, and their job was to listen for the quartermaster's bell and check the navigation lights. After they answered with their own bell, they called out together, "All's well and lights burning brightly!" Their watch was almost over.

Someone had forgotten to equip the crow's nest with binoculars, or misplaced them, but no matter; many a sailor had remarked that the best tool at sea was the naked eye.

THE *TITANIC*'S À LA CARTE Restaurant was an enormously successful innovation. First-class passengers, mostly prominent American businessmen, tended to prefer private dining room service and food served at odd hours. This approach wreaked havoc with the tight schedule necessary for a small kitchen to provide meals for a large ship; Ismay's solution had been to provide a private room with a staff of French waiters, open at all hours of the day and well into the night. Passengers could plan private engagements and request specific dishes at a moment's notice; the ship's printing office produced menus and, if necessary, invitations. The pressure on the kitchen staff was relieved, and prominent passengers enjoyed the same service as they would at a first-class hotel in London or New York.[20] All the waiters were male, but two young Englishwomen, Miss Martin and Miss Bowker, served as cashiers and hostesses. They sometimes hid in the kitchen to gossip about who sat with whom and at what table.

At seven-thirty P.M., Captain Smith entered the À la Carte and briefly adjusted his sleeves before advancing to the long table where he was due to dine with Harry Widener and his parents, George and Eleanor; Maj. Archibald Willingham Butt, assistant to President William Taft; John and Marion Thayer; and William and Lucile Carter. Miss Martin, blushing slightly, led him to the table. Heads turned as they passed.

At a nearby table Emma Bucknell turned to Margaret and whispered, "Shouldn't he be on the bridge? I've heard rumors of icebergs and such."

"Nonsense." Margaret privately suspected Emma of a fearful imagination. Since their departure from Cherbourg, Emma had scarcely slept. "He often dines with first-class passengers."

"It does seem that the ship is moving more southwest than due west," Dr. Brewe commented. "Although that may be due to fog. In any case, Captain Smith is the best captain we have. He's never encountered a problem at sea. They always assign him to the maiden voyage of a new ship."

They had a leisurely dinner, Emma sipping a bit more wine than usual, and afterward retired to the Palm Court, a long, narrow room with upholstered chairs. The women wrapped heavy furs over their gowns and Dr. Brewe wore a long coat over his tuxedo as they sat at a small table under leafy fronds and listened to the *Titanic*'s band play ragtime.[21] The setting reminded Margaret of Newport, where she would soon be summering once again. A steward brought a tray carrying a silver pot of coffee and fresh cream, which Margaret declined.

In his cabin, Quartermaster Robert Hichens prepared for his watch on the poop. His job was to note the reading on the dial of the patent log fixed to the taffrail, telephone it to the bridge, and enter it into his logbook. He also ran messages, trimmed the lamps in the standard compass, read the thermometer and barometer, checked the water temperature, and sounded the bells every half-hour for the men in the crow's nest. His first duty this evening was to advise the carpenter to check the fresh water before it began to freeze, and to turn on the heaters in the officers' quarters.[22]

AT EIGHT-FIFTY P.M., Captain Smith rejoined Lightoller on the bridge. The sea was astonishingly calm and flat, with no sign of a moon but brilliant, piercing stars. "The air is quite brisk," Captain Smith remarked, and Lightoller agreed. "The stars are so bright that we'd likely see the reflection of an iceberg," he replied.

"Yes," mused Captain Smith, who felt full and tired and was looking forward to his bunk. "But if you are the slightest degree doubtful, let me know."

"I will, sir." Lightoller had little reason to worry. Only one ice warning had been posted, although, unbeknownst to him or any of the other officers, numerous warnings had been received from four other passing ships.

FREDERICK FLEET WAS an ambitious man and a good sailor. In 1888 his mother had left England for a better life in America, leaving behind her infant son. Years spent in orphanages had made him nothing if not resourceful, and after being commissioned to a training ship at age twelve, Fleet, now in his midtwenties, had worked his way up from deck boy to able seaman.[23]

Just before ten P.M. he took a cup of strong coffee to brace himself and climbed the ladder to assume his watch in the crow's nest. The ship was moving swiftly at 22.5 knots, the air temperature near freezing, growing cooler as the *Titanic* began to enter the influence of a large Arctic high moving in a southwestward direction. The brisk north wind had diminished. The night was clear, although tiny splinters of ice caught the lights off the deck and glittered in the air like confetti. Fleet solemnly stood his post in front of the long brass bell, nearly two feet in length, that hung just above his head. In a moment Reginald Lee, an older fellow from Threefield Lane, Southampton, joined him. At her cabin, Margaret unlocked the door and reached in to switch on the light. She could remember a time when she had to fumble in the dark to light a single lamp, never mind all the lights that burned brightly now just for her. One could stay up as late as one wanted. She sat on the brass bed and unbuttoned her shoes, then pulled her gown up over her head and hung it smoothly in the wardrobe. She put on her fleece gown and brought a book to bed, first checking for the roll of crackers she kept in the mesh netting hanging on the wall, a convenient spot for her books, handkerchief, and the small tin of balm she kept for her hands. Sometimes she woke up hungry in the middle of the night but rarely indulged in more than a few crackers or, when home in Denver, a bowl of cold porridge.[24] She loved her cozy stateroom; it was almost as nice as staying at the Ritz-Carlton.

Her room swayed ever so slightly. Tonight the vibration of the engines seemed stronger than usual; the *Titanic* was steaming faster than at any other time since they had sailed from Southampton.

Up in the wireless room, operator John ("Jack") Phillips jerked the headset from his ears. The static was nearly deafening; after ten hours on the job his energy had waned and his patience was thin. The ship was passing Cape Race, and he still had hours to go before transmitting all the messages that lay piled before him, most of them from first-class passengers eager to check on news from home or simply to relay a message to friends using the marvelous new technology. A ship less than twenty miles away, the *Californian*, sent a curt message: *We are stopped and surrounded by ice.*

"Shut up, I am busy," Phillips furiously typed back. "I am working Cape Race." He returned to the pile of scribbled notes. The *Titanic* continued on at 22.5 knots, the highest speed she had ever achieved.[25]

The steady pull of the engine was just enough to make it difficult for Margaret to keep her eyelids from dropping. In a cabin just down the corridor, Emma Bucknell, despite her frightening dreams, was sound asleep. In third class, where the victualing crew was housed, Miss Martin was still whispering with Miss Bowker. It had been a most interesting evening, and both agreed that young Harry Widener sounded exceedingly well read, in addition to being rich and handsome.

At eleven-forty P.M., just after seven bells, Frederick Fleet continued to peer ahead. The heavens were bright with stars, but everything below the horizon was liquid black. Suddenly he tensed. The air changed; the moist, clammy smell that filled his nostrils reminded him of a cave, deep and dark, filled with rock and ice. He strained to see into the black. A hole appeared in the space ahead, at first small, then looming, an empty black void against the thickly studded sky. He reached forward and rang the bell thrice, then lifted the phone and called the bridge.

A calm voice answered. "What did you see?"

"Iceberg right ahead."

"Thank you." The line went still.[26]

Down below, in the wheelhouse, young Cornishman Robert Hichens stood at the wheel, twenty minutes away from the end of his shift. He nearly leaped out of his boots when the officer of the watch barked, "Hard-a-starboard!" The engines stopped and the order was given to reverse them. Hichens put the helm hard over, his heart pounding.

Thirty-seven seconds stretched into eternity. Fleet gripped the rail and watched in grim horror as she sluggishly turned and shouldered her side up against the dark wall. Chunks of ice crashed and splintered onto the forward well deck and slid across the floor, scattering like shards of broken glass. The smell of ice was acrid and ancient. As if propelled by its own power, the dark bulk bumped and scraped along the length of the ship. Then it was gone.

Fleet and Lee stood in disbelief.

MOST *TITANIC* PASSENGERS felt little more than a bump or heard a faint grinding noise. Margaret Brown, deep in a book in her cabin on Deck B, felt a crash overhead and was knocked to the floor. Numerous ocean journeys had made her a seasoned traveler; she was startled but not frightened. She rose, put on her dressing gown, and ventured out into the corridor. Earlier she had heard several men enter their state-rooms, saying that the cold night air had forced them to retire early from the smoking rooms. Now these same men stood in the gangway in their pajamas, and a few women in kimonos poked their heads out from behind their stateroom doors. "Are you prepared to swim in those things?" joked one man, jostling another in the side.[27]

Nothing seemed amiss, although she noticed that the engines had stopped. For the first time the ship was truly silent. Margaret returned to her room and began reading again, the lamp at her shoulder burning steadily. Through the wall next to her she heard someone say, "We will go up on deck and see what has happened." Again she rose, donned her dressing gown, and poked her nose out into the corridor. An officer and several stewards stood quietly conversing. The situation seemed well under control. Once again she returned to her warm bed.

Abruptly she was startled by a pounding noise. The curtains at her small window moved slightly, and a face appeared. She sat up straight— it was Mr. McGough from Philadelphia, a Gimbels buyer she had met earlier on deck.[28] His face was blanched, eyes protruding like those of a fish, and he seemed out of breath. He looks absolutely haunted, she thought. "Get your life preserver!" he gasped.

Second Officer Lightoller had been roused from a heavy, exhausted sleep, not by a jolt but by a grinding vibration that could have been a thousand different things. He waited tensely in his room—his orders were to stay put until called for duty—but finally pulled a sweater and trousers over his pajamas and bounded to the bridge. Captain Smith stood grimly giving orders to his officers, his breath hanging in brief clouds of steam. "Uncover the lifeboats!" he bellowed. Lightoller glanced at his watch. It was twelve midnight, sharp.

Margaret Brown was filled not with fear but with practicality. She laid her nightgown across the bed and quickly dressed in a black velvet two-piece suit with black-and-white silk lapels, one she'd scarcely worn.[29] She had been saving it for New York. But warmth, not style, was foremost in her mind, and this was her warmest piece of clothing. Over her sturdy legs she pulled seven pairs of woolen stockings, one over the other. She put on the sable stole J.J. had given her years ago, wrapped a silk capote around her head, and glanced quickly around her cabin. Her clothes, her books, her favorite Parisian shoes (thirteen pairs total, including slippers)—all would be left behind. From her room safe she quickly took $500 in bills and folded them into a small wallet she carried around her neck under her clothing. She strapped on her lifebelt, the cork stiff and straps awkward and difficult to fasten, and took the blanket from the bed. At the last moment she seized the three-inch turquoise-colored Egyptian statue she had bought in Cairo and slipped it into her pocket for good luck.[30]

Just as she emerged from her cabin, an officer strode by, followed by the young steward who rapped on her cabin door each morning to wake her at six. "Good evening, Mrs. Brown," he said, standing politely in his black suit and boots. "I'm sorry to inform you that the captain has ordered everyone to go to the boat deck."

"I'm ready." she said. She climbed the stairs to Deck A, where about fifty passengers were strapping on lifebelts. Emma Bucknell joined her immediately. "Didn't I tell you something was going to happen?" she whispered. They watched in horror as the crewmen struggled with the lifeboats, and an officer ordered the group to descend to the deck below. There a lifeboat had been lowered flush with the deck, and another officer began helping passengers step across the gap into the unsteady craft.

Down below in the gymnasium, the floor was beginning to list decidedly. Mr. McCawley had secured his equipment as best he could; he now stood at the door with a young man from first class whose lifebelt was so tight that his suit was bunched like crepe paper. "No, not for me," Mr. McCawley declared. "I won't wear a lifebelt. It will only slow me down as I swim."

John Jacob Astor sat on an exercise horse next to Madeleine, her maid, Rosalie, hovering nervously nearby. With a pocketknife he deftly cut open a lifebelt to prove how sturdy it was, how solidly designed, and held out the pieces in his hands like fine porcelain. "But we'll stay here for now," he said. "With all the watertight compartments, there is no chance this ship can sink. It's perfectly safe."

In cabin C-104, Maj. Arthur Godfrey Peuchen of Montreal, the president of Standard Chemical Company, at first thought a strong wave had struck the boat. He was a military man, having long served with the Queen's Own Rifles, and didn't mind a little excitement. His steward, James Johnson, found him down in the dining saloon. "Sir!" he cried. "We have struck an iceberg!" Peuchen needed no further encouragement; he bounded up the grand staircase to his cabin, pulled on warm clothes, and placed his yachtsman pin prominently on his lapel. A tall, broad-shouldered man with a closely cropped handlebar mustache, he felt ready to meet whatever fate might deliver.

In their cabin, Miss Martin and Miss Bowker were interrupted by a knock on the door. "Women up on the boat deck!" the voice cried. "Get your lifebelts!" There was no time to change clothes; each girl grabbed a wrapper and cloak. As they dashed down the passageway they looked back to their colleagues, all male: the French waiters, chef, chef's assistants, bakers, sauce makers, fish cooks, wine butlers, barmen, coffeemen, soup cook, and sculleryman. Sixty-four men total, not allowed to leave the corridor.[31]

After roving the decks and seeing a few young cutups from third class playfully kicking and throwing the snow and ice that had landed on the lower deck, Major Peuchen decided the situation was rather more serious than he had thought. He returned to his stateroom. While fastening his lifebelt, he looked down at a tin box on the table filled with $200,000 in bonds and $100,000 in preferred stock. What to do? He slammed out of the room, only to return a moment later to take a good-luck pin and stuff three oranges into his pockets. He left the box on the table.[32]

Lightoller had been ordered to take charge of the even-numbered boats on the port side. Following orders wasn't easy. The air was filled with the blast of steam; every safety valve had been lifted, and the noise was deafening. He shouted at the top of his lungs and attracted the attention of no one. Finally, using hand signals, he began loading Lifeboat Four. Almost immediately he ran out of passengers; no one seemed to be taking the situation seriously. In frustration he raised his fist to the sky; the windows on Deck A were locked, requiring the passengers, some terrified, some nonchalant, to go back down one deck and come up the stairs. There had been no rehearsal with the new equipment, and each minute seemed to stretch into an hour as passengers were coaxed or coerced into their seats and the lifeboats were lowered. The din and confusion were unbearable; he had little idea what his colleagues on the other side of the ship were doing. Lifeboat Six hung ready to go: more passengers appeared, and he began to order them into the boat. "Women and children only!" he cried. The women hung back, unwilling to leave their husbands or the ship itself, or convinced that the whole thing was unnecessary.

Margaret Brown stood amidst the din and thanked God that Helen had decided to stay in Paris. Suddenly her acquaintance Madame de Villiers appeared, wearing nothing but a short nightdress, slippers, and a long motorcoat over her bare, shivering legs. Abruptly the safety valves closed and the air was still. "Into the boat!" Lightoller called, his voice suddenly crystal clear.

"No!" Madame de Villiers cried in her thick French-Canadian accent. "I have to go back to my cabin!" She turned back to the stairs.

"Get into the lifeboat, Madame," Margaret cried, and grabbed her arm. "You should do what the officer says."

"But my money and jewelry! I haven't even locked the door!"

"It's only a precaution, dear. In a few minutes we'll all be able to return to the steamer." Margaret pulled the other woman toward Lightoller, who stood drenched in sweat and steam despite the cold air and his unconventional dress. "Your steward will lock your door. Don't worry."

"No!" Madame de Villiers cried, seeming not to comprehend what was happening. Margaret pressed her forward. "It's going to be fine," she said.

"Get into the boat," Lightoller growled, and Madame de Villiers stumbled, sobbing, over the edge. At the last moment, Margaret held back: perhaps what John Jacob Astor had said was true. The *Titanic* itself was probably much safer. And even if it wasn't, she was quite a fair swimmer.[33]

AT TWELVE FORTY-FIVE A.M., the first of eight distress rockets was fired from the starboard side of the bridge. Five minutes later another was fired, then another, a thunderous shot high in the dark that sent sparkling white stars cascading over the black sea. Ten miles away, two separate members of the crew of the *Californian* took brief note but decided it was probably nothing important.[34]

HELEN CHURCHILL CANDEE, like Margaret Brown, was traveling alone. Nevertheless, she had made many new friends, among them Edward Kent, fifty-eight, an architect from Buffalo, New York, and Col. Archibald Gracie IV, fifty-four, a writer and historian. Many on board knew her name; she was the author of several books, including the controversial 1900 volume titled *How Women May Earn a Living*. With Gracie, Kent, and several others she had formed an informal writers' group for the duration of the *Titanic*'s journey. The news of her son's accident in an airplane—and certainly very few people could boast of a son who piloted an airplane—had unexpectedly put her on the ship. When she heard the order to go to the boat deck, she ran to her room to retrieve an ivory miniature of her mother, which she gave to Mr. Kent for safekeeping.

"Surely you will be much safer here than I will be out there!" she declared almost gaily, the situation for the moment seeming almost surreal. After some discussion he finally agreed to accept the portrait; surely the matter was academic, he said, as the crisis would clearly pass. He kept his true thoughts to himself; privately, he doubted whether he would survive.[35]

The steward came by, helped Mrs. Candee don her lifebelt, and securely locked her cabin. "And now," she said to the ruddy-faced young man, "it is time for you to look out for yourself."

"Oh, there's plenty of time for that, madam," he said. "Plenty of time for that!" He watched her climb the steps to the deck and then disappeared down the corridor. She never saw him again.

Just as Mrs. Candee came up to the deck, a throng of men blackened with soot and coal dust emerged from the other side, dunnage in hand. A fine mist rose from their bodies as they hit the bitter air. Stokers and trimmers, she thought, and nearly a hundred of them! As a group they moved toward a lifeboat, and immediately an officer appeared. "Go back!" he shouted. "Go back down!" Like a military unit they turned on their heels and marched back down the steps. Surely there are special lifeboats for them, Mrs. Candee thought, further down below.

Just behind Lightoller, who could barely contain his frustration with the reluctance of the people whose lives he was trying to save, stood Julia and Tyrell Cavendish, an English couple in their midthirties. Julia wore only a wrapper, her husband's long overcoat,[36] and a pair of thin shoes. They had barely spoken to each other since the first order to come up on deck; there seemed nothing to say. Their lives appeared suddenly truncated. Finally Lightoller turned to them; Mrs. Cavendish gazed for a moment into her husband's eyes and then took Lightoller's hand. When she had precariously found a seat in the lifeboat, she turned to look for Tyrell; he was gone. A sense of urgency now gripped the crowd.

The next woman into the boat was Mrs. Candee. She arrived with an encouraging word and a vigorous hoist from Lightoller and happened to land on the oars lying lengthwise in the black depths of the boat. She mentioned to no one the fact that she had fallen heavily and injured both of her legs.[37]

Lightoller ordered as many women as he could find into the boat. Just as the lashings of the mast were cut and the boat began to lower, Margaret Brown, who had decided to walk around and see how things were going on the other side of the deck, was grabbed from behind by two determined men and unceremoniously dropped four feet down into the boat. "You are going, too!" one growled. She scrambled for a seat and tucked the extra stole she had brought behind her feet. Confusion swirled in the darkness as people called back and forth to one another, trying to ascertain who was in the lifeboats and who was still on the ship. The boat rocked wildly.

"We've only one man in this boat!" cried Helen Candee to Lightoller. "Only one man!" Hichens, the quartermaster, sat silent at the lifeboat's prow.

Major Peuchen stood at the rail. He had been helping unravel the tackle of the lifeboats, which seemed hopelessly difficult, and was waiting for just this opportunity. "If you like, I will go," he said.

"Are you a seaman?" Lightoller called back.

"I am a yachtsman." Although it was almost impossible to see in the dark, he pointed to his pin. He wasn't vice-commodore of the Royal Canadian Yacht Club in Toronto for nothing.

"If you are sailor enough to get out on that fall—a difficult thing, for you must get over the ship's side, eight feet away, and make a long swing on a dark night—if you are sailor enough to get out there, you can go down," Lightoller answered.

Peuchen was sailor enough. He swung wide and landed heavily in the boat, quickly tallying the occupants. "We need more seamen!" he yelled.

Captain Smith appeared at the rail next to Lightoller. "Here's one," he called, and lifted out a boy of twelve or fourteen. For a moment it seemed he might fall into the sea. The boy crumpled into the bottom of the lifeboat. He was lucky; most male children over ten were considered man enough to stay with the ship.[38]

"We're listing!" cried Helen Candee as the bow of the boat swung crazily, high in the air. Margaret clung tightly, fully expecting to greet the icy water face first. Abruptly the bow dropped and the boat jerked down, and now the opposite end hung precariously high. "The other side! The other side!" cried Helen. By a series of jerks and pulls they came down beside Deck D, and Margaret noted with horror a gush of water spouting from an opening on the side of the ship. She slid an oar out from the bottom of the boat and braced it against the shell of the ship, holding the side of the lifeboat out and away.[39] They dropped into the water with a splash, nearly capsizing. The black air was perfectly silent except for the shouting above. Margaret looked up to the deck rail, where a small group of stewards stood smoking as if basking in the sun of a warm afternoon. She saw for a moment, in the odd brightness of the light, the stoic face of Captain Smith in his whiskers, jacket, and cap. He gestured out toward the sea and bellowed, "Row to the light! Row to the light! And keep all the boats together!"[40]

As the boat pulled away, shots were heard. Later Margaret would be told that it was the sound of officers shooting to prevent people from the lower decks from jumping into the lifeboats. At the time it sounded as if the boilers were exploding in a series of pops. She looked out to the smooth ocean surface, almost indistinguishable from the black horizon. There was no light.

LIFEBOAT SIX WAS the first to pull away from the port side; equipped to carry sixty-five passengers, it held twenty-four.[41] Only three men were aboard, and two of them could scarcely comprehend their role in the unfolding disaster—fate had dealt them a cruel hand. Robert Hichens, quartermaster, had been at the *Titanic*'s wheel when given the order to turn hard a-starboard.[42] The turn had been too late, too slow, too wide. Now he sat at the stern of a lifeboat, cold terror gripping his heart. Unbeknownst to anyone, Fred Fleet, the lookout who had been the first man to see the iceberg, sat huddled in quiet angst on the starboard side. He should have seen it sooner. He should have rung the bells faster.

Major Peuchen clambered toward the front of the boat past the legs and wraps and blankets and stumbled over the boy. "What do you want me to do?" he shouted at Hichens.

"Get down and put that plug in." Hichens shivered uncontrollably. Peuchen dove into the belly of the boat where Hichens pointed. He frantically felt across the bottom, although his hands were so cold they had almost no sensation. "I can't find it—it's too dark!"

"Hurry, damn you!" Hichens cried.

Peuchen rose to his knees. "It would be better for you to do this and me to do your work." His voice swelled with authority. "You get down and put in the plug, and I will undo the shackles." Hichens dropped the blocks tethering the lifeboat to the ship and sank to the floor. He couldn't find the plug either; finally, with the help of two women sitting nearby, he located the plug and fitted it into the bottom of the boat.[43] He leaped to help Peuchen with the shackles. "We've no time," he gasped. "This boat is going to founder!"

"Our boat?" cried Miss Martin. Margaret turned to look at her in surprise; just a few hours ago they had bidden each other good-night in the À la Carte Restaurant.

"No, no!" Hichens shouted angrily. "The big boat! The big boat!" Together the two men put the rudder down. "Now you, sir, should go forward and take an oar." Hichens glowered at Peuchen. I'd like to take this man to task, Peuchen thought, but he dropped back and took a seat on the port side, across from Fleet. Fleet refused to look at him. He'd scarcely been noticed.

"My son!" Madame de Villiers cried. "I must find my son!"

"Row! Row as hard as you can!" Hichens cried. "We need to get away from the suction!" He stood over the rudder, a tall, thin figure in the dark, shivering like an aspen tree. Margaret placed an oar in the oarlock. "Will you hold this while I slide it into the other side?" she asked Miss Martin. Two women who sat huddled between them quickly reached to help slide the oar across the middle of the boat.

"I've got it!" Miss Martin cried. The oar locked into place, and together Margaret and Miss Martin braced their feet against the bottom of the boat and pulled full strength.

"Row now, row!" Margaret cried.

"Harder!" Hichens barked. "Otherwise we won't make it. She's so large that when she sinks, she'll pull everything down for miles around."

"We'll make it," Peuchen growled.

"You row like a galley slave!" Margaret gasped to the young girl beside her, pulling hard, her breath in short bursts of white mist steady as a steam engine. All the women in the boat were at oars; Margaret felt a quick rush of triumph. The boat began to pull away. They were going to make it after all.

"Ah, faster!" Hichens moaned. "If we're not pulled down, once they're under, those boilers will burst and rip up the bottom of the sea. These icebergs will be torn asunder and completely submerged. We'll be lost!"

His voice was cut short by the sharp blast of a whistle from the deck.

Hichens froze. "Stop rowing!" he shouted. Immediately the oars fell silent. He peered out into the dark. "That was an officer's call. I thought I heard the captain say, 'Come alongside.'"

"I didn't hear anything," Miss Martin said.

"Be quiet!" Hichens snapped. He stood and listened. "We need to go back."

"My son!" Madame de Villiers moaned again. "We must go back for my son!"

"No," Helen Candee said. Her voice was calm and oddly logical. "The captain's final orders were to keep the boats together and row away from the ship."

Hichens stood in anguished indecision. Margaret felt murderous. Go, go! she thought. My life depends on this miserable creature. After an interminable pause Hichens said, "Yes. Row. Yes. Let's pull away from the ship." When the oars were once again engaged he became vehement, standing at the bow like a preacher before a recalcitrant congregation. "Faster! Faster! If you don't make better speed with your rowing, we'll be pulled down to our deaths!"

"Wouldn't it be more profitable," demanded Major Peuchen, "if you were to come down here and row and let one of these women steer the boat? The water is perfectly calm."

"You row, sir, and I will remain in command of this boat," Hichens retorted. "I want each person on this boat pulling full speed. You, there, why aren't you rowing?" He pointed to a dark figure huddled in the bottom of the boat.

The boy raised his head, his jaw clenched to control his emotion and pain. "I would row, sir, but I've only one arm." With his right arm he raised his left, the limb jutting out at an odd angle. "It broke in the fall," he said. Poor lad, Helen Candee thought. He looks consumed by his own guilt. She was thankful that her own pain had subsided as her legs became numb with cold.

"Ah, useless!" Hichens moaned. "We are doomed."

A FINAL ROCKET leaped off the starboard deck, and Margaret saw that Decks E and C were completely submerged. The nose of the ship gently tipped into the water.

"Someone will come; another ship will save us," a voice cried, and it seemed true simply because what was happening seemed so impossible. The deck lights still burned, and in their false brightness Margaret saw a throng of people suddenly burst onto the boat deck. Where were the lifeboats? Were the lifeboats gone? The sound of barking dogs and shouting, so much shouting, and children crying—children? Surely all the children had been taken off in boats. Margaret looked out onto the water and saw nothing except one other lifeboat, matching them stroke for stroke.

Hichens abruptly stood. "What's that? A light?"

"No," Peuchen answered. "It's only a reflection."

"It must be a boat, a boat of some kind," Hichens cried. "Or a buoy!

By God, it's a buoy!" He waved his arms at the other lifeboat. "I say, do you know of any buoys around here?"

How perfectly absurd, Peuchen thought. The man's a raving idiot.[44]

"There are no buoys in the middle of the Atlantic Ocean," Margaret muttered to Miss Martin, and despite the fact that they were rowing so hard they could hardly breathe, Miss Martin smiled. All seemed quiet except for the slap of oars and the heavy panting of the rowers, and the ship seemed nearly a mile away.[45] The lifeboats quickly became separated as they maneuvered around the floating chunks of ice, losing sight of each other quickly in the velvet darkness. Tiny glittering crystals stung Margaret's cheeks, and with each breath she felt as if she were filling her lungs with ice. Don't look back, she thought. Don't look back. Abruptly Major Peuchen stopped rowing and let his dripping oar, rest in the water. Shouts and cries of terror filled the air.

"What is it?" cried Margaret.

"The ship," Peuchen whispered.

"No," said Hichens. "It is only the men on the collapsible lifeboat."

"Look," Peuchen said. Margaret let her oar come to rest and squinted in the dark. Already she could feel her gloves rubbed clear through, and despite her velvet suit she was soaked. Frosty tendrils clung to her hair and nostrils. Just stopping for a moment made her shiver.

The distant cries ceased, and suddenly a great rumbling noise filled the air. "The boilers!" Hichens cried. "Ay, there they go!"

In one long, booming slide, the contents of one side of the ship slid to the other: twenty-nine boilers torn from their beds, hundreds of dining tables and wicker chairs, five grand pianos, countless china cabinets, scores of potted palms, gymnasium equipment, thirty cases of tennis rackets, fifteen thousand bottles of stout and ale, eight thousand cigars, steamer trunks filled with clothes and books and personal belongings, thirty thousand fresh eggs, forty tons of potatoes, warm croissants still baking in their ovens, and hundreds of tons of coal.[46]

"Dear God," Margaret gasped, and stood. She did not have the strength to look away. The ship rose at the stern, and the lights flickered and then abruptly cut. The calm, flat water carried shouts and cries of terror from the fast-sinking ship. The rumbling stopped, and for a moment the ship seemed to break in two, one half airily suspended like the iceberg itself, an enormous black blot against the starry sky. Later

Margaret would write, "Suddenly there was a rift in the water, the sea opened up, and the surface foamed like giant arms that spread around the ship."[47] The image burned itself into her soul.

For a long moment, the occupants of the lifeboat remained as mute as the dead, all standing erect, clustered in the middle of the boat. "Oh my God," gasped Julia Cavendish, and dropped her face into her palms. "Tyrell!"

"Edgar!" Leila Meyer, a recently married woman in her twenties, leaned against the two young sisters standing beside her. "Father!" they cried together. "What about Father?" Almost every woman in the boat had the name of a loved one on her lips. Margaret thought of Emma and Dr. Brewe. The *Titanic* had simply disappeared as if it had never existed. Voices mingled and intensified: a man shouting, a woman screaming, the high, thin wail of a child. Hundreds of anguished criers filled the air in a cacophany of terror.

"We must go back!" Helen Candee demanded.

"Yes, go back! Go back!" Miss Martin cried. "We can fit a great many more people in this boat!"

"No!" Hichens cried. "It is our lives now, not theirs. Row, damn you. Our boat will immediately be swamped if we go back into all that confusion."

"But there are a great many people in the water," Julia Cavendish cried.

"No!" Hichens shouted. His face was violently red. "We would go to our own deaths! They would only pull us down. Row! Row!"

"We have to go back," Margaret said. She couldn't bear it. If only she could close her ears, her eyes. "We can't leave them!"

"There's nothing in the water but a great many stiffs," Hichens barked.

Julia Cavendish choked back a sob. Reluctantly the passengers returned to their oars, some quietly sobbing. Soon the heavy rhythm of the oars had a balmlike effect. Thank God Helen is in Paris, Margaret prayed. Thank God.

FOR TWO HOURS they rowed with no light in sight, only stars. Margaret stripped six pairs of stockings one by one from her legs and handed them out to the other women. Occasionally she noticed a brief flare from another lifeboat, as if someone had lit a match for a moment, but then it was gone.[48] There was no way to tell how many lifeboats were out there, or how many people in them. Her face and hands were numb from the bitter air, her legs soaked nearly to her knees with icy water, but her torso was soaked with sweat. She knew that if she stopped for a moment she would freeze. The women called or sang to each other to keep rowing.

She watched Hichens standing on his pinnacle, trembling, with an attitude like someone preaching to a multitude, fanning the air with his hands. "We're likely to drift for days," he predicted. Everywhere they were surrounded by ice and icebergs, and a castle of ice, perhaps as high as seventy feet, loomed in the distance. "There is no water in the casks, and we have no bread, no compass, and no chart," he exclaimed.[49] He shook his arm against the sky. "If a storm should come up, we are completely helpless! We will either drown or starve. That is our fate."

Margaret felt the exhaustion in her limbs. She felt as heavy as lead, as if she could drop right through the bottom of the thin-skinned boat to the sea floor. Next to her Miss Martin swore softly under her breath.

"Be quiet!" Margaret cried. "Keep it to yourself if you feel that way. For the sake of these women and children, be a man. We have a smooth sea and a fighting chance."[50]

"I don't even know what direction we're rowing," Hichens retorted.

Helen Candee paused and pointed to the north star immediately over the bow. "We are rowing north, sir." Hichens didn't reply.

Leila Meyer passed a silver brandy flask to her partner in oars.

"I might have a bit of that!" Hichens cried. "I'm frozen."

"You're not rowing," Major Peuchen muttered.

"I doubt you need this, sir," Leila said, and replaced the flask in her cloak. "I expect you'd finish it all yourself." Nevertheless, she unwrapped the steamer blanket from around her shoulders and draped it over his huddled form. Another woman wrapped a second blanket around his waist and limbs. "Now," Leila added, "you've got more blankets than the rest of us."

"If you were to row, you might keep yourself warm," Major Peuchen said.

"Listen, you on the starboard side there," Hichens snarled. "This boat might move a little faster if you kept your oar up in the water at the right angle."

❧

ANOTHER HOUR AND a half passed. At regular intervals Margaret's voice—as well as the voices of other women in the lifeboat—urged everyone to row, row, row. The boy lay huddled in the bottom of the boat, exhausted but unable to stop shaking long enough to fall asleep. One woman slipped from her seat and lay prone; no one could revive her.[51] Margaret's eyes played tricks on her; the air itself seemed liquid black, the stars cold and piercing. She couldn't judge time or distance. Every once in a while Major Peuchen called out the time until someone told him to stop. Better to feel beyond the boundaries of time and space than to consider how many oar strokes an hour could claim, with no hope of a destination.

A thin line of gray light tinged the horizon, which melted into a pale, leaden dawn. Suddenly, to their relief, another lifeboat drew near, this one fairly full. Margaret could see the number 16 on the side.

"Let's tie up!" cried Hichens. "Throw us a rope!" A man sat stiffly in the bow, dressed only in white pajamas, his hair tinged with frost, his teeth chattering violently.

"Start rowing, man!" Margaret called to him. "Get your blood in circulation!"

"Shut up!" yelled Hichens. "Will you please let me do my work here? Throw us a rope!"

A rope landed near Hichens's feet, and he quickly tied the boats together. "Now we rest," he gasped. "Everyone drop your oars and lay to. Rest."

His order was immediately obeyed. The sense of exhaustion was palpable. Margaret looked over to the other lifeboat, faces becoming clear in the dawn. The pale light disclosed the horror of their situation. They sat in the middle of a field of ice. Mountains and spires of ice stood like points on a landscape. Icebergs appeared in every direction, some lying low in the water, others tall as ships.[52] No one spoke. There was so much to say, and no one spoke.

An icy blast of wind rocked the boats, knocking them together, and then another.

"If I sit here for one more minute I'll utterly freeze to death!" cried Helen Candee.

"Yes, let's keep rowing," Julia Cavendish said. "It is our only hope."

"I'll decide when we're to row!" Hichens cried. "Besides, we've no men at our oars." He looked over to the other boat. "Surely you can spare us one man if you have so many." The pajama-clad man nodded briefly, and a stoker was ordered to leap between the boats and take the starboard side. Margaret thought the stoker looked nearly as frozen as the man in pajamas. Black and covered with coal dust, he was dressed only in thin jumpers, his legs exposed from the knees down. She took her sable stole and wrapped it from his waist down around his limbs, tying the tails around his ankles.[53]

"Cut us loose," Margaret called to the frozen man in pajamas.

"I'll decide when to cut loose!" Hichens howled. "Indeed, if we do, I'll likely be thrown overboard! We need to rest."

"I'll toss you over myself," Margaret snorted, and rose from her seat. Hichens jumped back. Miss Martin put a hand on Margaret's shoulder. "Don't," she muttered. "He's likely to tumble in of his own accord if you so much as approach him."

"Sit down, damn you!" Hichens cried. His voice was high and thin. "Don't you know if there's a scramble, you'll knock the plug out? By damn, I wish you'd keep your place!"

The stoker, with Margaret's stole around his legs, protested in a thick accent. "Say," he said, "don't you know you're talkin' to a lady?"[54]

"I know to whom I am speaking, and I am commanding this boat!" Hichens snapped.

Nevertheless, the pajama-clad man tossed the rope into the boat. Margaret sat down and took up an oar; at least her anger made her forget the cold. "Row!" she cried. "Row! Row! Or else we'll freeze!" They backed away from Lifeboat Sixteen and pulled out into the vast expanse of water.

Another hour and a half passed. The women tried spelling each other, to give their arms a rest, but to sit still for too long was to court death.

Suddenly Miss Martin gasped, "Look! There is a flash of lightning!"

Hichens squinted up into the sky. The stars were still visible against a thin veil of dawn. "No, it's just a falling star. It's nothing."

"It's the light glinting off a pinnacle of ice," Leila Meyer said.

"It is a ship," someone cried. The light became brighter and was multiplied by others stretched in a distinct row. A deck. The deck of a ship. It seemed miles away.

"It's likely to be the *Carpathia*," said Fleet. Margaret turned and looked at him in surprise; he had sat completely silent during the entire ordeal. "That would be the closest ship," he added.

The precise British accent of Julia Cavendish rose high and clear over the voices of the occupants of both boats. "Where those lights are lies our salvation," she said. "Shall we not go towards them?"[55] The reply was a murmur of approval, and they all fell to the oars with renewed vigor.

"Let this boy here guide the rudder, the one with the broken arm, and you take an oar!" Helen Candee cried to Hichens.

"I am the quartermaster, and I will guide the rudder," Hichens replied sullenly. The other women teased and jeered, but Hichens refused to move.

"Will the *Carpathia* come and pick us up?" Miss Martin asked.

"No, my dear," Hichens said icily. "She is not going to pick us up; she is here only to pick up bodies."[56]

The stoker again intervened. "No, no. She's a good ship; she'll help us."

Margaret looked around and saw several other lifeboats struggling in the gray air. None of them were full. As the day continued to lighten, the sea grew choppy. A good wave would tip this boat with no problem, Margaret thought. Finally they drew close enough to see the deck, lined with anxious crew members and curious passengers whose journey had been unexpectedly interrupted. By now a heavy sea was running, and despite their desperate paddling, they couldn't get close to the ship.

"Wouldn't it be smoother to go 'round on the other side?" Major Peuchen asked.

"No," Hichens said, "for then we stay longer in the cold sea. We can't stand any more exposure."

Three times they tried to approach the ship, and three times they were dashed against the keel, bounding off like a rubber ball. Finally they managed to nudge up alongside. From the deck a man threw down a rope spliced in four at the bottom; Major Peuchen and the earnest stoker fumbled with frozen fingers to make a Jacob's ladder. A wooden seat, two feet long and a foot wide, was trundled down. The lifeboat rocked mightily with each swelling wave, and the men steadied the wooden seat while the first woman climbed on. Once again, Margaret thought, a good dousing seemed likely. Above them gathered a dozen of the *Carpathia*'s officers and crew. Again and again the seat was hoisted up, with a rope looped around each passenger's shoulders in case anyone fell. As they scrambled onto the deck, crew members caught each one as tenderly as if they were children.[57]

Just before Major Peuchen hoisted himself onto the seat, he glanced at his watch: eight A.M. Hichens, pale, too exhausted to speak, was the final man up the ladder.

Met with blankets, hot coffee, and stimulants, the half-clad survivors were strangely quiet. Each man, woman, and child achingly scanned the deck for a familiar face. The *Carpathia*'s Captain Rostron quickly made a count of the survivors crowding his deck: over seven hundred people from thirteen lifeboats.

The mood was strangely calm and otherworldly. Margaret looked out to the sea, a flotilla of jagged ice. She had heard that in the north Atlantic one could actually smell ice before seeing it. She smelled it now, pungent as a steelyard, a damp, venomous vapor.

A Legend Born
April 1912, and Aftermath

SEVERAL HUNDRED MILES off the coast of Newfoundland, the tiny lifeboats had bobbed up and down in a sea that had grown uneasy with the dawn. Quivering from cold and shock, the *Titanic* survivors were pulled one by one up onto the deck of the *Carpathia*. Firsthand accounts describe a methodical calm compared to the terrifying chaos of just a few hours before. Some survivors were no doubt too hypothermic or injured to do much more than allow themselves to be hoisted aboard; others were dazed or stupefied, unable to grasp the enormity of what had happened. Harold Bride, one of the wireless operators, had been pulled onto an overturned collapsible lifeboat just as he "felt like sinking." Eventually he was pulled into another lifeboat, and by the time the *Carpathia* arrived his legs had been soaked to the knees in icy water for hours. He "tried the rope ladder. My feet pained terribly, but I got to the top and felt hands reaching out to me. The next I knew a woman was leaning over me in a cabin, and I felt her hand waving back my hair and rubbing my face." First-class passenger Elizabeth W. Shutes described being pulled up against the side of the *Carpathia* "like a bag of meal. My hands were so cold I could hardly hold onto the rope, and I was fearful of letting go. ... At last I found myself at an opening of some kind and there a kind doctor wrapped me in a warm rug."[1]

Lawrence Beesley, a young science teacher from London, described the enormous relief no doubt felt by all lifeboat passengers as the *Carpathia* steamed into sight. "It meant deliverance at once: that was the amazing thing to us all. ... Here only a few hours after the *Titanic* sank, before it was yet light, we were to be taken aboard. It seemed almost too good to be true." As the sun began to rise, Beesley was struck by the remarkable serene beauty of the massive ice field as pinnacles glistened in the rosy flush: "First a beautiful, quiet shimmer away in the east, then a soft golden glow. ... The sky turned faintly pink and in the distance the thinnest, fleeciest clouds stretched in thin bands across the horizon. ... And next the stars died, slowly—save one which remained long after the others just above the horizon; and near by, with the crescent turned to the north, and the lower horn just touching the horizon, the thinnest, palest of moons."[2]

Margaret Brown was exhausted, arms and shoulders sore, fingers frozen, legs and feet wet and numb. No doubt she, like others, felt a panicky, guilty relief at being rescued, coupled with a sense of disbelief that turned to anger and action. Her gratitude to the people on the *Carpathia* would be expressed again and again. "Catching hold of the one thick rope," she wrote, "we were hoisted up to where a dozen of the crew and officers and doctor were waiting. Stimulants were given to those who needed them and hot coffee was provided for all the survivors. Everything was done for our comfort, the *Carpathia* passengers sharing their staterooms, clothes, and toilet-articles, they, then retiring to the far corner of the ship, where their deck-chairs were placed, giving the lounge up completely to the survivors."[3]

If a census were to be taken of all those who survived—and the sea had been most capricious—Margaret would put Quartermaster Hichens in a category all his own. "We had in our boat one creature—I will not call him a man, for we had no way of knowing it except by his clothes, so craven was he," she wrote. "This creature kept crying out that all was lost, that we might as well give up: and he was quartermaster of the ship, think of that. [As soon as] we pulled into the boat a poor, half-frozen stoker, we had evidence of manhood. This almost naked man I wrapped in my sable stole, and when the craven creature, the quartermaster, talked impudently to me, and when, tired of his complaints, I threatened to have him thrown overboard, the stoker rebuked him."

Hichens was quick to try to establish his own version of events. Margaret spotted him standing in the dining saloon shortly after the rescue, where most of the survivors had gathered. "He was wildly gesticulating," she wrote, "trying to impress upon them what difficulty he had had in disciplining the occupants of his boat. On seeing a few of us near, he did not tarry long, but beat a hasty retreat." Later, at the formal investigation, Hichens avoided any mention of Margaret Brown but noted that Leila Meyer had accused him of using bad language, taking the blankets in the boat for himself, and drinking all the whiskey. "Which I deny, sir," he stoutly declared to the court, claiming that he had done his duty and made sure every lady on his lifeboat was hoisted aboard the *Carpathia*.[4]

Once aboard, survivors were first asked their name and class and then briefly examined by a doctor. Sleeping places were assigned according to gender, class, and general physical condition. Most of the women and children settled in the dining rooms and surrounding corridors; men found space on the deck in steamer chairs or in the smoking room. Some people doubled up in staterooms to provide the less sturdy survivors with beds; a few steerage passengers slipped down to the lower parts of the ship, where they would be least visible. Every nook and cranny of the *Carpathia* was taken. Mrs. Astor, Mrs. Widener, and Mrs. Thayer, the three most prominent first-class survivors, were given Captain Rostron's personal quarters.

AS SOON AS a relative level of orderliness had been achieved, Captain Rostron returned to survey the ice field for any remaining survivors. There were none. Floating sheets and crests of ice stretched across the horizon in all directions. He declined an offer by the nearby *Californian* (a ship that earlier had presumably missed or misinterpreted the *Titanic*'s call for help) to relieve the *Carpathia* of some of its passenger load, and the *Carpathia* began its bleak journey back to New York.

Margaret Brown's first act was to go to the wireless room, where the lone *Carpathia* operator, Harold Cottam, labored furiously. She scribbled a message for her daughter, Helen, in London to let her know that she was safe.[5] Her message apparently never got through; Cottam was busy tapping out the names of survivors to a disbelieving world. Later Margaret would return again to the wireless room to try to send messages for friends as well as other second- and third-class survivors, many of whom did not have the funds to pay for such an extravagance. She paid for them all, but ultimately none of the messages were delivered.[6]

Some degree of ceremony seemed appropriate, and able passengers were called to gather in the first-class dining saloon, where Captain Rostron organized an impromptu service for the hundreds—he had no idea of the exact number—who had been lost. An Episcopal clergyman was found among the passengers, and he struggled to find appropriate words. Many survivors continued to cling to the hope that husbands, sons, friends, or crew members had been plucked off lifeboats or icebergs by other passing ships. With the minister's words, that hope began to fade. One survivor described this service of thanksgiving and

grief as "one of the most harrowing scenes I ever saw."[7] Months passed
before the captain himself admitted his own fears of those early hours:
"When day broke, and I saw the ice I had steamed through during the
night, I shuddered, and could only think that some other Hand than
mine was on that helm during the night."[8]

Those who had been fortunate enough to survive relatively unscathed
now turned their attention to helping others. Happily, the *Carpathia*'s
primary ports were on the Mediterranean, and Margaret reported that
with respect to the quantity and variety of food, "there was nothing
left to be desired." The ship's barber was soon relieved of extra tooth-
brushes, soap, combs, and other toiletries, and the *Carpathia*'s passengers donated clothing, socks, bedclothes, and whatever else they could
think of. Margaret set out to distribute supplies for the women and
children who were sleeping in the dining rooms and corridors. "Sprinkled among the affluent," she wrote, "were our sisters of the second
class, and for a time there was that social leveling caused only by the
close proximity of death." This social leveling apparently caused some
consternation, for Margaret also reported that the ship's doctor tried to
keep her and other first-class women from helping the poorer women:
"'They have blankets cut up for them,' we were told, 'so they are all
right.' 'Blankets indeed!' I replied. 'You can't calm those tortured minds
with blankets.' And we got to them, you may be sure."[9]

Margaret joined a group of women who scoured the *Carpathia*'s
cabins for extra blankets and bedclothes, cut them up, and stitched
them together for the rescued children. Her travels in Europe now
proved useful as well as her fluency in French and conversational skills
in German and Italian. She hardly slept a wink on that long trip to
New York, consoling survivors from second class and steerage who
spoke little English. Everything had been lost: husbands and children
and friends but also clothes, money, valuables—all that was necessary
to start a new life in a new country. Immigration law forbade indigent
immigrants to remain long on American soil, and even the wealthier
foreign women were apprehensive about being turned back to their
homelands for lack of funds. "They were terrified at their being subject
to such humiliation," Margaret wrote.[10] Those fears proved groundless,
at least temporarily: once the *Carpathia* reached New York, customs
regulations were fully suspended, and customs officers helped survivors
locate relatives and friends.

Despite all good intentions, some survivors were not prepared to receive consolation from anyone. "Go away," said two women to Mrs. Louis Ogden, who had brought them steaming cups of coffee. "We have just seen our husbands drown."[11]

At breakfast the morning after their rescue, Margaret looked around at her fellow first-class survivors and suggested that perhaps some action should be taken on behalf of the "poor foreigners who, with everything lost, would be friendless in a strange country." The idea was met with general enthusiasm, although few felt inclined to actually commit to the bottom line. Later that morning, while walking on the deck, Margaret approached several first-class women who were stretched out on deck lounge chairs and tried to interest them in contributing to the fund. One woman replied, "Why, Mrs. Brown, why worry? I will be met by representatives of the Waldorf, who will take me at once to the hotel, and you, of course, will be greeted by the Ritz-Carlton, so why bother?"

"But all these people will not have a Ritz-Carlton or a Waldorf to receive them," Margaret exclaimed in astonishment. The women nevertheless refused to help.[12]

By afternoon, however, a committee had been formed consisting of Margaret, Emma Bucknell, and Mrs. George Stone, among others, with Margaret acting as chair.[13] A meeting of all the survivors was once again called in the dining saloon at three P.M. "Resolutions of gratitude, first to God, then to the Captain and officers, were framed and read," Margaret wrote. Next a subscription list was started, and $4,000 was pledged immediately. The names and contribution amounts were promptly typed up and tacked on the wall at the foot of the stairs, with an open list for those who as yet had declined to contribute. Social pressure must have taken its toll, for by the time the *Carpathia* reached New York, the committee secretary informed Margaret that nearly $10,000 had been pledged.[14] Other records indicate that more than $15,000 was pledged; Madeleine Astor, although severely ill, immediately wrote a check for $2,000.[15]

Time stretched interminably on that short trip. Survivors had to deal with overwhelming grief as well as the anxiety of knowing that friends and family back home would have little knowledge about who had been rescued and who had drowned. Unbeknownst to those on the *Carpathia,* false reports circulated wildly, including rumors that the *Titanic* was being towed safely to shore, or that all passengers had been saved, or that all passengers had drowned. The media frenzy was at a high pitch.

The maiden voyage of the stately *Titanic* had begun in a white blaze of publicity. Newspapermen were welcomed aboard and proudly paraded around the ship; the White Star Line believed in cultivating the press and a bit of free advertising. However, on the cold, rainy night of April 18, 1912, four days after the *Titanic* first set sail, the press was less than welcome. As the *Carpathia* steamed into New York Harbor, despite police orders to the contrary she was immediately surrounded by tugs, ferries, yachts, and just about anything else that could float. Reporters called through megaphones and held up huge placards bearing names from *Titanic*'s passenger list. Beams of light swung out across the water, and opportunists shouted out sums of money for anyone who would be willing to sell his or her story to the right newspaper. Captain Rostron did his best to protect his human cargo, but his efforts were largely futile. One plucky reporter managed to scramble on board the *Carpathia* just before the quarantine section and was promptly apprehended and put under "house arrest."[16]

The wonder and terror of the event was not lost on Margaret, who had already learned to endure the capriciousness of public scrutiny, or on the three terrified Irish girls she had brought up on deck when she found them hiding in steerage, wrapped only in blankets. "Newspaper men and photographers impeded the progress of the *Carpathia*," she wrote. "The excitement of this and the Captain calling through a megaphone to the pilot to disperse the drafts or he would be unable to reach the docks, and the seeing and hearing of the multitude of humanity on the wharf, so frightened these [Irish] women that they refused to quit the ship."

The first act of the *Carpathia* was to deposit *Titanic*'s thirteen lifeboats at the White Star pier, Pier 59, which took nearly an hour. Then the ship shouldered up to Pier 54, where a huge throng of humanity, over thirty thousand people, pushed forward in the cold, driving rain. Police barricades were knocked down, and mounted police officers proved mostly useless. More than five hundred automobiles and carriages, alongside flashing ambulances from local hospitals, were parked next to the pier. Finally the gangway came down, and the first survivors to touch terra firma were met with an explosion of white magnesium powder as news photographers jockeyed for the best shot.

In the wireless room, Harold Cottam and *Titanic* operator Harold Bride had been transmitting, practically nonstop, the names of those rescued. Not even aware that they had docked, Harold Bride—his feet still heavily bandaged from frostbite and the severe wrenching they had endured in the lifeboat—stopped tapping only when William Marconi, the inventor of wireless technology himself, entered the room with a reporter from the *New York Times*. "There's no need to send that now, son," Marconi said gently. With a stroke of the reporter's pen, a hero was born.

Down the gangway the survivors straggled, some to be whisked off in limousines, some to slip away invisibly into the night. Those willing to talk to the press, however briefly, found their names in headlines the next morning. Some embellished their stories; others were pleased or dismayed to discover that someone else had done the embellishing for them. Ever conscious of such matters, the newspapers reported that despite the sanctioned distinctions of class on the *Titanic,* survivors descended the gangway in haphazard fashion, "with no regard to rich or poor."[17]

MARGARET BROWN CHOSE to stay with the ship until the following day, keeping close to those she had been watching over. She still wore the two-piece velvet suit she had donned the night of the sinking, now somewhat worse for wear, and kept her tiny Egyptian statue safe in her pocketbook. "Feeling a duty to remain after the army of Red Cross doctors and nurses, White Star officials, and general Aid Corps [primarily the Travelers Aid Society] had taken leave of the ship, we found it was necessary to improvise beds in the lounge, so I remained with them on board all night," she wrote. "There were many who had friends on the dock, but did not know them, so with each one was sent an escort and the names called out." As soon as a contact had been established and confirmed, Margaret wrote down the destination of each survivor, and this list was given to White Star agents.[18] She was then met by her brother, Daniel Tobin, who had hastily taken a train from Denver, and her New York friend Genevieve Spinner. Once she had learned that her grandson was faring well—the primary reason she had booked her passage on the *Titanic*—she delayed her return to Denver and set up temporary headquarters in New York City. From their rooms at the Ritz-Carlton,

Margaret, Daniel, and Genevieve helped foreign-born survivors by directing them to various consuls in New York, contacting friends and relatives, and sending a flurry of telegrams. They also tried to ensure that donations of cash and clothing were directed to those who needed them most. "This took some days afterwards," Margaret reported. All of New York City strove to help the survivors, and donations began to pour in from all over the world. Six members of the New York Stock Exchange showed up with $20,000 they had collected that very day.[19]

The committee that had been formed at breakfast on the rescue ship continued its steady work; indeed, Margaret's position as chair of the Survivors' Committee was one she would continue to hold until her death twenty years later. On behalf of the "much overworked" crew of the *Carpathia*, the committee raised an additional $5,000 to be distributed evenly among the crew members. They also pledged to continue to pressure the White Star Line to keep its promise to adequately accommodate surviving passengers and crew.

Back in Denver, Margaret's estranged husband, J.J. Brown, and all of Denver waited anxiously for news of Margaret and Hugh R. Rood, the only other Denver resident on the *Titanic*. J.J. and Margaret had filed for a legal separation; nevertheless, their children, complicated financial affairs, and strong Catholic faith kept them closely connected. Finally the news reached Denver that Margaret was safe and Hugh Rood, sadly, had been lost. Any relief that J.J. might have felt was reportedly hidden in a quip to a friend: "She's too mean to sink."

The rest of the city welcomed her with open arms, however, and Mrs. Crawford Hill, the most prominent of Denver socialites, hosted a luncheon in her honor. The *Denver Times* quoted Margaret as saying, "I think I have been misrepresented to my Denver friends. I simply did my duty as I saw it. I knew that I was healthy and strong and was able to nurse the suffering. I am sure that there was nothing I did throughout the whole affair that anyone else wouldn't have done. That I did help some, I am thankful and my only regret is that I could not have assisted more."[20]

On May 29, 1912, Margaret returned to New York for a formal ceremony in which, on behalf of the Survivors' Committee, she presented each *Carpathia* crew member with a crimson-ribboned medal and Captain Rostron with a silver loving cup. Not a single *Carpathia* crew member was forgotten, with six gold medals going to Captain Rostron, Chief Engineer A.B. Johnson, Surgeon F.D. McGee, Purser

E.G.F. Brown, and the first and second officers. Twenty-six silver medals and 284 bronze were presented individually to the remaining crew members. Captain Rostron insisted that all the credit should go to his loyal men. "Captain Rostron," one reporter wrote, "blushing like a school boy who had been praised in the presence of the whole class, tried his best to look stern—and failed miserably. Officers and crew were scarcely less embarrassed than the skipper; many of them tried to hide themselves behind their mates."[21] To Captain Rostron personally, Margaret made a gift of the tiny turquoise-colored Egyptian statue, her good-luck charm, which he cherished the rest of his life.

The photograph of Captain Rostron and Margaret Tobin Brown made newspapers around the world.

As the foremost example of progress in modern shipbuilding and first-class luxury, the *Titanic* was one of many steamers that ambitiously sought the patronage of American industrialists, European aristocrats, and other prominent social and political figures. Millionaires may have walked the top decks, but it was the hundreds of passengers in steerage, in the belly of the ship, who mostly picked up the tab. As on other steamers, obvious barricades and less obvious instruments of design ensured that first-class, second-class, and steerage passengers were carefully segregated. When the lifeboats were lowered, what mattered first and foremost was gender and economic status—along with a bit of luck. Of the 337 first-class passengers, all but one of the children, approximately 97 percent of the women, and 34 percent of the men were saved. Second-class passengers numbered 271; all of the children, 84 percent of the women, and 8 percent of the men were saved. Steerage passengers numbered 712; most were emigrants from Ireland, England, France, Poland, Scandinavia, Italy, and the Middle and Far East. Only 30 percent of the children, 53 percent of the women, and 12 percent of the men were saved (the difference in number between women and children was likely due to the fact that some families chose or were forced to stay together). The *Titanic* and her passengers required 915 crew members to keep things running smoothly, including 517 people to provide cooking, cleaning, and other services. Only eighty-five members of the total crew were experienced sailors. Most of the crew went down with the ship.

The final tally of lost souls was over 1,500. The world was stunned.

Reaction was swift. Such a loss was unfathomable, and newspaper reporters, editors, ministers, and politicians cast about for an adequate list of human sins to hold responsible for such cosmic vengeance. The White Star Line's determination to set a new record for speed demonstrated the foolhardiness of human ambition and the brashness of technological advancement. Most significantly, to boast that the *Titanic* was "unsinkable" arrogantly mocked God and Nature both. Some were quick to note that humankind no doubt deserved such a disaster. Rev. Dr. Charles A. Eaton of the Madison Avenue Baptist Church echoed the words of many when he cried that more than anything else, the disaster "dispelled the wretched selfishness and sleepiness of our age."[22] At the American hearing held shortly after the sinking (the British held a separate inquiry), Senator William Alden Smith of Michigan declared that the disaster resulted from capitalistic greed and aristocratic luxury. "We're running mad with the lust of wealth and of power and of ambition," Smith said. "We are separating society into castes. It takes a terrible warning to bring us back to our moorings and senses." Smith was a strong opponent of J.P. Morgan, the financial agent behind White Star.

Though *Titanic*'s first-class passengers enjoyed the final excesses of the Gilded Age and the technological advantages of the new industrialism, the ship traveled between two troubled shores. Its sinking became an uneasy metaphor for indisputable disparities in wealth and class in both the United States and England. People opened their newspapers to read that the net worth of *Titanic* victims John Jacob Astor, Benjamin Guggenheim, Isidor Straus, and George Widener was over $200 million. Most Americans could not even begin to imagine such wealth. The United States was struggling to grow from a rural to an urban society, and the problems of rapid industrialization were apparent. In 1910, 40 percent of New York City's population was foreign-born, and since then the city had continued to grow exponentially. Factory work was common, with women and children working twelve to fifteen hours a day, six or even seven days a week. Strikes occurred frequently, sometimes violently. A typical example of labor-related strife was the 1909 fire at the Triangle Shirtwaist Company in the garment district of New York City, where most of the employees were young Jewish and Italian women. Following a strike, doors were locked during working hours. A fire broke out, and over one hundred women died in the flames; forty-six jumped from windows to their deaths. Although immigrants from eastern and western Europe provided much of the labor for America's new factories, they were often considered a threat to the American way of life. On the opposite shore, *Titanic*'s maiden voyage had been jeopardized by a coal strike in Britain that left many ships standing at their docks. In fact, many of *Titanic*'s steerage passengers had never intended to board the *Titanic* at all; they had been transferred when their previous arrangements had been canceled due to the coal shortage.

The stern words of ministers and politicians about the *Titanic*'s fate were somewhat mitigated by greatly exaggerated tales of the actions and sentiments of the first-class male passengers who went down with the ship. Patriarchal noblesse oblige reached a high pitch as stories began to circulate on both shores. Maj. Archibald Butt, President Taft's military aide, had booked passage on the *Titanic* after a few weeks of much-needed rest away from Washington. Although little is known of the exact circumstances of his death, it was reported that Major Butt, "thinking always of others rather than himself, joining gentleness, serenity, and firm authority with loftiest sacrifice, mingled the finest pulses of his race and creed, and wrapping the mantle of English Sidney about his knightly shoulders, went down to immortality."[23] Some writers held that Captain Smith shouted to his crew from a megaphone on the bridge, "Be British!" Once the ship slipped beneath the surface, legend claimed that Smith swam out to pluck a baby from the icy water and deposit it safely in a lifeboat before sinking to his own death. Even John Jacob Astor, who had fled New York with his new wife after being thoroughly villainized in the press for divorcing his first one, was morally redeemed by Rev. Johnston Myers of Immanual Baptist Church: "People are better than we think they are," he said. "Only a few months ago public opinion condemned as unfit one of the men who died as heroes and today is acclaimed. The millionaires are not all bad men as it turns out."[24]

The press expressed some empathy for the passengers in steerage as well, although attitudes tended toward condescension and echoed the prevailing notion that people in the lower decks were not quite as noble as those higher up. "Men whose names and reputations were prominent in two hemispheres were shouldered out of the way by roughly dressed Slavs and Hungarians," one writer proclaimed, echoing similar attitudes in other books and newspaper stories.[25] Popular belief held that men of money deserved their wealth and status owing to superior moral constitution; those in steerage were numerous, anonymous, and of dubious character. It wasn't only the newspapers that perpetuated false assumptions about the classes; the account of the British inquiry into the tragedy noted that many "foreigners" perished in steerage because they didn't want to be separated from their luggage. Some *Titanic* survivors were quick to protest this elevation of the moneyed class: the science teacher from London, Lawrence Beesley, exclaimed, "Major Butt and Colonel Astor and Mr. Straus died as brave men died, but did not John Brown and Wilhelm Klein and Karl Johanssen? And yet they are not chronicled, and no newspaper has columns on their self-sacrifice and personal courage. But we know these things were true, and we can bear testimony now to every brave man who perished in the steerage, even if we knew not his name."[26]

Margaret Brown's reaction was forthright and to the point. "The *Titanic* disaster," she said, "was a tragedy that was as unnecessary as running the Brown Palace Hotel into Pike's Peak."[27] While the rest of the world waxed poetic about God's will, Nature's retribution, and the nobility of the great men who had died, Brown laid the blame squarely on the shoulders of the White Star shipping line. She told the *Daily News*, "More lives would have been saved only for rank carelessness and lack of discipline. Not once was there a drill on the vessel, and this in itself was the cause of many a soul going down with the steamer." The "craven" quartermaster, Robert Hichens, was not the only White Star employee to bear her wrath. Bruce Ismay, director of the White Star Line, had been a somewhat reticent occupant of collapsible Lifeboat C. After Ismay was rescued, the ship's doctor told him to go to the dining saloon and get something hot to drink. He refused. Believing Ismay was suffering from shock (which certainly was likely), the doctor led him to his own room, where he dosed him with opiates. Ismay hung a "Don't Knock" sign on the good doctor's door and refused to see anyone.[28] He made an exception for Captain Rostron, who suggested that Ismay send a wireless message to New York. Ismay agreed and scribbled, "Deeply regret advise you *Titanic* sank this morning after collision with iceberg, resulting serious loss of life. Full particulars later. Bruce Ismay."[29] His only other communication was a request to White Star officials in New York to arrange for his immediate return to England along with the other surviving officers.

Ismay was an obvious and perhaps somewhat undeserving target for the torrent of grief and rage held in check by the doctor's cabin door;

his decision to retreat may have exacerbated rather than alleviated his predicament. Margaret thought his behavior unfathomable. She held Ismay indirectly responsible for the accident due to his "mania to break all records on the water," and reportedly told Ismay to his face that in her hometown of Leadville, Colorado, he would have been strung up on the nearest pine tree.[30]

Her next line of attack struck a deep chord in American and British values. "The attitude of the men who were rescued was indeed pathetic," she wrote. "It was noticed how they all tried to explain how it came about like a miracle that they were saved, with an expression of apology, as though it were a blight on their manhood."[31] Benjamin Guggenheim, who did not survive, wished his wife back home to know that he "played the game out straight to the end. No woman shall be left aboard this ship because Ben Guggenheim was a coward."[32] Guggenheim and his valet reportedly disappeared and then reemerged on deck in formal attire, Guggenheim declaring, "We've dressed in our best, and are prepared to go down like gentlemen." Major Peuchen, who shared a lifeboat with Margaret, went so far as to obtain a chit (voucher) from Second Officer Lightoller stating that he had entered the boat only in response to a direct order.[33] Later, at both the American and British inquiries, nearly every male survivor maintained that he had obtained passage on a lifeboat only through the most extraordinary circumstances, either by direct order from an officer of the ship or by going down with the *Titanic* itself and being pulled into a lifeboat afterward. "They told me of the navigation laws restricting men from the boats when women and children were on board," Margaret wrote. "I replied that such must have been the ancient law, and now that equal rights existed ... their conscience on that score should be relieved."[34]

The greatest tragedy of the *Titanic*, in Margaret's opinion, was that families were needlessly separated. "'Women first' is a principle as deep-rooted in man's being as the sea," she stated in an interview. "It is world-old and irrevocable. But to me it is all wrong. Women demand equal rights on land—why not on sea?" These words were echoed by feminist and political activist Emma Goldman, who was lecturing in Denver when the *Titanic* sank. Brown and Goldman shared more than just their opinions regarding the *Titanic;* both were founding members of the Woman's Party, Goldman in New York and Brown in Denver. The women on the *Titanic*, Emma Goldman stated, should have elected to die with those they loved. By accepting "man's tribute in time of safety and his sacrifice in time of danger," women allowed themselves to be treated as subordinate to men.[35] She scathingly criticized each female survivor for succumbing to the "centuries of her training as a mere female." Furthermore, she said,

> With all the claims the present-day woman makes for her equality with man, her great intellectual and emancipatory achievements, she continues to be as weak and dependent, as ready to accept man's tribute in time of safety and his sacrifice in time of danger, as if she were still in her baby age. The men stood aside to let the ladies go first. What about the ladies? What about their love superior to that of the men? What about their greater goodness? Their demand to equal rights and privileges? Is this to be found only at the polls, or on the statutes? I fear me very much that the ladies who have so readily accepted the dictations of the men, who stood by when the men were beaten back from the life-boats, have demonstrated their utter unfitness and inferiority, not merely to the title of man's equal, but to her traditionary fame of goodness, love and self-sacrifice.[36]

The gender debate raged in the newspapers, from the pulpits, in drawing rooms and street pubs. Dr. Henry Van Dyke, in an address on April 18, 1912, in Princeton, New Jersey, explained that "on the average, a man is stronger than a woman, he is worth more than a woman, he has a longer prospect of life than a woman. There is no reason in all the range of physical and economic science, no reason in all the philosophy of the Superman, why he should give his place in the lifeboat to a woman." Only the law of God, Dr. Van Dyke declared, saved the human race from the evils of materialism and "selfish expediency."

Margaret, who was a strong Catholic yet at every juncture of her life had challenged the church's definition of appropriate female roles, took a more practical and straightforward approach. She snapped at a reporter,

> I wonder if I make myself understood? What I mean is that many men went down with the ship who should have saved themselves for their families' sakes. I do not condemn the men utterly for doing what by education and training they have been made to consider themselves irrevocably bound to do, but I say it is a false standard of conduct they adhere to and, analyzed to the bottom, it means nothing but selfishness. Consider those widows left behind, many of them almost as helpless without their

husbands as they would be without their limbs. Their husbands went down to practically painless deaths, while they are left to suffer living deaths, for nobody knows how many long, weary, anguished years are to come. Women whose husbands and children were with them should have held back and declined to be saved.[37]

At a critical time for women's suffrage, the *Titanic* disaster reignited all of the difficulties of early feminist dialogue with respect to articulating the rights of women. Many supporters had been won to the cause of women's suffrage by the argument that women inhabited a higher moral ground than men, which morality would be reflected in society to a greater degree if women were allowed to vote. However, this argument also marginalized women and emphasized certain traits that were believed to make them unsuitable to participate in business or other endeavors outside the home. By arguing that women were helpless without their husbands, Margaret inadvertently played into the ideology of antifeminist men and women who defended traditional gender roles, many of whom were working to collect donations for a memorial dedicated to "the chivalry of American manhood."

Indeed, the one woman in first class who did stay behind with her husband, Ida Straus, became a hyperbolic example of woman's strength through deference, not equality. True to the noblesse oblige expected of his gender and class, Isidor Straus, founder of Macy's Department Store, declared, "I am not too old to sacrifice myself for a woman," and refused to leave the ship.[38] His wife, after some indecision (she entered a lifeboat and then got out again), decided to stay behind with him and reportedly said, "I've always stayed with my husband, so why should I leave him now?" At a time when the *Titanic* disaster stood for so many social ills, the Strauses became a symbol for conventional roles in marriage and the importance of a woman's devotion to her husband. "In an age of domestic disloyalty and divorce [the Strauses] have wreathed a fadeless beauty around the deathless tie of marriage," one author proclaimed.[39] And in a parting shot, Emma Goldman said, "It is to be hoped that some there were among the steerage victims at least, who preferred death with those they loved to life at the expense of the loved ones." The dilemma of social roles, differences in gender real or imagined, and personal commitment and integrity continue to haunt us today.

〜

PEOPLE GENERALLY BELIEVED that almost all of the survivors were women and children and most of the drowned were men. However, statistics prove otherwise. Overall, regardless of class, members of both genders survived (315 men and 336 women were saved, although there were substantially more men than women aboard the ship). Of 105 children, only 52 were saved.[40] George Bernard Shaw, in a May 14, 1912, essay in the *Daily News and Leader,* noted that in the lifeboat of one first-class survivor, Lady Duff Gordon, there were ten men and only two women. Newspaper reports of the disaster, he wrote, fostered a false sense of heroism and "outrageous romantic lying" and laid the blame on fate when human negligence was responsible. Shaw felt that the unruly behavior of second- and third-class passengers had been exaggerated to amplify the chivalrous actions of the wealthier class.[41]

Margaret held her ground and soon antagonized both the lower and upper classes with a few more biting observations. She noted that first-class passengers had ready access to the lifeboats, while most steerage passengers had been prevented from reaching the upper decks until it was too late. Some had reportedly even been trapped behind closed doors in the bowels of the ship. One crew member stated that when the doors to the watertight compartments were closed, more than fifty steerage passengers had been trapped in a "steel prison from which escape was impossible,"[42] but this statement was never verified.

Furthermore, she declared that death was not necessarily met in a noble manner by anyone. "Aristocracy and class distinction were there even in the dread face of death," she wrote. "That mighty leveller of human destinies did not bring the rich man to the poor man's level — they met death together, but the barrier of class was ever there." She was quick to criticize first-class women who seemingly took no one's fate but their own into consideration and the unjust class structure that meant inevitable death for most of the steerage passengers. But she also reproached those who had the least amount of power with which to prevent their own deaths: the crew. Of the seventy stewards who survived, none, she claimed, "attempted to warn those in the staterooms of their danger,"[43] and the officers themselves played a deadly role. "Certain officers," she stated in an interview, "boasted that they would make those damn American Millionaires take their chances with the rest of humanity. Several prominent men went down to their deaths with plenty of opportunity for being saved because those officers wanted to show them their places."[44] Margaret further described in a later written account how on the third day on the *Carpathia* she talked at length with one of the *Titanic* officers who had five lifeboats in his command and "preened his feathers" over how there was only one "rich nabob" who got into a boat without the officer knowing it. "He displayed his weapon," she wrote, "and told how he made one [man] who persistently attempted to get in the boat with his wife ... go chase himself around the deck." The only apparent regret this officer displayed was that he had used oaths toward some of the women in the boats.[45]

In the final analysis, however, we are left with one indisputable and unforgivable fact: there were far too few lifeboats for far too many people, and many of the lifeboats were lowered half empty. The words of first-class passenger Elizabeth Shutes ring true to the present: "The horror, the helpless horror, the worst of it all—need it have been?"[46]

IT WAS ONLY a stroke of luck that Margaret's daughter, Helen, had avoided a trip on the *Titanic*. In 1912, at the age of twenty-three, Helen was an accomplished young woman, nearly finished with her studies. She had been given the choice of attending an American women's college or spending a couple of "not too intensive" years of study at the Sorbonne in Paris.[47] Margaret preferred Europe; Helen wanted to stay in America. However, Helen also feared that she might feel constrained by the restricted curriculum and limited social life afforded college-minded young women in the states. She decided on the Sorbonne and quickly befriended another young American woman with whom she shared a common complaint: "a strong-minded mother determined to marry her daughter to the kind of husband she considered suitable."[48] Helen had planned to accompany her mother on the return voyage but at the last minute changed her mind and decided to stay in London for a few days with friends. Years later she told her own children that if she had boarded the *Titanic*, she believed she would have drowned. "Most persons were in their cabins when the iceberg struck," she said. "I would have been content to wait till morning to learn what had happened."[49]

A favorite family story is one that Helen told about Margaret's beloved seal-skin coat, the first luxurious gift she had received from her husband. Margaret's grandson, James George Benziger, wrote, "For more than two decades she had carried it from continent to continent as a small child carries with it its dearest and oldest teddy bear. My mother [Helen Brown Benziger] never told her she had left the coat in a closet in Paris."[50]

Margaret had to count among her losses her friend Dr. Brewe, whose new wife had emerged from their apartments at 43rd and Chestnut in Philadelphia confident that her husband had taken a different ship. Captain Smith was gone, a man with whom she had made many ocean journeys, as well as her undaunted gymnastics instructor, Mr. McCawley. Both Margaret and Mr. McCawley had thought they could swim away if necessary; Mr. McCawley had to put his belief to the test. The tremulous Mrs. Bucknell and her maid, Albina, survived in Lifeboat Eight. Mrs. Bucknell rowed next to the Countess of Rothes while at the other end of the boat their personal maids rowed together. Mrs. Bucknell's large family at first believed she had perished because her name was absent from early survivors lists; they were ecstatic to learn she had survived. Mrs. Thayer of Philadelphia, a close friend of Margaret's, thought both her husband and son had drowned but "to her supreme joy" was met by her son's embrace when she was brought up on the *Carpathia* deck. Margaret wrote, "In her great thankfulness in having one spared her, for the rest of the voyage not more than a few minutes at a time would she permit him to be separate from her."[51]

Frederick Fleet, the unlucky lookout who had kept a low profile in Lifeboat Six, soon discovered that the White Star Line looked upon the surviving officers and crew as embarrassing reminders of the disaster. He survived eight days of questioning in Washington during the American inquiry, then eventually left the company and built a long career working for other shipping firms, years later becoming a paper salesman in Southampton.

Of the other women in Lifeboat Six, Margaret Martin, whom Margaret had said could "row like a galley slave," and Ruth Bowker, her fellow cashier at the À la Carte Restaurant, both survived—two of only three survivors of the sixty-six-member restaurant crew. Helen Candee, who reputedly broke both legs in her fall into the lifeboat, went on in 1913 to publish *The Tapestry Book* to favorable reviews, and during the 1920s became a travel lecturer, escorting tours to China and Southeast Asia. Her book *Angkor, the Magnificent* was honored by the French government and the king of Cambodia. Mrs. Candee's writer friend,

Col. Archibald Gracie, wrote one of the most significant accounts of the *Titanic* disaster (with Margaret Brown's assistance), although complications from exposure ended his life a few months after the sinking.

Julia Cavendish, the daughter of a wealthy Chicago merchant and a socialite in her own right, lost her husband, Tyrell, but was grateful that her two-year-old child had been left at home.[52] The *Denver Times* considered the Cavendishes one of the most prominent and poignant couples on board and splashed their photos across the front page. Leila Meyer later told a reporter that she had made her husband, Edgar, promise that he would not ask her to leave him, but at the last moment they decided they couldn't leave their baby, waiting at home, without a parent. Her husband continued to help others into lifeboats once he'd seen his wife off safely.[53] One report states that Madame de Villiers, who had spent the greater part of the lifeboat journey calling for her son, later saw him safe and sound in Montreal; he had never been aboard the *Titanic*. Another report claims that Madame de Villiers was really a Belgian woman traveling under an assumed name who saw her luckless fiancé go down with the ship.

Madeleine Astor, nineteen years old and a bride of less than a year, was met at the dock by her stepson, Vincent Astor, whose age was not far from her own. The following August she gave birth to a son whom she christened John Jacob. Her husband, standing in the starboard forecastle area, was reportedly crushed by the *Titanic*'s first funnel when it shook loose and tumbled into the ocean. Madeleine inherited a $5 million trust fund and the use of homes on Fifth Avenue and in Newport, but under the terms of her first husband's will, she relinquished everything when she decided to marry again. That marriage, as well as a third to a champion prize-fighter, ended in divorce, and she died at age forty-seven in Palm Beach.

The "haunted" face that had appeared at Margaret's cabin window was that of James R. McGough from Philadelphia. He survived the disaster, along with J.K. Flynn, who was also a buyer for Gimbels. Hugh Rood, the other Coloradan on board the *Titanic*, was thought to have perished in the sinking. For years his widow, once a belle of Denver society, waited for his return and dropped wreaths over his ocean grave. When he was finally declared dead, his widow inherited $2.5 million and went on to marry a commander in the U.S. Navy. However, according to some reports Hugh Rood had never been aboard the *Titanic* at all.

In November 1932, the Bureau of Missing Persons at the Denver Police Department received a curious note inquiring whether his widow was alive. "Don't let her know anyone is seeking her. Just let me know if she lives," the letter said. The note, mailed from a small town outside York, England, sparked interest in the notion that perhaps Rood was still alive. Detective Tom Lahey of the Bureau of Missing Persons was quoted as saying, "It has always been supposed that Hugh Rood was alive—that he never boarded the *Titanic*. ... If he had, Mrs. J.J. Brown who was aboard would have seen him—she knew him well. But she never did—and I've always been convinced that he, for some reason or other, just dropped from sight after he heard the *Titanic* had gone down."[54]

Robert Hichens, Margaret's "craven quartermaster," remained an irascible figure, reportedly later serving time in jail for shooting a man. Historians have not yet decided whether Major Peuchen was a help or hindrance to the plucky women of Lifeboat Six. Some accounts claim he provided strong arms and ready leadership; others report that he, like Hichens, had to be urged by the women, including Margaret, to row when he became tired. When interviewed by reporters in New York, Peuchen condemned the actions of Captain Smith but later changed his mind and denied his previous allegations at the Senate hearing in New York. On May 21, 1912, he was promoted to lieutenant-colonel in the Queen's Own Rifles and awarded the Officer's Long Service Dedication. He died in 1929 in Alberta.

White Star Director Bruce Ismay, despite his plans to the contrary, was detained at the *Carpathia* dock by American officials; weeks would pass before he could return to England. The Senate hearing established that Ismay did, directly or indirectly, influence the *Titanic*'s high rate of speed through the ice field, but the British press came to his defense and tried to prevent one man becoming the scapegoat for the entire affair. False reports that Ismay had committed suicide circulated on both continents; in the spring of 1913 he retired from the White Star Line and lived the rest of his years quietly in northern Ireland.

Perhaps the most astonishing story is that of Second Officer Lightoller, who loaded the passengers into Lifeboat Six. Before April 14, 1912, his fortitude had been tested by three separate disasters at sea. He went down with the *Titanic*, but a blast from the boilers thrust him back to the surface, where he grasped the capsized collapsible Lifeboat B. The crash of the forward funnel of the ship, which killed John Jacob Astor, missed him by a hair. Lightoller climbed on top of the overturned life-boat, joining thirty others who tenaciously matched their wits against the cold Atlantic. During the night three men slipped into the sea, but Lightoller proved once again that he was a man of fortitude. After the *Titanic* disaster, his career in the Royal Navy included the apt handling of three more disasters at sea and a daring evacuation of Allied troops from Dunkirk in 1940.

Like other survivors of the *Titanic,* for the rest of her life Margaret would be haunted by the cries of those hurled into the icy waters of the Atlantic, calling for rescue that never came. She rarely spoke of it except to mention her fitful dreams and, later in life, to describe how the exposure seemed to have affected her health. Second Officer Lightoller wrote, "Fortunately, the scene that followed [the sinking] was shrouded in darkness. Less fortunately, the calm still silence carried every sound with startling distinctness. To enter into a description of those heart-rending, never-to-be-forgotten sounds would serve no useful purpose. I never allowed my thoughts to dwell on them, and there are some that would be alive and well today had they just determined to erase from their minds all memory of those ghastly moments, or at least until time had somewhat dimmed the memory of that awful tragedy."[55]

SURVIVING THE *TITANIC* disaster afforded Margaret Tobin Brown a pivotal chance to step back and evaluate the purpose and direction of her life. Her children were grown: Lawrence was married and had a new baby son, and soon Helen, nearly finished with school, would marry as well. Despite her staunch Catholicism and the fact that she did not believe in divorce, she and J.J. no longer hid their differences. Their devastating legal separation had taken its toll emotionally and financially and resulted in a bloodbath in the newspapers, but she was now untethered by a husband who disagreed with her personal and political views and preferred her to stay at home. What she had just witnessed had shaken her, but she had done more than just survive. She had responded with action, and her convictions were stronger than ever. Her political involvement blossomed into maritime reform, the rights of workers, children's rights, and further involvement in suffragism and the new feminist movement. The publicity attending her *Titanic* experience provided her with a ready platform to voice her concerns.

On a cultural level, however, the myth of the "Unsinkable Molly Brown" had now taken root. Margaret's energetic personality and forthright political opinions brought a backlash from the press as her words and actions were amplified and exaggerated. Reporters ridiculed her dress, her speech, her opinions; in post-Edwardian America, Margaret Brown pushed the boundaries of appropriate behavior for women, particularly "society" women. Twenty years later, after Margaret's death, overblown newspaper stories turned into sensationalized magazine articles. These articles—fiction, not fact—turned into books; books turned into Broadway plays and Hollywood movies that had almost nothing to do with the *real* story of Margaret Tobin Brown. Soon the myth threatened to swamp and ultimately overtake the story of the real woman, whose story would be lost as surely as if she had indeed sunk with the ship.

CAROLINE BANCROFT, one of the first writers to embellish and popularize the story of Margaret Brown, began by commenting that it was a "strange story" she was about to relate. The story grew more strange with each retelling. Sister Mary Laetitia, Margaret Brown's granddaughter, wrote that Margaret had exercised great caution with the press after the *Titanic* disaster because so many false stories had been printed about her. But even then it was too late. Margaret Brown was the nearest thing to royalty that Denver had ever had, and the city gleefully seized upon its new heroine. The *Denver Post* gushed, "It was she who remained on the ship for two days after the landing at New York to comfort the sick and weary and it was she who spent more than a week in New York seeing that no one had been overlooked and that all of the needy survivors were comfortable." One overblown report described Mrs. Brown as personally nursing Madeleine Astor back from the brink of death; another related that she had commanded Lifeboat Six entirely by herself. Suddenly the life of Margaret Brown became fodder for melodrama, which, perhaps not surprisingly, happened to many *Titanic* survivors who told their tales to the media. However, a boost from Hollywood was necessary to make the myth endure.

Margaret Tobin Brown died of a brain tumor in 1932, but her legend had just begun. Gene Fowler's 1932 book, *Timberline*, and Caroline Bancroft's 1936 biography, *The Unsinkable Mrs. Brown*, both highly fictionalized Margaret's life story but came to be accepted as fact. These books became the basis for the Broadway play *The Unsinkable Molly Brown* and the 1964 Metro-Goldwyn-Mayer (MGM) film of the same name. Director James Cameron relied on the same sources to develop the character of Molly Brown in his 1997 film *Titanic.*

In *Timberline,* Gene Fowler, a reporter for the *Denver Post,* wrote a highly entertaining description of Mrs. J.J. Brown that certainly helped to sell his book, a wry, dry, tongue-in-cheek account of early Denver history. The *Post* was famous for pillorying local politicians, socialites, businessmen, or anyone else in a position of prominence unless they were useful for the newspaper's own aspirations; in fact, J.J. Brown once threatened to toss owners F.G. Bonfils and H.H. Tammen down the back stairs of his office. Fowler began his description of Mrs. Brown's adventure on the *Titanic* by describing how she enjoyed "amusing some and terrifying others with pistol-feats, one of which consisted of tossing five oranges or grapefruits over the rail and puncturing each one before it reached the surface of the sea." On the fateful night, Mrs. Brown "came from her cabin prepared for battle with the night sea air. She had on extra-heavy woolies, with bloomers bought in Switzerland (her favorite kind), two jersey petticoats, a plaid cashmere dress down to the heels of her English calfskin boots, a sportsman's cap, tied on with a woolen scarf, knotted in toothache style beneath her chin, golf stockings presented by a seventy-year-old admirer, the Duke Charlot of France, a muff of Russian sables, in which she absentmindedly had left her Colt's automatic pistol—and over these frost-defying garments she wore a sixty-thousand-dollar chinchilla opera cloak!"

Fowler erred on the side of fact when he wrote that at first Mrs. Brown, like many others, did not believe the ship was actually sinking. Once aboard the lifeboat, however, she is described as assuming command, and Fowler's colorful description became the basis for the role Debbie Reynolds would play thirty years later. "Keeping an eye on the rowers," he wrote, "she began removing her clothes. Her chinchilla coat she treated as though it were a blanket worth a few dollars. She used it to cover three small and shivering children. One by one she divested herself of historic woolens. She 'rationed' her garments to the women who were the oldest or the most frail. It was said she presented a fantastic sight in the light of flares, half standing among the terrified passengers, stripped down to her corset, the beloved Swiss bloomers,

the Duke of Charlot's golf stockings and her stout shoes." She sang
from various operas, and told stories to keep the minds of her fellow
survivors occupied. "'Some of you people—the guy here with heart
trouble that I'm curing with oars—are rich. I'm rich. What in hell of it?
What are your riches or mine doing for us this minute? And you can't
wear the Social Register for water wings, can you? Keep rowing, you
sons of bitches, or I'll toss you all overboard!'"

Caroline Bancroft, a colorful personality and local legend in her own
right, conjectured a "Mag" Brown who spent every waking moment
dreaming of how she might enter the ranks of the "Sacred Thirty-six,"
Denver's most elite social group. "Maggie spent money as if she were
married to a Croesus in an effort to make the social grade," Bancroft
wrote, and claimed that "Maggie" strode down Seventeenth Street to
try to impress the "distinguished occupants who might be looking out.
These men soon developed a by-word which they passed along to each
other: 'Here comes Colorado's unique fur-bearing animal!'"

Early Denver writers who sniped at Margaret Brown were motivated
by political and social reasons, not the least of which was the "salty,"
exaggerated style of journalism popular in those days, particularly in
writing about prominent people. In early Denver, news events focused on
the provincial and often on the trivial, and a colorful or provocative story
sold newspapers much more successfully than any adherence to fact.
"The best editors in the West were masters of vigorous English." wrote
historian David Dary. "They knew or concocted virile expressions. They
applied the barbed epithet when they thought it would do the most good.
They understood the value of editorial abuse in attracting readers ... or
show[ing] their indignation about rival editors or people they did not
like." Nevertheless, in the case of "Molly" Brown and other legendary
Colorado women such as "Baby Doe" Tabor or "Silver Heels," a type
had been established. Women who lived relatively independent public
lives—and stood for the cause of suffrage, as both Margaret Tobin Brown
and Elizabeth McCourt Tabor did—were cast as aggressive, flamboyant,
"unnatural" women whose physical characteristics were described as
overtly masculine or excessively erotic. Despite the existence of voluminous primary sources, subsequent historians relied upon these often
bawdy stories without looking much further for facts or verification.

A Night to Remember, produced in 1958 and directed by Roy Baker,
was the first major cinematic effort to interpret the *Titanic* disaster.

Essentially a fictionalized documentary based on the book of the same name by Walter Lord, the film was largely accurate but broke form with the character of Mrs. Brown, taking its cue from Fowler and Bancroft rather than more reliable sources. The first scene in which Mrs. Brown appears shows a robust, overdressed woman at a finely set table, speaking loudly enough for everyone in the restaurant to hear. "Leadville Johnny, they called him," she bellows, "and he was the best gol-durn gold miner in Colorado. Fifteen I was when I married him."

"Really?" a young, refined English gentleman inquires.

"He didn't have a cent," she cries. "Well, three months later, he struck it rich and we was millionaires. You know what he did?"

"Yes?" The young man, clearly offended by her vulgarity and pretentiousness, draws back.

"He built me a home and had silver dollars cemented all over the floors of every room!" she declares. The camera moves on; the entire room has found her offensive in a mildly amusing way.

This scene establishes several interesting untruths: "Leadville Johnny" was not J.J. Brown but rather John Campion, a prominent and well-respected business associate of the Browns. Margaret was not fifteen when she married J.J. but nearly twenty. It took them years, not months, to make their money, and the story of silver dollars embedded in the floors was invented by Gene Fowler. The most interesting detail in this passage is Mrs. Brown's speech. She no doubt had a slight Missouri accent when she first came to Leadville, but in addition to studying speech and languages in Denver and later at the Carnegie Institute in New York, she played minor dramatic stage roles in New York and Paris. She almost certainly never said "gol-durn."

Nevertheless, an archetype was born, and a fun one at that. In the film, as the lifeboats are lowered, Mrs. Brown bellows to a steward, "Hey, steward. Cancel my appointment with the hairdresser, will ya? Tell her I've gone boating!" Once in the lifeboat, she tucks a stole around the shoulders of a woman with a baby and coos, "Here you are, sister. This will help keep you warm. Don't you worry about me—I got plenty of fat!" The scene would not be complete without the cowardly quartermaster, whom she chides like a strict schoolmarm: "Don't get fresh with me, son. I'll throw you overboard!"

The movie that popularized the name "Molly" and truly made her unsinkable was, however, *The Unsinkable Molly Brown*, produced by MGM in 1964 and starring Debbie Reynolds as Molly and Harve Presnell as Johnny, based on the earlier Broadway play starring Tammy Grimes. The movie follows the life of "Molly" from her birth to the *Titanic* disaster; it was enormously popular in its day and a turning point in Debbie Reynolds's career. On the lifeboat, Molly once again emerges as the dominant figure, slapping a woman and then pulling her close to control the woman's hysterics. As another woman cries, "We're going to sink!" Molly yells, "Not with Molly Brown on board. That ship may be down, but not me! I'm unsinkable! I survived the Colorado floods when I was six months old, so this is nothin'!" She urges all the women to row, leads them in song, and again chastises the quartermaster (the original script called for her to label him a "rat-gutted, chicken-livered, bare-bottomed coyote"). By this point the legend obviously had little to do with the real Margaret Brown; the "Molly" of the film has bright red hair, a well-bosomed figure, and an accent that proves she never saw the four walls of a schoolhouse.

The movie's *Titanic* scene concludes with an English butler in Molly's mansion back in Denver reading aloud from the newspaper to an admiring circle of family and friends. "Denver's heroine, our own Mrs. J.J. Brown, who is now known throughout the world as the Unsinkable Molly Brown, returns to Denver today," the butler reports gleefully. "When interviewed during her triumphant week in New York, she made light of her heroism despite the glowing reports from her fellow passengers. She said, 'I sure as *blank* wasn't ready for a *blank-blank* watery grave, so I just *blank* well took the others along with me!' On her last day in New York, the Unsinkable Mrs. Brown was decorated by the British Government for her courage. When asked about the medal she said, 'A girl can always use another piece of jewelry!'"

Some of the myths perpetuated by the MGM movie appear to be composites of various experiences or of actual people. Although Margaret Brown did not lead her lifeboat in song, as Debbie Reynolds did in the movie, survivors in several different lifeboats reported that people sang to drown out the moans and cries of those who had been thrown into the water or merely to keep themselves alert and alive. Many women in Lifeboat Six acted nobly, regardless of class; the movie combined all of the heroic actions into the character of Molly Brown, and the rest of the women appear helpless and weak. There is no real evidence that Margaret Brown ever referred to herself as "unsinkable," a fact that was verified by

Meredith Willson himself, who wrote the music and lyrics for the Broadway musical. The name "Molly" was invented by Richard Morris, writer of the book on which the movie was based. As time passed, however, and the distinction between fact and fantasy became more obscure, history books held that Margaret herself had changed her name from Maggie to Molly to make it sound less Irish, less lower class, and "more American."

The year 1997 brought a new version of Molly Brown to the screen in the James Cameron movie *Titanic,* in which the character plays a minor but pivotal role. Cameron touches more directly on some of the class issues that played out on that fateful April night and again uses the character of Molly Brown as a catalyst. Rose, a first-class passenger set to marry a pretentious, emotionally abusive socialite, falls in love with Jack, a passenger in steerage. Rose survives the sinking, while Jack predictably does not (although the point, of course, is that their romance survives the greatest of all disasters). An elderly Rose, looking back on her *Titanic* adventure, describes her first sighting of Molly Brown: "At Cherbourg a woman came aboard named Margaret Brown, but we all called her Molly. History would call her the Unsinkable Molly Brown. Her husband had struck gold someplace out west, and she was what mother called 'new money.'" "New money," of course, doesn't spend the same as "old money," and Molly Brown is an impostor, a "Western spitfire" who doesn't understand conventional standards of class and gender. The script notes that Molly Brown is a "tough-talking straightshooter who dresses in the finery of her genteel peers but will never be one of them."

Molly, although despised for her vulgar ways, becomes the medium through which first-class Rose and third-class Jack find their love. After Jack nobly prevents Rose from flinging herself into the ocean in despair over her engagement, Rose's fiancé invites Jack to dinner in the first-class dining saloon, against the wishes of her mother and other first-class passengers, hoping to humiliate him. The scene is set for Molly Brown to come to his rescue. "Son," she says, "do you have the slightest comprehension of what you're doing?"

"Not really," he glibly replies.

"Well, you're about to go into the snakepit. I hope you're ready. What are you planning to wear?"

Jack looks down at his clothes. This is something he hasn't considered.

"I figured," Molly says, and takes him down to her stateroom, where she has dozens of stylish men's suits, supposedly purchased for her son.

Jack finishes dressing. "My, my, my," Molly exclaims. "You shine up like a new penny! Ain't nothin' to it, is there, Jack?"

"Yeah, you just dress like a pallbearer and keep your nose up!" Jack responds.

"Remember," she advises, "the only thing they respect is money, so just act like you've got a lot of it and you're in the club."

There is little in this scene that relates to the real Margaret Brown. But what is most interesting at this point is how a type has clearly been established that plays a pivotal role in several distinct ways.

Storytellers, whether in print or on screen, generally try to bring a sense of purpose or closure to the most complex and often painful human experiences. Narrative structures reflect our attempts to make sense out of seemingly nonsensical situations. Yet the way in which we as a culture tell our stories also reflects the fears, phobias, and uppermost concerns of the times, explicitly or implicitly. The sinking of the *Titanic* is an event that no amount of objective reasoning or creative imagining could adequately explain or soothe, in 1912 or in any year since then. The legends that grew around certain *Titanic* personalities not only worked to obscure or at least temper the real human tragedy but allowed us to continue to fall back on familiar, conventional stereotypes that obfuscated the substantial social, political, and economic changes that were occurring in both British and American culture. Now, decades later, we can begin to look at what these stories represented and misrepresented and what they say about American culture both then and now.

The tall-tale character of Molly Brown crystallizes class and gender tensions in such a way that we laugh with her and at her—and the story of a sinking ship needs comic relief. As court jester and Western-style clown, Molly can poke fun at others and also make fun of herself; she's a fish out of water but doesn't care what people think. In Cameron's film, one scene that ended up on the cutting-room floor (owing to time constraints) shows Molly sitting in the Palm Court just as an iceberg can be seen though the window behind her, passing ominously. Molly pertly raises her glass to a nearby waiter: "Hey, can I get some ice here, please?"

A less successful scene takes place with Molly in the lifeboat, urging the other women to row. Just as the *Titanic* sinks into the frothy sea, Molly quips, "Now, there's somethin' you don't see every day!" The joke falls flat—the tragedy too real at that point for such an off-the-cuff remark—and her character dissolves into triviality.[56]

Another curious aspect of the legendary Molly Brown is her court-ship of European culture and taste and how this taste contributes to her alienation from American culture. American-European tensions were fanned by the *Titanic* disaster and played out most tellingly in the two very different investigations of the sinking, each country eager to shift blame to the other. Margaret Brown moved easily in social circles in both New York and Europe, and the legend incorporated this element of her story in a very interesting way. Molly may have found acceptance and cultural stimulation in Europe, but the movies and books show this as a weak side of her character, as a degenerate and un-American trait, very nearly a betrayal of the American dream she supposedly represented. She may have been accepted in a king's court and counted royals among her friends, but Americans were supposed to know who she really was: a belligerent, unmannered impostor trying to force her way into society.

On stage and screen, Molly Brown is cast as unschooled, unman-nered, wild, and very "Western." There are positive and negative aspects to this role: the positive is that she represents a gutsy fortitude and forthrightness that we admire; the negative is that we never have to take her seriously. The character of Molly Brown represents what we want to believe about the West just as the real West seems to be disappearing. The western frontier embodied America's desire to believe in a "pure" West and a "pure" Western character, strong, independent, unfettered by culture. But this frontier has always been a vanishing ideal, just on the edge of our imagination. Readers and moviegoers alike want Molly Brown to wear miner's boots under her satin dresses, speak with a crude accent, and forget to notice the dirt under her fingernails when she's having tea with the queen. Like the stereotype of the Western prosti-tute, Molly has to be rough, tough, and wild but must also possess an independent spirit and an untarnished heart of gold.

Most importantly, the legendary character of Molly Brown provides a useful intermediary or interstitial link between classes and genders. She represents the American dream that anyone can make it from the bottom rung of society to the top if they just try hard enough and allows us to believe—at least for a moment—that America was and is, ultimately, a classless society. She is the perfect agent to help Jack fall in love with Rose. She is also a woman who behaves like a man, and thus her courage and strength can be explained in ways that don't threaten society's idea of what a truly proper or feminine woman should be. These exaggera-

tions of the point that she was an exception to the rules, not like other
women, indeed abnormal or unnatural (a theme that is most apparent in
magazines and journals of the 1940s and 1950s) prevent her from being
a threat to men or women. She moves easily in both circles because she
belongs to neither.

The real Margaret Brown understood that a certain degree of wealth
and education allowed a woman to take a stand against patriarchal
culture, and she used those benefits to her own advantage as well as
to help others politically and culturally. Wives of prominent men,
particularly those who strode the first-class decks of the *Titanic,* were
often considered nothing more than elegant adjuncts of their wealthy
husbands. Economic and social change meant that a new, albeit small,
window of opportunity existed for some women: they could move
beyond the conventions of the past and begin to turn their lives in very
different directions. Even on the *Titanic,* conventional social behavior
had begun to change. Tradition dictated that men's and women's social
rooms be separate: men spent time in the Smoking Room, women in
the Ladies' Writing Room. However, the ship's designer, Thomas An-
drews, planned to remodel the Ladies' Writing Room into more first-
class staterooms and cabins once the ship returned to England because
it simply wasn't being used enough. Women refused to be segregated;
men and women were socializing together.

Does Cameron's film, or any film about the *Titanic,* tell it like it was?
No, nor should it. But it does make us remember history the way we see
it on the screen. Books and films always take liberties with history; they
must and should. But a curious cultural phenomenon occurred with the
Broadway play and Hollywood film *The Unsinkable Molly Brown* that
may be a precursor to the controversy surrounding more contemporary
films such as Oliver Stone's *Nixon* and Steven Spielberg's *Amistad.* As
any biographer or reader of biography knows, historical characters are,
ultimately, unknowable beyond the most conspicuous aspects of their
lives, and the interpretation of history and the personal lives involved
can be highly subjective. Nevertheless, we hold a certain responsibility to
unravel the distinctions between history and myth as best we can and to
continue to ask ourselves why certain myths and stereotypes fascinate us.

The *Titanic* disaster proved to be an interesting turning point in
American history. In the years following the disaster, America faced the
first world war, incipient labor and women's rights movements, and the

beginning of a national income tax. The vehemence of Senator William Alden Smith at the Senate hearing on the *Titanic* disaster was echoed in the words of newly elected president Woodrow Wilson. In his message to Congress on April 8, 1913, almost a year to the day after the *Titanic* sinking, Wilson proclaimed, "We must abolish everything that bears even the semblance of privilege." America truly was changing.

In Margaret Brown's life, the *Titanic* proved an interesting catalyst as well as she turned her attention from her children and the more provincial aspects of Denver and Leadville to events on a grander scale. But now we return to her beginnings. The legend of Molly Brown began with a cyclone that left the newborn babe with no home, no mother, and a goat as a wet nurse. Margaret Tobin began her life no less auspiciously in 1867 in the small town of Hannibal, Missouri.

Raised on the Milk
of a Nanny Goat

1867–1886

ON JULY 18, 1867,[1] in a modest immigrant's cottage in the bustling riverside town of Hannibal, Missouri,[2] a daughter was born to John and Johanna Tobin. They named her Margaret and called her "Maggie." The child was part of the new life her parents had established for themselves in a town already made famous—first by the new railroad, an important stop for miners bound for the goldfields of California, and then by the pen of young Samuel Langhorne Clemens, who became known as Mark Twain. In Charleston, Virginia, John Tobin had left behind the grief surrounding the death of his first wife, Bridget, and come to Hannibal with his eleven-year-old daughter, Catherine Bridget, in tow. Johanna Collins, whose marriage to John Reading had also come to a sad conclusion upon his death, left Pennsylvania with her daughter, Mary Ann, who was a year younger than Catherine. In Hannibal they found not only each other but also a vibrant, close-knit Irish Catholic community in which they soon established themselves. They had four children in addition to the daughters they each brought to the marriage: Daniel in 1863, Margaret in 1867, William in 1869, and Helen in 1871. The siblings remained close throughout their lives.

The Tobin home, perched on a small hill on the corner of Denkler Alley and Prospect Street, was only blocks from the banks of the Mississippi River. The four-room cottage, with a kitchen, bedroom, front room, and larger room on the lower level set back into the hillside, not only housed the growing Tobin family but had enough land to support one cow, several chickens, and a small vegetable garden.[3] There were many such cottages along Denkler Alley, and the children were across the street from Mary O'Leary's grammar school on Prospect Street (run by Johanna's sister, Maggie's aunt) and near the Hannibal Gas Works, where John Tobin worked as a laborer. Living quarters may have been a bit cramped, but the Tobins had no less than their neighbors, and the children reveled in the thick woods surrounding the town, the nearby caves (later made famous in the book *Tom Sawyer*), and the excitement of an occasional riverboat chugging up to berth at Hannibal's bustling dock.

Years later Margaret would reminisce that adventure—and politics—ran in her blood. John Tobin was born in Fermoy, Ireland, in 1823.[4] The early years of the potato famine and Fenian violence in Ireland likely precipitated the Tobin family's decision to emigrate to the United States. As a boy John came to America via Canada with an uncle, joining other members of his family on a farm not far from Harpers Ferry, West Virginia. He eventually took a position with the government, met Bridget Pickett, and married her. Soon he was caught up in the politics of the times and joined the efforts of abolitionist John Brown to liberate slaves. Family lore claims that he worked at a station on the Underground Railroad and helped slaves escape across the Pennsylvania state line.[5] After the premature death of his wife, like many other immigrants John may have dreamed of following the call of the gold camps to the west, but he liked what he saw in Hannibal and decided to stay.

John Tobin met a kindred spirit when he met Johanna Collins (who apparently dropped her married name, "Reading," after her first husband's death). Johanna, born in Ireland in 1825, felt staunchly that education—something that had been largely denied to them both—was important, and she shared John's faith in a society striving to be free of repression and prejudice. Johanna had spent most of her childhood in Pennsylvania and was a descendant of O'Donovan Rossa, an Irishman exiled to America for his militant efforts in the Irish resistance.[6] The Tobin family was fiercely proud of its Irish roots, and Johanna Tobin was known for her strong spirit and involvement in Hannibal's Irish Catholic community. Until the age of thirteen or so, each of the Tobin children attended the private grammar school run by Mary O'Leary and her daughter Margaret, less than a block away. Many years later Margaret would recall that Johanna rarely read but loved to be read to; whether that preference was because of failing eyesight or the possibility that she never acquired the higher reading skills she demanded of her children is impossible to say.

For twenty years John Tobin worked for the Hannibal Gas Works, firing coke furnaces and performing other types of manual labor.[7] At one point, perhaps during his early years in Hannibal, he also apparently worked in the office of one of the riverboat companies.[8] Next to the tobacco factories, the Hannibal Gas Works was one of the largest employers in town. Just a few blocks from the Tobin home, the company occupied a significant plot of land. One large stone building contained the coal and coke house, a condensing room, and a purifying room. Another brick building held furnaces and a meter room; a coke-crushing building and stone valve house stood nearby. A storehouse stood on the corner of Third Street, with a round gas-o-meter tank. Hours were long and the work rigorous; an average worker's wage at the time was $1.75 to $2.00 per day.

Despite the long hours necessary to keep his family clothed and fed, John Tobin found his new home town an exciting place, for Hannibal was a bustling community. At the beginning of 1850 Hannibal's census recorded 1,996 "whites," 282 "slaves," and 41 "free persons of color," for a total population of 2,319. Ten years later the population had nearly tripled to 6,324. The nine saloons were outnumbered only by the lawyers—ten. There were nearly as many physicians, along with two music teachers, two dentists, and two undertakers. Seven family groceries dotted the town, along with several mills and factories, a carriage and wagon factory, three hotels, and one steam sawmill. The nine saloons were rivaled by nine churches of various denominations; one brewery kept the saloons well supplied. Hannibal was not just a port but boasted its own shipyard as well. The town had come a long way from its quiet beginnings in the early 1800s.

The first people to arrive in Hannibal were primarily Southerners from Virginia, Kentucky, and Tennessee, with a few coming from Pennsylvania in the 1830s. The Irish didn't come to Hannibal until the railroad days, beginning in 1852, but by then economic lines were drawn and social hierarchies established. The Irish, although they arrived in significant numbers and were an integral part of early Hannibal, nevertheless were marginalized to a great degree and tended to keep to themselves. Their influence in the town increased as their numbers grew; however, historians note that it wasn't until World War I that this early ostracism disappeared.[9] Catholic missionary Father John Canon O'Hanlon—who became a good friend of the Tobin family—arrived in Hannibal in 1848 and not only kept a detailed journal but established the first Catholic records. The first organized Catholic parish, Immaculate Conception Parish, was started by Reverend Patrick Fleming in 1851.

The small group of families that made up the first congregation eventually erected a small brick church at 512 Church Street, and by 1859 the membership had grown to 1,500. The entire town swelled in size during the next ten years as first- and second-generation immigrants from Ireland, Germany, France, Italy, and other western and eastern European countries arrived in significant numbers.

John Tobin might have anticipated a more tolerant racial climate in Hannibal than he had experienced in Virginia, but similar problems were brewing. Nowhere was this situation more evident than in education. In 1847 a law had been passed in Missouri making it illegal to teach "Negroes" or "mulattos" to read or write. This measure was intended primarily to thwart the efforts of abolitionists, who distributed pamphlets that some Hannibalians feared would incite a slave rebellion. Although the penalty for breaking this law was a $500 fine or six months in jail, officials in Hannibal tended to look the other way as white sympathizers visited the homes of "free Negroes" and continued to teach them to read and write.

Nevertheless, when civil war erupted in 1861, Hannibal was caught, geographically and politically, in the crossfire. Trade was diverted to nearby Quincy, a secure Union town, as Confederate sympathizers and Union organizers struggled over their differences in Hannibal streets and neighborhoods. The mood of buoyancy over growth and prosperity was quickly lost as the town grappled with the effects of the devastating war: failing businesses, the constant presence of soldiers, residents' fears for personal safety and the potential loss of their homes and property, and the deaths of family members and friends. Ultimately the war claimed the lives of over 600,000 men, and no family was untouched. Industries were paralyzed; many businesspeople closed their doors and simply left town. The citizens of Hannibal lived under martial law, and no one was allowed to enter or exit the city limits without a pass. Wealthier families sent their daughters East to stay with relatives. Even the venerable John Garth, owner of the hugely prosperous Garth Tobacco Company, quietly closed shop and left town. Unemployment rates skyrocketed.

During the Civil War, the state of Missouri supplied 40,000 men for the Confederacy and 110,000 for the Union forces and recorded a total of 1,162 military engagements. Despite strong local sentiment on both sides of the war, there were no major engagements in Hannibal itself.

Union troops were primarily concerned with guarding the Hannibal–
St. Joseph Railroad, which was used for transporting troops and
arms, and preventing or slowing the recruitment of Southern troops.
Confederate troops attempted to destroy bridges and occasionally took
shots at passing trains. Nearly a century later James Benziger, Margaret
Brown's grandson, wrote that his great-grandfather John Tobin had
joined a local regiment during the war, but beyond that little is known
of John Tobin's wartime activities.[10]

By the time Maggie Tobin was born, the Civil War had ended, but
its devastating effects were still evident. Food was more plentiful on
shopkeepers' shelves, and her father was safe at home, but the family
had struggled. John Garth's sons, John and David, returned and reestablished the tobacco factory, but it would never fully return to its
former prosperity. Some men returned to their families; many did not.
Growing up in the decade after the Civil War made an impression on
young Maggie, fostering an incipient political awareness and belief in
basic human rights that years later she would vocalize in the women's
and workers' rights movements. Helen Brown Benziger, Margaret's
daughter, echoed the sentiments that John and Johanna Tobin had
passed on to Margaret, who then passed them to her children, when she
remarked during the Harlem riots in the 1960s that she was "delighted
that the colored people were standing up for their rights at last."[11] The
family had not forgotten the proud role John Tobin had played at
Harpers Ferry one hundred years earlier.

ANNIE OVER, Dare Base, Run Sheepy Run, King Arthur, London
Bridge—the games Maggie Tobin played with her siblings had been
passed down for generations. At that time Palmyra Avenue (named for
the palmyra palm whose fiber was used to make rope, and now called
Mark Twain Avenue), near where the Tobins lived, was a rocky, winding
road crisscrossed several times by O'Meara Creek. It was almost impas-
sible by stage or carriage, but the thick line of trees along the road, many
hung with rope swings (hemp was raised in Hannibal, and there were
a number of rope yards), was popular with children and made a grand
playground for Maggie and her siblings. Maggie would have played
marbles and mumblety-peg with her older brother, Daniel, and as her
younger sister, Helen, grew the two girls became inseparable as well.

Although physicians were readily available for severe illnesses, broken limbs, and childbirth, folk remedies were popular. Mothers protected their children from childhood disease with homemade asafetida bags, worn on a string around the neck from early fall to late spring. Asafetida, purchased from the local druggist, was tucked into a rectangle of cloth and sewn into a square bag about an inch in diameter. These bags were thought to ward off everything from colds and sore throats to stomach aches. (Roberta Hagood, a Hannibal historian, notes that the bags reputedly were "smelly when new and more smelly as time passed!")[12] Children and adults alike drank sassafras tea to ensure good health and "thin the blood." The roots were dug and cut into two- to three-inch lengths and steeped in boiling water, and even babies were given an occasional sip to strengthen their constitutions.[13] Though no one can be sure, Johanna Tobin likely employed many such remedies in her family.

During her early years Maggie Tobin watched a number of significant changes take place in Hannibal. A railroad bridge across the Mississippi River was completed in 1871 and brought not only increased transportation but a flurry of opportunity for investment and speculation in the town of Hannibal itself. Various fees were imposed for its use: pedestrians crossed for five cents; a horse and rider were charged fifteen cents; a two-horse carriage paid thirty cents. Four-legged crossers were also charged: hogs, sheep, or goats cost three cents each; horses, cattle, or mules were double that rate. In May 1878 every resident in Hannibal turned out to celebrate the opening of the streetcar line; the first car, driven by John Fortner, was pulled by a mule team along the newly laid tracks. Once the car reached the end of the line, the mules were deftly unhitched and switched to the other side for the return trip.

The first telephone exchange was established in 1879, and Hannibal vied with St. Louis to be the first in the state with telephone service (Hannibal won—but the difference was only a few hours), though the Browns likely did not have a telephone for years afterward. Few women worked outside the home; however, a whole new field of employment blossomed in the wake of an interesting exchange that occurred one night in a bar. In 1879 Hop Flynn and Harry Ballard were the first and only Hannibal telephone operators; Harry took the day shift, and Hop worked at night. One night Hop took a call from Hoffscheimer's saloon and endured a string of epithets that made his ears burn. He promptly put on his coat and went downtown to investigate who was on the other end of the line. They vigorously resolved the problem with their fists. Shortly thereafter the company elected to hire only female telephone operators to encourage more appropriate behavior from its customers.

Along with the other Tobin children, Maggie attended school in the home of her aunt, Mary O'Leary. Mrs. O'Leary at first taught classes herself, then, when her daughter Margaret was old enough, turned them over to Margaret. Margaret Tobin and Margaret O'Leary were close friends as well as cousins and occasionally traveled overseas together years after Margaret had left Hannibal. A number of private schools were available for Hannibal children, and public schools had been established in 1859. However, the lines of color remained firmly drawn. The first private school for African Americans in Hannibal was established in the mid-1850s by Rev. Tom Henderson and held in the back room of a Baptist church. Students of all ages attended, and tuition was $1 per month. In 1870 a public school, Douglassville School, was established for African American children, although all the teachers were white. It wasn't until 1874 that the first three African American teachers were hired.

As Maggie grew, fashions for women were changing as well. The first bathing suits for women were introduced in the 1870s, consisting of long pantalettes of heavy cotton covered with a knee-level skirt and topped by a full blouse with dropped shoulders, puffed sleeves, and a high ruffled collar. Only the most daring women ventured forth in them, an early indication of changing attitudes by and toward women.

As the Tobin children grew, they were expected to eventually help support the family. The census taker who appeared at the door of the Tobin household on June 4, 1879, wrote down the names of John Tobin, no age (he would have been fifty-two); Johanna Tobin, age fifty; Daniel Tobin, sixteen; Maggie Tobin, twelve; William Tobin, eleven; and Ellen (Helen) Tobin, eight. (Their names were carefully entered in the "White" column; the other categories were "Black," "Mulatto," "Chinese," and "Indian.") Maggie's half-sisters, Catherine and Mary Ann, after helping raise their younger siblings, had left the house on Denkler Alley to work and start their own families.

Daniel, the oldest son, took a job selling newspapers at the railroad depot, which provided not only a much-needed steady income but a good deal of excitement as well. The railroad had transformed Hannibal from a sleepy little river town into a busy trade center. By 1859 track had been laid to nearby St. Joseph, but stagecoaches still ran to the smaller towns. Hannibal fought to get on the line (Judge John Marshall Clemens, the father of Mark Twain, was one of the initial organizers), and the final piece of track was laid at seven A.M., February 13, 1859. The next day the first train reached Hannibal from St. Joseph, a distance of 206 miles completed in just twelve hours forty-five minutes. Eventually, so many railroad lines made Hannibal their destination that citizens began to rally for the construction of a depot, which was completed in 1882 and became a well-known architectural landmark.

Small newspapers at the time tended to have short lives or to quickly merge with competitors. It's likely that Daniel sold various incarnations of the Hannibal *Clipper Herald* and *Morning Journal*. With a cotton bag slung over his shoulder, each morning and evening he hawked papers to passengers coming in, going out, or just passing through, walking up and down beside the cars while the trains stood steaming on their tracks. He sold newspapers in the sheds where the trains were loaded, keeping informed as to what cargo was being loaded or unloaded and where it was headed. He spent his days talking to the steady stream of travelers heading west to the goldfields and silver strikes that were just beginning to make newspaper headlines. In 1870 the first train to Denver left the Hannibal station, and many Hannibalians watched their sons and daughters leave their riverside hometown for the "wild West." The year 1878 marked Horace Tabor's infamous Colorado silver strike, and everyone was talking about a place called Leadville.

ON FEBRUARY 13, 1879, a good portion of the Hannibal Irish community gathered at the Immaculate Conception Church to watch Father O'Hanlon perform a wedding ceremony for Catherine "Katie" Bridget Tobin and John A. Becker.[14] John Becker, who was to make a lasting impression on Hannibal, hailed from the Alsace-Lorraine region of France,[15] and the couple was remembered for Katie's soft Irish brogue and John's slight French accent. The young Beckers bought a large two-story brick house at 322 North Street, within walking distance of the Tobin home. They spent their entire lives in this much-beloved house. John Becker owned a confectionery on Broadway, a small shop that sold fruit, tobacco, small household necessities, and all sorts of sweet delights and became a vital stop for children on their way home from school.

Maggie spent many happy hours at the home of her half-sister Katie, and a good amount of time at the confectionery as well. John Becker was known throughout Hannibal as "Johnnie" and was loved by children and adults alike. He roasted peanuts in the back of the store in a small roaster with an engine that featured a tiny painted mechanical man on top who turned around and around with the circling of the drum.[16] When the weather was agreeable, he moved this operation out onto the sidewalk and sold nickel bags of piping hot nuts, often to eager dock or ship workers who strolled up from the river. On their way home from school, children stopped to buy licorice root, penny candies, all-day candies, and yellow buttercorn. Johnnie patiently stood by while each child declared a desire for "two of this" or "three of that," and, in the words of a customer who recalled her business there years ago, "if a child had as much as a nickel to spend all at one time, Johnnie really made a sale."[17] As a young bride, Katie Becker wore a huge apron gathered at the waist, which covered her from waist to foot, and presided over neat rows of pins, needles, tape, and sewing goods for industrious housewives. She also sold oversized sugar cookies for a penny apiece. Not quite as forgiving as her husband, Mrs. Becker gained a reputation with some of the more conniving young customers for being "Argus-eyed" and—although gentle by nature—could spot a young thief in a second.

The Beckers eventually had three children: Elizabeth, Frank, and George. George didn't survive infancy; years later Frank Becker would work for J. J. Brown in his mining operations based in Denver. Elizabeth Becker stayed in Hannibal and married a man named William Frier, whose family was from Limerick, Ireland. Upon their marriage, Elizabeth and William moved into the house next door to the Beckers at 314 North Street, and the home has remained in the family to the present day. In 1954 Rose Drescher Weatherly, an early Hannibal resident who still clearly remembered her childhood visits to the Becker store, recalled, "These people were utterly without any formal education, but their children were outstanding in our schools ... Johnnie was known by all the town, and beloved by its children."[18]

Long after she had grown up and moved away, Margaret made a point of visiting the Beckers at least once a year. (The Frier children vividly remember Mrs. Brown as being "quite a dresser" and carrying a "stately walking stick."[19]) The two half-sisters enjoyed sitting on the porch and looking out toward the river, watching the riverboats pass by. Margaret always brought gifts, including a delicate pair of mother-of-pearl opera glasses from Paris, a present for young Elizabeth, which is still cherished by the family. When both Katie and Johnnie Becker passed away in the late 1920s, Margaret sent white crosses made of Carrara marble with red-and-black trim from Italy to put on their graves.[20]

WHEN MAGGIE COMPLETED her final studies at Mary O'Leary's school, she too was faced with the prospect of finding work. At thirteen, Maggie, who now preferred to be called Margaret, though her family and friends continued to use the old nickname for some time, went to work at the Garths' tobacco factory along with scores of other young Irish girls and women who had few other choices.

The Garth tobacco company, now owned by Messrs. D.J. Garth & Bro., occupied an immense four-story building on Palmyra Avenue. The company processed over 500,000 pounds of leaf tobacco annually. Manufactured tobacco—which took various forms, including plug, twist, chewing, and smoking tobacco—was sold to dealers in Illinois, Wisconsin, Iowa, Tennessee, and other parts of Missouri. Leaves and stems went to the market in St. Louis, and tobacco strips were shipped to England. The first two floors of the Garth establishment were used for stripping and rolling tobacco, the third floor contained casing and sorting rooms, and the fourth floor had beds for employees who needed an emergency place to stay.

Work at the tobacco factory was seasonal, and during harvest time girls and women were employed for leaf stripping, which was most likely Maggie's job there. The rolling of cigars was primarily reserved for men (although at the Red Star Cigar Company, a minor competitor, a woman named Lola Harro was able to work her way up the ranks to become a packer and finally a cigar maker). Every morning a bell that could be heard all over Hannibal rang to summon the workers to their jobs. In the mornings the cigar makers used knives, molds, and cutting blocks to process the tobacco and band it with binders or "first wrappers." After lunch the men would fit the tobacco rolls into special molds to tailor the shape and then carefully wrap them again. The Garth company was proud of the fact that each cigar was rolled by hand, not by a machine.

Women and girls were hired to strip the parchment-like leaves from the stiff, prickly stems and prepare the tobacco for processing or packaging.

Workers brought their lunches of bacon, corn dodger, bread, and butter-milk in dinner pails. The days were long; the rooms were hot and humid; and a young girl would have made significantly less than a cigar roller, who was paid $1.75 to $2 a day. Margaret, although she talked often of her Hannibal days, never spoke of her experience in the tobacco factory and—unlike her mother and father—never took up the tobacco habit, although it was common for children of the time to try a bit of "chaw," against their parents' admonitions. Although no records of the Messrs. D.J. Garth & Bro. Tobacco Company exist, it's probable that Margaret Tobin worked there for several years and eventually was joined by her sister, Helen. Then Margaret's life took an unexpected turn.

Various myths have given credit to Mark Twain for talking young "Mólly" into going west. But the real culprit may have been an innoc-uous young man named Jack Landrigan, who happened to fall in love with Margaret's half-sister Mary Ann. Jack was an enterprising young blacksmith, and when he married Mary Ann, he sought to convince her that greater opportunity might lie in Colorado than in Hannibal. In the fall of 1883, along with his bride and her twenty-year-old half-brother, Daniel, he boarded a train bound for Denver. From Denver it was nearly a full day's train ride to Leadville, which had suddenly become the fastest-growing city in the country. Jack wasted no time in estab-lishing a blacksmith shop at 529 East Fifth Street while Mary Ann set up housekeeping.[21] The Landrigrans quickly became stalwart members of the extensive Irish Catholic community in Leadville, and Mary Ann became pregnant with the first of their eleven children. (Years later, when Mary Ann returned to Hannibal for a visit, her nephew Albert Frier reported that she looked "tired and weather-beaten.")[22]

Daniel liked what he saw in Leadville but felt the weight of his responsibilities in Hannibal and a growing newspaper career. Likely his heart was also influenced by a young Hannibal girl, Mary Brophy Grace, whom he had left behind. He returned to Hannibal, and a newspaper clipping saved by Margaret indicates that he expanded his newspaper business to become a contractor for the C.B.&Q. Railroad. This same clipping states, "Rumor hath it that an arrow directed from Cupid's west side fort had had its effect on Mr. Tobin and a trip to Hymen's altar is among the certainties for the near future."[23] But Cupid would have to wait. In late 1885 Daniel boarded the train to Colorado again, but this time he was ready. For the first few months he stayed with Jack and Mary Ann, but soon he moved into his own home at 722 East Fifth Street, just up the street from the Landrigans.[24] In the early spring of 1886 he wired money to Hannibal for railroad tickets for his sisters Margaret and Helen (although Helen was just to visit, as she was only fifteen). He was considerate enough to include an overnight stop in St. Louis so the girls could buy new clothes.[25]

Margaret Tobin Brown would look back on this period of her life as one of anticipation, struggle, and tremendous ambition on the part of all her family members. It was hard to leave her parents and younger siblings behind, but she, along with her brother and half-sister, was determined to build a better life and help her family, particularly her father. "I longed to be rich enough to give him a home so that he would not have to work," she later said. "I used to think that the zenith of happiness would be to have my father come to his home after a pleasant day and find his slippers warmed and waiting for him. It was a little thing to want, I thought. Of course we could have had his slippers ready for him in those days, you will say, but father was too tired when his work was done to enjoy any comfort. His life was bounded by working and sleeping."[26]

Her wish would come true.

When Margaret Tobin boarded a train for Leadville in 1886, she had experienced what most young Irish girls likely experienced in Hannibal at the time. Her life was not particularly remarkable. Her family was strong and close knit, unusually firm perhaps in its political convictions, and a bit more ambitious than most. More than most parents, John and Johanna encouraged their daughters as well as their sons to go out and make lives for themselves in the world. But nothing so far had indicated that fifty years from that auspicious day when Margaret stepped aboard a train bound for Denver, writers and historians would look back to her youth in Hannibal to seek some early sign of what made her life so unusual for a woman of her day. The first writers, Gene Fowler and Caroline Bancroft, strongly influenced by the colorful, inflammatory tabloid style of journalism in the late 1930s, found few facts to feed their stories. So they invented, and a folk legend was born.

As folklore, the legend of Molly Brown rivals the stories of Calamity Jane, Billy the Kid, and even Paul Bunyan. First penned by the sardonic hand of Gene Fowler, the story—written a year after Margaret's death in 1932—is as strange and telling as the wild tempest that heralded Molly's birth. The newborn babe, Fowler wrote in *Timberline,* arrived two months early and, with all odds against her, refused to die. Nature acknowledged the unnatural birth by sending a giant tornado to ravage the town. The twister descended so swiftly that mother, father, and two sons fled to the cellar, leaving the poor babe alone in her wind-rocked cradle, and the tornado "tucked their shanty under its arm and raced like a monstrous half-back over a gigantic field."[27] When the terrified family finally emerged, they discovered that the house had disappeared, but the baby was unscathed, joyfully gurgling in her little berth. Nothing as trivial as a tornado could scare Molly Brown, even when she was just a few hours old.

Molly's father, "Old Shaemus," was a poor, drunken Irishman but resourceful nonetheless. He took stock of the situation and fashioned a crude incubator, or cradle, of wood and nails. With the help of his two sons, he pounded together a shack of loose timber and tin cans left in the wake of the storm. His wife proved less tenacious. Molly's premature arrival "was in key with her aggressive temperament"[28] and boded ill, especially for a girl child; the mother died of shock and grief over her unnatural offspring. Shaemus quickly recovered from his loss and borrowed a nanny goat for a wet nurse.

The plucky child spent the first two months of her life in her father's wooden box. When she emerged, Molly demonstrated a maturity remarkably beyond her years and required little along the lines of parental guidance, which was fortunate, as her father enjoyed his homemade whiskey. She grew from toddler to child without the fetters of proper clothing or social habits and ran wild in the woods like the wide-eyed deer that ventured into the Tobin yard. Schoolwork did not appeal to her, or the friendship of other girls in town who wore shoes and frocks and attended Bible study. She disdained housework, "particularly in a shanty," and instead spent long days by herself hunting and fishing along the banks of the Mississippi River. The local truant officer made sure Molly spent some time between the four walls of a schoolhouse, but it "didn't take very well"—she was too busy climbing trees and skinning her knees and acting like a tomboy. Joining up with her older brother's gang of local insurgents, she learned to chew tobacco, shoot marbles, and spit farther than any boy in town. Most of all, she learned to brag and make up stories about herself, a habit she nurtured her entire life.

One of the tales Molly loved to spin was that her father was an Irish nobleman come all the way from Ireland itself. But, Fowler reports, "he was just old Shaemus Tobin, a tin-roof Celt of the Missouri River bottoms. Old Shaemus was a man more ready of song than cash, red-haired and tempestuous."[29] And the Tobin family was famous for red hair, Molly most of all, her hair a bright lick of flame that meant trouble to the gentle folk of Hannibal.

As Molly grew, her troubles deepened. Another version of the story relates how Molly, at nine years of age, was playing innocently on a Mississippi mudbank when she was startled by a storm bearing down upon her with terrifying intensity. The tornado swept her up in its furious twists and swirls and "literally whizzed" her onto Pearl Island, where another Hannibal legend was attempting a leisurely afternoon of fishing at the Pearl Island Fishing Club. "Naturally bewildered," the child looked up to see a "benevolent, white-haired stranger" coming to rescue her. To her boundless delight she discovered that he was a dear old friend of the family. "Where the devil will I find you next?" Mark Twain muttered gruffly.[30]

Indeed, it wasn't long before the two infamous characters would meet again. One afternoon Molly was once again doing her best to avoid the truant officer and decided to go fishing. She tied together a few logs for a raft and set out with her fishing pole. Mark Twain had the same idea, although his boat was somewhat more conventional. They passed each other on the river, and Twain "saw her at once for what she was, a female Huckleberry Finn."[31] Twain admired her bright blue eyes and flaming red pigtails and invited her to scout fish from a more reliable vessel. She happily accepted. The first thing that Twain discovered was that Molly "didn't have the remotest idea that she was a girl. She could whistle like a calliope, and before Mr. Clemens could gather his celebrated wits together, she had disrobed completely and dived over-board, with an absence of mock modesty that characterized her entire life."[32] Molly leaped and rolled in the water, as natural as a porpoise, but her laughing and diving brought her to grief. Her head got stuck ostrich-fashion in the famous Mississippi mud, and Twain had to pull her out most unceremoniously by her famous tomboy feet. But Mr. Twain couldn't be more forgiving. Although noticing that she looked like some "weird clay model," he scraped the mud from her eyes, helped her on with her clothes, and sent her on her way.[33]

Despite Molly's best efforts to remain a tomboy, she began to grow into a young woman. By her teens, Molly was a "most attractive, bosomy redhead with an aggressive personality and exaggerated ambitions."[34] There was never enough food in the Tobin cupboard, and finally Molly was forced to go to work at the local tobacco factory with all the other poverty-stricken Irish girls. As soon as she turned thirteen (or fifteen, depending on whose version of the story you consult), she managed to land a job as a waitress at the fashionable Park Hotel in Hannibal. Working at the Park Hotel gave Molly first peek at any celebrities who came to town on the train, and luck would have it that her old friend Mark Twain once again made an appearance. He was seeking material for a new book and stopped in at the Park Hotel for lunch. Mark Twain wasn't an overnight millionaire like all the gold and silver kings Molly had heard of, but he was famous. Molly envied fame even more than riches. She begged the manager to allow her to wait on him, since "she loved celebrities and he loved an audience, even an attractive and worshipful waitress."[35] They met, lunch was served, and Twain spun tales of his days in the mining camps of Nevada and California. New strikes were made every day, he said, and a young girl like Molly could make a life for herself that certainly would be better than life in Hannibal. Or better yet, find herself a rich husband! The richest strikes were in Leadville, the Cloud City of Colorado, where gold and silver nuggets could be plucked from the ground as easily as spring flowers tugged from their roots. Every man, no matter how humble his birth, became a millionaire or knew one, and mining camps were notoriously short of females. Molly's mind was made up—she would run away from home.

Poverty, youth, and inexperience meant nothing to a soul determined to take fate into her own hands. Molly returned home that evening and secretly packed all her belongings into a single carpetbag. Waiting until her drunken father and shiftless brothers were sound asleep, she slipped out in the dead of night. But who wanted to wait for a train? Molly threw caution to the wind and took a galloping stagecoach all the way to Leadville, where she knew in her heart she would meet the man of her dreams and make her fortune.

DESPITE THE MANY variations of this myth that made it into plays, books, movies—and history books—there are a few interesting elements that hold a shade of truth.

The Park Hotel did exist in Hannibal and indeed was very reputable during the 1870s and 1880s. One interesting overlooked fact, however, is that the hotel hired only male waiters for its formal dining room and almost certainly would not have hired an Irish girl at that time, except perhaps as a housemaid. Samuel Clemens, not yet known as Mark Twain, left Hannibal in 1853 at the age of seventeen—fourteen years before Margaret Tobin was born. Years later he did return to Hannibal during his 1868 and 1869 lecture tour; however, he never stayed at the hotel but rather put up at the six-hundred-acre, sprawling Victorian-style mansion owned by the Garth family, with whom he was good friends. He visited Hannibal again in 1885,[36] just before Margaret left for Leadville, but it seems unlikely that they met.

Nevertheless, it's important not to dismiss the influence Mark Twain did have on Margaret's life and how important she was to his legacy. John Tobin claimed that he was acquainted with Mark Twain's father, Judge John Marshall Clemens, and there seems to be no reason to disbelieve this statement. Mrs. Matabelle Kettering, Mark Twain's niece, was good friends with Margaret Tobin Brown, and they visited each others' homes, with Mrs. Kettering coming to Denver for an extended summer stay in 1904.[37] On June 9, 1905, Margaret published an extensive article in the *Denver Times* titled "Mark Twain's Boyhood Home" and lectured on this subject in Newport, Rhode Island. During World War I, Margaret was credited with initiating the translation of Mark Twain's work into braille and French, work for which she was recognized by the French government. And in 1927 she participated in the dedication of a Tom and Huck statue in Hannibal and, with the help of Twain's descendants, made sure some of the great author's personal mementos were given to the museum in Hannibal.

Gene Fowler's imaginative story was amplified again and again. But fact or fiction, one aspect of the story remains the same: a young Irish girl left Hannibal and ventured west to achieve a dream, and that dream came true. Margaret Tobin left Hannibal, but she never forgot it, and returned time and time again.

Better Off with a Poor Man

1886–1894

LEADVILLE RISES NEARLY two miles into the Colorado sky. Resting on a high bench of the western slope of the Mosquito Range, the city's elevation measures 10,152 feet above sea level; from one of the surrounding mountainsides it looks like a tiny toy village in the middle of an enormous frying pan. Lofty epithets have always been common: the Cloud City, the Magic City, the Carbonate Camp, the Greatest Mining Camp in the World. The mountains that ring the town are covered with thick pine, much of which was cut down when the city was first built, but now, to a certain extent, the forest has reestablished itself. The beauty of Leadville's surroundings is breathtaking, but winters are long and cold and summers brief. Before the age of pavement, springtime turned the main street of town into a sea of clinging mud. Miners burrowed into every nook of every mountainside and even under the very town itself; it wasn't uncommon for a sinkhole to suddenly appear in someone's backyard (an event that still occasionally occurs today). In Leadville's early years the people who lived there liked to compare themselves to the delicate, brightly colored flowers that stubbornly grew between the rocks on the vertical hillsides: hardy, independent, determined to survive.

Leadville was a city that literally sprang up overnight. Encouraged by what was happening in the goldfields of California and a strike on the banks of the South Platte at Cherry Creek, where the city of Denver now stands (a strike that amounted to only a few hundred dollars, magnified substantially with each retelling of the story), prospectors began struggling their way up to California Gulch as soon as the snows melted in the spring of 1859. A few found a bit of luck, and word traveled fast; by the summer of 1860 over five thousand people were camped out in the valley, and Oro (Spanish for "gold") City was established. By the mid-1860s, however, placer mining, involving small claims and limited mining methods, had fairly exhausted the sources of gold that could be reached by such means. It wasn't until the late 1870s that the "black cement" that had interfered with early gold-mining efforts was recognized as silver-bearing lead ore, or carbonate, that could be refined to silver-lead bullion and shipped back east for refining. The carbonate boom was on, and by 1880 Leadville was not only "the most important mining center in Colorado" but the second largest city in Colorado.[1]

The people who settled Leadville, rich and poor alike, came from all over the world. Early miners were Mexicans from the silver and copper mines of northern Mexico; tin miners from England; Cornishmen, or "Cousin Jacks," with sophisticated skills for working the deeper lodes that were being discovered; Danes, Norwegians, and Swedes; and, in great numbers, the Irish. Some miners were the sons of wealthy Eastern families, determined to make strikes on their own; others came with only the clothes on their backs. As the camp grew, immigrants from southern and eastern Europe tended to be pushed into lower-paying jobs in smelters and ore-reduction plants. The Chinese and Native Americans, particularly the Ute and Cheyenne, were considered outcasts, and even though the Chinese helped build the railroads, they weren't allowed to ride the trains. The Utes had been "relocated" to southern Utah in 1881, but residents swapped stories of occasional "strays" reputedly showing up at back doors and begging for biscuits. These Indians were considered nothing like the "noble red man of fiction," and the *Carbonate Weekly Chronicle* went so far as to declare, "If you are particularly handy with a rifle, bring along a good one and shoot the first Ute you find."[2] Women, although they filled a number of various roles in the growing community by operating boardinghouses and working as nurses, cooks, housemaids, laundresses, teachers—and yes, saloon girls—were denied participation in the most prosperous aspect of Leadville's economy. It was considered a curse to allow a woman in a mine.

In 1880 the Irish were the largest ethnic group in Leadville,[3] but by then the game had changed. Gold had been so plentiful that millions of dollars were derived from the California Gulch area in the first year after the end of the Civil War. By 1878 silver production had nearly eclipsed gold, but the miner who made his fortune with a lot of hard work and a little dose of luck was pretty much out of the picture. Miners could no longer rely on carbonates near the surface. More sophisticated mining technology—and greater financial investment—was necessary to reach the more complex sulfides far below.[4] As mining corporations with strong Eastern backing were formed, mergers were enacted, and boards of directors made decisions regarding who owned what and who profited, the solitary miner saw his chances of riches slipping away and felt "trapped by a system he had come to the magic city to beat."[5] Large numbers of manual laborers became essential, and suddenly thousands were employed rather than hundreds, working six and sometimes seven days a week, ten to twelve hours a day, in conditions that were not only dangerous and sometimes terrifying but often inhumane. Historian Marcia Goldstein wrote, "The miner became an anonymous cog in the industrial wheel, a mindless body in a striking mob, a hardworking machine by day, a blithering drunk by night."[6] In the mines, lack of adequate ventilation combined with candles and explosives produced air high in carbon dioxide or monoxide. Dizziness and fainting contributed to a high accident rate, although most mine owners attributed such problems to workers' carelessness. Pneumonia, lead poisoning, and silicosis, caused by the inhalation of rock dust, were common complaints and often resulted in lingering deaths. Missing a day of work meant missing a day of pay, and a miner's family was often left with no income and large medical bills.[7]

As the "silver kings" flaunted their wealth with new carriages and fancy Denver mansions, the majority of Leadville's population struggled to keep food on the table and the wolf from the door. It wasn't uncommon for a woman to have two or more husbands and children by different fathers, not because the divorce rate was high but because mine accidents and the slow deaths caused by silicosis took their annual toll. Unions, which had never been able to gain much of a foothold, took on a new strength—the 1880 strike at the Chrysolite Mine was a harbinger of things to come. In the meantime, despite fervent speeches and heavy politicking in Washington, the price of silver continued to slowly decline—partly due to Eastern unease over Leadville's exuberant output and the new economic power of Leadville and the West. The stage was set for trouble.

But Leadville, despite its problems, provided a unique window of opportunity for men and women alike to come from nearly any corner of the globe and make their lives anew. For every life lived in despair there was the thrill of hoping for what many people considered the essence of the American dream: with enough "guts and gumption," and a little bit of luck, an earnest soul could rise above the boundaries of class, race, and gender and achieve some degree of prosperity. The man who wore miner's duds and couldn't rub two nickels together might in two weeks' time find himself keeping company with the likes of famous Colorado pioneers and businessmen Horace Tabor and David Moffat. A woman who had left behind a life of disillusionment or abuse could come to Leadville and make a new life for herself in one way or another, often with a child or two in tow. Some men made their fortunes honestly and others less so—a few sacks of good ore could be used to "salt" or line the bottom of a poorly producing claim for a quick and lucrative sale (although sometimes this strategy backfired and the new owner would indeed discover profitable ore a little deeper down). Many men made a tidy sum not in silver or gold but as bakers or butchers or owners of shops, and women found employment in local stores and businesses as well, in addition to managing boardinghouses and taking in laundry for miners. Sometimes women discovered opportunities for financial independence not found in other cities. "Mom-and-pop" stores were common,[8] and, as many of the early women homesteaders discovered, a Western town was sometimes more accepting than an Eastern community of a woman who ventured into the business arena. One unique aspect of Leadville's booming real estate economy was that a "proper" businessman might decide to build a nice Victorian home downtown and then discover that his next-door neighbor had the same idea but wasn't quite the neighbor he had in mind. It wasn't uncommon for a financially successful woman of the "underworld" to buy a city lot and build herself a nice house without the benefit of a wealthy husband. Some of them even became "respectable," willing to at least look the part of a proper nineteenth-century woman. Some of them didn't care.

TO EIGHTEEN-YEAR-OLD Maggie Tobin, Hannibal probably looked a little tame by comparison. In the spring of 1886, when she stepped off the train with her sister, Helen, Maggie encountered a city filled with infinite dangers and delights. Harrison Avenue was clogged with a steady stream of freight wagons, burro trains, two- and four-horse carriages, tramps, prospectors, speculators, street girls, day miners, tradesmen, fine-suited businessmen, and dusty cowboys. To the east of the town they could see the landscape of Iron, Carbonate, and Fryer Hills, all dotted with slapdash lean-tos and haphazard head frames as well as orderly operations as sophisticated as anywhere else in the world, all seemingly piled on top of each other. The saloons along Chestnut and State Streets stayed open all night, and just about any excuse seemed good enough to plan a holiday or parade. In preceding years the Fourth of July celebration had become particularly boisterous; the newspapers declared that a "season of discontent" had come to the small boys of Leadville, and a city ordinance was passed to prevent the shooting of firearms, firecrackers, or other "fizzin' things" inside the city limits from July 2 to July 5.[9] Adults were not subject to the same restrictions, although it was considered polite to use one's pistol somewhat discreetly. Disputes that began in the saloons were often resolved in the courts, with nice profits on both ends. In 1879 Leadville boasted 120 saloons, 59 boardinghouses, 3 daily newspapers, 2 weekly newspapers, 118 gambling houses and private club rooms, 36 houses of prostitution, and 147 lawyers. Four public school teachers and five ministers tended to the gentler side of life.[10]

But twenty-five years of civilization had not been for naught in Leadville. "Although Leadville had its vicious side of life strongly accentuated," one author wrote, "there was considerable development of refined social life as well."[11] Investors and capitalists from New York and Chicago visited Leadville with their wives and daughters and were pleased to find all their expectations of comfort and even luxury in the midst of "wilderness" happily met. Many stayed at the elegant Twin Lakes Lodge resort or the fashionable Tabor Grand Hotel and spent evenings at the Tabor Opera House, which attracted top talent from around the country and featured everything from Shakespeare to vaudeville. The Leadville Trotting and Running Association built a luxurious half-mile track on eighty acres, attracting trotters, pacers, and runners from as far away as Missouri, Iowa, and Chicago. Appropriate attire for afternoon races or evening theater was never a concern— Leadville's dressmakers, who came from all over the country, could sew gowns made from heavy grosgrain silk, the height of elegance, as well as brocaded satins and velvets just as fine as those found in Paris or New York. Dressmakers demanded Eastern prices for their work and got them: $25 to $40 for a plain princess gown and custom gowns made to order with custom prices. Milliners were equally popular and could charge as much for hats as women paid in the most fashionable shops in New York. Four jewelry shops kept the well-heeled stocked with appropriate jewelry, and diamonds were de rigueur.

Despite disparities of class—and labor tensions at the boiling point— Leadville had, for the most part, a good heart. Numerous charities were popular, and a strong coterie of earnest fund-raisers, mostly women, knocked on doors and stopped passersby for donations. Churches and civic clubs flourished. A free reading room on East Fourth Street was open to the public and very popular during the evening hours. Lottie Williams and Louise H. Updegraff established the town's first schools before the official name of Leadville had even been established.[12] One important early pioneer was Father Henry Robinson, from Salem, Illinois, who began his ministry in Fairplay in 1874, eventually moving to Leadville in 1876.[13] The first Catholic church, the Sacred Heart, was soon far too modest in size for the growing Catholic community, and the Annunciation Church, a towering structure on the corner of East Seventh and Poplar, was begun in 1879, with the first mass held on January 1, 1880. Father Robinson pleaded for nuns to come help build a hospital in the "wilderness," and three Sisters of Charity arrived to help him: Bernard Mary Pendergast and Mary Crescentia Fisher from the Mother House in Leavenworth, Kansas, and Francis Xavier from St. Joseph's Hospital in Denver. The sisters raised the money, hired carpenters, and masterminded the construction of the hospital, all within three months.[14] St. Vincent's Hospital opened on May 13, 1879, and had to be enlarged the following month owing to the booming population. In 1882 Sister Francis Xavier moved to Denver to help establish St. Vincent's Orphan Asylum, later one of J.J. Brown's favorite charities. Father Robinson rose to further prominence when he left Leadville to become vicar general of the Denver Diocese in 1889.

"There is no better place," said George Albert Harris, reputedly the first settler of Leadville, "for a poor man, a rich man, a wise man, a fool, a mean man, an honest man or a knave, than Leadville."[15] In Leadville, many of the buildings—as in other cities in the West—were false-fronted, but the enthusiasm of this new city was genuine. It was a good place to begin a new life.

MARGARET'S SISTER HELEN TOBIN returned to her parent's home in Hannibal, but she too had been affected by "Leadville fever" and would soon come back to stay. Some historians claim that Maggie worked briefly in a boardinghouse—and myth tells us that she went straight to work as a saloon girl with a flashy skirt and an ability to hold her liquor just as well as the "belly-up-to-the-bar" boys, as shown in the MGM movie *The Unsinkable Molly Brown*. What is certain is that she moved in with her brother Daniel, cooked his meals and tended his house, and made him as comfortable as she could while he struggled to make the stake. For $2.50 a day, Daniel was learning the mining business the hard way.

Jack and Mary Ann had quickly become a part of Leadville's Irish community, and Daniel and Maggie followed suit. Author Michael F. Donovan wrote that the Irish people who came to Leadville from 1860 on "retained their Irish characteristics and insisted on being called Irish." Not only were the Irish active in civic events, they also dominated local politics for decades.[16] The Annunciation Church was the cornerstone for much of the Irish community and held all the usual masses, weddings, baptisms, and religious schooling common to Catholic communities at the time. Irish wakes were formal affairs involving all the neighbors, although the men "often retired to the kitchen where a bottle of spirits was passed around." St. Patrick's Day was particularly notable in Leadville, involving a special mass attended by families and members of formal Irish organizations. The entire Leadville community participated in the St. Patrick's Day parade, speeches, banquets, and a fancy Grand Ball. The Irish were considered hard workers but also had a reputation for knowing how to have fun—some of the more rowdy Irish lads were referred to as "Utes" for their habit of emitting "piercing war whoops on their way to town on Saturday nights."[17]

In 1882 St. Mary's School was officially opened with an enrollment of 320 students. Four people managed the school and taught classes: Monsignor Robinson, Sister Mary Clare Bergen, Sister Joseph Dungan, and Sister Theodosia Roth. One sister remembered a young pupil who paid for books and tuition from the money he made working in the mines and who had a habit of bringing out his pipe, filling it, and smoking in class. He was eight years old and entering the first grade.[18] Most mining companies, however, claimed they wouldn't hire boys under the age of sixteen.

IT WASN'T LONG before Maggie began to look around for something a little more ambitious to do. She found it on a prominent corner of Harrison Avenue, occupied by the dry goods firm of Daniels, Fisher, & Smith.[19] The dry goods business was competitive in Leadville.

David May, a German Jew from Kaiserslautern, Bavaria, had come to Colorado to save his health and stave off the threat of tuberculosis. He started out in Manitou Springs and eventually ended up in Leadville, where he met Jake Holcomb, also seeking a healthier climate after a bout of malaria. The May Company, as it came to be known, met stiff competition from W.B. Daniels, W.G. Fisher, and Joel W. Smith, three men who, like David May, found a ready market for two new fads: riveted overalls made by a man named Levi Strauss and wool undershirts and drawers the miners liked to call "long johns."[20] Over time the two highly competitive companies not only resolved their differences but merged to form May D&F department stores, a company that still exists today in a further incarnation as Foley's.

Maggie was hired to work in the carpet and drapery department, where she made fast friends and was remembered for her thorough work. Years later Lawrence Brown, her son, was disturbed by Hollywood depictions of his mother as a course, hard-drinking, uneducated saloon girl and set out to find people who had known his mother in her youth. Thomas Cahill, although quite a bit younger than Maggie, had worked as a delivery boy for Daniels, Fisher, & Smith and remembered her well. In a 1947 letter to Lawrence Brown, Cahill wrote, "I knew your Mother well. … We both worked for the firm of Daniels, Fisher, and Smith. Her work was in the Carpet and Drapery Department, her duty being to sew carpets, draperies, and shades. She was a very capable and pleasant employee, and her work was very satisfactory to her employers, and all her fellow employees were very fond of her." Cahill recalled that even long after the Browns had moved to Denver, Margaret would always "come to the store to greet her old co-workers and visit her friends."[21]

A young girl set on making a life for herself, as well as hoping to help support her father in his old age, had few obvious choices. Sewing draperies provided a subsistence lifestyle at best, and every day Margaret saw Daniel's health and ambition sorely tested as he worked ten- and twelve-hour days in the mines. Between the two of them, they could barely make ends meet. Daniel's salary was around $60 per month, and Maggie's was likely less than half that. Grocery costs alone were high: 30 cents for a can of milk, $3.50 for a sack of flour, potatoes at 4 to 5 cents per pound, and beef up to 15 cents a pound. Boarding houses charged $7 to $15 per month; renting a private house, as Daniel and

Maggie did, cost more. The cost of heating was high as well: coal oil averaged $4 per gallon.[22]

Maggie couldn't help but dream of marrying a man wealthy enough to help her and her family out of their straitened circumstances. But despite her adamant intentions, she fell instead for a man whose situation was scarcely different from her own. James Joseph Brown was a tall, personable young Irishman, and—like Maggie—intelligent, gregarious, and very ambitious. He was smitten with the auburn-haired Irish girl he first met at a Catholic picnic. But he was poor.

JAMES JOSEPH BROWN, known as J.J. or Jim to his close friends, was born in the town of Waymart in Wayne County, Pennsylvania, on September 27, 1854, and was thirteen years Maggie's senior. J.J. was also the child of immigrant parents, John and Cecilia Palmer Brown, and nurtured the dream of someday returning to his father's hometown in Ireland once he had made a success of himself in America. John Brown had immigrated to Pennsylvania in 1848 via Canada, where he met Cecilia Palmer, a schoolteacher, and they married and had several children. Shortly after James's birth, the family moved to Pittston, Pennsylvania, between the towns of Waymart and Avoca. The Browns lived on the corner of Vine and John Streets in the Irish section of town, and young J.J. was schooled by his mother and eventually attended St. John's Academy on William Street.[23] J.J. later spoke fondly of his childhood and felt strong ties to his beloved hometown. In a letter years later, he wrote, "Pittston, Oh how I love it so. I dream at night of its splendor, the kind I experienced during my childhood."[24]

In February 1877 J.J. left Pennsylvania at the age of twenty-three to pursue a mining career. He had his first taste of the West on a farm in Nebraska, where he worked for a short time to bolster his finances.[25] But he dreamed of being a miner and knew—as everyone did—the fantastic fortunes that could be made in gold and silver if one believed the newspapers. J.J., however, wasn't a speculative sort and believed in hard work more than good luck. From Nebraska he traveled to the Black Hills of the Dakotas, where he found work in the placer mines in the southern part of that area. He later described occasional skirmishes with Indians as the miners tried to work their claims there.[26] Two years in the mines provided him with some solid experience but began to take a toll on his health, which he disregarded at the time. In the early spring of 1880 he took the train to Colorado, spending the month of June in Georgetown and then moving on to Aspen, settling in the area around the mining town of Ashcroft. It was a happy period of his life. J.J. loved the work, the landscape, and the companionship, which included his brother, Edward, who had also moved west from Pennsylvania. For two years he worked in the Aspen area, gaining experience and establishing an important network of contacts in the mining business. Years later, in a letter to a friend, he wrote, "I do remember dear old Sam Houston and the year of 1880 in our camp at Aspen ... Oh, what a jolly good crowd we were!"[27]

But two years was a long time for a mining man to stay in one place. One early diarist recalled, "The miners are a queer impulsive sort of folk. If they find they are making some three or four dollars a day when somewhere else they can make seven or eight, the whole lot of them pull up stakes and leave for richer mines. Sometimes they are obliged to desert their entire town when the mines give out."[28] In 1882 J.J. left Aspen County to prospect briefly at Alma, Fairplay, and Red Cliff, finally deciding to head to Leadville. Contrary to popular opinion, success in mining was not a matter of luck, he decided, particularly now that most of the surface finds were gone and it took a combination of ingenuity and knowledge of geology to know where to sink a shaft. J.J. took it upon himself to study everything he could find on geology, ore deposits, and mining techniques and "gained a special genius for practical and economic geology."[29]

J.J. was probably less awed than Maggie when he first came to Leadville, which was a larger and less restrained version of what he'd already experienced in the booming town of Aspen. For two years he worked as a day miner and studied his books. He had gained valuable mining experience in the mines of his native Pennsylvania; the Black Hills of South Dakota; and Gunnison, Park, Pitkin, and the Lake Counties of Colorado. With his knowledge, experience, and growing network of contacts to bank on, in 1885 he landed a job as shift manager for the conglomerate of mines owned by mining moguls David Moffat and Eben Smith.

Moffat and Smith were well respected in Leadville and beyond. Moffat, with Horace Tabor, was one of the original investors in the Little Pittsburg mine and used his fortune to construct roads and railroads. He dreamed of building a more direct transcontinental route for the railroad by constructing a tunnel through the continental divide, a project that proved to be more problematic than he anticipated. He died in 1911 with his dream of a great tunnel unrealized (seventeen years later the tunnel was finally completed at a total cost of nearly $18 million). In 1852, the young Eben Smith had left his home in Pennsylvania to prospect in California. Over thirty years later he ended up in Leadville, where in 1883 he hooked up with Moffat and became manager of the Maid of Erin properties.[30] Their experience and substantial financial resources made them a formidable team.

Eben Smith was impressed by J.J. Brown's competence and over the course of the next few years promoted him from shift boss to foreman to superintendent of the Maid and Henriette Mine, one of the largest mineral producers in the district. For fourteen years Brown would work with Moffat and Smith, developing some of their most valuable properties. But not even he could anticipate what would happen with a stubborn little gold mine called the Little Jonny at the height of Leadville's depression.

IN LATE MAY or early June 1886, Maggie Tobin and J.J. Brown met at a Catholic church picnic. It's probable that Maggie attended with her half-sister Mary Ann; Mary Ann's husband, Jack; and one or two of the Landrigan children. Daniel was likely there as well. Maggie had firm ideas about the type of man she hoped to find and clearly understood the stakes—she had no formal education and few options beyond working in the carpets and draperies department at Daniels, Fisher, & Smith. The choice and caliber of a marriage partner was crucial. James Joseph Brown was no different than hundreds of other mining men in Leadville, working long hours and harboring dreams of success. But J.J. Brown was—as she described him later—irresistible: personable, charming, a man with many friends. He wasn't wealthy, but he had a steady job. And the fact that she had met someone through the church would please her family. She agreed to a date.

One family story holds that J.J. first arrived at Maggie's doorstep in a modest single-horse carriage that had decidedly seen better days. She refused to go out with him. The next night he returned with an elegant two-horse affair that better suited her expectations. However it began, theirs was a whirlwind courtship in a community that presented a few challenges to couples out for a night on the town. Despite the general lawlessness and disregard for social custom in some sectors of town, late-Victorian social etiquette was at its peak. Nonetheless, occasional holdups were common, and a young man would often comfort his female companion by remarking that he was "well heeled," a polite way of saying that he carried a small revolver in his pocket or belt should any trouble arise.

From the elegant dining room at the Tabor Hotel to the Evergreen Lakes Lodge, a fine dinner could be had in Leadville as easily as in Denver or even New York. J.J. no doubt squired Maggie to the Tabor Opera House, where they discovered that they both loved the theater, a passion they would share for many years. Both were also excellent dancers. But given J.J.'s modest salary and Maggie's circle of family and colleagues from work, they likely spent many pleasant evenings taking a carriage up to Twin Lakes or playing card and parlor games that were popular at the time. Maggie's friend Thomas Cahill wrote, "It is easy to understand that at about this time the handsome young Jim Brown fell in love with her. ... Everybody in Leadville thought it a wonderful match."[31] Weeks turned into months, and soon Maggie found herself in a dilemma. "I wanted a rich man," she said, "but I loved Jim Brown." She felt torn between the hope of helping to support her father versus following her heart even though it might mean a lifetime of struggling to keep food on the table in an isolated mountainside cabin where long, bitter winters were the rule. "I thought about how I wanted comfort for my father and how I had determined to stay single until a man presented himself who could give to the tired old man the things I longed for him," she said. "Jim was as poor as we were, and had no better chance in life. I struggled hard with myself in those days. I loved Jim, but he was poor. Finally I decided that I'd be better off with a poor man whom I loved than with a wealthy one whose money had attracted me. So I married Jim Brown. I gave up cooking for my brother and moved to Jim's cabin, where the work was just as hard."[32]

ON SEPTEMBER 1, 1886, against a backdrop of distant mountaintops already covered with snow, Margaret Tobin and James Joseph Brown were married in the tall-spired Annunciation Church with a large congregation attending. The ceremony took place at two in the afternoon and was performed by Father Henry Robinson. Maggie was nineteen; J.J. was thirty-two. Most of Maggie's family attended, although Hannibal must have seemed very far away indeed.

Attendees recall that the best man was Thomas Greeley, a barber, and the bridesmaid was Margaret Boylan, a "housemaid" (a woman who likely worked in a boarding house).[33] J.J. and Maggie's miner friends presented the couple with a set of solid silver. The society editor of the Leadville *Herald Democrat* duly noted the occasion: "A wedding which attracted considerable attention took place at the Church of the Annunciation at two o'clock in the afternoon. The contracting parties were James J. Brown, the popular superintendent of the Louisville mine, and Miss Maggie Tobin, the accomplished young saleslady from whom the patrons of Daniels, Fisher, & Smith will invoke the richest blessings."[34]

After the ceremony friends and family went to Evergreen Lakes, where they enjoyed a "magnificent repast." Standard fare at the time would likely have included imported mussels or oysters on the half-shell as an appetizer, fresh trout from local streams, Colorado corn and peas, locally picked raspberries in big bowls with frothy cream, home-made pie, and strong coffee. The Browns enjoyed a brief honeymoon at Evergreen Lakes, which featured not only an elegant dining room but Oriental gardens and first-class rooms.

Thomas Cahill wrote that J.J. and Maggie "started housekeeping in a modest little home and were very happy,"[35] and indeed both J.J. and Margaret would remark years later that the period of their courtship and early marriage, when their children were born, was a very happy time. The couple stayed briefly in town and then moved up to J.J.'s two-room cabin on Iron Hill, known as Stumpftown, which was closer to the mines. (Even though most of the mines were within a ten-mile radius of Leadville, this location made a significant difference to J.J.'s commute, particularly in winter.) Cahill continued to work as a delivery boy at Daniels, Fisher, & Smith and recalled occasionally taking packages to the Brown home. He wrote to Lawrence Brown, "I can remember often taking packages from the store to their home and your Mother always asked me to come in, sit down, and have a piece of her homemade cake or pie. You can easily imagine what a hit that would make with a little boy. I was so impressed with her kindness and thoughtfulness that the memory of her has remained with me always."[36]

After her marriage there are almost no references to Margaret as "Maggie," with the exception of one 1905 entry in the Denver Woman's Club register. Likely she was called Maggie by a few close friends, but to the rest of the world she was known as Mrs. J.J. Brown or, less formally, Margaret.

Life in Stumpftown was simpler than life in Leadville, perhaps, and certainly less commodious, but the community was close knit, and Margaret made many lasting friendships. In Leadville's early years, dozens of small communities surrounded the city, built by miners who wanted to live within walking distance of the mines. Stumpftown was reportedly named after Joseph Stumpf, an engineer for the Ibex Mining Company; other small hillside communities were Finntown; Ibex City; Chicken Hill, where most of the Scandinavians lived; and Evansville. Most of the Irish community settled in Strayhorse Gulch, just down the hill from Finntown.[37] Stumpftown could be reached by following Seventh Street up a steady grade to a small valley to just past the point where the road leveled out. There were no sidewalks and only one main dirt road. Most of the buildings were constructed without foundations and consisted of weathered boards, although a few of the nicer homes had been painted. Rooms were often lined with newspaper for warmth and to keep out the wind. Stumpftown had several saloons (one with a bowling alley and pool table); a livery stable; a candy store; one lodge; and a small school, District Thirteen, which was located in the back of the lodge. One old-timer recalled that "the town got its personality from the pool hall."[38] Houses and cabins were built haphazardly across the surrounding hills, creating a nighttime blanket of scattered lights. Although the railroad ran from Leadville up Johnny Hill to Ibex City and on to Conley Lakes, only ore taken from the mines was hauled; passengers were not allowed. Groceries and supplies were delivered from Leadville by the John King Mercantile or the Zaitz Mercantile Companies, which occasionally provided free lifts to Stumpftown residents. Paid transportation consisted of the Seppi family's horse-drawn wagon, which ran back and forth between Leadville and Stumpftown. Two or three homes had telephones, as did the saloon and livery stable.

Life was not quite as easy as it had been in town. There was one pump in the main part of Stumpftown where people could draw their water. Baths were taken in washtubs, and water was heated on the stove; the creek was available for those who weren't so fussy. Clothes were washed in washtubs and scrubbed on washboards. Coal- and wood-burning stoves kept homes and cabins warm; coal could be purchased from a boxcar at the section house. Throughout the summer wood was collected for wood-burning stoves and stacked neatly against outside cabin walls—for this and other reasons, fire was always a danger. Although electricity was used in many homes, there was no sewer system; most homes had outhouses.

Stumpftown residents reported few encounters with wild animals, although the yapping and howling of coyotes could be heard nearly every night. The hillsides were famous for their springtime flower displays: bluebells, buttercups, round white "snowballs," and delicate blue and purple columbines. Many Stumpftown homes featured hardy little gardens of lettuce, turnips, and radishes, and "everywhere there were yellow sulfured mine dumps, sprinkled with sun-glinting fool's gold and splintering wood mine head frames."[39]

Despite the rigorous climate and isolation of the mining communities, art and literature were not forsaken. Helen Hunt Jackson and Mary Hallock Foote, both important early women writers in the West, lived for a time in mining communities near Leadville and wrote about their experiences. Many writers came through Leadville as they traveled from coast to coast. Oscar Wilde made an indelible impression on the local literati when he gave a lecture in Leadville in 1882, rather ironically titled "The Ethics of Art."

Both Margaret and J.J. were determined to better educate themselves, and almost immediately after their marriage Margaret began lessons in reading and literature with a tutor in Leadville. She also studied music, piano, and singing with an instructor named Mrs. Wooster.[40] Shortly thereafter, apparently while still living in Stumpftown, the Browns hired Mary A. Fitzharris Nevin to help with household duties. Mary had been born in County Wicklow, Ireland, in 1866 and had come to Leadville when she was seventeen. Margaret always appreciated company, and she took Mary along on her daily trips to the tutor in Leadville. Both women studied with the tutor five days a week for about three hours a day.[41] Mary stayed with the Brown household for almost two years, after the births of both children, and then was married herself. The women remained close friends even after the Browns moved to Denver.

In the summer of 1887, less than a year after her marriage, Margaret returned to the Tobin home to be with her mother for the birth of her first child. On August 30, 1887, Lawrence Palmer Brown was born in Hannibal, the name "Palmer" chosen to honor J.J.'s mother. Lawrence was baptized by Rev. M.J. McLaughlin on September 13, 1887, two weeks after his parents' first-year anniversary, and Daniel Tobin and Margaret O'Leary were his sponsors. At that time childbearing—regardless of location—was a potentially life-threatening experience and was particularly perilous in remote mining communities. Twenty-six percent of all women born in Colorado in 1890 were dead by 1910—a significant percentage dying in childbirth.[42] If a young girl survived the common illnesses of her own childhood in those days before antibiotics, she faced another two decades of potentially fatal situations if she chose to have children. And the lack of effective or dependable birth control methods often eliminated the luxury of making that choice.

When Margaret returned with the new baby, the family moved back to Leadville, briefly occupying a house at 320 East Ninth Street and then later settling in a home at 322 West Seventh Street as their family grew. This house has since been demolished and another one moved to that site. However, a pen-and-ink drawing of the house remains,[43] and the interior is described as having a living room, a formal parlor with a fireplace of fine tile and hand-carved wood, several bedrooms, a large kitchen, and high ceilings. The Browns lived just two blocks from Jack and Mary Ann Landrigan and Daniel Tobin, and all three homes frequently hosted visitors, friends and family alike, from Hannibal.

The year 1888 was a memorable one in Leadville, described by one resident as a winter of sleighing parties. Colorful sleighs, each pulled by six high-stepping horses, drove through the streets with bells merrily ringing, partygoers bundled up in brightly colored robes. A common outing included a sleigh ride to Twin Lakes for an afternoon of ice skating, followed by an evening at the Interlaken Hotel for games and a gourmet supper. J.J.'s career as a mining superintendent brought him into contact with notable businessmen from Denver, Chicago, and the East, and the Browns were swept up into a whirlwind of social activities. A.V. Hunter, who was to become an important long-term business associate of J.J. Brown, and his wife became early social leaders of Leadville, and the Browns and Hunters were well established in local social circles. Masked balls and "theme" balls had been popular since as early as 1880. Outlandish costumes were the rule, and writer Edward Blair noted how remarkable it was to consider "those bachelors working ten-hour shifts and then preparing for a ball as Louis XIV, or Falstaff." Women apparently largely preferred the "princess look." The Hard Times Ball charged only ninety-nine cents for admission, and men dressed in business suits or a miner's worn bib overalls, while women came in house dresses.[44]

Despite the hard work and good times, Daniel Tobin never forgot the girl he'd left behind. In June 1889 he returned to Hannibal to retrieve his waiting fiancée, Mary Brophy Grace. Mary was the daughter of William and Sabina Grace, who had moved from Quincy, Illinois, to Hannibal in the early 1870s. The Grace family lived on Palmyra Avenue, just a few blocks from the Tobins, and the families had known each other for years. Daniel Tobin and Mary Grace were married in Hannibal at the Immaculate Conception Church, with more than three hundred guests attending the wedding. Daniel brought Mary back to his home on Fifth Street in Leadville, where he had advanced his position in the world, forsaking work as a day miner to pursue and develop his own mining interests. This same year John and Johanna Tobin sold their home in Hannibal and followed their children west, bringing Helen, now seventeen, and Will, aged nineteen. (There is some speculation in the family that the Tobin home was sold to finance J.J.'s mining interests, but there is no proof of this notion, and it seems unlikely.) John and Johanna rented a home at 708 N. Hemlock in Leadville, and John, now in his sixties, accepted a position as watchman at the Maid and Henriette Mining Company, where J.J. worked as a superintendent. Will worked as a cigar maker in town,[45] a skill he had likely learned from his father or his brother-in-law, Johnny Becker, back in Hannibal. J.J.'s family had also joined the growing Leadville clan. In addition to J.J.'s brother, Edward, his sister, Helen Brown, came to Leadville, met her future husband, and decided to stay. Her daughter, Lucille Brown Caraugh, was a goddaughter of Margaret's.[46]

The Browns' second child, Catherine Ellen, was born on July 1, 1889. This time there was no reason for Margaret to return to Hannibal, as the entire Tobin clan, with the exception of John and Katie Becker and their children, was now in Leadville. The baby was fondly nicknamed Helen after Margaret's sister, Helen. (J.J.'s sister was named Helen as well, but apparently she wasn't as close to J.J. and Margaret's family as Helen Tobin.) On July 21, 1889, Catherine Ellen was christened at the Annunciation Church. Her godparents were Patrick Shovelin and Helen

Tobin—and Helen proved to be a most devoted aunt, in later years looking after the children when Margaret and J.J. were traveling. The two sisters, along with baby Helen and Lawrence, now a toddler, celebrated the occasion by having their photograph taken at a fancy Leadville studio.

LEADVILLE WAS A city that seemed to contradict itself at every turn. Famous, or rather infamous, for its "Wild West" reputation, it tried to capitalize on that fame while at the same time promoting culture and social refinement. Feeling a little intimidated by Eastern money and Eastern influence, Leadville citizens stewed over the belief that it was a city without a past, situated in a part of the country that didn't yet have a viable history (of course the white settlers felt that Native American history didn't count). Consequently, legend and folklore superseded fact as Colorado writers and storytellers, feeling somewhat defensive, embroidered their stories with vivid details born of imagination, not fact. Even newspaper writers felt free to embellish wherever hyperbole was deemed necessary or profitable. Yet during the late 1870s and 1880s a list of notable characters did make at least short appearances in Leadville: Tom Horn, Frank and Jesse James, Bat Masterson, Wyatt Earp, and Doc Holliday, to name just a few.[47]

The legends, although entertaining, left a damaging legacy by creating an intricate web of myth and actuality that is almost impossible to unravel. The stories of real people, particularly women and ethnic minorities, were largely lost. But at the very least these legends reveal the complexities of a swiftly changing society and the sort of character deemed necessary to not only survive but benefit from rapid social and economic change. One theme that rang true was that the economic development of the West presented unique opportunities to those who were savvy enough to recognize them—people such as Margaret and J.J. Brown.

With two children in tow and a good companion in Mary Nevin, Margaret entered into the charitable causes in which most women in her position—not wealthy but better off than most—were expected to engage. Some women might have been content to help organize church picnics and volunteer at the hospital, but Margaret brought to Leadville not only an enormous amount of energy but a strong social conscience as well. Her father's experience in Harpers Ferry and her own humanitarianism gave her a sense of compassion and conviction.

Her leadership qualities, evident even then, put her at the forefront of the causes she chose. A common observation was that if Margaret Brown had been a man, she surely would have had a wonderful career in business or mining. But she was a woman, married to a man who, she quickly discovered—like most men of his generation—had specific ideas about a woman's proper role. So she did what many women did— spoke her mind when she could, and made compromises. Like many other people in Leadville, she was concerned about education, and by 1893 the Leadville *Herald Democrat* could boast that "no town of its age and size in the country can boast of better schools than Leadville." But Margaret's primary interest was in the miners and their families. Both she and J.J. knew only too well the cost a miner paid to do his job and earn his paycheck. But Margaret's interest went beyond the pragmatic—and no doubt consuming—work that J.J. did just to keep his employees on the payroll each week.

Leadville, like many other mining communities in the West, was a microcosm of contentious race and labor relations just before the turn of the century. In proper society, the distinction between "old" and "new" money might be only a decade or so, sometimes less. A similar distinction was applied to the term "American," which was used somewhat capriciously. Everyone in Leadville was a newcomer to a certain extent. Nevertheless, most miners fell under the category of "Mike the Finn and Jansen the Swede and Hansen the Dane and Giuseppe the Dago and Pat the Irishman," and as such were considered "un-American." Additionally, the rapidly changing economic base of Leadville meant that a few people at the top exercised enormous control over a large population of "day miners" who had little political clout—and in some Colorado towns, miners were not only limited in where they could work but were forced to live in company houses, buy food and household goods at company stores, and send their children to company schools. In the early days few miners attempted to influence local politics, and unions were slow in gaining power, not only because of the influence of mine owners but also owing to the attitudes of the mine workers themselves. One miner represented the opinion of many when he said, "I don't want this thieving gang telling me how long I can work and where I can buy with a swat in the jaw and a knife in my back for daring to say my soul is my own and sticking to it against orders of the union." Many workers felt that the unions hoped to make the miners "senseless tools" for their own designs, planning to "knock employee and manager heads together" for their own benefit.[48]

Margaret Brown found herself in a curious position, empathizing with the miners' plight yet married to a prominent mining engineer who often necessarily found himself defending the position of the mine owners. All around her she observed the great inequities of society: men who made a fortune overnight and families left destitute by the brutal effects of the boom-and-bust, growth-at-all-costs Leadville mining industry. She resolved to do what she could, and with young Lawrence and Helen in tow organized relief soup kitchens for impoverished miners and their families.[49]

THE POLITICAL LANDSCAPE of Colorado was changing in other ways as well. The women's suffrage campaign in Colorado was launched in a big way by Ellis Meredith, a journalist for the *Rocky Mountain News*, and Leadville—growing faster than Denver at this point—was a focal point of that movement. In August 1893 the Colorado chapter of the National American Women's Suffrage Association set up regular offices in the Tabor Opera House building on Harrison Avenue, in rooms donated by well-heeled member Mrs. Elizabeth Bonduel McCourt Tabor, whom history has nicknamed "Baby Doe." One of these rooms was an office for a full-time secretary; another was a meeting room "large enough to hold several hundred persons."[50] There is no extant record of who attended these meetings, but it seems likely that Margaret was a participant and at least an acquaintance if not a friend of Elizabeth Tabor, though Elizabeth was somewhat older. Elizabeth's brother Peter McCourt, as manager of the Broadway Theater in Denver, was active in Denver society, and Margaret entertained Peter and his wife on numerous occasions, including a large society dinner party on December 13, 1902.[51] Helen and Lawrence were friends of the McCourt children. Many years later, in 1927, when Elizabeth McCourt Tabor had fallen on hard times at the infamous Matchless Mine, Margaret came to Leadville to visit Lorraine Brown Schuck, a niece on J.J.'s side of the family. After hearing of Elizabeth's plight, Margaret asked Lorraine and her husband to take her up to the Matchless Mine, where she visited for some time with "Baby Doe" and consequently tried unsuccessfully to help Elizabeth redeem her $14,000 mortgage.[52]

The women's suffrage campaign in Colorado was successful. In 1875 a constitutional amendment had awarded voting rights to African American males. It would take another forty-five years for women to be granted the same right on a national level with the Nineteenth Amendment to the Constitution. However, Colorado women were allowed to vote in school board elections as early as 1876, and in 1893, after an extensive campaign led by Carrie Chapman Catt, they won full suffrage in a popular referendum. Indeed, some women had been allowed to vote in elections for governments of the early mining camps.

Margaret also began to make connections with other women that would eventually lead to the formation of the Denver Woman's Party. Many women took an active role in early Colorado politics—a fact that has often been overlooked by historians. In 1893 Mary C. Craig Bradford, a teacher in the fledgling Leadville school system, became involved in the suffrage movement. In 1894 she ran for state superintendent of schools and lost but didn't give up the fight. Clara Cressingham, Carrie C. Holly, and Frances Klock became the first three female legislators elected in Colorado in 1893. Holly, a Pueblo lawyer, remarked upon her election to one term in the House that "I have noticed among the warmest friends of equal suffrage a feeling of uneasiness as to the advisability of electing a woman to office. They seem to think the women would legislate themselves a large collection of bonnets or some equally foolish measure."[53]

At the same time, J.J.'s reputation had begun to spread. Thomas Cahill recalled that J.J. "was considered a top flight mining man in Leadville when we had the best mining men in the whole country."[54] But J.J.'s ambitions went beyond his successful management of the Maid and Henriette. In 1891 several prominent Leadville mining men—John F. Campion, William Byrd Page, August R. Meyer, Max Boehmer, and A.V. Hunter—had formed the Ibex Mining Company. J.J., who knew these men well, was a minor stockholder. The board was interested in having J.J. use his well-known expertise to oversee their mining operations, and among the many properties they decided to develop was one called the Little Jonny Mine.

A.V. Hunter became a lifelong friend of the Brown family. Originally from Missouri, he had worked for James McFerran, owner of the Colorado Springs People's Bank, and married one of McFerran's daughters. With his father-in-law's backing, he helped found the Miners

Exchange Bank in Leadville and eventually became chairman of the board of directors of the First National Bank of Denver and president of the Carbonate National Bank in Leadville. Likely he was the most sedate member of the foursome.

John Campion, also a long-term friend of the family, had a more colorful reputation. Originally from Prince Edward Island, he was known about town by the nickname "Leadville Johnny" and acted as organizer, promoter, and general manager of the Ibex Mining Company.[55] Evalyn Walsh McLean, whose father was a friend of John Campion, recalled his habit of wearing a black patch over one eye and always making a memorable impression.[56] Over the years, historians have confused J.J. Brown with "Leadville Johnny" or stated that Margaret Brown claimed to be associated with the Campion family rather than the Browns. These statements are not only untrue but rather ironic considering how close the families were, in business as well as friendship. James J. Brown and John F. Campion, both "educated, hard-driving professionals," were crucial elements of Leadville's extraordinary success in the late 1880s and early 1890s and, according to historian Edward Blair, "took the reins of the Cloud City's metals industry."[57] The Leadville *Herald Democrat* proudly reported that James J. Brown was considered "one of the best mine superintendents in the district."[58]

The Browns, although not wealthy compared to those in the highest echelons of Leadville's silver barons, nevertheless enjoyed their modest success. A popular entertainment on a hot summer afternoon in Leadville was to watch the daily parade of fancy carriages along wide, dusty Harrison Avenue. Mrs. Eben Smith, wife of J.J.'s manager at the Maid and Henriette, was noted for her "magnificent and speedy animal whose sorrel coat is studded with spots of ebony."[59] Mrs. J.J. Brown herself caused somewhat of a stir. "On the dirt streets, you could hear the differences of commercial vehicles of one or two horses," said Louise Day, who was a child at the time. "Mrs. Brown had a Victoria with a folded-down top, two beautifully groomed black or very dark brown horses, a coachman driver sitting high in front, and a footman standing at the back. She always wore a great big picture hat, another one every day." Despite her admiration, Louise Day remembered her mother's disapproval. "My mother wouldn't speak to Mrs. Brown as she thought Mrs. Brown coarse because Mrs. Brown painted her face," she said. "Real heavy paint."[60] Although the use of makeup by women has been glorified or vilified at different historical times, in late-nine-teenth-century America, it was considered risqué. Twenty-some years later, Margaret's daughter, Helen, would try her hand at a newfangled commercial product for women—mascara—and even then it would be considered somewhat daring.[61]

The "shady ladies" of State Street—some of whom had managed to amass sizable economic foundations—drove their carriages in the early evening after the more respectable women had retired. They were said to be "usually intoxicated and smoking long black cigars, with a grand ability to hold the ribbons over the flanks of their fine, high-stepping animals"—expensive horses that were often gifts from the husbands of the "nice" ladies who had paraded earlier.[62]

Not all such women fared as well, however. Prostitutes could be found in the "fancy houses" on West Third and West Fifth Street, but the lower end of State Street contained rows and rows of cribs that housed girls as young as twelve or thirteen of black, Hispanic, Indian, and Anglo de-scent. Some presumably chose their path, but most of these women and girls found themselves—through desertion, divorce, or a turn of fate—in a situation they found impossible to escape. Some girls had run away from home and couldn't find a way back. Drug abuse and suicide, partic-ularly by "poisoning," as the newspapers termed it, was common. Some reports estimated that there were as many as two hundred prostitutes in the State Street brothels alone, where violence, drunkenness, and abuse were a way of life. Perhaps the most horrible aspect of Leadville prostitu-tion was Stillborn Alley, just south of State Street, where bodies of men, women, and children were occasionally found, as well as the tiny forms of unwanted infants that gave the alley its name.[63] There were many fine days in Leadville, but State Street served as a constant reminder of how quickly, through an ill wind of fate, a woman could slip out of her place.

THE GENERAL PROSPERITY of the 1880s was not to last. Until 1873 the United States had always followed a policy of bimetalism, or the coinage of both gold and silver. In 1873 a policy of following a gold standard emerged, and the government halted the production of silver dollars, which initiated a call for "free coinage" of silver from the western min-ing states, particularly Colorado. Lobbyists worked—unsuccessfully—for passage of a law that would allow for unlimited coinage of silver, although the Bland-Allison Act of 1878 and the Sherman Silver Purchase Act of 1890 alleviated some of the problem. The Silver Purchase Act, sponsored by Senator John Sherman, authorized the government to purchase 4.5 million ounces of silver monthly and boosted the price of silver. But it was a temporary fix, complicated by larger factors such as an overbuilt cross-country railroad system that was losing money fast and increasing tensions between the eastern and western states.

On May 15, 1891, President Benjamin Harrison visited Leadville to great fanfare and a main-street parade. Everyone hoped that Harrison, an advocate of the gold standard, would take a more kindly interest in Leadville's silver-based economy after his visit. But Harrison's impressions of Leadville, whatever they were, proved inconsequential. In 1892 the citizens of the United States elected Grover Cleveland as their new president. Cleveland was a man who firmly believed in the gold standard, and in October 1893 the Sherman Silver Purchase Act was repealed. In four days the price of silver dropped from eighty-three cents an ounce to sixty-two. Investors panicked as the price dropped even more. Banks, businesses, and mining operations came to a standstill, and by midsummer 1893, a full 90 percent of Leadville's labor force was out of work.[64]

The people of Leadville scrambled to ride out the disaster. Many miners packed up their families and left town. The mine managers and the existing union, the Knights of Labor, agreed to lower miners' wages to $2.50 per day. Soup kitchens were reestablished. The repeal of the Sherman Silver Act had far-reaching consequences—not just Leadville but every city west of the Mississippi was plunged into a deep economic depression. Leadville was waiting for something good to happen, and it did.

BROADWAY AND HOLLYWOOD insist that "Leadville Johnny" discovered the Little Jonny Mine for his new wife, "Molly," a saloon girl turned gold digger eager to spend his riches. The story about Molly burning up all of Johnny's money in the woodburning stove is folklore at its best—never mind the fact that paper money wasn't used in mining camps until decades later. Johnny's determination to "just go out and find some more," and his good luck in "striking the Little Jonny the very next day," is far from the truth but not, perhaps, far from the spirit.

Indeed, there may be a small element of truth to the story. Years later, in a conversation with a cousin, Margaret Brown reportedly mentioned that she had once hidden coinage in a stove, but the story had become greatly exaggerated over the years. When asked if she was upset that the newspapers had distorted (and enjoyed) the story so much, she is said to have remarked, "I don't care. It makes a damn good story!"[65]

The real story is somewhat complicated. Historian Edward Blair noted that "the discovery of the Little Jonny seems lost in a maze of conflicting stories, deals, and trades," and the Arizona heirs of a man named Samuel Christy Robertson claimed that *he* actually discovered the Little Jonny.[66] J.J. himself had many ties in Arizona, so this story does not seem completely implausible. However, what is true is that regardless of who discovered it, the Little Jonny was one of the properties owned and managed by the combined efforts of Brown, Campion, Page, and Hunter, doing business as the Ibex Mining Company. They operated a number of shafts in an area a little over three miles up the hill from Leadville's Harrison Avenue, and Ibex No. 1 shaft was the Little Jonny Mine.

In 1893 the company appointed J.J. Brown as superintendent of all the Ibex properties, a position he held for the next ten years. What happened next was a fortuitous combination of ingenuity, timing, and good luck. Despite dismal economic conditions, the Ibex Mining Company decided to make another attempt at mining the Little Jonny—for gold, not silver. The Leadville *Herald Democrat* declared that "when John Campion said that he proposed to make a gold mine out of the Little Jonny, there were probably 1,000 men each of whom had 25,000 reasons why gold should not be found there."

The cynical predictions came true when almost immediately they hit a dense layer of slippery dolomite sand that made it impossible to drive and timber a shaft. Never mind fancy equipment—J.J. took a common-sense approach. He used bales of hay supported by stout wooden timbers to hold the sand back. The shaft—which one professional estimated would take over $100,000 to build—held. Mining operations began, and not only were they successful but the Ibex company's highest hopes were met. On October 29, 1893, the Leadville *Herald Democrat* admitted with pride that "the Little Jonnie [sic] is shipping 135 tons of good ore per day." Professor Tilden of the Colorado School of Mines, representing the Venture Company of London, examined the Little Jonny and exclaimed, "It is practically a lake of ore, with some of the vugs yielding as high as $60 to the pound in gold."[67] Leadville suddenly woke up and began to pull itself up by its bootstraps. "Little Jonny Strike to

Revive Leadville," the newspapers screamed, causing one reporter to wryly note that "Leadville has more lives than the legendary cat."[68] The city rallied around J.J. Brown's unexpected success, and by the end of 1893 nearly all of Leadville's larger mines were in full production. All of America was watching; the story of resourceful J.J. Brown and the lucky Little Jonny Mine "captured the country's imagination."[69]

The company paid $1 million in dividends. The Ibex Mining Company rewarded J.J. with 12,500 shares of Ibex stock (which had been capitalized at 100,000 shares) and a seat on the board.[70] J.J. had been working—and dreaming—nearly twenty years to reach this point; the Browns had been married seven years and had two growing children. This was no overnight success.

The Brown family celebrated by touring the southern and eastern states to see the sights and visit family. After months of traveling, they spent four weeks in Chicago for the Columbian Exposition of 1893, which historians agree was one of the most significant cultural events of the Victorian era. It was a memorable experience for Margaret as she gathered ideas for events she would later plan in Denver.

Called the "White City," the exposition encompassed the Chicago fairgrounds and was designed in the beaux-arts neoclassicist architectural style. Innovative in their emphasis on middle-class material culture, the exposition's buildings and exhibits highlighted essential aspects of the American urban economy: railroads, machinery, manufacturing, agriculture, mining, transportation, and electricity. One building housed exhibits related to women and children, with three model kitchens demonstrating the benefit of electric appliances. The first electric washing machine as well as the first phonograph made an appearance. The "Midway" celebrated America's cultural diversity, with booths representing Teutonic, Celtic, Arabian, Asian, African, and North American Indian cultures, among others. This aspect of the exhibition made a deep impression on Margaret, and she would later re-create this multicultural approach in her Carnival of Nations fund-raiser in Denver. The most impressive exhibit was George Ferris's wheel, a "bicycle wheel in the sky." Other new products at the Columbian Exposition included Aunt Jemima Pancake Mix, Juicy Fruit Gum, Shredded Wheat, and a new type of beer called Pabst Blue Ribbon. For a growing family with money to spend, the fair must have been a heady experience indeed.

The Brown family returned to Leadville in time to spend Christmas with family and friends. On the eve of December 17, the Leadville *Herald Democrat* reported that the Browns had attended a party at the home of Mrs. Frank Mullen, where they played cards until midnight. Whatever obscurity the Browns had enjoyed before, their wealth—and the circumstances that led to it—would rob them of any degree of privacy.

By late 1893 J.J. and Margaret had begun to seriously entertain the idea of moving to Denver. Their home was a bit crowded: John and Johanna lived with them most of the time, and there was a constant stream of nieces and nephews from both sides of the family. In Leadville summers were short and winters long, and sometimes the snow was so deep that sidewalks became snow tunnels. Many silver-baron families divided their time between the social circles in Denver—where the snow quickly melted—and summertime Leadville society. The Browns could now afford the same option. Briefly they rented a home, and then on April 6, 1894, J.J. Brown purchased a modest-sized but elegant house, designed by architect William Lang, at 1340 Pennsylvania Avenue. Pennsylvania Avenue (now called Street) had become a fashionable, upper-middle-class neighborhood and was just a few blocks from the capitol. The house was originally built for Isaac and Mary Large. However, Mary Large's health was poor, and the family had decided to move to the more rural community of Montclair. Isaac Large sold the house to James Joseph Brown for $30,000, with the exception of "a certain trust deed for $12,500" (likely earnest money, or an amount paid after the sale date). The Brown family celebrated their first snowfall in Denver—a late spring snow—by driving a sleigh up and down Pennsylvania Avenue and Colfax Avenue, singing Irish songs at the top of their lungs.[71]

ONE OTHER NOTABLE event occurred in 1893. On January 9 a child christened Grace Loretta was born to Daniel and Mary Brophy Grace Tobin in Leadville. She would be the first of three Tobin daughters— and although Margaret was a proud and devoted aunt, she could not anticipate the impact this child and her sisters would have on her life.

Despite a new house and a growing bank account, a small dark cloud cast its shadow over the Brown household. J.J.'s business required him to travel almost constantly to mining towns throughout Colorado and Arizona, and Margaret began to hear disquieting rumors. One reporter sniped that "J.J.'s life in Leadville was always full of gossip, as he had a reputation for being a ladies man and was extremely popular."[72] Similar comments had been printed about other gold and silver barons, and society tended to politely disregard such behavior. (A woman, however, rarely received the same latitude.)

Unlike her Hollywood persona, Margaret Tobin Brown was no saloon girl, gold digger, or social butterfly. Her life was not unlike the lives of many other women in Leadville at the time: raising children, keeping house, trying to improve her own education. She was bound by the same constraints as all women during the Victorian era—denied the rights to vote, receive equal pay for equal work, or venture beyond the domestic domain. Cultural restrictions on women's social behavior were severe. Yet along with her husband, Margaret had enjoyed a brief moment of fame with the success of the Little Jonny Mine. As she grew older, her strong social and political beliefs—and her willingness to express them—grew even more resolute. She began to care less about what other people thought of her than what she herself considered to be the essential ingredients of a meaningful life, regardless of appropriate social roles for women. As the end of the century approached, her life embodied the conflicts many women faced as they sought to embrace the role of the "new woman"—a woman who could vote, own property, and even run for office—and yet wrestle with the heavy baggage of the past. Margaret's next moment of fame would occur on a much bigger stage.

In his latter years, Lawrence Brown was disturbed by the presentation of his mother on radio and stage as an illiterate, uncouth, social-climbing schemer. He wrote to people who had known her during her lifetime to determine the facts. Thomas Cahill was quick to answer his inquiry. "As to whether she was illiterate, uneducated, and without schooling, I wish to emphasize most decidedly she was anything but that," he wrote. "She was exceptionally bright, a most interesting conversationalist, had a charming personality and this coupled with her beauty made her a very attractive young woman." Even if we take into consideration the fact that Thomas Cahill was recalling the emotions of a starry-eyed young delivery boy, his final comment has been echoed by many Leadville residents of the time. He wrote, "Long after your Father had made his fortune and they moved to Denver to live permanently, your Mother would come back to Leadville and always come to the store to greet her old co-workers and visit her friends. Her wealth never seemed to change her one iota. She was always democratic and kind. This was the keynote of her personality."[73]

An Unfortunate Disposition

1894–1906

THE HISTORY OF the Brown family in Denver has been colored by writer Caroline Bancroft's 1963 assertion that the Browns were shunned by Denver society, particularly the "Sacred Thirty-six," a contingent of Denver's most wealthy elite, who found Margaret to be too Irish, too Catholic, too outspoken, and lacking the proper bloodlines. Bancroft and others referred to a small but weighty publication titled *What Makes Social Leadership?* by Agnes Leonard Hill, in which Hill wrote, "The world is full of dowdy ill-bred women who fancy that if they only had money enough they could take society by storm."[1] However, as in the woodburning stove story, the facts don't support the myth. For one thing, *What Makes Social Leadership?* was written in 1892 and published in 1893, and the Browns didn't move into their Denver home—or appear on the Social Register—until 1894. From 1894 to the early 1920s, the Browns took up more space in Denver's society pages than nearly any other Denver family and were regularly listed on the Social Register. Margaret and J.J. were not ostracized by Denver society—they *were* Denver society.

As with all legends, however, there is a drop of truth to be distilled. Despite their popularity, the Browns were indeed excluded from the Sacred Thirty-six, as were many other notable Denver families. Furthermore, Margaret no doubt turned a few heads by quickly becoming a "mover and shaker" in the rough-and-tumble mining camp that had become one of the fastest-growing cities in the country. And she never hesitated to speak her mind.

During the 1890s Denver, known as the Queen City of the Plains, sought to establish itself as a city worthy of comparison to Chicago or even New York, and architects played a key role. In just seven years, from 1886 to 1893, architect William Lang established an estimable reputation with work that included St. Mark's Episcopal Church, built in 1890 at Twelfth and Lincoln, as well as a number of notable homes. Before the devastating panic of 1893 he built houses for Denver's growing upper middle class in the area called Capitol Hill, just east of the state capitol building, which extended from Sherman to Madison Avenues and Eighteenth to Seventh Avenues. Each home was slightly different, incorporating diverse architectural styles to reflect the personalities of the owners. The three-story home the Browns bought at 1340 Pennsylvania Avenue was Queen Anne style with Romanesque arches. The house contained four fireplaces—for aesthetic purposes only, as the house, like most homes along Pennsylvania Avenue, had central heating. Other modern conveniences included indoor plumbing, electrical wiring, and a new hand-crank telephone. When they moved in the Browns decided to alter the front of their home by building a retaining wall at the sidewalk level and constructing a new, longer walkway up to the porch, which they framed with sandstone columns. The wooden shingle roof was replaced with trendy, fireproof French tiles, and two small porches in the back of the house were combined into one large, enclosed brick veranda. Eventually the carriage house out back held a horseless carriage instead of a horse. The Pennsylvania Avenue house was elegant but modest—yet a far cry from the Browns' two-room cabin in Stumpftown. Two stone lions guarded the front. (It wasn't until 1900 that Pennsylvania Avenue became Pennsylvania Street, the name by which it is known today.)

After the night of their joyful sleigh ride down Colfax Avenue, the Brown family settled into a new lifestyle, and from 1894 to 1909 both Margaret and J.J. were prominent in Denver social and business circles. It is certainly fair to say that being Catholic, Irish, and of humble origin were not badges of merit in predominantly Protestant early Denver society; nevertheless, the boom-and-bust cycles of the Colorado mining economy had built enough fortunes and broken enough hearts to keep society somewhat flexible, or at least fairly forgiving. In 1894 the notoriety the Browns had earned in Leadville with the success of the Little Jonny Mine allowed them to enter society under the aegis of Mary Matteson Grant, wife of former governor James Benton Grant (who held office from 1883 to 1885). The *Denver Times* reported, "Social annals record that when Mrs. Brown first made her bow to Denver society it was under the friendly chaperonage of Mrs. J.B. Grant. When the wife of the millionaire mine owner first came to the city it was the Grants who were the first to welcome her. It was in their box at the theater that she was the observed of all observers. It was the Grants' carriage that might be seen at any day and hour waiting before the Brown residence while the owner visited with the witty young matron from the mountains who had yet to make her way into Denver society."[2] Others who welcomed the Browns into early Denver society were Edward Costigan and his wife, James and Annie Goodell Whitmore, and Senator Edward Wolcott and his wife.

However, three people in particular had a significant impact on Margaret Brown's life in Denver: Judge Benjamin Lindsey, an outspoken reformer for the rights of juveniles; Mrs. Leonel Ross O'Bryan, a journalist whose early pen name was "Polly Pry"; and Mrs. Crawford Hill, née Louise Sneed, a transplanted Southern belle who appointed herself queen of Denver society.

Beyond doubt the most significant and long-standing of these relationships was Margaret's friendship and partnership with Ben Lindsey, which resulted in the establishment of the first juvenile court in the country. Both Lindsey and Brown became embroiled in politics, and their notoriety was partly owed to the fact that they embraced some of the most liberal and controversial positions of the time. Polly Pry, a society gossipmonger who eventually became a respected journalist, changed in quick order from foe to friend and became a partner in Margaret Brown's reform efforts. Mrs. Crawford Hill has played the cruel villainess in the Molly Brown legend, but the truth is much more complex as well as less severe. For all the grandstanding she did during her reign in Denver society, Louise Sneed Hill kept the gossip mills going with her own melodramas.

Once the Browns settled into their new home, J.J. established his mine management business in Denver, eventually hiring nephews Frank Becker and Ted Brown to handle the day-to-day details of his office. His mine ownership expanded into various parts of Colorado, particularly the Creede area, and he managed or held interests in mines and property in other states as well. His Denver holdings included several residential properties and the Colfax Hotel. Daniel Tobin, Margaret's brother, supervised many of J.J.'s properties in Leadville and the surrounding areas, and the two men exchanged sometimes heated letters regarding the handling of various properties. Nevertheless, the families remained close. In the late summer of 1898 Margaret's sister-in-law Mary Brophy Grace Tobin came with her four children to stay with the Browns for several months while Daniel traveled around Colorado to check various mines before the snows set in.[3] To welcome Mary into society, Margaret gave a luncheon party and invited twelve of Denver's most prominent society women to meet her. The *Denver Times* dutifully reported that "the appointments of the entire affair were perfect to the minutest detail."[4] Mary and Daniel's family had grown: Grace Loretta was born in 1893, Frank in 1894, Florence in 1896, and Helen Marie in 1898. One more son, Daniel, was born just before the turn of the century but didn't survive infancy.[5] Family lore holds that the baby died of diphtheria.[6]

After their extended visit the Tobin family briefly remained in Leadville, then moved to the mining town of White Pine (sometimes spelled Whitepine), where a large body of magnetic zinc had been opened in the Erie Mine. White Pine was notorious for its isolation: the first prospectors who established the community were forced to return to a lower altitude for the winter. On the trek down the mountain, they went snowblind.[7] Nevertheless, by 1900 White Pine was a fairly substantial town with a general store, hotel, theater, and school.

Any family member from either the Brown or the Tobin side who had an interest in the mining industry was brought under J.J.'s paternal wing; some stayed, some didn't, but even as the family eventually spread itself over two continents ties remained close, and the Pennsylvania Avenue home was never dull. The eclectic side of Margaret's nature became apparent as she filled her home with mementos of her travels and Victorian art as well as fond reminders of their life in Leadville (including mounted antelope heads on the walls). An infamous white polar bear rug occupied the parlor. Although the origin of the rug has never been determined, it appears in many photographs as a dramatic backdrop for family photographs and social functions and was obviously a much-loved belonging.

The Browns had architectural plans and dreamed of building a rural home where their two children could play freely and they could entertain on a grander scale. In late 1895 they purchased two hundred acres on Bear Creek, approximately nine miles from the city of Denver. A year later J.J. acquired the C.F. Reed farm directly south and a forty-acre tract on the east boundary, for a total of four hundred acres.[8] It would take another two years before their foursquare Victorian home and large brick barn— with a hardwood floor for dancing—would be completely finished, but everything was built exactly to their specifications. (Unfortunately, there is no extant record of the name of the architect.) The surrounding grounds featured terraced lawns, a tall fountain encircled by flowerbeds, a broad drive, and a pond for fishing. For nearly ten years the Brown family spent winters in Denver and summers at their ranch, announcing to their social circles that during the summer months they would formally receive visitors at their country home two days a week. Guests generally arrived by train, disembarking at Sheridan Junction and then taking a carriage, hayrack, or later an automobile up to the Brown home. It was common for guests to stay for days or even weeks, and visitors hailed not only from Colorado but also from Hannibal, Chicago, New York, Paris, London, and even Russia. The society columns noted a particularly popular expedition for guests of the Browns: parties would travel out to the farm in the evening and then be up early the next morning for a carriage ride up Turkey Creek Canyon. After a picnic lunch the group would journey to Troutdale, twenty-eight miles from Denver, and enjoy one or two nights in the quaint cabins next to the lake. Fishing, climbing, and hiking by moonlight were popular diversions.

In addition to tending to his blooded thoroughbred horses (both he and Margaret loved to ride), J.J. tried his hand at farming. The January 1899 supplement of *Kings and Queens of the Range* described a hundred acres of hay (timothy, alfalfa, and wheat), over a thousand · fruit trees, and an experimental crop of sugar beets.[9] In many ways the Browns were ahead of their time — even in ranching. The idealistic side of J.J.'s personality came to the fore in his attempt to raise "natural," or "pure," chickens. Even after the formation of the Chicken Growers' Association in 1875, chickens were in constant demand by Denver restaurants. In conjunction with a friend, William Newton, J.J. built a "chicken village" consisting of small houses built of straw, including a hospital building, recreation yard, and large bathhouse for daily baths. The *Rocky Mountain News* reported J.J.'s claim that he would use "every facility under the sun that will add to the best care of the choice fowls."[10] The chickens were fed a specialized diet, with recipes carefully detailed in a cookbook. Custom-built heated incubators housed the chicks. Johanna Tobin, Margaret's mother, reportedly liked to tell stories about the ardor with which J.J. cared for his beloved chickens.[11]

Both Lawrence and Helen loved the farm, and for Helen some of the happiest hours of her childhood were spent here as she groomed her pony and spent hours driving her pony cart across the rolling hills with the blue Rockies in the distance. Even when the family stayed in town, the bounty of the farm — fresh milk, butter, buttermilk, smeerkase (cheese), chickens, and fruit — were sent daily on the train to arrive in time for breakfast at the Brown household.[12] Margaret loved the sprawling landscape and the fresh air, which was far from the "smoke" of the city. Denver, with its high concentration of smelters and factories, was already beginning to earn a reputation for air pollution.

What to name this grand estate? The Browns settled on the name "Avoca." Margaret chose it for the Thomas Moore poem "The Vale of Avoca," a favorite of hers that she felt conveyed the appropriate sentiment. The poem begins by describing a valley so sweet and lovely that all cares are chased away and ends with the lines:

> Sweet vale of Avoca, how calm could I rest
> In thy sweet bosom of shade with the friends I love best
> Where the storms that we feel in this cold world should cease
> And our hearts, like thy waters, be mingled in peace.

"Avoca" was agreeable to J.J. not only because he too loved the poem but because he had lived near the town of Avoca in Pennsylvania. Avoca was the name of a town in Ireland as well.

Even the *Rocky Mountain News* gushed about the beauties of the Browns' country paradise. One reporter wrote,

> It lies on Bear Creek about a mile beyond Loretto Heights, in a lovely spot, which presents a varied aspect of rich, rolling farm land, grove and stream, bounded in the distance by the foothills, dark and blue. ... The house stands halfway up a long hill. It is a big, roomy structure of red brick, with white trimmings, and long porches surrounding the two sides. Inside there is room to accommodate a house party, which is where the Browns propose to entertain often when the place is in perfect order ... in the dining room there is a mighty fireplace, where Mr. Brown proposes to burn great logs when he visits his country place in winter. But at present he could rather sit on the porch and watch the light and shade chase each other over the beautiful country that stretches for miles around.[13]

The writer predicted that many such estates would be built along the foothills of the Rockies as wealthy Denver families discovered the advantages of country life. "Gentleman farming" became a trend. Other notable country homes included the Edward Wolcott home, Wolhurst, and the A.G. Reynolds home, Haddaway, in Littleton; J.C. Osgood's castle in Redstone; and the W.E. Hughes Pine Cliffs home in Castle Rock, among others.[14]

Although the Browns fared well in the mid-1890s, many of their friends and associates were still recovering—or never recovered—from the panic of 1893. Denver had been particularly hard hit. As mines closed, businesses shut their doors, and people lost their jobs, the banks collapsed. People rushed to withdraw their money before it was too late, but many watched helplessly as financial institutions sank and took everything down with them. There was no federal bank insurance in 1893. Architect William Lang was financially and emotionally devastated by the panic and slid into alcoholism and despair. He was killed in Illinois when hit by a train as he was walking along the tracks.[15]

With the discovery of gold in the Little Jonny, however, Leadville had taken the lead toward economic recovery—and the city was ready to boisterously commemorate the fact. Not only had the panic of 1893 ended but Leadville produced more silver in 1895 than in nearly any other year in its history. Residents wanted to celebrate and—in typical fashion—to celebrate in a way that would attract worldwide attention. What to do? For years Leadville had been watching cities such as Montreal and St. Paul build "ice palaces," grand but temporary structures that housed skating exhibitions and civic events. The city's coffers had never been substantial enough to consider such a frivolous event. But on a Friday evening, October 25, 1895, a meeting was held at the Vendome Hotel on Harrison Avenue. Those in attendance included wealthy citizens Tinsley S. Wood, A.V. Bohn, and J.J. Brown. Most were in favor of the fantastic event, but a second meeting four days later confirmed the predictions of the cynics: such an endeavor would be enormously expensive—$20,000 was needed just to begin construction. The project was stalled until J.J. Brown came forward. "Gentlemen," he said, "it is useless to talk longer until we have some money in sight. I subscribe $500." Tinsley S. Wood and John Campion donated similar amounts, and by the end of the evening $8,000 had been raised toward the construction of Leadville's Ice Palace.

It was indeed a grand event, and people generally agreed that "the West's greatest mining camp could support nothing less than the world's greatest ice palace."[16] Hopes were high that hordes of tourists would descend upon the town and spend money at hotels, bars, and restaurants. Construction began with huge blocks of ice cut from local ponds and streams, with more ice hauled in by train. By December a great Norman castle with archways, parapets, and towers had been raised, the smoke of smelters reaching into the sky providing an incongruous backdrop. Several dining rooms, a dancing room, and a large clay-based skating rink hosted exhibitions, ice sculptures, and costume and skating contests. Mary Nevin, Margaret's first domestic helper, had married and stayed in Leadville but remained a close friend of Margaret's. Mary's younger sister was awarded the title of Queen of the Ice Palace.[17]

Alas, the life of the Ice Palace was cut unnaturally short. Colorado weather has always been fickle, and the old adage, "If you don't like the weather, wait a minute," carried a cruel truth when the temperature began to rise unseasonably. On December 12, it reached sixty-five degrees. The Ice Palace limped along until the end of March, but it never attracted the crowds or the dollars people had hoped it would. Nonetheless, in the Brown family the Ice Palace came to represent not only a magical time but an instance of J.J. Brown, usually pragmatic and rather particular with respect to his spending habits, letting his imagination get the best of him.

TO CELEBRATE their new prosperity, the Browns embarked on an extended family tour of Europe. Lawrence was eight, Helen six. They traveled by train from Denver to New York and on March 28, 1895, sailed to Naples, arriving on April 10. The family stayed several months in Italy and then spent another several months traveling through England, Ireland, and Scotland.[18] Margaret discovered three things about herself: she liked to travel, she enjoyed learning new languages, and she especially loved Paris. She also determined that her children, when they were old enough, would attend the best schools Europe had to offer.

When they returned to Denver, Margaret found herself caught up in the grassroots movements that were struggling to cope with the city's rapidly changing scene: a burgeoning population; growing disparity between economic classes; concern about the stubborn social ills of alcoholism, gambling, and prostitution; and the increasingly active women's rights movement. Barred from entering most business and professional arenas, women turned to "club work" as a way to gain recognition and power and work toward social change. The women's reform movement included such groups as the Woman's Christian Temperance Union (1880) and the Young Women's Christian Association (1887); clubs devoted to literature and culture included the Denver Fortnightly

Club (1881) and the Tuesday Musical Club (1891). Small philanthropic groups spread throughout the city, and the *Rocky Mountain News* declared, with a combination of hope, pride, and perhaps some trepidation, that "Denver is a city of women's clubs."[19] Margaret became a charter member of the Denver Woman's Club (DWC), a group that sought to position itself as an umbrella or turnkey organization for all the other organizations and hence to represent women's voices and goals in a more focused manner. Many of these women's clubs, in Colorado and across the nation, began as literary or social clubs and eventually metamorphosed into formidable forces for political change.

First established in 1894, the Denver Woman's Club was incorporated in 1897 by a group of charter members that included journalist Minnie J. Reynolds and prominent society women Mary Matteson Grant, Elizabeth Byers, and Margaret Evans in addition to many other names that appeared regularly on the Social Register. Once established, the club quickly expanded to include women from various social and economic backgrounds. Sarah Platt Decker served as the first president, a position she held for five years. The purpose of the club was ambitious: it hoped to encompass political, educational, and social issues in a nonpartisan and egalitarian manner. Specific goals were to "present and consider practical methods for securing to women higher physical, intellectual, and moral conditions with a view to the improvement of all social and domestic relations; to study and to encourage the study by women of matters relating to the home, domestic relations, education, art, literature, music, science, philosophy, philanthropy, sociology and reform; and generally to adopt and carry out such plans and use such means as may tend to secure women higher physical, intellectual, and moral conditions and to improve all social and domestic relations."[20]

In 1898 the directors proudly declared the club "no longer an experiment." Its accomplishments included a traveling library and art exhibit for schools, community vegetable gardens to help feed the impoverished, and public health clinics. Furthermore, the directors wrote that "no spirit of clique or exclusiveness mars [the club's] efficiency. It holds out hands of cheer and sympathy to all women, and it endeavors, in the spirit of genuine democracy and helpfulness, to widen the sphere of its influence by friendly ties, not only with clubs in our own city and state, but in other states as well."[21] Dues were five dollars per year, and the board met every second and third Friday from October to July at ten A.M., first at the homes of members and later at a building owned by the club itself.

In 1898 Margaret Brown was elected chair of the Art and Literature Committee. The DWC yearbook[22] for that year recorded that "the growth of this department is sufficient evidence of its popularity." Margaret was recognized for organizing monthly entertainments at the Working Girls' Home and the YWCA as well as a Christmas dinner and tree for the "fifty little ones" at the DWC Day Nursery. The committee raised $875 for art in the public schools and secured books and subscriptions to newspapers and periodicals for the DWC Reading Room. The women also distributed reading material to various institutions throughout Denver and were strong advocates of literacy. In the evenings Margaret taught a course on the city of London. Despite the committee's busy schedule, the yearbook dutifully noted that "at each meeting tea has been served."

On a personal level, Margaret was perhaps most affected by her involvement in the River Front Park project, in which club members built a playground and summer school for five hundred indigent children. In the year-end book, the secretary of the club recorded, "The experiences of the summer have left a deep impression not only upon the children into whose colorless lives has been brought a new and wholesome element, but upon the women who in serving here have come to know the people in their comfortless homes and have entered into the almost hopeless struggle of their lives. They have been brought in touch with conditions that call for charity when *justice* might avail. Through the work of River Front we have been brought face to face with the burning questions of the day, and we cannot lightly turn from them again." Soon Margaret would meet Ben Lindsey—who was passionate about helping children living on Denver's streets—and she would have the opportunity to carry this cause into the courts.

In June of the same year the DWC held its biennial convention, with representatives from numerous Denver clubs as well as women from all over the country. Each day featured a series of lectures, presentations, and meetings. The recording secretary noted, "The Open House Committee of the Woman's Club welcomed each day hundreds of tired visitors to their attractively decorated club rooms." Margaret hosted a luncheon at Avoca, which years later would be recalled by gossip columnist Polly Pry as particularly memorable because the food ran out too soon (Margaret declared that she had been misinformed regarding how many guests to expect). Numbers overall had increased substantially: membership now totaled 920 members, up from 638 the year before.

By 1905 the Denver Woman's Club could add a number of political achievements to its record of achievements. Child labor laws had been introduced or revised throughout the country, largely due to "investigations" and political pressure exerted by the DWC and its larger umbrella organization, a national network of Woman's Clubs. More women had been appointed to school boards and various philanthropic and reformatory organizations, and 4,655 traveling libraries had been established throughout forty-five states.[23]

IN 1898 THE Denver Women's Press Club (DWPC) was established, and Margaret became an associate member of that group as well. The DWPC was a little more discriminating than the Denver Woman's Club, declaring that "no woman shall be admitted to the club who is a bore; who holds out on newspaper reporters; who has not a proper respect for the power of the press; and who cannot do something to drive dull cares away." Copy readers (a term used at the time for copy editors) and proofreaders were banned from membership. Although in 1898 Margaret had not yet published her own work, she went on to publish several lengthy travel essays, including "The French Woman Seen with American Eyes," "Mark Twain's Boyhood Home" (1905), "The Life and Shadows of Hindu Life," "Crossing the Alps in Modern Times" (1908), a full account of her *Titanic* experience, and an autobiography titled "The Course of Human Events."[24]

By 1898 Margaret and J.J. Brown were members of the Denver Country Club, and J.J. enjoyed the exclusively male benefits of the Denver Athletic Club. They both loved theater and opera. Each season they had their own box at the Broadway Theater, J.J. attending with his nephews when Margaret or Helen couldn't go. Helen, even as a young girl, enjoyed the theater and dreamed of becoming an actress. On one particularly elegant evening, Margaret was described as wearing blue lace and a string of emeralds "worth a king's ransom," while Helen, who had not yet made her formal debut in society, wore a white dress with a white rose tucked into her copper hair. J.J. had brought down with him from Leadville a family friend and several children from Leadville, who greatly enjoyed the show.[25]

The Browns' social events at Avoca were highlights of the season: the *Denver Times* reported that "Mrs. J.J. Brown is giving a series of luncheons in the country. No invitation received by any one of her friends is more eagerly anticipated than an invitation from this charming entertainer."[26] The newspapers regularly described Mrs. J.J. Brown's elegant gowns, which were made in Paris and often set the trend for Denver. At the 1899 spring bachelor's ball held at the Brown Palace Hotel, to which only "members of exclusive society" had been invited, seven of society's most eligible young bachelors greeted partygoers at the door. Dancing, which lasted through the night, included grand promenades down the long corridors between dance sets, and Margaret wore a "Paris creation of white brocaded satin rose point lace, accented with a collar of pearls."[27] Margaret was always fashionable but didn't necessarily follow fashion rules. One story claims that after a party, a friend of Margaret's pointed out another woman and remarked that it "wasn't proper to wear diamonds in the daytime." Margaret retorted, "I didn't think so either, until I had some!"

On August 27, 1898, Margaret hosted a huge social event at Wolhurst, the country home of Edward Wolcott, a prominent lawyer and U.S. senator who was a stalwart member of upper-crust Denver society (at least until 1900 or so, when his occasional patronage of the Navarre, an infamous Denver house of ill repute, was revealed, and his marriage and reputation crumbled). Margaret held a series of organizational meetings at her Pennsylvania Avenue home, dutifully noted by the press, with the intention of raising money to be given by the state of Colorado to the surgeon general for "wounded and sick soldiers." The event was considered a resounding success and led to Margaret's name heading the list of society women who could be called upon to organize elegant parties and raise substantial amounts of money as well.[28]

J.J. was also philanthropic, but in his own way, and generally liked to keep his generosity out of the newspapers. In December of this same year, and for many years thereafter, J.J. presented the boys at St. Vincent's Orphan Asylum with Christmas gifts.[29] Each boy received a new suit coat, vest, trousers, undergarments, hat, and gloves—as well as something extra such as a pair of ice skates, a sled, or a yo-yo. J.J.

reportedly "felt he owed these children something for the loss of their fathers in the mines."[30] Every Christmas both Margaret and J.J. sent gifts and supplies to the miners' families in Leadville.

Lawrence and Helen grew quickly, and it wasn't long before they saw their own names appear in the Social Register. The children's first school was run by Lucy Green, a Boston woman who had traveled west with her brother in hopes of curing his tuberculosis. The school eventually failed, and Miss Green lived with the Browns for a time, tutoring Helen and Lawrence in reading and likely instructing Margaret as well.[31] Both children attended the Sacred Heart College, a Catholic school in Denver, and eventually would be sent to boarding schools in France: Helen to the Convent of the Notre Dame and Lawrence to Jean D'Arc College.[32] As her children developed their own lives and interests, Margaret became increasingly involved in church activities and in helping the Catholic church cope with its expanding congregation. Partially due to the success of the event at Wolhurst, in April 1899 she was appointed president and head of the executive committee for the Catholic bazaar to raise money for the expansion of St. Joseph's Hospital. Margaret again held planning meetings at her home and began collecting donations.[33] Her approach was egalitarian—the paper reported that committee members included "the exclusively fashionable element, the club women, [and] the church aid societies."[34] Despite warring elements associated with different local newspapers, the planning of the bazaar was followed closely by all the Denver papers.

Unfortunately, however, just before the bazaar was about to begin, Margaret's father died. John Tobin, who had survived nearly fifty years of hard labor and lived a life that took him from the depths of poverty in Ireland to the height of luxury in Denver, died in the Brown home on April 20, 1899, at seventy-six years of age. The coroner determined the cause of death to be heart disease. The family was devastated—J.J. had spent many happy hours in his study with his father-in-law, smoking cigars and telling stories, and all of the Tobin children and grandchildren loved John Tobin. James Benziger recalled many stories that his mother, Helen, had passed down about her grandfather. "Grandfather Tobin was the favorite of all," he wrote. "Much of his time was spent with his son-in-law [J.J.] in the library at the back of the house. Favorite topics were politics, baseball, and questions of strategy raised by the memoirs of a Civil War general. My mother, a great reader from childhood, spent much of her time in a rocking chair in this room."[35] Margaret had been particularly close to her father. Although greatly saddened by his death, she was glad that she and J.J. had been able to make the last years of his life more comfortable. Along with her children who lived in Colorado—Daniel, Margaret, William, and Mary Ann—Johanna traveled with the body back to Hannibal, where John was laid to rest in the family plot. Johanna, who had been married to John for nearly forty years, returned with Margaret to Denver and over the next few years divided her time between the households of the two daughters who were closest to her, Margaret and Catherine.

Margaret quickly picked up the pieces and went about finalizing preparations for the Catholic bazaar, scheduled for May 12–20 at Denver's new Coliseum hall. Denver merchants donated impressive prizes, including a brand-new 1899 Studebaker Carriage and a Columbia Chainless bicycle. Food booths ranged from Japanese fare to chocolates and other sweets donated by Denver candy makers. The fair was more successful than anyone had imagined. A sketch portrait of Margaret appeared in the *Denver Republic,* which reported that she was "so busy that it is almost impossible to find her anywhere, and whatever success the fair attains will be due in no small degree to her energy."[36] The *Denver Times* elaborated, "The moving power in the whole scheme is Mrs. J.J. Brown, the president, whose organization of the various committees … has been remarkably successful."[37]

At the end of the bazaar, despite the fact that the fair had been enormously successful, a number of items remained unsold. Consequently, Margaret and her committee members organized a "mammoth" euchre tournament for June 18, 1899, at the Denver Armory, and promptly sold 1,500 tickets. Merchant donations for this event included a diamond ring, an onyx clock, and household furniture. This endeavor garnered a new round of support for the hospital from the community. "All classes of citizens, and especially the physicians of the city, are interested in seeing the sisters of charity able to erect the addition, which is so much needed at their building, and which will enable them to accommodate so many more patients," a *Denver Times* writer explained.[38] Once again the event was a success. On the Sunday afternoon of July 24, 1899, a crowd gathered to acknowledge the large cut section of stone that would become the cornerstone of the new hospital wing. Governor Charles S. Thomas and flour-mill magnate J.K. Mullen gave eloquent speeches. Five Catholic priests spoke and led prayers for the success of St. Joseph's Hospital. Mrs. J.J. Brown was formally recognized for her work as well as Mrs. J.K. Mullen, Mrs. John F. Campion, Mrs. W.C. Daniels, and Mrs. Joseph Thatcher.

While Margaret was expanding her circle of friends and connections in Denver, J.J. was already thinking of moving on. He returned to Denver after the Catholic bazaar closed, just when Margaret was busily organizing the euchre benefit, exhausted and discouraged. He had been traveling almost constantly—to New York, Pennsylvania, Florida, Arizona, California, and even Cuba and Mexico—to review his mining investments and in an attempt to regain his health. Although he loved the Colorado mountain landscape, the cold winters were brutal to his constitution, and he apparently had suffered a partial stroke some months earlier. Although a large and vigorous man, years of work in the mines of Pennsylvania and Colorado had taken their toll. He remarked to friends that between the rigors of hard underground labor and the stress of managing properties, he felt that he had practically worked himself to death. In a newspaper interview he mentioned that he was definitely thinking about leaving Denver, erecting a mansion on Fifth Avenue in New York, and possibly summering in Newport, Rhode Island, where months earlier the Browns had visited friends. He also said that owing to poor health, he had "practically withdrawn" from the active mining business.[39] His physician advised him to retire, at least temporarily, and J.J. felt that even though he was only forty-six, he was ready to turn most of his business over to his nephews and take a long respite. Margaret, at the age of thirty-one and just beginning to enjoy a more independent role, wasn't ready yet to retire. And the children were still young.

Nevertheless, the *Denver Times* reported that as a result of J.J.'s declining health, the Browns would be living in Ireland for four years. The *Rocky Mountain News* further claimed that J.J. was buying a permanent home near the lakes of Killarney. "When I was in Ireland," J.J. said, "I saw a little spot in the neighborhood of Killarney where I thought I could enjoy living. There is where I am going." He transferred the title of the Pennsylvania Avenue home into Margaret's name and in mid-July 1899 consolidated all of his properties under the Jefferson Mining and Investment Company, with mines in Colorado, Utah, and Arizona and additional real estate in Salt Lake City. Avoca was given over to tenants. Margaret arranged for the children to attend school in

Paris while she stayed with J.J. in Ireland. J.J. had no desire to travel on
the continent and planned to leave that task to his wife and children; he
wanted only to rest in the land of his ancestors, far away from the trials
and tribulations of his Denver and Leadville business affairs.[40]

But for reasons they kept to themselves, the Browns lasted only a
year in their Irish getaway. Likely J.J. felt too removed from his mining
business and Margaret too far away from her whirlwind of activities.
They both missed their family and friends and by August 1900 were
back in the house on Pennsylvania Avenue. J.J. resumed control of
most of his mining interests, and Margaret was once again included
in a busy round of social and political events. "There is no such thing
as real comfort in Europe," she remarked to a journalist, although she
may have been referring more to J.J.'s feelings than her own.[41] Together
they took the train to Leadville to visit friends, staying at the elegant
Vendome Hotel (previously called the Tabor Grand), and were warmly
welcomed. "Mr. Brown likes to get back to Leadville every so often
and meet his old mining friends," a reporter noted. "Mining to him is
about the best business on earth, and while he does not feel inclined
to do any active mining anymore, he is constantly getting interested
in propositions with his old friends." The Browns were astonished to
discover that Leadville, delirious in its efforts to mine at any cost, had
decided to prospect beneath the actual city streets. "Mrs. Brown, whose
immense wealth has enabled her to travel the world over with the 'smart
set,' is still inclined to enjoy the life of the mining camp, and was greatly
interested in hearing about the advancement made in the mining industry in Leadville since her husband became wealthy and left the city for
Denver," the *Denver Times* reported. "The idea that companies were
organizing to mine under the principal streets of the city was so novel
and surprising to her that she looked on the enterprise with great favor,
and said she believed she would go into the business herself, if she could
get enough pin money together."[42]

THE HOUSE ON Pennsylvania Avenue was once again boisterously
full. Helen and Lawrence were back in school, Helen attending the
prestigious Wolcott School in Denver. Founded by Anna L. Wolcott,
the Wolcott School for Girls has not only survived but thrived over
the years (existing today as the coeducational Kent Denver School).

Even in the beginning it was a high-grade, fashionable school from which graduated some of the most influential women in Denver. Helen Brown's friend Mary Phyllis Campion, John Campion's daughter, attended Wolcott, as did the daughters of other prominent early Denver families. Many close friendships ensued—scrapbooks from around the turn of the century reveal that one of the most notorious secrets of the school was OTX, a secret girls' society. Despite the efforts of the school administration to outlaw it, OTX survived for seventy years.

Also living at the house during this time were Mary Bondestal, a sixteen-year-old relative from California and legal ward of the Browns, and Frank A. Becker, eighteen, who worked for J.J. and listed his profession as a stenographer. Johanna Tobin, now seventy-five and spry as ever, had her own room upstairs. Mary C. Mulligan, aged thirty-six, was Mrs. Brown's housekeeper and dressmaker, and Harry Reynolds, a young man of twenty-five, was hostler and general caretaker. At 1361 Pennsylvania, just a few doors down the street, additional relatives from both sides of the family were housed.[43]

Harry Reynolds cared for the Browns' horses and kept the carriage ready. Originally from Missouri (possibly Hannibal), he was a horse-shoer by training and lived in a small apartment above the stable in the carriage house. Mary Mulligan was the Browns' primary servant from 1900 to 1904, and more than one society column dryly noted that Mrs. Brown treated Mary more like a friend than a domestic. Mary's responsibilities included baking bread, canning and preserving fruit, making sausages and head cheese, washing, ironing, and general housecleaning. She was an accomplished dressmaker and often accompanied Mrs. Brown when she went out. Most Denver domestics were first-generation Americans, and Mary Mulligan, like Mary Nevin, was no exception. She had been raised in Nebraska and Kansas by Irish-born parents, came to Denver as a young adult, and had worked as a domestic since the age of twenty-one. Mary never married or had children and, once she left the Brown household, continued working for various Denver families until she retired at age sixty-six.

Although the Denver papers often paternalistically mentioned the lack of reliable household help for wealthy families in Denver, a steady influx of young immigrant women kept those positions filled. Domestic work—albeit low paying and usually quite restrictive (women were typically not allowed a social or family life of their own)—was more respectable than other jobs at the time. Only 20 percent of American women were in the paid labor force, including factory workers, maids, cooks, laundresses, and nurses. Factory work for women generally paid $5 to $6 a week; household help was sometimes paid as low as $2 per week, or room and board only. In Denver around the turn of the century, the average salary for domestic help was $6 to $7 per week plus room and board.

After her retirement in 1930, Mary moved to St. Rosa's Home for Working Girls, a Catholic home for women who could no longer support themselves and had no living relatives. She then moved to Mullen Home, run by the Little Sisters of the Poor, where she lived until her death in 1941. Although she only worked for the Browns for four years, Mary was one of Margaret's closest friends and allies. When Mary left in 1904, Mrs. Ella Grable eventually replaced her, and the number of the Browns' household help increased to five, including a cook and another stablehand.

With Mary's help in creating fashionable gowns patterned after dresses Margaret brought back from Europe, Margaret's social influence continued to increase. In September 1900 the society page described a "musicale luncheon" of Mrs. Brown's that included prominent guests from Chicago and New York as well as local social luminaries. At a charity ball several weeks later, Margaret topped the list of society women, and her French gown "attracted admiration immediately. The bodice was a chic little Prince Albert coat, hand-painted in delicate pink rosebuds and foliage. Around the edges, fringe-line silk threads gave a touch that was decidedly Parisian. The skirt was flounced with accordion-plaited chiffon, with draperies of Brussels lace on it. Around her firm, white throat several strands of pearls were clasped."[44]

The high cost of photographs meant that newspapers had to rely on sketch drawings or detailed descriptions, and the specifics of this description, taken from an evening at the opera, would have allowed any dressmaker to attempt a copy. The *Denver Times* reporter wrote,

> One of the most brilliantly attractive and richly gowned women was
> Mrs. J.J. Brown. Her hair was dressed in a quaintly artistic fashion, built
> high and finished with a gilt snake coiled about an aigrette in which
> glittered two large solitaires and a cluster of opals and diamonds. Two
> long curls, of the sort that do not repose on the toilet table at night, fell
> over her beautiful bare shoulders. Her gown was just imported from
> Venice and the artistic touches of the clever modiste were apparent in

every detail. The material was ivory white satin brocaded in large chry-santhemums. The front of the skirt was embroidered in gold thistles and flounces of accordion pleated chiffon edged the skirt. The bodice was se-verely plain in cut, the beauty of it consisting in the richness of the mate-rial. A fichu-like drapery of gold embroidered lace finished the bodice at the top, and a chou of narrow velvet ribbons gave a touch of black which is so distinctly Parisian. The girdle was of chiffon, and was tied at the left side and the pleated ends reached to the hem of her skirt.[45]

Another article described Margaret's hair ornaments, one of which was set with diamonds. The society editor wrote, "Some raved about it and some didn't like it, but it's fashionable, so many will copy."

Although J.J. accompanied his wife to almost all of her evening social engagements—and was a very fine dresser himself—the newspapers would never have described a man's attire with the same painstaking attention to detail that they devoted to women's. This point highlights an interesting distinction between spheres of influence in society as dictated by gender at the time. Men achieved power—and the attention of the newspapers—through business deals and the accumulation of wealth. Women, who were generally not allowed to advance or even participate in business or political circles, could achieve social distinction only through high-profile charity work or extravagant dress. Hence the newspapers, though perhaps inadvertently, contributed to the strict social limitations of nineteenth-century women by focusing incessantly on clothing and style.

Margaret's work on the Catholic bazaar had not gone unnoticed. On October 1, at a meeting presided over by Father Calahan, Margaret was appointed general manager of the upcoming fall Catholic Fair intended to raise money for a number of charitable purposes.[46] The *Denver Times* reported that "Mrs. J.J. Brown has been asked to engineer another ba-zaar, the one she gave two years ago being such a great success." The date was set for the last two weeks of November, and the event was scheduled to take place at the old tramway power house at Colfax and Broadway. Tickets were presold at $1 apiece. Once again Margaret held meetings at her house, and one of the first steps she took was to involve Jewish as well as Catholic women.[47] By November the *Denver Times* was reporting that the fair had assumed a "most encouraging outlook," and "with Mrs. J.J. Brown's indomitable pluck and energy at its head, it is certain to be a great social and financial success." One of the most unique fund-raising booths Margaret planned was a doll booth, featuring a silent auction of dolls sewn or donated by well-known people. A number of notable people made donations, including the wives of President William McKinley, Theodore Roosevelt, and William Jennings Bryan, and the dolls began to come in "thick and fast. Mrs. Teddy Roosevelt sent a violet and black gowned little lady doll that will be a great attraction in view of the fact that Mrs. Ted made the little garments and dressed the doll. Mrs. McKinley has written that she would send her contribution, and Mrs. Bryan's doll is already on the way." The newspaper added that "it is seldom that so much unsolicited interest is being shown in an affair of this kind. Mrs. Brown has received assistance from people all over the state."[48]

Participation was accelerated by the fact that the newspaper printed a long list of all the individuals and businesses that had donated time or money to the event; the list quickly doubled after publication. Mrs. Brown involved as many civic clubs as she could, read an open letter to all members of the DWC, and established a special day for them at the fair.

The Catholic Fair opened with a grand march led by ten-year-old Helen Brown, looking "every bit an elfen queen" in a white satin dress with a red velvet cloak trimmed in ermine. A young consort dressed as Prince Albert walked by her side. "It seemed as if all the little tots in Denver and at least half of their mamas and papas were at the Catholic fair yesterday," a reporter wrote.[49] The event once again was a huge success, with crowds so large that people "could move neither one way nor the other." Mrs. Brown was in her element. "No one wore a happier smile nor seemed in a gayer mood than Mrs. J.J. Brown, the woman who possesses the button that controls the entire fair. She seemed to possess an astonishing ability to be many places at once, and no one, to have seen her, debonaire and mischievous, would have dreamed that it has been long past midnight before she has been enabled to seek her downy couch for a number of nights past."[50]

Mrs. Brown did not give up her involvement in politics. On July 9, 1896, at the Democratic National Convention in Chicago (which J.J. and Margaret likely attended), William Jennings Bryan had given his "Cross of Gold" speech, arguing against the gold standard and calling for international bimetalism. His speech eloquently articulated the broader issues of Eastern money versus Western expansion and demanded whether the Democratic party sided with the "idle holders of idle capital" or the "struggling masses." He argued for the "hardy pioneers who have braved all the dangers of the wilderness, who have made the desert to blossom as the rose—the pioneers ... who rear their children near to Nature's heart, where they can mingle their voices with the voices of the birds." He cried, "Our war is not a war of conquest; we are fighting in the defense of our homes, our families, and posterity."

Bryan underscored his speech with the infamous words, "You shall not press down upon the brow of labor this crown of thorns, you shall not crucify mankind upon a cross of gold." The popularity of this speech led to Bryan's Democratic presidential bid in 1896, and then again in 1900 and 1908. The silver platform held enormous consequences, not only for the Browns but for the entire state of Colorado. Both J.J. and Margaret supported Bryan's campaign, and when Bryan was in Denver in early November 1900, Margaret was prominently listed on the front page of the newspaper as a member of the Grand Silver Rally of the Woman's Bryan Club.[51] Unsuccessful in all three of his bids for the presidency, Bryan, a fundamentalist, later became famous as the prosecutor at the Scopes trial in 1925, winning over defense attorney Clarence Darrow against teaching the theory of evolution in the schools.

Although women had won the right to vote in Colorado in 1893, the fight continued for nationwide suffrage and Colorado became a focal point for heated rhetoric. Despite Margaret's support of the Catholic church, she and other women were singled out by church officials in strong language admonishing them for their suffragist activities. Father O'Ryan, speaking before the female members of the Denver Philosophical Society, caught his audience off guard by taking the opportunity to speak against women's suffrage. His words made newspaper headlines. "I would like to see the question put to a vote again in Colorado and have it voted down," he said. "I voted for woman suffrage when it was presented to us, but now I feel that I ought to throw a white sheet about myself and stand in front of the church door and do penance for it. It is working harm to the women of the state. I have been shocked to see them engage in political work as they have, in precinct canvassing and on election day at the polls. The women are losing their womanhood through it." Mrs. Scott Saxton, an outspoken suffragette who is known to history only by her married name, immediately stood and sarcastically thanked him for his "compliment to women."[52]

O'Ryan's words differed little from those of a Presbyterian minister who had spoken in 1877, when the movement for suffrage was just beginning to gain momentum. On October 1, 1877, a huge gathering at the Lawrence Street Methodist Church allowed a public forum for the views of feminist Lucy Stone, among others. The next day, in a sermon titled "Woman Suffrage and the Model Wife and Mother," the minister declared, "God intended woman to be a wife and mother and the eternal fitness of things forbade her to be anything else. If women could vote, those who were wives now would live in endless bickerings with their husbands over politics, and those who were not wives would not marry." The city of Denver immediately became a hotbed of suffrage debate, which would continue well into the twentieth century.

Margaret had philanthropic interests as well as political ones. J.J. looked after the orphans at St. Vincent's; Margaret—in conjunction with Benjamin Guggenheim—helped plan a Christmas dinner and toy fair for underprivileged children at the Brown Palace Hotel. "What pleasure it is to see the dear little children so boisterously happy!" she declared.[53] When asked by a reporter to reminisce about her own childhood Christmases in Hannibal, she recalled, "All of my Christmas days were happy ones."

WHEN THE CATHOLIC FAIR ended, Margaret had already made plans for the next step in her life. Despite the fact that she had received no formal education beyond the age of twelve, was a female in her thirties, and was married with two children, she had a goal: to go to college.

Through her connections in New York and Newport, Rhode Island, Margaret had been watching with great interest the development of Andrew Carnegie's dream project, the Carnegie Institute. The Carnegie Institute was founded on the belief that anyone—regardless of gender, race, or economic or social status—could go to college and study not only subjects related to a trade but such things as drama, literature, and painting. Margaret was determined to become one of the institute's first students. Just after Christmas in 1900, she took another trip to France with her children and installed Helen once again in the Paris convent. (One family story relates that Margaret demanded some special considerations for her daughter, including the right to have a bath once a week and a daily glass of fresh milk—a request that was vetoed.[54]) Margaret brought thirteen-year-old Lawrence back with her to the East Coast. After settling Lawrence into St. John's College in Fordham, New York, which he would attend for two years (spending his summers in Denver), Margaret started taking classes.

For most American citizens in 1900, education—especially adult education—was still a privilege. Between 1880 and 1910 only about 5 percent of Americans between the ages of eighteen and twenty-one had attended a college, university, or "female seminary." However, powerful political forces were at work to change the face of education in America. The federal government promised land to states that provided university-level education, including "industrial classes" as well as courses in the liberal arts. However, the real sources of educational growth in America were the deep pockets of the barons of the Gilded Age. Although much discussed, income tax (permanent in Britain since 1874) was not levied on individuals or corporations until the Eighteenth Amendment was passed in 1913. Just before the turn of the century philanthropy became fashionable, and "Gilded Age millionaires" sought to invest in the future of America by establishing universities bearing their names. Colleges such as Cornell, Drew, Johns Hopkins, Stanford, Vanderbilt, Duke, and the University of Rochester were all founded through the gifts of moguls. John D. Rockefeller, who in later years was acquainted with Margaret Brown, donated millions to the University of Chicago. But Margaret was most attracted to the Carnegie Institute, which specifically supported the education of women.

Founder Andrew Carnegie had emigrated with his family to the United States from Scotland at the age of thirteen. He began his business career as a bobbin boy in a cotton factory, and—aided by the discovery of oil on the family farm—he slowly began to build an empire that would eventually put him at the helm of a monopoly of the entire U.S. steel industry. Known for his aggressive business practices, he astonished the world by selling Carnegie Steel Works to J.P. Morgan and retiring to Scotland, where he began to divest his fortune of an estimated $350 million. Schools, libraries, and various other institutions benefited from his benevolence, and Andrew Carnegie set about establishing the Carnegie Institute and the Carnegie Endowment for Peace.

Founded in 1900, the school was known for the first twelve years as the Carnegie Technical Schools. Arthur A. Hamerschlag served as the first president, and the twelve professors, assisted by six administrators, were divided into four faculties: the School of Apprentices and Journeymen, the School of Science and Technology, the School of Fine and Applied Arts, and the Margaret Morrison Carnegie School for Women. At the time that Margaret enrolled, most students attended on a part-time basis, but the school grew quickly. Although no class or attendance records from that period exist, Margaret wrote that she studied literature and language, and it seems likely that it was at Carnegie that she had her first instruction in drama—an experience that would change her life and deeply affect the lives of her daughter and nieces. (Indeed, in 1917 the Carnegie Institute distinguished itself by awarding the nation's first undergraduate degree in drama.[55])

Margaret spent the year studying at Carnegie, traveling briefly with her cousin Margaret O'Leary after Christmas. On May 15, 1901, she returned to Hannibal for the funeral of Margaret O'Leary's mother, Mary O'Leary, who was Margaret Brown's aunt and had been the grammar-school teacher for all the Tobin children.[56] Once again she stayed with the Becker family in Hannibal. Margaret summered in Denver and then traveled East with her children again. In the fall of 1902 Lawrence was enrolled in the Pennsylvania Military College in Chester, Pennsylvania, a school he attended for two years. Helen attended school in New York. Like many other Denver families, the Browns believed that the best education was to be obtained at prestigious Eastern schools or boarding schools in Europe, although J.J. was less partial to European schools than Margaret.

Margaret spent the fall semester at Carnegie once again. When she returned to Denver in time for Christmas, she discovered an unhappy surprise—J.J. was being sued for $50,000 by Harry D. Call, the stenographer of well-known Colorado silver baron W.S. Stratton, for alienation of his wife's affection. Described as a "tall blond with a splendid figure … lighted only by the eyes that laugh," Maude Morton Call had reportedly met J.J. Brown at a health resort in Pueblo and subsequently decided to leave her husband and three-year-old son. Mr. Call moved in with his mother and presented his complaint to the press. After much publicity, the case was settled out of court.

Margaret was devastated and was particularly upset that the event received so much press coverage. The Browns withdrew, temporarily, from society. Partly to repair their marriage and partly to escape Denver's gossip mills, they decided to take a long trip together. J.J. had tired of European culture and wanted to see some of the rest of the world—Margaret agreed. From 1902 to 1903 they rented their Pennsylvania Avenue home to Governor James Orman and his wife and on April 16, 1902, embarked on an around-the-world tour. J.J.'s passport described him as forty-nine years old with a "rather high forehead, blue eyes, straight nose, medium mouth, and square chin." Listed as nameless traveling companions were one wife and one servant, presumably Mary Mulligan. Margaret, who loved to travel and kept mementos of every trip, later carefully pasted a copy of the passenger list from their steamship, the *Konig Albert,* into her scrapbook as well as a June 10 program from a charity bazaar the Browns attended at the U.S. Embassy in Paris.

They were gone for nearly a year, with Margaret's sister, Helen, looking after the children's interests and nephews Frank Becker and Ted Brown watching over the business. (Years later, Helen Brown would recall that her Aunt Helen, though stunningly beautiful, lacked Margaret's wit and charm and had a penchant for cleanliness and order. Any child who opened a drawer or closet door was confronted with a curt note reading, "CLOSE ME."[57]) When the Browns finally returned to Denver, Margaret wrote a lengthy article for the *Denver Republic* describing life in India. "There is no place in the whole world where so many temples or places of worship exist as in India," she wrote. "Not even a little village exists without its temple, and it is a proverb among the Hindus that people cannot live and prosper where there is no temple."

However, Margaret was deeply disturbed by the caste system. "The English have made some very wise laws in India, giving employment to a few outcasts and making them legally free, but socially the pariahs are in a greater state of degradation than any other people in the world," she wrote. "It seems a great waste of power that so many millions of strong and fairly intelligent men and women should be cut off from their fellow-countrymen and allowed to drag on an existence almost as elementary as that of the brute creation."[58]

Despite the fact that their marriage of seventeen years was beginning to show signs of strain, both Margaret and J.J. enjoyed the trip. Years later J.J. would speak of how much he had loved Japan and longed to return. Margaret brought back beautiful reminders of her Japanese experience: embroidery, silk kimonos, and exotic gifts for family and friends. She astonished New York and Denver society with a new Japanese-style coiffure and elegant, albeit unusual, clothing.[59] Nevertheless, she was a confirmed advocate of French language and culture. J.J., on the other hand, had nothing good to say about the French, and this issue became one of many differences between them.

When the Browns returned to Denver, they made an unpleasant discovery, which somehow made the front page of the society scandal sheet published by Polly Pry. Polly gleefully reported that when the Browns reoccupied their home, Mrs. Brown called the attention of the governor's wife to the fact that the walls and rugs were in a significantly less-than-perfect condition. Mrs. Orman retorted, "But you didn't furnish cuspidors!"[60]

IN 1903 MARGARET MET a man who was to make an enormous difference in her life: Judge Benjamin Barr Lindsey. Few men have stirred up so much controversy in Colorado politics—or accomplished as much long-term benefit for the state. Called "the Kids' Judge" by his advocates and "the Bull Mouse" by his enemies (he was rather short),[61] Ben Lindsey rose from an obscure county judgeship in Denver to national fame and captured the country's imagination, admiration, and wrath.

Ben Lindsey was only twenty-five when he was admitted to the Colorado bar in 1894, but his passion for the plight of juveniles had begun years earlier. The son of a former Confederate Army captain in Jackson, Tennessee, he had come to Denver at the age of eleven when his father took a job managing telegraph operations for the railroad. His adolescence in Denver was interrupted by a visit from a recruiter for the elementary school department of Notre Dame University, who promised free transportation if Ben's family would send him off to school. Lindsey's two years at Notre Dame were not only memorable but allowed him to form a close friendship with another Denver boy, Edward P. Costigan. Years later Costigan would run for the Colorado governorship as a Progressive candidate and become a leading supporter of New Deal legislation in the United States. Costigan and his wife also became close friends of Margaret Tobin Brown.

Lindsey was forced to give up Notre Dame when his father lost his railroad job, and he and his brother, Chal, went to live with their grandfather in Tennessee. When he returned to Denver, Ben was shocked to discover that his father was in very poor health. Ben and Chal took full-time jobs rather than applying to the newly built East Denver High

School. One morning just after Ben's eighteenth birthday, he went down to the family coal cellar and discovered that his father, despondent over poor health and rising debts, had committed suicide.

For three years Ben worked three jobs to support the family: delivering newspapers, doing accounting work, and working nights as a janitor. Chal eventually found a job working for R.D. Thompson, a successful Denver lawyer. Ben—who aspired to a career in the legal field—convinced his brother to switch jobs with him. Despite an atmosphere of "exasperated misery" at home and a seemingly endless path of poverty, Lindsey gradually became "more of a clerk and less of an office boy."[62] Even though he had yet to gain admission to the bar, the bright and ambitious Lindsey was allowed to argue two cases that shaped his career.

The first case involved a man who had forged his credit references. Ben Lindsey argued persuasively, and the jury deemed the man guilty. But Lindsey was almost immediately overcome by the consequences of the decision: the man, married with dependent children, could not support his family while incarcerated, and his wife and children were forced to live on the streets. Lindsey asked the judge for a suspended sentence; his request was denied.

The second case made an even deeper impression. The same judge asked the idealistic young law clerk to defend two indigent men accused of burglary. Lindsey encountered what he thought were his two clients, a safecracker and a horse thief, playing pool with two little boys. Lindsey "feared he had a very difficult assignment since the men had the look of hardened criminals and the encouragement they were giving to the two little boys to gamble hardly improved the impression they made."[63] Then Lindsey learned that the children, who had been accused of breaking into a railroad section house and stealing some tools, were his real clients. They had been jailed for two months because their parents couldn't afford bail. Why, Lindsey asked, were the boys in a cell with such hardened criminals? The warden patiently explained that there were often children in jail, and not enough room to accommodate even the adults. Ben Lindsey made a personal resolution: "Here were two boys, neither of them serious enemies of society, who were about to be convicted of burglary and have felony records standing against them for the rest of their lives. ... The state was sending them to a school for crime—deliberately teaching them to be horse thieves and safecrackers. It was outrageous—and absurd." Lindsey was determined to help the boys have a chance in life. "I saw only vaguely then what afterward became clearer to me—that my first fight with the state was not just for those two boys but for millions like them," he wrote. "I had made up my mind to smash the system that meant so much injustice to youth."[64]

This time the judge listened to Lindsey and released the boys on the condition that they provide regular, satisfactory reports demonstrating that they had mended their ways. In 1894 Lindsey entered into practice with Fred Parks on Champa Street in West Denver, representing people who traditionally had been powerless in early Denver society, including cases related to employers' liability and industrial accident claims. One of their first cases involved a mother whose young son had been struck and killed by a streetcar. The court, unable to determine the prospective economic "services" of the child, denied compensation to the mother. Frustrated by the legal system, Lindsey and Parks decided to go into politics and change the rules.

Lindsey's political career began with his appointment to the Capitol Hill precinct in 1898. The following year he was appointed public administrator and guardian and worked as guardian of abandoned orphans and other dependents of people who had died. He held this position for two years, in addition to building his law practice, and in 1900 was appointed to fill the unexpired term of Judge Robert W. Steele, who had been elected to the state Supreme Court. Now thirty-one years of age, he quickly earned the nickname "the Kids' Judge," a role he would fill for twenty-six years.

Ben Lindsey was characterized as a dreamer and a visionary, and his uncle scolded him by saying law was a sorry profession for such a sensitive young man. But Lindsey was a tough reformer. He made a dramatic impact on the formation of juvenile law in the United States and changed the way Colorado, and the nation, treated children. But he needed someone with as much vision and compassion as he to make it happen—and someone who knew how to raise money and make connections. Margaret Tobin Brown and Ben Lindsey made a formidable team.

By 1904 Margaret was holding a series of regular fund-raising events for Denver's juvenile court. On April 30, 1904, a theatrical benefit at the Broadway Theater was a "bona fide society affair." Young women from the Wolcott School sold candy, flowers, ices, and punch to playgoers, and society columnist Polly Pry was quick to point out that Helen Brown was one of the prettiest. The "Smart Set" looked on from their private boxes, and the long list of society elite included Mrs. Crawford Hill, the J.K. Mullens, and the J.S. Browns (of the Brown Palace Hotel).[65]

The event was so successful that another was planned for July 1904, to take place at Avoca. The Jane Oaker stock company closed their summer season at the Broadway on August 29 and agreed to stay in town long enough to do a special production of Shakespeare's *As You Like It*, starring Eugene Ormande and Jane Oaker. At Avoca construction began on a special stage of a "decidedly unique and original character" and a long supper table that would encircle the fountain on the west side of the house. A miniature farmyard and orchard were planned, with table decorations of painted animals and real miniature fruit trees. Little girls dressed like milkmaids would help serve the guests, and young men home from colleges back East were to be ushers.

Margaret sent out six hundred invitations, including the members of the Denver Woman's Club and Denver Women's Press Club. Despite the fact that some members of Denver's elite did not agree with Margaret Brown's and Ben Lindsey's liberal politics, many of those among Denver's "choicest society" promised to attend. Polly Pry declared, "The entertainment is on the order of the fashionable fetes given at Eastern summer resorts and will be the first of the kind ever attempted in Denver"; she even wrote a poem titled "Vers de Societie" to encourage all to attend:

> A club for juveniles is planned
> And will be built, I understand,
> With proceeds from a splendid fete
> That Mrs. Brown has planned of late.
> Avoca lodge, that day, will be
> A scene of social revelry.
> There is no doubt that Mrs. Brown
> Will do her best to win renown.
> And, by the way, here's just a hint:
> She's often getting into print;
> And, ere the summer passes by,
> Will entertain folks standing high
> In Gotham's most exclusive set—
> Some real aristocrats, you bet!
> I would not be surprised if she
> Became the *leader* locally![66]

But the event did not come to pass. Mr. H. Hamilton of Hamilton & Summerfield, who managed the Oaker company, came out to Avoca to inspect the facilities and agreed to present the play. Invitations were sent out and "vast advertising" followed. However, once Hamilton realized the scope of the event, he changed his mind and decided that neither Jane nor the company could possibly "lift an eyelash let alone their voices for less than a thousand dollars cash." Margaret was forced to cancel the whole thing. Polly Pry was quick to chastise Hamilton: "Wow! Is the honor of coming to 'Avoca' nothing? Is a recognition of mere player folk nothing in the balance? Go to, likewise, fie!"

Polly Pry had not always been such a strong advocate of Margaret's philanthropies. Known for her sharp, tongue-in-cheek columns about society, Polly Pry is credited with much of the negative publicity about the Brown family. (In fact, it could be said that it was a mark of high society to get into Polly's paper—she wrote only about the most elite circles.) The truth, however, is that Polly Pry quickly moved from being one of Margaret's adversaries to become a friend and a strong supporter of her charitable and political causes. Although Polly began her career as a writer of gossip and scandal, she used her wit and intelligence to become a respected reporter not only in Denver but in New York and beyond.

Leonel Ross Campbell—the real name of Polly Pry—was born in Kentucky on November 11, 1857, to a family that would be devastated by the Civil War. At age fifteen "Nell" eloped with her much older paramour, George Anthony, the son of a wealthy Kansas railroad family. They traveled to Mexico, where George, representing a Boston banking firm, was commissioned to help build the Mexican Central Railroad. Nell learned Spanish and, as the wife of a prominent man, entertained Mexican diplomats and dignitaries. But she tired of the re-straints imposed by her role and her marriage and decided—alone and unemployed—to try for a journalism career in New York. Her first interview was with John Cockerill of the New York *World,* a publisher who also happened to know her father. "I ought to spank you and send you back to your husband!" he scolded. Nevertheless, she was hired for $6 a week. Eventually the paper made her a foreign correspondent and sent her to cover events as far away as South America.

Then Nell's brother became ill and like many others was advised to go west for the healthy climate. On a train to visit her brother, Nell met the gregarious Frederic Bonfils, cofounder of the *Denver Post.* By the time they reached Denver, Leonel Ross Campbell had been hired as Bonfils's first female reporter.

It wasn't long, however, before Nell's enthusiasm got her into trouble. While writing a story on Colorado's treatment of prisoners, an exposé she titled "Our Insane Treatment of the Insane," she met a gaunt man who at first refused to speak—the infamous Alferd E. Packer, imprisoned for cannibalism after he and five other men were stranded after a blizzard and Packer reportedly survived by consuming the bodies of his companions. Packer's escape from prison and sensational 1883 trial were legendary. (Judge Melville Gerry of Lake City, when sentencing Packer, reportedly burst out: "There were seven Democrats in Hinsdale County, and you ate five of them!")

But the reclusive Packer, now elderly, eventually talked to Nell. "I am innocent," he said, "of the hideous crime with which I am charged." Nell believed his claim, and also believed that the full circumstances of his actions had not been taken into account. The unwritten law of the sea, she noted, allowed cannibalism in extreme conditions, and surely the same applied in a blizzard. She wrote to Governor Charles Spalding Thomas, received a curt reply, and decided to conduct her argument in the pages of the newspaper. Bonfils and Tammen of the *Denver Post* hired attorney W.W. Anderson, known as "Plug Hat," to help Nell's cause. Plug Hat promptly visited Packer in jail and relieved him of the $1,000 Packer had carefully saved over the years from weaving hair ropes and horse bridles to sell to cowboys.

Nell, Bonfils, and Tammen were incensed. "Let's sic Packer on him!" Tammen suggested, but instead they sent Nell across the street to inform Plug Hat that they were terminating his services. When she returned, Plug Hat was hot on her heels.

"You're a damned robber!" Tammen yelled.

"He's got a gun!" Nell shrieked. In the subsequent brawl, both Bonfils and Tammen were struck by bullets. Nell rushed between them, her hat and full skirts complicating matters considerably. "You'll get it next," Plug Hat hissed.

"Go ahead," Nell replied. "And you'll hang for it!"

Others arrived on the scene. Plug Hat calmly walked down to police headquarters, where he turned himself in. He figured he'd killed "those two skunks" and saved the city of Denver a lot of trouble, a deed worth hanging for (both men survived). At Plug Hat's trial—in which he was ultimately acquitted—Alferd Packer was a witness. And on January 7, 1901, Alferd Packer was paroled.[67]

Now that she had created a reputation for herself as a journalist of some substance, Nell's next assignment involved the impending labor crisis in the mines. She was sent to Telluride's Smuggler Mine to report on the murder of a mine worker and was promptly advised that women weren't allowed underground. Nell put on pants and tucked her long blond hair into a miner's helmet, took a pick and lantern, and followed a night shift down the tunnel. Her subsequent articles attacked labor leaders for their aggressive tactics and even accused them of advocating murder. The union retaliated by boycotting the *Denver Post.* Despite the fact that she had stood between him and a bullet, Bonfils—always a staunch believer in Nell—suddenly withdrew his support.

Nell accused Bonfils of being a coward and quit. She decided to go into business for herself. Working out of her home, she took the pen name "Polly Pry" and published a weekly magazine of the same name. "Denver was just big enough and just lively enough and just naughty enough to need a weekly paper," she declared, "as desperately as a lively boy needs his Saturday-night tubbing."[68] Polly poked fun at everyone—society leaders, political figures, members of the elite and the underworld. Her sharp wit and political savvy gave her writing an edge that, even when it was complete fabrication, made Denver squirm. Her paper sold like hotcakes. And one of her first targets—although they had never met—was Mrs. J.J. Brown.

On Sepember 5, 1903, nine years after the Browns moved to Denver, Polly Pry wrote, "Mrs. Brown was Irish, when Leadville saw her first, with a certain charm and frankness that went well with the face full of irregular features, and laughing blue eyes, [although] the mouth generally smiling was not altogether lacking in good qualities. There is a craze these days among folks to know what you are and from whence you came, why not carry one's escutcheon on one's face as well as to blazon it on the doors of one's chaise?" Polly also made fun of the word "Avoca," the name of the Browns' country home. "From whence is the word derived? Toward what limb of the philologic tree must endeavor crawl in order to pluck the bloom? What's the use of asking? It is here, gracing our poverty-stricken vernacular—and Mrs. J.J. Brown was the originator."[69]

It is a credit to Margaret Brown that she overlooked or forgave these early attacks by Polly Pry, and later, as the women became friends, Polly's columns took quite a different bent. Nell and Margaret shared a tendency to take the side of the underdog—and neither hesitated to speak her mind. Historian Mary Lou Pence wrote, "Although [Polly] tried to cover up with the crispness of her style and the sharpness of her tongue and typewriter, her stories spread sympathy like jam on toast for the plight of the frustrated and downfallen."[70]

Nell's second marriage to Denver attorney Harry O'Bryan allowed her to entertain in "proper" Denver society; nevertheless, many considered her too outspoken and even offensive. At one point the situation became extreme. On January 16, 1904, Polly Pry wrote, "For the past several weeks I have been receiving anonymous letters warning me ... that I would be killed and my office blown to atoms." Sure enough, one night a stranger knocked at her door. Shielding herself with the door, she opened it slowly, and "a bad light, a black dress and a poor marksman saved my life." The city's corps of newsboys, who adored Polly Pry, arranged a twenty-four-hour security watch around her house, and the magazine continued for another two years. "I am going to keep right on running my magazine and writing what I think proper," she declared.

Once they became allies, Polly Pry regularly reported on Mrs. Brown's successes and her more colorful endeavors. In 1904 she noted that the Countess de la Castlemardno of Rome, the Countess Leary of New York, and Mrs. Patton-Glover of Washington (sister to General Corbin) all stayed at the Brown home. Mrs. Matabelle Kettering, Mark Twain's niece, also stayed with the Browns that summer. She had been busy traveling back and forth from Hannibal to St. Louis for her work with the 1904 St. Louis World's Fair, an event the Brown family attended twice that year.[71]

Margaret and Helen frequently traveled abroad with the Count and Countess de la Castlemardno. Prior to her marriage, the Countess—who, like Margaret, loved to ride—had been Edith Van Buren, who had met her count in Rome when her uncle was ambassador to Italy. Margaret often stayed with her in New York.[72] The Countess Leary was the person who first introduced Margaret Brown to Newport society in 1903. Anna Leary, whom the newspapers described as the daughter of a New York hatter, had not come by her title through marriage. In October 1902, due

to her extensive work and many philanthropies related to the Catholic
church, the pope had conferred upon Anna Leary the distinction of the
title Countess of the Holy See. A chapel was named after her as well.
Archbishop Corrigan announced, "So far as is known, it is the first time
the distinction had been conferred on any woman in this country."[73] In
addition to her Newport mansion, Countess Leary owned a home on
Fifth Avenue in New York and counted among her closest friends the
Vanderbilts, Astors, and much of "old" New York society. She had a
private box at the Metropolitan Opera and invited both Margaret and J.J.
to join her when they were in New York. When the countess came to
stay with the Browns for a month, Margaret took her all over Colorado,
showing her the natural wonders of the state. Polly Pry once again waxed
poetic and wrote of the countess,

> The Countess Leary's here!
> We'll envy, them, the favored few
> Whom she puts down in her "Who's Who."[74]

Polly Pry, who had no children of her own, was captivated by young
Helen. Noting that Mrs. Brown was off to New York with a party of
friends and would spend the penitential days (Lent) in Cuba, she wrote
that Margaret "did not take her stunning little daughter, who might
have made a sensation with her Titianesque beauty, even if she is only
a little girl in short frocks."[75] Helen had not only impressed Denver
society with her red-auburn hair and charm, she had also set her heart
on the stage. She played parts in small theatrical productions, including
An Intimate Acquaintance in 1905. Polly Pry extolled her looks, writing, "Helen carries herself with a *Vere-de-vere* poise, although only the
blood of Brown and Tobin courses through her veins. Her hair is the
coppery color we read about, but seldom see; her skin the tint of mag-
nolia flowers; her eyes great twilight pools of gray. When her lips turn
up instead of down she will be incomparable."[76]

On April 29, 1904, another benefit at the Broadway Theater raised
money to send Judge Lindsey's boys "away from the city to help them
become self-sustaining youngsters." Two plays were presented, William
Dean Howells's *Room 45* and T.B. Aldrich's *The Set of Turquoise,* with
two prize-medal winners from the Wolcott School for Girls giving rec-
itations between the plays. A concert beforehand and lunch afterward
completed the day. Despite his political differences with Judge Ben

Lindsey, Denver Mayor Robert W. Speer—and all of Denver society—attended. The *Denver Times* reported that once again Mrs. Brown was "working like a Trojan" and that a "neat sum" was realized for the children. Following this event, a "Juvenile Improvement" organization was formed. Margaret Brown and Judge Lindsey drafted a formal fund-raising letter, and two of the people they convinced to sit on the board were J.J. Brown and Crawford Hill.[77]

In November 1904 the annual juvenile benefit was an art show featuring over one thousand drawings, landscapes, and "sentimental studies," which was held at the Brown Palace Hotel and lasted five days. Polly reported that the event was supported by a "literal who's who list of Denver society ... [with] names potent enough to insure sufficient appreciation to keep the boys going for another year." The following year Margaret organized another benefit at the Broadway Theater. Branches of pepper trees decorated the entire theater, and a children's pony was raffled. Mrs. Peter McCourt, sister-in-law of Elizabeth McCourt Tabor, sold raffle tickets. Helen Brown, once again referred to as a "Titianesque beauty," had a part in the play. "Here's luck to the annual Lindsey-bad-boy-Mrs.-J.J.-Brown show. We'll all be there, Molly darlin'," Polly wrote. (This instance is an example of the Irish diminutive "Molly" being used as a term of affection—Margaret was never called Molly in person.) The drama was so well received that Polly rhetorically asked whether Mrs. J.J. Brown was planning to take her theatrical troupe and talented daughter on the road.

Clearly both Nell and Margaret enjoyed a good story and a tart remark. In a column filled with details of society Christmas parties, Polly Pry wrote, "Some of our society matrons have a pretty quick wit of their own—especially when enhanced by an Irish quickness to see an opportunity and take advantage of it." She reported that a "foolishly daring male person" at a social function was privileged to serve Mrs. J.J. Brown a cup of tea.

> Bending over the teacups, the man whispered thrillingly, "Do you know, you have eyes that would send a man to hell!" There was no answer possible at the moment, and later this same male person ostentatiously asked permission to call. "My husband is away," said Mrs. Brown, "and in his absence I do not receive gentlemen—and my daughter is not out yet."
> "I have a stunning auto," he insisted; "let me come and take you out for the run of your life!"

"Thank you!" said Mrs. J.J. very distinctly. "When I want to go to hell, I will send for you!"[78]

AROUND THE YEAR 1895 Mrs. Crawford Hill set about changing the scenery of Denver society. A Southern belle, Louise Sneed married Crawford Hill, son of smelter king Nathaniel Hill, in 1895 and wasted no time assuming her proper role. Her background, her husband's wealth, her grand mansion on Sherman Street, and her father-in-law's status earned her the self-imposed title "arbiter of Colorado society." Nathaniel Hill owned the *Denver Republican,* a staunch conservative, big-business, antilabor newspaper that Judge Ben Lindsey called "a corporation organ." The alternative to the *Republican* was the *Denver Post,* Gene Fowler's eventual employer, which in its early years seldom felt bound by fact and sold newspapers through red-ink sensationalism. "Many hated the *Post,* but practically everyone read it," historian Tom Noel noted.[79]

In the opinion of Mrs. Crawford Hill, Denver society—although bound by its own "natural" prejudices against certain ethnic and economic types—was entirely too egalitarian. Early Denver had relied upon morals rather than wealth to determine social standing, and Mrs. Hill sallied forth to set things straight. Her first step was to "captivate all of Denver with her charm, wit, and beauty." Then she announced the order of necessary requirements for social standing: "First, you have to have money. Then you must have the knowledge to give people a good time." She frostily declared that there were only sixty-eight people in all of Denver whom she dared invite to her own parties—and then narrowed the list even further by establishing the "Sacred Thirty-six," a list of names from Denver's wealthiest echelons. Understandably, many members of Denver society were miffed, and tensions between the rival newspapers intensified. Despite her social standing, however, even the venerable Mrs. Crawford Hill had a few crosses to bear. In later years she earned a few headlines herself with her extramarital liaison with Bulkeley Wells, which rocked Denver's innermost social circles.[80]

Nevertheless, in the society pages much attention was paid to whose social events Mrs. Hill determined to grace with her presence. For many years Margaret Brown and Louise Hill attended parties and served on committees together in relative peace, despite the fact that Margaret and J.J., although listed in the Social Register, were not included in the Sacred Thirty-six. Mrs. Crawford Hill was a stalwart member of the Daughters of the American Revolution (DAR), even serving as president, and despite the fact that Margaret's bloodlines didn't qualify her for membership, she was always invited to DAR functions. Often Mrs. Brown and Mrs. Hill good-naturedly tried to outdress each other. After a November 1904 charity ball, Polly Pry described Mrs. Brown's elegant gown as looking like a "full-blown tiger lily" and Mrs. Crawford Hill as wearing her "beautiful pearls, which she never takes off." But social snubs were common all around, and Polly Pry always took careful note of such things—informing all that one notable person donated a mere $10 to the cause; that certain husbands were there without their wives (and vice versa); and that a few prominent people chose not to attend. "Everyone was there, with just a few exceptions, and we all knew the reasons for the exceptions," she wrote.[81]

On March 7, 1906, however, social tensions came to a peak. Margaret had organized an event for the Denver Woman's Club, featuring "the best musical talent in the city," to raise money for art in the public schools, but it became known that Mrs. Hill and Mrs. Whitmore would not attend. Despite the overwhelming amount of club and charity work she had done and her citywide support, the two primary dictators of Denver society, Annie Whitmore and Louise Hill, still considered the Browns—and Margaret in particular—unqualified for Denver's innermost society circle. The reasons were many: Margaret and J.J. were Irish, Roman Catholic, and still considered "new money." Margaret's politics were liberal, in stark contrast to those of the conservative Crawford Hills, and she rarely hesitated to speak her mind. Denver was a hotbed of politics at the time, with the newspapers fanning the slightest innuendo into a flaming bonfire.

The situation was complicated by the fact that Mrs. Whitmore was running for the presidency of the Denver Woman's Club—and most members of the club supported Margaret. "A few are interested in the affair for the work's sake," a society reporter wrote. "Scores of society women will drop in incidentally for the cup that cheers, but really to discover if Mrs. Grant and Mrs. Whitmore are recognizing Mrs. Brown's efforts. ... The desire to see them clasp hands and exchange the soft salutations of polite society will put many half dollars into the treasury."[82] The reporter added that the situation was certainly embarrassing to all involved, but Mrs. Brown had reassured everyone that things would go smoothly. Attendance at the event was unprecedented—but there was no sign of Mrs. Whitmore or Mrs. Hill.

Margaret and her supporters rallied, and a new idea was born: the Carnival of Nations. Not only would it become Denver's largest and most memorable fund-raising event to date but its liberal, prolabor, multicultural approach would turn much of conservative Denver society on its ear. With an eye toward filling the coffers of those who needed it most, Margaret planned her revenge.

TEA PARTIES AND social status, however, were not the only focuses of Margaret's life. In January 1903, after a long illness, Mary Brophy Grace Tobin died at the age of thirty-seven. Margaret and J.J. were at her bedside when she passed away, and her funeral service was held at the Annunciation Church in Leadville. She was buried next to Michael Brown, J.J.'s brother. She left behind a grieving husband and four young children: Grace, eleven; Frank, nine; Florence, seven; and Helen, five. Margaret and J.J. were present at Mary's mountaintop funeral, and then Margaret brought all four children home to Pennsylvania Avenue to rear them herself. Daniel Tobin continued working for J.J. in the White Pine area and regularly visited his children on Sundays, often taking them to the Orpheum Theater. Margaret raised her nieces as if they were her own daughters and became particularly close to Helen, the youngest. (Frank Tobin lived with other relatives but frequently visited the Brown home.) The children attended Catholic schools in Denver, and Margaret included them in her social events, including dancing parties at Avoca for Helen and Lawrence when they came home from school for holidays. Helen Brown looked back on those boisterous days when the house held five growing teenagers—four of them girls—as happy and joyful ones, and remarked, "When Larry [Lawrence] and I were young, we thought we had the best mother in Denver." She also noted that her mother had a "particular gift" for arranging parties for them all.[83] Margaret's dancing parties became famous among Denver's social "young set." A common excursion was for a group of twenty or thirty to leave Denver about noon, enjoy a dinner and boisterous dance in the Avoca barn (which had a special floor for dancing), and return to the city by horseback and carriages in bright moonlight. Both Helen and Lawrence gained the reputation of dancing nearly as well as their mother, and Grace, Florence, and Helen learned the social graces that would eventually serve them well in Newport, New York, and Paris.

On April 10, 1905, Margaret's mother, Johanna Tobin, died at age seventy-five.[84] She had struggled with her health for years and six weeks earlier had suffered a stroke. Johanna had divided her time between the Becker home in Hannibal and the Brown house in Denver; for the previous two years she had lived with Margaret. Not only had she been a constant and gentle—albeit colorful—presence in the home, she had also helped with the care of Daniel's four children. During the period of Grandmother Tobin's ill health—and her almost constant pain near the end of her life—-the children were responsible for carrying her meal trays up and down the stairs. If they ever complained of their grandmother's crankiness, Helen recalled, they were scolded by Margaret. Grandmother Tobin was known to "stage a miraculous cure" on Sundays, just in time for mass, when she emerged from her room in her best dress. "If there was any crippling arthritis," James Benziger later wrote, "it seemed to disappear as she marched down the aisle, proud and erect."[85]

Two funerals were held, one in Denver and one at the Becker home in Hannibal. Margaret took her mother's body back on the train, and Johanna was laid to rest in St. Mary's cemetery with her husband.

BUT MARGARET WAS never far from her work. She turned her energies away from the DWC and instead concentrated on Lindsey's juvenile court. In May 1904 she held another outdoor benefit at Avoca for the Denver Women's Press Club, the Sisters of Loretto, and the social set from nearby Fort Logan, with donations once again going to Judge Lindsey's wards. Her interests had expanded in other directions as well. By now completely enraptured with French culture and fluent in the language, in 1903 Margaret had helped organize the Denver chapter of the Alliance Française, a "distinctly French-speaking club" dedicated to the study and discussion of French culture. She campaigned for members and used her House of Lions home for French-language classes and Alliance Française assemblies. Phases of French life, as well as life in Paris, were topics of discussion.[86] The following fall she made headlines in the *Paris Tribune* not only with her stunning gowns but with the fact that she hired an elegant carriage and pair of horses to take her to the Grand Prix.

The idyllic summers at Avoca would soon come to an end. By 1905 the Browns were no longer spending time at their country home, and the farm was sectioned off, leased, and eventually sold to various parties. A Denver newspaper lamented,

> Would anyone like to buy a country place with several thousand little chickens in the garden? To be sure yes. Several residents of this city are casting sheep's eyes at Avoca lodge, the place where the good dollars of the J.J. Browns are tied up. … Mr. Brown is in New York and they do say he has lifted up one end of the Stock exchange and put a chunk under it. … His fad of raising chickens at Avoca Lodge and shoveling money into a country place to make it interesting as well as beautiful may now be abandoned for the joys of making the bulls and bears sit up, lie down, roll over, and play dead.

The same article reported that the Browns were heading off in different directions: Mr. Brown was going to New York, Mrs. Brown was taking Helen abroad, and Lawrence was being tutored to apply to Yale.[87] J.J. continued to enjoy a steady stream of profit from his mining investments. But the tense situation with miners and labor unions continued to simmer like a slow pot coming to a boil.

IN THE 1906 Denver Social Register, Mrs. Crawford Hill penned a list of appropriate behavior for Denver's upper crust. She also listed several characteristics that doomed a person, particularly a female person, to the lower rungs of society. Foremost among these attributes was "an unfortunate disposition," a term that carried all the social codes of appropriate behavior for women in late Edwardian society. Women were expected to be nice, quiet, refined—and to keep their names out of the newspapers, except for the society page. Margaret Brown certainly did not fit the mold. Nevertheless, the *Denver Times* had long before declared Mrs. J.J. Brown one of the "smartest gowned women in Denver," adding that "Mrs. Brown's vivacity and merry disposition is a most refreshing trait in a society woman of her position, for in the smart set any disposition to be natural and animated is quite frowned upon."[88]

Despite her disposition, Margaret would soon find herself on the upper rung—and not just in Denver.

Left: Johanna Tobin, Margaret's mother, an Irish immigrant, *c.* 1899. The death of her first husband left her with one daughter. *(Molly Brown House Museum) Right:* John Tobin, Margaret's father, also an Irish immigrant and a widower with one daughter, *c.* 1885. *(Roberta Hagood)*

Above: The Hannibal, Missouri, train station, early 1880s. *(Roberta Hagood) Right:* The restored Tobin family home in Hannibal, just blocks from the Mississippi River. The addition on the left was added later, after the Tobins had raised six children. *(Vicki Dempsey)*

Helen Tobin, Margaret's sister, who remained close to Margaret her entire life and helped raise Helen and Lawrence Brown as well as Grace, Florence, and Helen Tobin, c. 1900. Helen was said to have the most colorful life of all the siblings. *(Denver Public Library, Western History Department)*

Daniel Tobin, Margaret's brother, who eventually became a successful mine broker, c. 1890. When his wife Mary died, Margaret raised his three daughters as her own. *(The Colorado Historical Society)*

Margaret Tobin Brown as a young bride, just as she was beginning to assert herself in Leadville society. *(Denver Public Library, Western History Department)*

Margaret Tobin Brown (left) and her sister, Helen, with young Lawrence in Leadville, c. 1889. *(Denver Public Library, Western History Department)*

Helen and Lawrence Brown in school in Paris, *c.* 1900. Margaret wanted the best European schooling for her children, but argued for special privileges, such as a daily glass of milk for Helen. *(Estate of Peter Benziger)*

The Brown family in Leadville, *c.* 1892. The Browns' attire reflects upper-middle-class standards; young Lawrence wears an Irish kilt. *(Colorado Historical Society)*

The photo Margaret used to first announce her candidacy for political office. *(Colorado Historical Society)*

The successful James Joseph Brown, *c.* 1910, who rose from his job as a day miner to owning and managing a network of mining properties. *(Colorado Historical Society)*

The House of Lions on Pennsylvania Street in Denver (right), *c.* 1890, beloved by both Margaret and J.J. *(Denver Public Library, Western History Department)*

From left to right, James Joseph Brown, Helen Brown, Lawrence Brown, and Margaret. This portrait was likely taken in 1906, just prior to their departure for an extended European visit. *(Denver Public Library, Western History Department)*

Over ten thousand people fill Denver streets for the dedication of the Cathedral of the Immaculate Conception on October 27, 1912, a church Margaret helped to build. For many years she devotedly occupied pew number six, and rarely failed to attract attention. *(Colorado Historical Society)*

Titanic survivors in Lifeboat Six, including Margaret, steadfastly row toward the rescue ship *Carpathia*. This photo was taken from the deck of the *Carpathia* on the morning of April 15, 1912. *(Don Lynch Collection)*

As chairperson of the Survivors' Committee, Margaret Tobin Brown presents a silver loving cup to Captain Arthur H. Rostron of the rescue ship *Carpathia*, May 29, 1912. *(Colorado Historical Society)*

The Egyptian talisman Margaret carried in her pocket on the *Titanic* for good luck, which she later gave to Captain Rostron of the *Carpathia* to thank him for saving her life. *(Stanley Lehrer Collection)*

The medal Margaret presented to each member of the *Carpathia* crew illustrating the *Carpathia* steaming past icebergs. *Titanic* buffs now call these the "Molly Brown" medals. *(Stanley Lehrer Collection)*

Fairview Cemetery in Halifax, Nova Scotia, where hundreds of *Titanic* victims are buried. Margaret and her nieces placed a wreath on each grave in August of 1920, and sought to keep alive the memory of the victims. *(Vollrath Collection)*

Margaret standing with a pine bough for a memorial wreath, August 1920. Identities of many victims were unknown and their headstones remained nameless. *(Vollrath Collection)*

George Benziger, Helen Brown's husband, of the Benziger Brothers publishing family, 1913. *(Estate of Peter Benziger)*

Helen Brown Benziger with her two sons, James (left) and Peter, in the early 1920s. Like her mother, Helen loved to travel and spent a great deal of time in Europe. *(Estate of Peter Benziger)*

Left: Eileen Horton Brown, Lawrence Brown's first wife, who married and divorced him twice. *(Emelie Lyons Wilson)* **Middle:** The silent film actress Mildred Gregory, Lawrence's second wife. Lawrence forayed briefly into the business of film production. *(Colorado Historical Society)*

Lawrence Brown, set to make a name for himself in the world despite his famous parents. *(Colorado Historical Society)*

Lawrence Brown with his classmates and fraternity brothers in 1918 at Colorado School of Mines, Golden, Colorado. Lawrence is second from right in the bottom row. *(Colorado Historical Society)* ·

Grace, Helen, and Florence Tobin, Margaret's three nieces, at the beach in Newport, 1914. *(Vollrath Collection)*

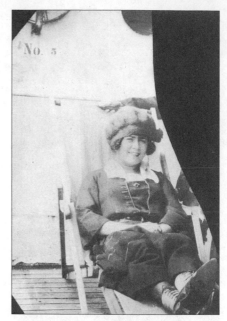

Florence Tobin returning to America after studying with the dancer and outspoken feminist Isadora Duncan in Darmstadt, Germany. Florence was renowned for her athletic ability. *(Vollrath Collection)*

"To the dearest Auntie in all the World." Helen Tobin, Margaret's youngest niece, who became an actress. *(Colorardo Historical Society)*

An elegant Grace Tobin not long after her marriage, 1916. *(Vollrath Collection)*

Margaret Tobin Brown and daughter Helen in Cairo, Egypt, early spring, 1912, just before Margaret left for France to board the *Titanic* at Cherbourg. The inscription across the photograph reads "ships that pass in the night." Just prior to this photo, an Egyptian palm reader warned Margaret of impending disaster. *(Vollrath Collection)*

A theatrical production in Paris, where Margaret studied in the Sarah Bernhardt tradition. Margaret is standing at the far right; her niece Helen Tobin, who shared her aunt's passion for the stage, at the far left. Although Margaret loved the stage and encouraged the creative talents of her offspring, she disapproved of it as a paying profession for her young wards. *(Vollrath Collection)*

The fashionable Mrs. Brown during her high-profile days in Newport and New York. *(Denver Public Library, Western History Department)*

Margaret Tobin Brown in court contesting J.J. Brown's estate. Emotional battles over the various issues surrounding the estate divided Margaret and her children for years. *(Denver Public Library, Western History Department)*

Margaret's beloved cottage "Mon Etui" in Newport, Rhode Island, 1914. With the exception of J.J., Brown and Tobin family members came for regular and extended visits. *(Vollrath Collection)*

The 1925 fire at the Breakers Hotel in Palm Beach, Florida. Margaret led a group of hotel guests down a fire escape to safety. *(Henry M. Flagler Museum)*

The *Titanic* memorial in Washington, D.C., erected by Margaret Brown and other prominent women including Mrs. Harry Payne Whitney and Mrs. William Howard Taft. Designed by Gertrude Vanderbilt Whitney, it stood in storage for fifteen years before a site was agreed upon. The statue and inscription stirred up a new round of vigorous feminist debate. *(Muffet Laurie Brown)*

Why Be Mildewed at Forty?

1906–1912

THE CARNIVAL OF NATIONS was the most elaborate, expensive outdoor extravaganza ever attempted in Denver. The idea blossomed when
a mining investment turned sour. Denver's burgeoning Catholic congregation desperately needed a larger structure, and the dream of building a new, spectacular cathedral whose spires would rise dramatically
above the city had been born over twenty-five years earlier. In 1880 the
Immaculate Conception Cathedral Association, chaired by J.J. Brown's
old friend John K. Mullen, was formed. J J. Brown, along with Mullen,
John Campion, and Dennis Sheedy, chipped in for the $28,000 needed to
buy eight lots at the corner of East Colfax Avenue and Logan Street. But
as of 1906, all that stood of the grand design was an enormous hole in the
ground with a fence around it. Despite the fact that a groundbreaking ceremony had been held in 1902, and the foundation had subsequently been
completed, the project was stalled. The cathedral association discovered
the building fund had been invested in Cripple Creek mining properties
that had failed, and there was no money to continue the project.[1]

The turning point occurred in 1906 with the combined efforts
of Margaret Brown and an ambitious young priest named Hugh L.
McMenamin, affectionately called "Father Mac." Margaret and Father
Mac had many things in common in addition to their desire to build a
new cathedral. Hugh was one of thirteen children, his father was an Irish
coal miner, and—like J.J.—he had grown up in Pennsylvania. The family
moved to Denver, and Hugh became a student at Sacred Heart College, a
school Margaret's children also attended, and eventually became a priest.
In 1906 the young priest was assigned the job of infusing the cathedral
building fund with enough time, energy, and money to get things started
again. John K. Mullen, chair of the building committee, also had a few
things in common with Margaret and Father Mac. Born in Ballinasloe,
County Galway, Ireland, Mullen's family had fled the potato famine
when he was a child. At age fourteen he was apprenticed to a Denver
flour miller and eventually saved enough money to purchase the Star

Mill, an old local flour mill. In time, Mullen built the mill into a modern $5 million enterprise with eight hundred employees and became one of Denver's major philanthropists.

Father Mac initiated a Catholic Fair to raise money for the beleaguered cathedral building fund. In a general meeting at the Logan Avenue school, the assembly unanimously chose Mrs. J.J. Brown to be general manager of the fair. Margaret had a firm reputation as a good organizer and fund-raiser, and no one could doubt her positive attitude. The newspaper reported that Mrs. Brown "had long ago eliminated the word 'fail' from her lexicon, and with the assistance of so many energetic workers and the generosity of the people of Denver, she did not believe she would have to introduce that unpopular word again. The applause that followed showed that they were all of the same mind."[2]

But Margaret had something even bigger in mind. On March 22, 1906, she made a proposal during a meeting at the bishop's residence for an event she called the Carnival of Nations. No doubt influenced by other extravaganzas she had attended, including the World's Fair, her dream was to have as many nations as possible represented at the fair. She was captivated by the fact that America had become a cultural melting pot, and Colorado in particular comprised cultures as diverse as Native American, Mexican and Spanish, Chinese, Italian, Irish, "Colored," and many others. The bishop liked her proposal, and on April 1 a meeting was held in the Knights of Columbus hall. Present in the audience were all the prominent Catholic priests from the Denver area as well as Catholic society women, including Mrs. J.K. Mullen, Mrs. Frank J. Mott, Mrs. J.H. Butterfield, and Mrs. Elize De Bois. It was agreed that the fair would begin on July 10, 1906, the same week as the Elks convention, and run for four weeks. Walter S. Cheesman, president of the Denver Union Water Company, agreed to donate the land, and the Gas and Electric Company provided light fixtures. Lee Haney, former manager of the Orpheum Theater, contributed his technical skills in setting up lights. Many other city organizations, Catholic and non-Catholic, donated time and money; the plumber's union was "especially liberal" with its services before and during the fair. Prominent individuals such as railroad men Charles Kountz, Thomas Walsh, and John J. McGinnity contributed substantially. For prizes, Daniels & Fisher (Smith was no longer a partner), Margaret's previous employer in Leadville, donated an expensive punch bowl; Babcock Brothers donated a fur; and many other merchants chipped in. Margaret agreed not only to run the show but to cover a portion of the expenses herself.

The Carnival of Nations could be called Colorado's first example of what we today term "living history." Each nationality set up a "village" that represented their particular culture, and booth workers dressed the part to re-create particular scenes as authentically as possible. Margaret poured her heart and soul into creating an Irish booth that would show Denver the best that Ireland had to offer. With the help of Sister Aloysius, mother superior of a convent in Ireland, Margaret used authentic bogwood, peat, moss, Irish cherry wood, and blackthorn sticks to decorate the booth, with a pot of shamrocks center stage. She displayed a beautiful opera cloak of Irish lace, an identical copy of the one given to the queen of Spain at her recent marriage to King Alfonso. With her own reputation as a good dancer to stand her in good stead, she held an Irish dance at the dancing pavilion, with instructors for those who hadn't yet perfected the art.

Denver's African American population was well represented. Dr. J.W. Bailey, an eye doctor with offices on Larimer Street, wrote the newspaper to express his appreciation for Margaret's work on behalf of "Colored Catholics." Dr. Bailey was in charge of the "Colored Lyceum," which was rehearsing weekly to get ready for the big event. "A committee of our colored Catholic ladies," he wrote, "met with Mrs. J.J. Brown at the headquarters of the 'Carnival of Nations' to get a better understanding regarding their positions. As usual Mrs. Brown was not slow in arranging matters."[3]

Different booths were specially featured on different nights. On the evening that Margaret presided from the Italian Gardens, all of Denver's "Four Hundred"—a slightly larger circle than Mrs. Crawford's Sacred Thirty-six—attended. "Don't tell us that society people are not willing to help in a good cause," the paper enthused. "They are, and only await the chance to demonstrate the fact. Watch them during the Carnival!"

Two of the more controversial groups Margaret invited to the fair were Chinese and Native Americans. Indians, most likely Ute and Cheyenne, were brought in to set up and re-create the life of an actual Indian village. It had been only thirty-seven years since the last significant battle between the U.S. Army and the Plains Indians of Colorado, and the belief that "the only good Indian was a dead Indian" still lingered in many Denverites' minds. The Chinese, although they worked in the mines and helped to build the railroad system across the West, were still ostracized. The inclusion of these two groups caused some consternation. At the very least, a local newspaper said, people should attend the carnival as an "educational exhibit." Curiously, this controversy may be the origin of the myth that Margaret invited a tribe of Indians to camp out on her front lawn—a gesture that, according to legend, permanently alienated J.J.'s affections.

The booths were numerous, and Margaret designed a silk banner to display the daily receipts of each booth to "excite a profitable rivalry." Another rivalry she promoted was a "spirited although friendly" contest for the most popular priest in Denver. Tickets to vote were sold at ten cents each; the winning priest would receive a free round trip to Europe. The results were announced at midnight on the last night of the fair, when all of society was once again in attendance. Despite his hard work, Father Mac didn't take the prize—that went to Reverend Cornelius F. O'Farrell, assistant pastor of the new St. Leo's Church that supported Denver's growing Hispanic community. Father Mac came in a good-natured second and Reverend Percy Phillips a distant third.

The carnival ran into a political snag. Margaret had wanted it to run five weeks instead of four in order to raise the full $20,000 needed for the cathedral. But after only sixteen days the owner of the land, Walter Cheesman, claimed that a prior agreement dictated that the fair would have to close or move to another location. He claimed that a company was preparing to build a large skating rink and swimming pool on the Cheesman lots. Margaret proposed an alternative: let the carnival stay open one more day, she said, and the proceeds would benefit the Juvenile Improvement Association's project at Glenmoor Lakes up the Platte Canyon. The Glenmoor Lakes project, whose purpose was to "uplift the waifs of Denver by giving them an outing in the hills, a breath of untainted air and a glimpse of Colorado sunshine undarkened by the smoke of downtown streets,"[4] was in critical condition and needed $1,000 to continue. But she didn't anticipate Cheesman's reaction. A political opponent of Judge Ben Lindsey, Cheesman was angry over Lindsey's assertion that the heads of public utility corporations threw their weight around too much in the political arena. Lindsey, never afraid to speak his mind, had accused Cheesman of being part of Denver's "machine politics." Cheesman refused to allow any of the carnival's proceeds to be devoted to the Juvenile Fresh Air Fund, and an article in a local paper exclaimed that "spite was taken out at the expense of children."[5] In a flurry of controversial publicity, the carnival closed.

Nevertheless, despite these political snags and the fact that a steady rain dampened attendance records during the final days, people declared that "the carnival [was] to Denver what the World's Fair was to St. Louis."[6] Margaret didn't make her goal of $20,000, but profits were substantial: $6,000 in cash, an additional $5,000 pledged, and donations of a $3,000 altar and a memorial stained-glass window. The success of the Carnival of Nations enabled the construction of the cathedral to continue, and a new cornerstone was laid on July 15, 1906. In 1908 Father Mac was appointed rector of Cathedral Parish, a position he held until his death in 1947.[7] With his appointment, the pace of construction of the cathedral quickened, and the completed cathedral—to this day one of Denver's most beautiful and prominent structures—was dedicated and the first mass held on October 27, 1912. A reported twenty thousand people participated in the parade down Broadway and up Colfax Avenue, and the *Denver Republican* noted that "the completion of Denver's most beautiful church, and the spectacle of ten thousand souls kneeling outdoors to receive the Benediction of the Blessed Sacrament, was one never surpassed in the ecclesiastical history of the West."[8]

By 1913 the Cathedral of the Immaculate Conception boasted a congregation of over 3,500 members, a majority of whom were Irish American. Sunday mass at eleven was a social as well as a spiritual event; the Browns rented pew number six, and Margaret held the eyes of many as she walked up the center aisle with her tall European-style walking stick adorned with ribbons and flowers.

MARGARET DIDN'T REST on her laurels. A month after the Catholic Fair, she organized a lawn fete on the grounds of the old Tabor mansion (home of Horace and Elizabeth McCourt Tabor) to raise money for needy Italian children in Denver.[9]

If "fail" was not in Margaret's vocabulary, neither was the word "intimidation." She wasn't about to be undone by Walter Cheesman's caustic remarks. Ben Lindsey, in his continuing effort to "reclaim boys from their wicked ways," told Margaret that $5,000 a year would be enough to ensure the ongoing work of the Juvenile Improvement Association at Glenmoor Lakes. She promptly declared that she would

get twice that sum, and after "penning regrets to a round of fashionable functions"[10] set off for Cripple Creek, which—despite the fact
that some bad projects there had swallowed up the cathedral building
fund—was one of Colorado's most prosperous mining towns. Margaret
donned miner's pants, boots, and a sombrero and spent four days in-
specting nonworking mining properties. In several mines she had to
descend in a large iron bucket hung from a rope windlass, which she
hadn't done since she and J.J. had left Leadville long ago.

After taking samples of ore to an assayer, Margaret decided on a claim
on the Stratton Independence Mine. "Falling easily into the vernacular
of the miners who surrounded her," she stated that she would build a
new hoist and railroad spur, and shipping would begin the following
week. "But have you seen the owners?" called a man from the crowd.

"I have jumped the claim," Margaret declared. "No one in Colorado
will refuse me a lease when they know it is for the juvenile court. The
boys must have money and I must have this claim." Impressed with her
pluck, the man agreed to be her new mine superintendent. For good
luck, Margaret christened the mine the Little Jonny.[11]

Polly Pry, who for the most part was on Margaret's side at this
time, was quick to help garner support for the "Mine for Waifs." She
penned a poem titled "Our New Philanthropist," under the epithet "the
Observer," for her society column, "Town Topics":

> So Mrs. Brown has leased a mine
> To help the youngsters! Well that's fine
> All that it makes will go to aid
> The juveniles! When it has paid
> Enough to build a club house, then
> There'll be one for the "little men"
> In whom Judge Lindsey takes delight
> And "kids" will call it "out of sight!"
> I doff my hat to Mrs. Brown!
> Philanthropy is scarce in town!
> Not scarce, perhaps, but it might be
> Far more abundant here, and we
> Would never mind it! May the scheme
> Prove more substantial than a dream!
> May this one mine, at least, yield gold—
> More than the rest—an hundred fold!

Margaret was confident the venture would be a success. "Oh, I know it will pay, boys," she told the newsboys' club. "I told the owner, who already had a million, that it was sinful for him to have a mine idle while the little boys of Denver needed shoes. There seemed to be as much gold in his heart as in his mine, for we are to have the Little Jonny free for two years."[12]

Within six weeks the smelter receipts not only covered all operating expenses of the mine but had added $1,000 to the juvenile court fund. "The juveniles of Judge Lindsey's court have had no better friend than Mrs. Brown," a local paper declared. Her mission accomplished, Margaret took off on a trip to southern California with artist friends to visit the historic Catholic missions.

ALTHOUGH IT WOULD BE several years before the name *Titanic* became a household word, both Helen and Lawrence were enduring the trials and tribulations of establishing their own lives in the wake of their well-known parents. Helen, who had been presented to society not only in Denver but in New York, Newport, and Paris, made an impression far beyond the admiration of Polly Pry. With long auburn hair and a lively demeanor, she had many admirers on both sides of the ocean. She had traveled the world with her mother, frequently staying in Paris with friends while her mother returned to New York, Hannibal, and Denver. A year of study at the Sorbonne had not diminished her aspirations to the stage, first as an actress and then as a playwright. In November 1911, while staying in Surrey, England, she wrote to several New York directors, including William Jottesan at the David Belasco Theatre on Forty-fourth Street near Broadway. His answer was encouraging but cautionary. "It is a pretty hard fight for a beginner," he wrote. "The only thing to do is to be on the ground and get the first opening that may offer itself."[13]

Helen traveled frequently with her mother, often with one or more of her cousins along as well. In 1910 Margaret and Helen attended the coronation of King George V in Westminster Abbey. No doubt the zenith of Helen's social career was in the spring of 1911, when she was presented at the May drawing room of the English court.[14] Margaret apparently was to be presented at court two years later; while in Cairo she had a special train of silver woven by Egyptian hands, which went down on the *Titanic* with the rest of her wardrobe.[15] No record exists of whether she was ever actually presented.

Despite her desire for a life on the stage, Helen—now in her early twenties—was facing family pressure to marry. Even Lawrence wrote with some well-intentioned advice: "Sis, I don't wish you any hard luck," he said. "But if the right man came along I wish you could just share in the happiness this world has to give. Of course I wouldn't hurry matters any, but I would most certainly investigate all propositions that are surrounding this subject and all that sort of thing you know."[16] Helen had once already announced an intention to marry, which immediately set off a round of showers planned by her society-minded Denver friends, and a paper reported that Miss Brown was "scheduled to be one of the season's brides."[17] That event, however, did not come to pass, and it wasn't until Helen met George Benziger, thirteen years her senior, that she thought again of marriage.

Helen had seen George at social engagements, but they didn't meet formally until both were coincidentally on board the same ship, ironically passing over the exact area where a year later the *Titanic* would meet its iceberg.[18] Helen thought George pleasant, handsome, and certainly the caliber of man her mother would deem appropriate. The Benzigers were an old, highly respected family from Einsiedeln, Switzerland, who for nearly four hundred years had played a prominent part in the leadership of the Roman Catholic church. Benziger Brothers Publishing published all Roman Catholic catechisms as well as priests' concordances to the Bible; two prominent Benzigers were Mother Ursula Benziger, who lived at the Vatican and headed the Order of the Sacred Heart of teaching nuns, and her cousin Adelrich, a monk who managed church operations in India. George's mother was of the von Saarentein family and the daughter of a count and countess; his two sisters were married to Austrian barons.[19]

George Benziger's letters to Helen were witty (although his handwriting was hard to read), and his devotion was apparent. But Helen was in no hurry. She tucked his letters in a box along with the letters from all her other beaus, neatly tied with ribbons.

Lawrence did not attend Yale, as his parents had hoped he would. He took his own advice and fell in love with a society belle from Kansas City, Missouri, much to the consternation of his father. The relationship between J.J. and Lawrence had been strained ever since Lawrence's untimely eviction from the expensive college preparatory school his parents had sent him to—Phillips Exeter Academy in Pennsylvania. He had been in the middle of his second year at Exeter, with the goal of preparing himself to attend the Colorado School of Mines in Golden, one of the foremost mining schools in the country, when ill fortune intervened.

The incident seemed innocent enough at first. On his way back to Pennsylvania after a Christmas holiday at the House of Lions in Denver, Lawrence, along with seven companions, had an unexpected four-hour delay between trains in Boston. Four members of the group "went on a spree." The details of their adventure did not make it into the newspapers; however, it was enough to get those four expelled from the academy that very semester. After four months of deliberation, at the end of the spring semester the faculty decided to expel the other four boys as well, although many claimed that Lawrence Brown "was no more to blame than if he had been in another city."[20] Lawrence apparently neglected to inform his parents of the problem in advance because he planned to tell them in person.

News of the event had not yet reached the Denver society pages (although it wasn't uncommon for some of Exeter's more prominent young men to find their names in Newport's malicious society newspaper, *Town Topics*, which occasionally sent a "spy" to see what was happening with the offspring of New York's "Four Hundred"). Nevertheless, Lawrence returned to Denver with a heavy heart, knowing he would have to face the disapproval of his father first—Margaret was in Newport with nieces Florence and Helen. When Lawrence casually informed his father over dinner that he had been expelled, J.J.'s temper flared. He declared that Lawrence was not only a disgrace to the family but had become a "cigarette fiend." Lawrence jumped up to defend himself; the resulting argument apparently involved more than just words, and the authorities were called. Lawrence spent one memorable night in jail with a few drunken inmates, and the next day the story hit the newspapers.

Interviewed from his jail cell, Lawrence was quoted as saying, "My, but I regret this affair." He admitted that he and his father were of similar temperament and inclined to occasionally disagree. "I can hardly think of facing mother," he added. "I am very fond of her and Sis, and they will suffer most for what has occurred."[21]

Margaret took the first train back to Denver and arrived in time to issue a statement to the newspapers that the whole affair had been nothing more than a bit of Irish temper. Lawrence, she said, was the apple of his father's eye, and Lawrence was "absolutely dutiful" in his love for his father. Margaret noted that the state of J.J.'s health no doubt had contributed to his losing his temper, and a doctor verified that J.J.'s fits of anger were due to a sudden rush of blood to the head, a lingering effect of his stroke eight years earlier. The case was immediately dropped, by the newspapers as well as the court. Lawrence declared that he was writing a letter to his father expressing his regret over the entire affair. "I am mailing dad a letter to that effect," he said. "If he is anything like I know him to be, that letter will straighten things out."[22]

Despite his candor with reporters, Lawrence was deeply embarrassed by the publicity. Friends spoke up on behalf of his reputation. "Lawrence smokes a pipe in moderation like many boys of his age," one friend declared. "He has never been known to imbibe spiritous drinks of any kind and has never been known to dissipate in his life."[23]

Several weeks later J.J. underwent surgery for a severe hernia and spent over a month convalescing at a hospital in Los Angeles. Lawrence decided to let things settle down a bit with his father and spend the summer working on a ranch in the Northwest. But before he left, he accompanied Helen and Margaret on a trip to a summer ranch in Grand Lake, Colorado, a favorite family vacation spot. The scene was similar to the one J.J. and Margaret had experienced twenty years earlier—Lawrence was invited to a Catholic picnic and met a girl he couldn't forget.

Like Lawrence, Eileen Horton was on a trip with her mother, who was acting as chaperone to a group of girls from the Sisters of Loretto Academy in Kansas City. Eileen, valedictorian of her class, had graduated in the spring of 1909. She was just as impressed with Lawrence as he was with her, and they exchanged letters over the summer, calling each other by the nicknames "Laurie" and "Girl." In the fall Lawrence returned to Denver, and Margaret invited Eileen to come up from Kansas City and be properly introduced to Denver society. On September 19, 1909, Eileen joined Margaret, Helen, and Lawrence for a formal dinner at the House of Lions, where she was first presented to Denver's social circles, followed by a play at the Broadway Theater. The following day the group motored up to Troutdale for a day of fishing. Two days later Margaret held a luncheon in honor of Eileen and again took her guests to the theater, this time to the Orpheum. Eileen's trip was capped by a visit on September 22 to greet President William Taft, who was making an appearance at the Wolhurst mansion in Denver.[24]

Clearly Margaret approved of Eileen as a future daughter-in-law, but she counseled Lawrence to wait. J.J. too wanted to see his son go back to school, or at least settle into a career before he started a family. But after almost two years—with Lawrence still uncertain about his future and somewhat jealous of the fact that his two cousins were helping manage his father's business—the couple could wait no longer. At nine A.M. on January 16, 1911, Lawrence and Eileen were married against Margaret's and J.J.'s wishes. Neither parent attended the ceremony; Margaret was in Europe, and J.J., whose feelings were much stronger, chose to be absent.

When Eileen Horton had graduated from Loretto Academy, she had expressed a desire that her wedding, "whenever it should take place," be held in Loretto's beautiful chapel, performed by the chaplain with members of the faculty and senior class in attendance. The wedding did indeed take place in a part of the chapel, although Eileen had to obtain a special dispensation from the bishop of the diocese. A large gathering of Eileen's family and friends of the couple attended. The parents of the bride hosted a wedding breakfast, after which the couple boarded a train for Colorado. Lawrence and Eileen spent their first night together in Denver, staying at the House of Lions in Helen's "beautiful blue brocade room."[25] (Helen was in Europe with her mother.) The next day they took the train to Leadville, where they spent their honeymoon— likely at the same lakeside resort where J.J. and Margaret had spent their honeymoon twenty-five years earlier. Partly because of Lawrence's popularity in Newport, the news of his wedding made the *New York Times,* which reported that the couple had eloped after "strenuous opposition" from the groom's parents due to the "extreme youth of himself and his bride."[26] Eileen was twenty-one, Lawrence twenty-four.

J.J., angered that Lawrence had gone so thoroughly against his wishes, apparently told him he was cut off from the family fortune. Lawrence and Eileen moved to Victor, Colorado, where Lawrence took a job as a day miner. On November 21, 1911, Lawrence Palmer Jr., later known as "Pat," was born.

J.J. retreated to Arizona, where the warm climate helped him cope with his failing health. With Margaret and Helen out of the country, the newspapers were left with a dearth of stories on the Brown family, which now had a devoted readership and sold newspapers like hotcakes. A reporter was sent to Victor, near Cripple Creek, to report on the exiled son. The newspaper got its headline: "Rich Man's Son Toils in Mine to Feed Wife and Baby. Cast Adrift by Family. J.J. Brown of Denver Opposed Marriage of Heir to Kansas City Belle." Lawrence explained that he was making his start in life just as his father had—pounding rock in the depths of a mine. The reporter wrote that Eileen was coping magnificently. "Mrs. Brown has made quite a joke of washing her husband's flannel shirts and has listened longingly at the door of their cabin for his cheerful whistle when, lunch pail in hand, he has returned at the end of the day."[27]

Eileen, who was close to both Margaret and Helen and called Margaret "Mother Brown," wrote that she hoped Lawrence would eventually give up mining. "I have always been more or less against the mines and a series of accidents happening recently have finally persuaded him to see my point of view," she wrote.[28] With Eileen's encouragement, Lawrence began taking courses from the Scranton International Correspondence School. Tempers cooled with time, and the relationship between father and son eventually improved. J.J., impressed with the efforts of his son to make something of his life, began to send the struggling family small installments from a trust fund. Lawrence at first resisted, desiring to support his family on his own, but finally accepted his father's help.

Over the next eleven years the family moved twenty-two times, following Lawrence as he changed jobs again and again and struggled to build a career. Lawrence worked for a bricklayer, a lumber company, and a real estate company, several times attempting to start his own business. Eileen wrote to her mother-in-law that Lawrence's plan of building and renting houses, no doubt encouraged by his father, looked the most lucrative. "We may be millionaires yet," she said.

LAWRENCE WASN'T THE only one in the family to plan an elopement. Three months later, on April 17, 1911, nineteen-year-old Grace Loretta Tobin, the oldest of Margaret's nieces, eloped as well. Raised by Margaret as one of her own daughters, Grace was nearly as headstrong as her aunt—but ultimately chose a more conventional lifestyle than her two sisters.

Margaret had planned to take her nieces, Grace, Florence, and Helen, to England to watch daughter Helen's presentation at the English court. All three Tobin girls had made their debuts in Denver and Newport; indeed, Helen Tobin's introduction to society in the spring of 1910 had headlined Denver's society pages. Helen—who was only twelve at the time—enjoyed a garden party of eight hundred guests, including people who had come all the way from Colorado Springs. Tents were erected on the lawn and rugs thrown over the grass. Japanese lanterns burned brightly, a Hungarian band played on the balcony, and Loehman's orchestra accompanied dancing couples in the ballroom, which was decorated with masses of American beauty roses, peonies, and ferns. Prominent guests included Miss Ragnhilda Hobe of Washington, daughter of the Belgian minister, and Margaret's sister, Helen, who had married and was now the Baroness Von Reitzenstein of Berlin. The *Denver Post* declared the affair "a great success and most enjoyable."[29]

Helen Tobin, now a teenager, was determined to see all she could of Europe. Florence Tobin—who, like Helen Brown, had beaus on both sides of the ocean—had no desire to sacrifice her freedom for marriage. After the ceremony at the English court, she planned to travel to Darmstadt, Germany, and begin dance instruction with Isadora Duncan, a pioneer in dance movement and a prominent, somewhat controversial advocate of women's rights. But Grace Loretta Tobin met a man who convinced her to change her own plans.

Leslie Mortimer Carroll, the son of a Chicago millionaire, had received his inheritance at age twenty-one and decided to come west to invest it. He was staying with his aunt, Susan MacManus, at her home on Pearl Street when he first met Grace Tobin at a dinner party hosted by Mrs. MacManus. The *New York Times* reported, "One glance at her dainty blond beauty was enough for the young man of Chicago," and he declared that he couldn't rest until he had slipped a wedding ring on her finger. Grace demurred, saying she wanted to accompany her aunt and sisters to England. But Leslie Carroll persuaded her to stay, and on April 17, 1911—just after Margaret, Helen Brown, and Florence and Helen Tobin had set sail—Leslie and Grace were married by Reverend Hugh L. McMenamin, "Father Mac," at his Denver residence. The *Times* reported that back in Chicago, Mr. Carroll, when informed of his son's action, declared, "It certainly is news to me. I knew nothing whatever about it."[30]

Ruffled feathers were soon smoothed, however, and Grace and Leslie became frequent house guests of Margaret in Denver and Newport. They eventually had two children, Florence Helen Carroll (named after Grace's sisters), born May 8, 1916, and Dorothy Louise Carroll, born March 21, 1920. The children enjoyed very devoted aunts.

RELATIONS BETWEEN MARGARET and J.J. had grown increasingly strained. Seldom did they appear in society together, and both traveled almost constantly, J.J. spending time in California and Arizona and Margaret staying with friends in New York, Newport, and Paris. She continued the dramatic studies she had begun when she was at Carnegie and hired a voice instructor to improve her singing. Although it's unlikely that J.J. threw a fit over Indians camped on the lawn, it is true that the couple grew more distant as their lives took different directions. J.J. resented the fact that Margaret had become a favorite personality of Denver journalists. He felt that a woman's name should appear in the newspaper only four times in her life: at her birth, engagement, marriage, and death.[31] However, Margaret became one of the first real publicists in the country as she sought newspaper coverage for her political and social causes. Over time Margaret's opinions regarding women's and children's rights had grown even stronger; in the meantime, J.J.'s health problems and business worries contributed to what he called a "melancholy" disposition. He was often at odds with Daniel Tobin and was not particularly close to the three nieces living in his house. The House of Lions, as it eventually came to be called, was no longer a "dove cote," and even Margaret's best efforts to hide the fact weren't enough to keep people from noticing.

Now completely on her own, at least socially, Margaret sought solace for her marital woes through travel. She took Helen to the Schweizerhof in Lucerne, Switzerland, where they enjoyed an extended stay with other Americans, including William Waldorf Astor. On November 2, 1907, Margaret gave a musicale and reception in the "salle de musique" for her American and European friends, and after the main performance she herself sang Tyrolean songs accompanied by a zither. News of the event was carried in the *Paris Tribune* and picked up by the

Denver Republic, along with a remark about the unseasonable weather: "The glorious summer weather in Lucerne continues. For the past two evenings the Alpine glow has exceeded in beauty anything observed this summer."[32] Denverites who enjoyed following Margaret's exploits in the newspapers were experiencing snow.

Margaret had also established a reputation for yodeling, a feat that astonished and stupefied her American friends. She had met Martha Mesler, the "famous Swiss yodeler," at the St. Louis Exposition, and determined to learn the art. She engaged a teacher and practiced daily for two years, eventually performing in drawing rooms as prestigious as the Astors' and earning the title "the American warbler."[33] In 1909, with daughter Helen's assistance, she yodeled before an audience at Elitch Gardens in Denver.

A truly exotic affair was a dance held by the horse-racing committee at the Schweizerhof, at which Margaret and Helen made a striking pair. Despite the fact that over six hundred guests were in attendance, "at no time was the ballroom uncomfortably crowded." Several dinner parties were held in the restaurant before the ball, and Margaret presided over a table that included society leaders and American military dignitaries. Baron Gino di Morpugo escorted young Helen. Margaret's table was the most elaborately decorated in the room. In the center a judge's box was crafted of pink roses, with a porcelain racing judge perched on top. From the judge's chair floated long silk streamers, each attached to a miniature horse in front of each guest. Beside each place setting bands of silk represented the various racing colors, with the name of the guest and the names of the horses that were to run that day in gold lettering. A paper jockey's cap stood next to each plate.[34] Lawrence missed that affair but attended others. Before his marriage to Eileen he had taken an extended yachting trip along the coast of Ireland and motored with a friend through the chateau country of France before heading up to Geneva and Lucerne.[35]

When she returned to the United States Margaret continued her work with Judge Ben Lindsey. Lindsey's Juvenile Association for the Protection and Betterment of Children had become well known nationally and even internationally, providing the root for a juvenile court system throughout the country. Lindsey was responsible for the passage of numerous laws benefiting juveniles; however, his bold advocacy went beyond the walls of the courtroom. With Margaret's help he established a day nursery for impoverished children, public playgrounds to help keep children off the streets, a juvenile detention home so that youngsters would not be jailed with adult criminals, and even a bathtub in the basement of the courthouse for children who had been living on the street. He treated children in his courtroom with the utmost integrity, never breaking his word to them and placing them on their honor. In one particularly controversial move, he sent several hundred boys on their own—without guards—to the state industrial school in Golden, telling them it was their responsibility to show up at the institution, serve their sentences, and go on to lead productive lives. Only five boys disappeared on the way to the institution.

Lindsey was outspoken and often confrontational in his approach, a tactic that garnered him a loyal following as well as vehement enemies. He expanded his list of social causes to include not only juvenile delinquency but birth control availability, "companionate marriage," and—in a move that angered Denver politicians and led to an outrageous five-hour kidnapping episode on September 6, 1904—corruption in politics and the influence of public utilities companies over Colorado and Denver government. Lindsey, along with U.S. Senator Henry M. Teller, was kidnapped by Milton Smith, chairman of the state central committee of the Democratic Party, and Samuel Bedford, one of Smith's staunch lieutenants, in an attempt to force Lindsey to "serve the Democratic party in a more appropriate manner." Smith wished to coerce Lindsey to "decide the election contests, which had been filed by the Republican party in the county court shortly after the election of May 17 [1904], in favor of the Democratic party."[36] Lindsey refused, and the two men finally deposited him on his doorstep sometime after two A.M.

Because of the controversial nature of his opinions and his forthrightness in publishing them in books such as *The Beast and the Jungle*, which had been serialized in *Everybody's Magazine,* Lindsey was denied the opportunity to run on either the Democratic or the Republican ticket for reelection as juvenile court judge. In a move that delighted his supporters, he ran independently and soundly defeated his opponents. His run for governor on an independent ticket in 1906 was not as successful.[37]

Lindsey firmly believed that economic injustice was the root of crime and injustice in America. Although he and his wife were often invited to Denver's social events, many members of Denver's "establishment" took a dim view of his progressive ideas. By 1914, however, Lindsey not only was called "Colorado's World Citizen" for his far-reaching child protection laws but in a national poll was named one of the ten greatest living Americans.[38]

Margaret Brown provided the elbow grease and the social graces to help Lindsey achieve his goals. Her annual benefits for the Juvenile Aid Society (later called the Juvenile Association for the Protection and Betterment of Children) impressed Denver society with their ingenuity and success. At a benefit at the Broadway Theater in 1908, huge American flags and Japanese lanterns hung from the ceiling, and audience boxes were filled with pink and white apple blossoms and colored lights. As usual, the event was sold out. Tall green palms and dainty ferns—certainly not indigenous to Colorado—decorated the posts, and an apple tree made of pink and white tissue paper stood in the middle. Each blossom bore a slip of paper that could be purchased for ten cents. If the slip had a number on it, the owner won a prize. The Denver Elks purchased two hundred seats in the balcony and had as their guests orphans from "every orphan asylum in the city." Reflecting the country's current rage with fortune-telling, Madam Zoralda, the "celebrated Gypsy palmist," told fortunes in the gentlemen's smoking room.[39]

Margaret was also involved in the Colorado chapter of the League of American Arts, which was devoted to improving recognition and opportunities for American artists. On March 19, 1909, at the annual patrons' night at the Brown Palace Hotel, the club's exhibit filled the second floor and included a work by Lucius Wolcott Hitchcock that had won the bronze medal at the St. Louis World's Fair in 1904. Margaret lent a painting titled *Looking for Trouble* by J.D. Howland. Frederic Conger of New York was curator of the exhibit. The purpose of the exhibit, Conger noted, was to "stimulate the artistic appreciation of people and to bring local and other artists into prominence in this and other cities."[40]

Despite these successes, Margaret's attempts to keep her public life and the strife of her personal life separate were beginning to falter. On January 24, 1910, when the publisher thought Margaret was in New York and J.J. in San Francisco, the *Denver Times* emblazoned its front page with a headline stating that the Browns had divorced. "It has been an open secret for a year or more that there was anything but harmony reigning in the handsome house on Pennsylvania Street," the article revealed. "The prime cause of the trouble, it has always been understood, was the decidedly antipodal viewpoint of Mr. and Mrs. Brown as to the most congenial manner of life." The writer did not specifically condemn Margaret, noting that she "realized that social leadership required something more than the ability to pay a good chef and the taste to select a clever dressmaker." However, despite Mrs. Brown's admirable efforts in attending the Carnegie Institute, learning several languages, and becoming quite proficient "in the technique of the actress," J.J. was no longer in sympathy with his wife's social life and preferred the rough life of the mining camps instead.

Margaret was devastated. With her sister, Helen Von Reitzenstein, and daughter, Helen, she was indeed planning to leave for New York to attend the wedding of Carolyn Astor Drayton, granddaughter of John Jacob Astor, who was engaged to William Philips, first secretary of the American embassy. The event was to be a reunion of sorts; H. Coleman Drayton, Carolyn's brother and the "darling of the Newport set," was a close friend of Lawrence, who was still in school back East and intended to meet them in New York. But the women hadn't left yet; Margaret was home at the House of Lions when the newspaper hit the streets.

The reporter stood his ground, claiming that J.J. had declared to several of his business friends that the marital bond had been completely severed and the final decree signed just before Christmas. Margaret vehemently denied a divorce. "In the face of our Catholic religion," she said, "we could not think of divorce." She was forced, however, to reluctantly admit that a separation had occurred as a result of their home life being "not entirely compatible." J.J.'s friends blamed Margaret's drive and ambition. A friend of Margaret told the papers that since his stroke and paralysis several years before, J.J. had suffered from "peculiar delusions" and was "constantly pulling the family hearse as chief mourner."

Another newspaper accused the *Denver Times* of "meanness and mendacity," and the *Times* attempted to retract the story. But the damage had been done. Despite the fact that marital discord and even adultery were tolerated to a certain extent in Denver's most elite social and religious circles, they were allowed only under the condition that details remained absolutely private. Margaret canceled her New York plans and left Denver with Helen for a few days of respite in Florida. In an unusual outburst of her personal feelings to the press, she cried, "What I want to do most of all is get away from Denver for awhile and

all its painful associations. There has been no pleasure in being obliged
to listen to all these reports and to have to answer questions about conditions of which I myself am only too sensitively conscious. And I do
not care to talk about Mr. Brown and his condition, because it would
be evidence of poor taste on my part. I will only say this: that his pecu-
liarities have made it necessary for me to reach an adjustment of finances
so that we may live apart." She noted that Denver's high altitude aggra-
vated J.J.'s health, a condition that made him "likely to say anything. ...
He has absented himself from the house for months at a time and when
he has come back, we have humored him by not asking questions as to
where he has been or what he has done."[41]

Margaret had indeed signed a separation agreement, but it had been
months earlier, on August 10, 1909. It would be a year or more before
Margaret fully realized the extent of what she had signed. J.J.'s fortune was valued at about $238,000,[42] but with the help of an attorney
Margaret had agreed to a trust fund of $25,000 set up in her name with
the International Trust Company, from which she would receive $700
per month. She retained ownership of the House of Lions and the fur-
nishings within; J.J. specifically requested a steel engraving of Lincoln's
cabinet, a picture by Harvey Houn titled *Loaded Burros at Aspen
Mountain,* and two paintings by J.D. Howland, *Coyotes* and *Looking
for Trouble,* which was on exhibit at the Brown Palace Hotel.[43]

Despite everyone's efforts to keep the separation as congenial as possible, by late February 1910 the situation had polarized. Both Helen and
Lawrence took their mother's side, and Margaret promised them that
despite the fact that her share of the family fortune had been severely
limited, she would take care of them until they became established on
their own. She refused to let them see letters their father wrote to her
or to them. J.J. wrote angrily to a friend that Margaret had compelled
the children "to disobey me in all things and thereby [created] disorder
and doubt in the minds of the children. ... She has ruined them for any
earthly use."[44]

Margaret and Helen continued their round of social and political
engagements in Denver, and Mrs. Crawford Hill generously listed all
the Brown family members in her Social Register, albeit at separate
residences. Polly Pry fortunately steered clear of the situation. And in
the spring of 1911, an event occurred that lifted Margaret's spirits more
then she ever could have anticipated: Sarah Bernhardt came to town.

A stunning review of Bernhardt's performance in Denver's *Daily News* was written by none other than Helen Ring Robinson. Margaret was well acquainted with the young woman, who as a debutante had been a frequent guest at Avoca and since her marriage had assisted Margaret and Ben Lindsey in their work for Denver juveniles. She loved politics, and she loved to write. Little did anyone realize at the time that the bright young reporter, delegated to writing entertainment reviews for itinerant local newspapers, would one day become the first female senator in the country.

The *voix d'or* (golden voice), fluidity of movement, and fiery personality of Sarah Bernhardt had ensured her status as legend long before she graced Denver with her presence. The 1911 tour of Edmond Rostand's *L'Aiglon* was the second time Bernhardt had come to Denver to play the role and was one of six American tours Bernhardt organized after she broke with the Comedie Français in 1880 and established her own theater. (Edmond Rostand is most famous for the 1897 play *Cyrano de Bergerac.*) When she had visited Denver in 1901, Bernhardt had played at Elitch Gardens in the rain. In May 1911, when she arrived at her elegant suite at the Brown Palace Hotel it was already filled with flowers and cards from hosts of Denver admirers.

At the age of sixty-seven, despite the fact that she had suffered an injury to her right leg that made it almost impossible for her to stand unsupported (the leg was later amputated), Bernhardt played the part of Napoleon's son, a young boy kept in captivity after the fall of the empire. Audiences found her role more than believable—just before launching Edmond Rostand's *L'Aiglon* Bernhardt had played the leading role in a French production of *Hamlet. L'Aiglon* had first opened in Paris and had sold out every performance, becoming legendary for its financial success. But the actress's age was becoming more apparent. "Her ductile voice, a harp of a thousand strings, has lost some shade of its magical quality. The silver cord is a little loosened," wrote Helen Ring Robinson. "The death's head that lurks within every cooing baby's skull, behind every laughing girl's features, every burdened man's tired face, shows nearer the surface of Mme. Bernhardt's countenance than when she first played 'L'Aiglon' in Denver some ten years ago." Nevertheless, Robinson was entranced. "Oh Queen, live forever," she cried with a flourish at the end of her review.[45]

Sarah Bernhardt was one of the first major actresses to move from the stage to the screen, and in 1912 a motion-picture production of *Camille* came to Denver theaters. The *Denver Times* reported that a knowledge of French happily wasn't necessary to understand the story—the plot was so clear on the screen that even reading the book was unnecessary.[46] Those among Bernhardt's substantial following in Denver were satisfied.

Margaret Brown was entranced with the great actress's skill, presence, and perseverance despite her age. The image of an older woman playing the part of a young boy—and playing it well—burned itself into her mind. Their paths would cross in unexpected ways in Europe, and in 1914 Sarah Bernhardt would become a chevalier of the French Legion of Honor, an award Margaret would one day enjoy herself.

But for now, as 1911 drew to a close, fate dictated a different type of dramatic role for Margaret Brown—one that had nothing whatsoever to do with the stage.

AT THE END of the summer Margaret left Denver for Newport, where she stayed through the holidays. A close friend of three generations of the Astor family, she was invited to join a group that included John Jacob Astor IV and his new wife, Madeleine, on their travels through northern Africa and Egypt. Helen Brown, who had taken time off from her studies at the Sorbonne to stay with a family friend in Paris, Madame Rochrich, wrote to friends that she intended to accompany her mother on some of her travels before returning to the Sorbonne the following fall.

Margaret left New York with the John Jacob Astor party on January 25, 1912. The journey seemed ill fated almost from the beginning: while on a ship in the Indian Ocean, the entourage very nearly capsized during a violent typhoon. Margaret was apparently unfazed. The party traveled to Cairo, where it stayed for several days, and Margaret and Helen had themselves photographed sitting atop camels in their long, heavy Edwardian garb, the Sphinx and pyramids in the background. On the return trip they spent a few days in Rome, where Margaret bought casts of ancient cities that she intended to bring back for the Denver Art Museum.[47] (Historians have been unable to determine precisely what these casts or models were—and they now lie at the bottom of the ocean.) When Margaret and Helen returned to the Ritz Hotel in Paris, there was a telegram from Lawrence stating that the baby was ill.

Margaret had intended to part company with the Astors but instead abruptly changed her plans, at the last moment booking passage on the *Titanic* with the rest of the Astor party. Helen bade her mother adieu and remained in Paris for some social engagements with friends.

When news of the *Titanic*'s sinking hit the newspapers, only a few people knew that Margaret was on board. Helen was panic-stricken. Margaret attempted to send her a wireless message from the *Carpathia,* but all messages had been delayed. (She also tried to send messages to Madeleine Astor's mother and George Widener's family in Philadelphia, among others.)[48] Helen endured "three days of agony" before she learned that her mother had survived. "Dear Mother," she wrote as soon as she received the news. "When your wireless message from the Carpathia came it was 6:30 in the morning, after I had passed three utterly sleepless nights. It has been a frightful ordeal for me, but oh, the relief your message gave me! My chaperone is as good as gold. She was with me during all that time of sleeplessness and agonizing suspense, but thank God! you are safe. How you must have suffered from the cold—and you didn't have pneumonia."[49]

Lawrence was another person who knew his mother had been on board the wrecked ship. Once the lines were free he sent a telegram to Margaret on the *Carpathia,* also thanking God that she was safe.[50] Working on a farm near Montague, California (his aunt Helen Tobin Von Reitzenstein was living nearby in Portland), Lawrence too had to wait several days before hearing that his mother had survived. In a letter to Helen, he exclaimed, "All I can do is to thank God for [her] deliverance and beleave [sic] me I will do that much all my life."[51] To Margaret he wrote,

> Mother of Mine,
>
> God has surely been good to me. He has saved from a horrible death one of my greatest treasures and I will never cease thanking him. This nightmare has awakened a better manhood in your son and all his life will be spent in showing his gratefulness to his creator. I was away out on a ranch when the firm telephoned me a wire sent by Eileen that the Titanic had sunk and you were a passenger. Mr. Gadis [his boss] however said not to worry that all had been rescued. I couldn't stand the strain ... so I came into Montague and there I saw the first accounts in the paper. All were not saved and the paper did not have a list of the rescued; there the nightmare started. I had visions of all the horrible things

that happen to one in a crisis of this sort. Some kind soul helped by handing me a paper with the list of saved and there you were. Then the report came that many had died and from that time until I received your wire I was in misery ... the strain was too much and I couldn't stand this forsaken country any longer. ...

This has taught me a great lesson and I hope it will teach us all. After all who have we but our own in this world and why can't we be more to-gether? You must come to us. ... I must see you and I must hold you in my arms; please come. ... With all the love and good wishes in the world I am your son, Lawrence.[52]

Margaret's family in Hannibal wasn't sure what to think. Early wires had indicated that Mrs. John Jacob Astor had been saved, and the *Hannibal Courier Post* speculated that because Margaret had been traveling with the Astors, it seemed likely that she had been saved as well. However, her name was not on the early list of survivors, and neither was Helen's, who family members at first believed had also been on board. Margaret's brother Daniel, who had been visiting family in Hannibal, immediately departed for New York.[53]

Margaret's personal response to the disaster is exemplified by a letter she wrote to Helen once she reached the Brown Palace Hotel in Denver. On the evening of May 8, 1912, at eight-thirty P.M., Margaret wrote,

My dear child,

After being brined, salted, and pickled in mid ocean I am now high and dry. Enclosed clipping will tell all. I was the first one to leave a message at the Marconie on board the Carpathia, but the system was so glutted they couldn't get it through. ... I didn't think any one knew I was on board. Mrs. Spinner met the Carpathia and was ringing her hands crying Helen who everybody thought was on board. Thank Heavens you were not you truly would be in a predicament—I had a telegram from Lawrence on board the Carpathia and a wonderful letter—He was crazed with anxiety. His baby had never been sick a minute but is a healthy and wonderful beautiful kind. ... I have had flowers, letters, telegrams—people until I am *befuddled*. They are petitioning Congress to give me a *medal* and to inscribe my name on the monument erected in New York harbor—If I must call a specialist to examine my head it is due to the title of *Heroine* of the Titanic. Well I am thankful you were not along: consequently my hands and mind were free.

I am now struggling with reporters. ... I have been so bewildered I couldn't write you and do not know whether I will get a way out [to] where Lawrence is or not.

Love Mother

Inscribed across the top of the page was a request for Helen to go down to Margaret's hairdresser in Paris and get her favorite henna mixture ("the man will know").[54]

As soon as Helen received the letter, she changed her plans to remain in London until the fall semester started at the Sorbonne. She arrived in New York by the first part of June, meeting briefly with her father there before taking the train to Denver to be with her mother.

Clearly Margaret had regained her sense of humor. To one of her attorneys in Denver she wired, "Thanks for the kind thoughts. Water was fine and swimming good. Neptune was exceedingly kind to me and I am now high and dry."[55]

Margaret arrived in Denver at seven-thirty P.M. on the evening of April 29, 1912. She had remained in New York for several days caring for *Titanic* survivors; when she stepped off the train at Denver's Union Station, she was greeted by a crowd of Denver friends and newspaper reporters. Nieces Florence and Helen were most eager to see her; they were finishing their studies in Denver and living with relatives in a house at 1420 Clarkson Street. Florence had been awaiting Margaret's return so that she could accompany her on her next trip to Europe; they had tentatively planned to depart from Montreal on the *Virginian*, with Helen Tobin following later.[56]

Once she had settled herself at the Brown Palace Hotel, Margaret granted several interviews, although her voice was husky and she had lost it more than once in the past few days. "I haven't stopped talking a waking moment in the past month," she declared. She seemed almost obsessed with the story of Ida and Isidor Straus and had watched as Ida Straus got into a lifeboat and then got out, refusing to be separated from her husband. "Noble woman!" Margaret declared. "I will never, never forget her as I saw her last, holding fast to her husband's arm as the two walked away along the deck of that sinking ship." She was repeatedly asked the same questions about her reputed role as "Heroine of the *Titanic*" but summarized her own efforts by saying, "As I went on deck [when] the boats were being lowered, I found many opportunities to be useful and I was glad to be. The less you think of yourself at such times, the better off you are."[57] One reporter asked whether she regretted the experience. "I cannot say that I regret having been in it," she answered, "for I think I did do a little good to some unhappy soul[s], but when I think it all over—think of the suffering some of those poor people went through, the homes which have been broken up, and the hearts broken—I think I would rather have missed it."[58]

Despite the fact that Margaret was renowned for her elaborate gowns, the closets at her suite at the Brown Palace Hotel were empty—she had arrived with only the clothes on her back. A reporter from the *Denver Post* was quick to note the fact. "Oh, such things never did worry me a particle anyhow," she sighed.[59] The striped taffeta dress she wore was something she had picked up in a shop in New York, "ready made and marked down." "Really, we think too much about too many clothes," she said. "If you have only one suitable gown for each occasion, it saves no end of worry."[60]

Margaret had lost a substantial amount of clothing and jewelry that now lay at the bottom of the ocean. However, she had saved her Egyptian good-luck talisman, which she later presented to Captain Rostron of the *Carpathia,* and a large diamond brooch that had been pinned to her corsage at dinner. (This brooch, valued at $15,000, was later stolen from her trunk in a hotel lobby.) The only missing items over which she expressed extreme regret were the four cases of pictures and models of ancient Roman ruins she was bringing back for the Denver museum.[61]

The Brown Palace Hotel was already fielding numerous requests for Margaret to make public appearances. "Will I do it?" she asked rhetorically. "No. I hardly think I will. I don't mind telling things I know to people I am sure are deeply interested in it." However, after a moment of contemplation, she revised her answer with a gleam in her eye: "If I had a pretty gown, I have that much of a woman's vanity about me I might go before an audience and show it off."[62]

Margaret was, however, interested in testifying before the Senate committee that held hearings on the accident. "I am willing to go before the Senate investigating committee and testify to all I have said," she told a reporter. "Hundreds of lives were needlessly sacrificed in this great disaster; and I, for one, am eager to see justice done."[63]

She never got her chance. Almost no women were called to appear before the committee—of the fifty-seven who testified, just six were

women, and only two of those six, Helen Bishop and Mrs. J. Stuart
White, appeared in person in the courtroom. The other women provided written affidavits, and Eleanor Widener, a friend of Margaret who
had lost both her husband and son in the disaster, submitted only a brief
statement confirming that she and her family had dined with Captain
Smith on the evening of April 12 and that the captain had "no intoxi-
cating liquors of any kind."[64] However, the three prominent male members of Lifeboat Six were called to testify. *Titanic* lookout Frederick
Fleet and Major Arthur G. Peuchen testified on the fourth day of the
hearing; Quartermaster Robert Hichens, who had been the helmsman
at the critical moment, on the fifth. None of the women from Lifeboat
Six were called to testify despite controversial testimony by Hichens
regarding his own behavior and an unproven (and unlikely) claim by
witness Louis Kelin that Frederick Fleet had been asleep in the crow's
nest owing to intoxication.[65]

Nevertheless, Margaret made sure the world heard her story. She
published a detailed and eloquent account of her *Titanic* experience in
the *Newport Herald*, so lengthy that it had to run in three parts on May
28, 29, and 30, 1912. She not only described the event in a narrative style
that made for irresistible reading but managed to both commend and
condemn her fellow first-class passengers for their behavior. She was
also critical of the manner in which the White Star Line had handled
the disaster. Newspapers around the country reprinted the series. In the
fall of 1912 Margaret was contacted by Colonel Archibald Gracie IV,
another *Titanic* survivor, who was interviewing survivors in an effort to
publish a full account of the disaster.

A graduate of West Point and a retired colonel from the Seventh
Regiment of the U.S. Army, Gracie was already an established author
when he boarded the *Titanic* on his way home to Washington, D.C.,
where his wife and daughter waited. When the call came to begin filling
the lifeboats, he helped several women into the boats, including the
pregnant Madeleine Astor, and gathered blankets for them. He related
that while he was standing on deck, he and his friend Clinch Smith
were suddenly met with a "mass of humanity" that emerged from a
lower deck, "facing us and completely blocking our passage to the
stern. There were women in the crowd as well as men and these seemed
to be steerage passengers who had just come up from the decks below.
Even among these people there was no hysterical cry, no evidence of

panic. Oh, the agony of it."[66] As the *Titanic* foundered, Gracie jumped with the crowd into the teeming water and avoided being pulled under the surface by catching hold of the bottom rung of the ladder leading to the roof of the officers' mess. He kicked himself clear and with the help of his lifebelt swam to a floating wooden crate, which helped him navigate to the overturned collapsible Lifeboat B. Lifeboat B, however, was slowly sinking. Second Officer Lightoller ordered all the men to stand on top of the boat in a double column, facing the bow, and in this manner—drenched and frozen—they delicately balanced themselves on the open sea for approximately four hours.

Gracie survived, although lingering effects of his experience kept him mostly confined to his bed. He wrote to Margaret and asked her to relate her experiences for his forthcoming book, *The Truth About the Titanic,* and she immediately complied. In a letter dated November 13, 1912, Gracie wrote that his manuscript was nearly completed and would soon be in the hands of his publisher. In a second letter dated November 20, 1912, Gracie wrote, "I am very indebted to you for the loan of your manuscript containing your experience on board the *TITANIC,* and I have read it with the greatest interest. ... Mrs. Gracie has also just finished reading your manuscript with intense interest. The book you propose writing should, with all the experiences you have had, receive a wide circulation." And thus we have in writing the first mention—one of many—of Margaret Brown's autobiography, which apparently was written and submitted to publishers but has been lost to history.

Gracie wrote that as soon as the book was finished, he and his wife were closing their home to stay in New York for the winter, and his daughter was making her debut on Thanksgiving Day at the Gotham Hotel. Although Gracie completed his manuscript, he never proofread it. Just days after he wrote to Margaret, he died in New York of complications related to pneumonia.[67] *The Truth About the Titanic* was published posthumously in 1913.

DENVER DIDN'T HAVE TO wait long to get a close-up experience of the *Titanic.* By April 23, the first moving pictures of the ship, taken ten minutes before the *Titanic* sailed from Southampton, were shown in Denver theaters. Albeit brief, the reel showed Captain Smith confidently striding about the deck and passengers bidding farewell to relatives and friends.[68]

And it wasn't long before the entire event was restaged at Sloan's Lake, where a lighted model ship, "quite large," was floated out onto the water, run into a fake iceberg, and sunk with a park full of people from the nearby carnival grounds avidly watching.[69] The *Titanic* disaster provided a plethora of pithy themes for Denver's clergy, including "God and the Ocean Disaster," "Man's Condition in This Age, Illustrated by the Most Pathetic Disaster of the Century," "Lessons from the Shipwreck," "The Price of Error," and "What Would You Do if on a Sinking Ship?"[70] Denver couldn't get enough of the *Titanic.*

Margaret busied herself writing articles, planning the next juvenile court benefit, and taking issue with Father Vaughn, a local priest, regarding his most recent inflammatory remarks on women's suffrage. Undaunted by her recent brush with death, she made plans to sail from New York on the *Auguste Victoria* to see Helen in London. (Helen, however, beat her to the punch and was back in the States before her mother could set sail.)

The city of Denver wanted to hail its new heroine. The Denver Woman's Club, in a unanimous petition, requested the U.S. Senate and House of Representatives to "grant a recognition of Mrs. Brown's services to her fellow passengers in the form of a medal."[71] The club passed a dramatic resolution declaring that in those moments of darkness and despair were found "the finest types of manhood and womanhood the world has ever produced. ... Among those who faced the grim messenger reaching out of the icy waters was a former member of the Art and Literature Department of the Denver Woman's Club, Margaret Tobin Brown, whose only thought was to help save those in peril ... who took a place at the oar and who encouraged and ministered to the wounded ... forgetful of her own sufferings and exhaustion but obeying the divine command of the offer of the cup in His name."[72]

On May 2, 1912, barely two weeks after her harrowing ordeal, Margaret Brown was the guest of honor at a luncheon hosted by none other than Mrs. Crawford Hill, leader of Denver's "Sacred Thirty-six." The luncheon was described as "unusually smart," even by Mrs. Hill's standards, and Mrs. Brown's arrival at the Crawford mansion was greeted with loud applause. The newspapers noted that although Mrs. Brown had previously been a guest at Mrs. Hill's "snowy board," the times had been so few that she could count them on one hand, and she certainly had never been the guest of honor. "What years of moneyed siege and tireless ambition never brought about for Mrs. J.J. Brown, one night of peril-born heroism in an open sea and a few days of splendid self-sacrifice in the cause of penniless and heartbroken folk has accomplished," the paper crowed. "Mrs. Crawford Hill rules the social world of Denver with sceptered sway, and it is she who has let down the icebound metal bars and admitted Mrs. Brown within the inner sanctum."[73]

Margaret, although she no doubt enjoyed herself—and reciprocated with a smaller luncheon for Mrs. Crawford a few days later—was not as gratified by the event as she might have been a few years earlier. The *Denver Times* reported that Margaret "talked entertainingly and with an ease which indicated that after all, this woman who has basked in the smile of Newport's social deities, who has faced death without flinching, and who has shared strength and means with the humblest people of the earth whom fate made her companions in distress, eyes her attainment of the local social zenith with less awe than its older counterparts."[74]

But where does the epithet "Unsinkable" originate? Legend claims that Margaret, stepping off the *Carpathia* onto the safe shore of New York, boldly exclaimed, "Typical Brown luck. I'm unsinkable!" But in reality, the name apparently started with none other than Polly Pry. The *Newport Herald* reported that Mrs. Brown's heroic story—which, it smugly noted, *it* had been the first to publish—had become a "genuine thriller" in newspapers across the country. According to *Newport Herald* editors, "Town Topics," Polly Pry's weekly gossip column patterned after Newport's own mean-spirited society rag of the same name, was "probably miffed because it had been unable to print [Margaret's] story when it was fresh news," and consequently "unfeelingly referred to her as 'the unsinkable Mrs. Brown." Mrs. Brown's response was nonchalant. "Did she care?" the *Herald* asked. "Not a bit. She sent the clipping [back] to her Colorado friends, and the laugh was on the rude Town Topics."[75]

Called "Lady Margaret" by other women survivors for her role in the lifeboat and on the *Carpathia*,[76] Margaret had no idea how profoundly the *Titanic* episode would affect the rest of her life. Family lore relates that one year after the date of the sinking, the other women survivors of Lifeboat Six gathered for a surprise party at Margaret's home in Newport to thank her.

Margaret wasn't ready to sit back on her laurels. Twice, once in 1909 and again in 1911, she had made a nascent run for the U.S. Senate, encouraged by her friends Judge Ben Lindsey, Helen Ring Robinson, and others. Sentiment against women in politics as well as personal circumstances surrounding her marriage and family had held her back. But Margaret's *Titanic* experience had given her a media platform from which to voice her most deeply felt concerns—and she discovered that she was good at it. She would no longer let convention stand in her way. In an interview with reporter Zoe Beckley, she asked, "Why should a woman be mildewed at forty? That's the best time to start a real career. Assuming she is a mother, her children are launched by that time; if a childless wife, she has probably mothered her husband's activities to the point of success; if wage-earning and responsibility occupied her early years, she has won success and can afford to take a breath and look around a little." With a flourish, she declared that only the national Senate offered the widest possibilities for the intelligent woman of a mature age.[77]

Drum Major of an
Imperial Band
1913–1922

DESPITE MARGARET'S NEW attitude toward the unnecessary burden of an extravagant wardrobe, she soon regained her interest in clothing. On September 4, 1912, she made a striking appearance at the horse show at the casino in fashionable Newport, Rhode Island, wearing a white-and-black satin gown of chiffon and lace dramatically draped from neck to waist with a scarlet Elizabethan ruff. Her lace hat was trimmed with white osprey. Mrs. Vanderbilt was among the group of friends who enthusiastically greeted her arrival.[1] After the horse show, with all of society in attendance, Margaret hosted an informal musicale at the Muenchinger-King Hotel with entertainment by Harry Evans, the baritone who had sung at Westminster Abbey during the coronation of King George the previous summer.

Marital problems, social rebuffs, political scandals—all were left behind when Margaret came to Newport. A frequent visitor and part-time resident since 1909, Margaret in 1913 leased a large cottage (exceedingly modest in comparison to the "cottages" of her friends the Astors and Vanderbilts) and declared Newport her home away from home.

At the height of its reputation, Newport provided a cozy respite from the real world for those who could afford it. Although the resort had been famous since shortly after the Civil War, it wasn't until the 1890s that Newport came to represent, on an international scale, the essence of the Gilded Age. Newport society was an exclusive club, and despite the fact that their pockets were not quite as deep as their neighbors', Margaret Tobin Brown and her family—minus J.J.—became cherished members.

In his 1907 book *The American Scene*, Henry James devoted an entire chapter to the smug wealth and iniquitous excesses of Newport society. Returning to Newport after a long absence, he declared himself threatened by the condition "of having known it too well and loved it too much." Critical of Newport's ostentatiousness but nevertheless admitting in his mildly ironic, self-deprecating manner that he was part of that same society, James compared the seaside town to a "little bare, white, open hand … with the gracefully-spread fingers and the fine grain of skin, even the dimples at the joints and the shell-like delicacy of the pink nails—all the charms in short that a little white hand may have. It is the back of the hand, rising to the swell of the wrist, that is exposed—which is the way, I think, the true lover takes and admires it … the touchstone of taste." Describing the town as a mere opportunity for wealthy New York families to escape the heat and swim, boat, ride, and drive, "more or less [an] expensive riot," he wrote that Newport cottagers arrived to "put things into [the town], things of their own, and of all sorts, and of many ugly, and of more and more expensive, sorts; to fill it substantially, that is, with gold, the gold that they have ended by heaping up there to an amount so oddly out of proportion to the scale of nature and of space."[2]

Margaret too was acutely aware of the discrepancies of race and class that Newport represented (much to the chagrin of some of her neighbors, she thought the community was too exclusive and constantly encouraged "colorful" visitors). But like other Newporters, she had many reasons to enjoy the Newport scene, and despite her more than modest roots she made a smooth transition into the highest echelons of American and even international society. "Newport is thought by foreigners to be the axis upon which the American continent revolves," she wrote. "Happily placed as it is, in just the right latitude and longitude, its climate is largely tempered by the Gulf Stream. … On the whole, those living in Newport are favored much more advantageously than many living elsewhere."[3] But more importantly, Newport provided for some women—particularly those with a lot of ambition and at least some degree of wealth—a unique opportunity to lead respected and independent lives. Margaret found refuge in Newport. Divorce or separation, frowned upon in other circles, was accepted in Newport. Education for women was an accepted fact, even if it tended toward finishing schools designed to make a woman an attractive marriage prospect rather than toward personal or professional development. A woman's ability to carry on an intelligent, informed discussion was considered an asset, and her right to travel the world—on her own if necessary—was considered a right.

Following her *Titanic* experience and perhaps bolstered by the recognition she received after the disaster, Margaret took up her permanent summer residence in Newport at the Reitz Cottage, which she called "Mon Etui," at 44 Bellevue Avenue, just adjacent to the Muenchinger-King Hotel. The Muenchinger-King was a landmark in Newport, owned since 1845 by David King, the first president of the Newport Historical Society, who gradually added on to it over the following decades. In 1903 King's heirs sold the property to Gustave and Amanda Muenchinger, and they turned it into an exclusive hotel.[4] In 1914 Margaret moved next door to the Club Cottage, also adjacent to the Muenchinger-King at 40 Bellevue Avenue. For the next ten years she alternated between these two cottages, from 1915 to 1920 living at Mon Etui, from 1921 to 1923 at the Club Cottage. She was regularly listed in the Newport Social Index from 1913 to 1920 but continued to spend winters in Denver, most often staying at the Brown Palace Hotel when the Pennsylvania Street home had tenants.

On August 15, 1912, Madeleine Astor gave birth to a son. Margaret cabled congratulations, and the news seemed to cheer a town hit hard by the *Titanic* disaster. In memory of the *Titanic* victims and in honor of Madeleine, Margaret sponsored a fund-raiser at Mon Etui for a new maternity ward at Newport's hospital, featuring a program all in French titled "Songs of Old France." One hundred Newport women pledged sponsorship of the new maternity ward.[5]

Switching between the two cottages may have been a function of how much room Margaret needed to accommodate her family, though she quickly established a reputation for hosting large social events as well. With four girls under her wing, Margaret took her role as mother and aunt very seriously and understood well the paradoxical nature of a woman's role in turn-of-the-century America. As a feminist and a harbinger of social change, she wished her young wards to be well-educated, articulate, independent women. But she also understood the restrictions imposed upon most women's lives and knew that wealth could sometimes buy a certain degree of independence and exemption from conventional gender roles. With the exception of Grace, who had married in Denver, the three remaining young women—daughter Helen and Florence and Helen Tobin—were formally introduced to society with a strong suggestion from Margaret that they each make a "good match."

The role of debutante required not only a significant investment of time and money but an appreciation of the part to be played. In the 1906 book *The American Girl,* which glorifies the role of the "new woman" in ways that now appear suspiciously racist and elitist, author Howard Chandler Christy describes the new generation of "social princesses": "As each new Spring brings its harvest of flowers, so each social season sees the advent of the debutantes, the young heiresses of all that is most precious in our civilization."[6] A young woman's social debut, courtship, and subsequent marriage to a man of appropriate wealth and rank were considered the high point of her life, after which she was expected to settle into a domestic role that usually rendered her invisible to social and business circles.

Florence Tobin, now eighteen and ready to return to America after her studies with Isadora Duncan, was the first to dazzle Newport with her ability to play the role of debutante to full advantage. Margaret traveled to Germany to sail back with Florence in July 1913 on the S.S. *Imperator,* an exquisite ship built by the Hamburg America Line whose first-class rooms had been designed by Ritz hotel architect Charles Mewes. In Europe Florence had studied art, music, and dancing, and as a protégée of Isadora Duncan her dance career had included an appearance before the German emperor, who had presented her with a medal in appreciation of her performance. On board the *Imperator,* Margaret and Florence helped organize a benefit to raise money for the Seaman's Widows and Orphans Fund, and Florence performed a dance titled "Hindoo's Maiden Prayer," organized in four parts: Meditation, Adoration, Prayer, and Burning at the Stake.

When Florence arrived in Newport she continued to perform dances choreographed by Isadora Duncan and Lady Richardson and established a reputation as being not only pretty but athletic and "one of the best classical dancers." The *Newport Herald* marveled at how much she had accomplished at such a young age: "It seems a great deal to crowd into a period of 18 years, but Miss Tobin would not know how to be quiet for any length of time. At least she has never tried it."[7]

The first suitor to appear on Florence's doorstep was Prince Gennaro Caracciolo of Italy, who had come to the United States with the intention of studying American economic and social conditions. The prince first glimpsed Florence Tobin in the fall of 1911 when she was vacationing in Newport, and returned in the summer of 1912 to see her again. By 1913 Newport's society column announced that "another munificent international marriage" was imminent. Although the prince was nearly fifty—more than thirty years older than Florence—Margaret considered him a favorable match because of the old-world prestige and financial security he might give her young niece. Upon their return to Newport she hosted a dinner for him at the Muenchinger-King and then took her guests to a dance and midnight buffet sponsored by the commandant of the Narragansett Bay naval station for the officers of the German cruiser *Victoria Luise.*

The prince was frequently described as a master of the art of charming young women, and his adoration of Newport was complete. "Can one ever forget the beautiful and extensive Easton's Beach," he said, "with its throngs of pleasure seekers basking at ease through the long summer's day; and the smaller and exclusive Bailey's Beach, with its charming people enjoying their morning dip like one big family! And what can one say to fitly describe the Ocean Drive and the Cliff Walk!" But the prince nearly stumbled over his adjectives as he sought to express his admiration of Newport women. "How shall I describe my impressions of American women?" he cried. "A dazzling complexity of charming manners, combined with kindness and French loveliness: full of spirit, cheerful in conversation, with Spanish temperament and Parisian modishness, and an almost cosmopolitan sympathy that is, however, sometimes marred by an exaggerated conventionalism." Though he admitted that it was impossible to be critical of such feminine perfection, he did note that American women did not seem interested in the "questions that stir the world: politics, arts, letters, and science."[8]

Florence was not as impressed by the prince's charms as her aunt. The Denver newspapers frequently picked up stories about the Brown family from the *New York Times* and the *Newport Herald,* and Helen Brown—who considered Florence, Grace, and Helen Tobin more like sisters than cousins—in a rare move granted an interview to the *Rocky Mountain News.* "The prince is a harmless old man," she declared. "Florence doesn't care for the society of old men and we wouldn't consider him for a moment in the light of a husband."[9]

Indeed, Florence had her eye on an old childhood friend whom she had known since her days in Denver. William Harper, twenty-eight, a member of the family of well-known publishers, had moved on from Denver and was now president of the Harper Engineering Company in New York. On his mother's side he was related to Madame Backhmeteff, wife of the Russian ambassador and a good friend of Margaret Brown. Handsome and adventurous, he was good friends with Lawrence Brown and known for his exploits as an amateur aviator.

Spurred by passion or perhaps the fear that she would be pressured into marrying an "old man," Florence announced her intentions to her aunt. Margaret didn't argue—and enjoyed helping orchestrate the wedding plans. The engagement was announced at a dinner Margaret hosted for Florence and William at the Muenchinger-King, at which William, described in the newspapers the following day as "a typical young hustling American of business," was congratulated by his friends on the success of his whirlwind courtship. The wedding took place just eleven days later at Margaret's Newport cottage, with Rev. William B. Meenan, pastor of St. Mary's Catholic Church, performing the ceremony. The occasion had an Irish flair: Florence's wedding gown was of rose point and Irish lace, and Helen Tobin, a bridesmaid along with her sister Grace, wore a coat of Irish lace trimmed with sable. Margaret elegantly reigned in a pink gown trimmed with mother-of-pearl and silver and for a wedding gift gave her niece a diamond tiara studded with pearls. Neither J.J. nor Daniel Tobin was present, and Helen Brown's steady beau, George Benziger, gave the bride away. After a formal dinner at the Muenchinger-King, the couple left for a honeymoon in the West Indies and planned to return to Newport by the end of the summer "to try out several hydroaeroplanes which the groom has perfected."

TRAVEL BY SHIP was the only way to get from one continent to another, and Margaret refused to allow—outwardly at least—her *Titanic* experience to daunt her willingness to travel. Invited to Russia for the winter of 1912 by Princess Stephanie Dolgoruky, she sailed to Scotland from New York and, after an extended visit in St. Petersburg, visited India once again before meeting Helen in France in the spring.

Helen Brown was beginning to think of marriage herself but was not as interested in filling the society pages as Florence was. She told a Denver newspaper reporter that after her graduation from the Wolcott School in Denver and subsequent study abroad, she had decided to "live the life of the West rather than follow her mother's example and enter the social surroundings of Newport and the East."[10] Nevertheless, she traveled almost constantly, spending a great deal of time in France. In glowing letters to her father she described the delights of French food and culture. "You know I despise and hate every inch of Paris," he wrote, "and have no earthly use for any of the people. So I do not care to hear about them. ... I have little time for things that are foreign."[11]

Despite her nomadic lifestyle and busy social life, Helen's relationship with George Benziger blossomed. She announced her engagement in January 1913 in Tucson, Arizona, where she was visiting her father, and ·then sent formal announcements to her friends in Newport and Denver. Helen spent several weeks in Chicago selecting her trousseau, and in April 1913 she and George were married in Chicago by the Right Rev. S.G. Messmer. A wedding breakfast was held beforehand in the English Room at the Blackstone Hotel, and the ceremony was performed at high noon. Guests included Mr. and Mrs. George J. Benziger, George's parents; J.J. Brown; and Helen's good friend Ragnhilda Hobe of Washington, daughter of the Belgian minister. Margaret was in Germany and possibly chose not to attend so as to avoid a potentially uncomfortable encounter with J.J., although she definitely approved of Helen's choice of a husband and over the years became close to George's family in Switzerland. Helen and George honeymooned in Europe and returned to live in New York, where their first son, James George Benziger, was born on March 31, 1914. A second son, George Peter Joseph Adelrich Benziger (known as Peter), was born on December 26, 1917.

Though most of her friends were in Denver, Helen was deeply concerned about the attitude of Denver newspapers toward her family and chose to marry and live in New York not only because of her husband's work in publishing but because she felt it was impossible to live in Denver with any degree of privacy. Just after the news of her engagement reached Denver, she wrote to George, "Now you know what I mean when I wrote you long ago [about] how humiliated I felt over the attitude in the newspapers — and what a false ridiculous light they have always placed us in. We have the Denver newspapers to thank for all the nonsense ... the other papers have only copied them. If we had been married in Denver we would have been subject to far more ridicule." She was most concerned, however, with what the newspapers said about Margaret. "Every one in Denver is subject to the same thing more or less," she admitted, "but Mother unfortunately always seems to get in for the worst of it and the greatest quantity. ... They seem to love to make sport of her."[12]

George Benziger came from a prominent and wealthy European family, but in a family of many sons it was up to him to make his own fortune. Helen wasn't concerned; like her mother, she had married for love, not money. Just before her marriage she wrote, "If I were deeply concerned about money I would have married a rich man some time ago. Thank God I wasent [sic] and I waited. ... You will be with me soon, and never to go away again."[13]

With one daughter and two nieces now married (although not necessarily out of the house—they all came to visit often), Helen Tobin was the only one left under Margaret's wing. Helen soon established herself as one of the darlings of the social set and became just as famous as her aunt for wearing elegant gowns. She made her debut in Newport wearing a white crepe de chine dress, embroidered in large swirls of black and red, with a short, sleeveless black velvet jacket. Her outgoing personality and ability as an actress in local amateur productions increased her popularity. Margaret—who had begun to study the roles of Sarah Bernhardt as well as reading Lamartine, Racine, and La Fontaine— was pleased with Helen's success. In 1914 a full-page photograph of Helen Tobin appeared on the Newport society page with the headline "Newport's Most Beautiful Girl of the Season." "If Paris were to make his celebrated Choice of Beauty this season at Newport," the article read, "no 'Trojan War' would follow, for by general consent he would bestow the golden apple upon Miss Helen Tobin."[14]

Margaret's house was always full of family and guests. During the summer of 1914, the Newport social index listed as residents of Margaret's home Helen and George Benziger, Lawrence and Eileen Brown (with Margaret's grandson, Pat), Florence and William Harper, and Helen Tobin. By 1917 Grace and her husband, Leslie Mortimer Carroll, were regular guests as well.

As early as 1910 Margaret's presence in Newport had created a sensation. In 1913 one reporter wrote that Mrs. Brown "thundered into Newport. This season she is entertaining society in a lavish manner. (I mean she entertains them at her home, and not only by the things she says.) Newport is entirely conscious that she is present, and they say she is the best-dressed woman in the place."[15] Her New York–born and

—bred neighbors were fascinated by the West, and Margaret, who loved Western culture in all its multicultural complexity, was happy to oblige. Once again the line between myth and reality blurred as stories about her exotic tastes and high-spirited approach—combined with the fact that she didn't particularly care what people thought about her—filled the gossip columns. She decorated her house with Navajo blankets and a papier-mâché cave and entertained her friends at a special table she had designed with a sunken fishbowl in the center. The fact that she could not only sing but yodel impressed even the most unflappable guest. She wore furs—often keepsakes from Colorado hunting trips with her son, Lawrence—and enjoyed draping them over her bed and furniture. Long before public awareness of wildlife preservation, this custom was an important statement about her Western heritage to her Eastern friends.

Margaret also shocked her neighbors by being one of the first cottagers to take up the motorcar. At a Newport car show she surprised a salesman by ignoring the luxurious, high-priced cars and expressing interest in the little Twombly cycle car. Although the car cost a mere $395, Margaret purchased a special body and fittings to the tune of $1,000 and then gave it to Florence and Helen to use at Mon Etui. Many cottagers harbored suspicions about the dangers of motorcars. Indeed, Margaret and Helen were driving a single-horse sleigh one day when the runners caught in the line of frozen car tracks and the sleigh overturned. The women were fine, but the horse, which had been hired from a local stable, was badly injured.

Generally, however, Margaret preferred to walk. One snippy commentator in *Town Topics* noted that Mrs. Brown, along with Mrs. William K. Vanderbilt and Mrs. Cornelius Vanderbilt, managed to schedule her daily walk at the same hour that the officers from the Atlantic fleet were taking their physical walking test.

Gaining recognition as an educated and articulate woman who could hold a conversation with just about anyone, Margaret hired young readers to come read the foreign newspapers to her and was always up-to-date on national and international politics. The *Newport Herald* described her as one of the most unique figures in Newport social life, whose studio had become a rendezvous "for people of taste and accomplishment." Nevertheless, some were quick to discredit a woman who had not only educated herself to a great degree but formally studied language and literature in America and Europe. One reporter noted, "If you speak to Mrs. Brown of the Chaucerian period of English literature she will probably tell you that she is very fond of Zola, and if you change to Zola and descant on French realism she suddenly remembers that Scott is one of her favorite authors. Thus in trice you receive intimate knowledge of the tremendous scope of Mrs. Brown's excursions in literature."[16]

Despite the fact that Margaret was legally separated from J.J.—and J.J.'s romantic entanglements occasionally ended up in the newspapers— she apparently never seriously pursued another relationship. On more than one occasion, however, it was noted that Mrs. Brown had "come out so strong for suffrage" that some men found her a little overbearing.

ONCE SHE FELT satisfied that her duties as mother and aunt were nearly accomplished, Margaret felt ready to tackle some new challenges in her life. Over the years she had developed friendships with many long-established Newport residents, including the Astors, the Vanderbilts, and the staunch Mrs. Stuyvesant Fish. But the most fascinating, powerful, and influential of Margaret's friends was Alva Vanderbilt Belmont, a forthright socialite and feminist who had a profound influence on Margaret's life. As with Margaret Brown, historians have tended to diminish or dismiss Alva Belmont's significant activities regarding the American women's movement. Her strong personality and somewhat eccentric character, combined with a prevailing attitude that women with money viewed feminism as a hobby rather than as a serious endeavor, have marginalized her contributions, financial and otherwise, to the suffrage movement. But Alva Belmont and Margaret Brown made a formidable team.

Born in Mobile, Alabama, on January 17, 1853, Alva Erskine Smith was the daughter of Phoebe Ann Desha Smith and Murray Forbes Smith. At a young age she was sent to a private boarding school in France, and even as a child she could see that her life was to be conscripted. "I loathed girls' occupations and pastimes," she later wrote. "There was a static quality to a girl's life, a monotony and restriction in it from which I rebelled from the very first. ... I wanted activity and I could not find enough of it in the circumscribed life of a girl."[17] Furthermore, "My first experiences in life gave birth to my belief in militant woman suffrage. I found that even at the age of seven boys looked down upon girls. I can almost feel my childish hot blood rise as it did then in rebellion at some such taunting remarks as: 'You can't run.' 'You can't climb trees.' 'You can't fight.' 'You are only a girl.' But no young would-be masculine bravado ever expressed twice such slurring belittlements of me."[18]

Through a combination of poor health and bad luck, Murray Forbes Smith lost most of his fortune. But that didn't prevent Alva from pursuing one of the most eligible bachelors in New York—Willie Vanderbilt, the second-oldest surviving son of William Henry Vanderbilt. Alva was twenty-two when she married Willie in 1875, and despite her youth she was determined to become the reigning monarch of New York society, on a par with the renowned Mrs. Astor, a goal that she accomplished. But Willie Vanderbilt was like many other men of his class and time: wealthy, handsome, sophisticated—and unfaithful. Infidelity was tolerated as long as it was accompanied by discretion. But Alva rebelled against the typical pattern of upper-class marriages, and her and Willie's relationship was riddled with conflict. For the sake of their three children as well as their fortune and reputation, Alva struggled to keep the marriage together.

In 1885, upon the death of his father, Willie inherited $70 million. In a gesture perhaps indicative of reconciliation, he bought a steam yacht and named it *Alva*. The couple also purchased a Newport cottage, Marble House, that remains legendary today. It was nothing but a small cottage when the Vanderbilts bought it in 1888, but with the help of architect Richard Morris Hunt, Alva built Marble House into an architectural masterpiece, a "glittering, shimmering jewel box" that became a national sensation.[19] Alva and her Marble House—and the extraordinarily lavish parties that were held there—became a symbol of the New York money that Henry James claimed had spoiled Newport's innocence.

A beautiful house did not compensate for a dismal domestic situation. Locked into a marriage that had become a "horrible mockery," the Vanderbilts decided to embark on a ten-month cruise to India in November of 1893 aboard their second yacht, *Valiant*. In addition to a crew of fifty-three, there were twelve stewards whose only job was to look after the Vanderbilt family and servants and their five guests, one of whom was Willie's friend Oliver Hazard Perry Belmont.

The party reached Bombay on Christmas Day and took a private train to Calcutta. Alva felt about India as Margaret did—she was fascinated by the temples and ceremonies but couldn't tolerate the poverty and the oppressed condition of women. She and Willie decided to leave the rest of the group and spend a week at the Government House, where their arguments continued. Alva found a supportive ally in Oliver Belmont. The journey finally disintegrated in the spring of 1894, and against the counsel of her friends and attorneys Alva asked for a divorce. When the decree was granted in March 1895, Alva got to keep the Vanderbilt name and alimony of $100,000 a year and was offered the Vanderbilt home on Fifth Avenue in New York, which she declined. She also received full custody of her three children—Consuelo, eighteen; Willie Jr., seventeen; and Harold, eleven—and disallowed any contact with their father. By the time Margaret Brown came to Newport in 1910, divorce was more commonplace, but in 1895 it was still a scandal. Alva was ostracized by her long-time society friends, although she noted that it was the women who needed divorce the most who condemned her most vehemently. Within a year after her divorce, she said, many other women had found the courage to follow suit.

Once again taking society by surprise, on January 11, 1896, Alva married Oliver Hazard Perry Belmont. Because they both had been divorced, no priest or minister would conduct the ceremony, and they finally asked New York Mayor William L. Strong to marry them. Alva then closed down Marble House and joined Oliver Belmont at Belcourt, also in Newport, so he could be near his beloved horses. Their parties at the turn of the century were the most elaborate in the country, with the great hall at Belcourt accommodating over three hundred guests. Then, without warning, Oliver died in June 1908 after a routine appendectomy. He was fifty years old. Alva was devastated.

Always an adamant liberal and supporter of human rights, Alva threw her time, money, and energy into the women's suffrage movement. Suffrage was not a new idea in New York or Newport; Ida Husted Harper, historian and friend of Susan B. Anthony, came to Newport to lecture, as did Carrie Chapman Catt. In 1909 Alva became a delegate to the International Women's Suffrage Alliance Convention in London and established a suffrage headquarters on Fifth Avenue in New York at her own expense. She founded the Political Equality League and served as its president, establishing several New York branches, including locations at the Harlem Club; the New York Physicians and Surgeons League; and Brookholt, which she converted into a training center for women farmers. Along with Margaret Brown, Alva Belmont became involved in the National Women's Trade Union League, an organization that teamed women in the work force with upper-class women who supported their drive for an eight-hour day and minimum wage for women as well as adequate and affordable child care. Women like Alva Belmont and Margaret Brown were critical to the success of this movement, particularly during the garment industry strikes from 1909 to 1911, as they not only provided great personal and financial support but were able to attract the attention of the media.

Like Margaret, Alva not only began to make speeches around the country but wrote newspaper articles on topics ranging from the rights of women and minorities to fashion, business, travel, and health. In the early stages of the Prohibition movement, its supporters advocated healthier lifestyles, including diet, and in an article for the *Denver Times* Alva—who sometimes had a tendency to become stout—advised women to forsake alcohol, watch their posture, and keep in mind that it wasn't really *what* they ate but *how* they ate it that was important to a healthy diet.[20] Modern technology held many promises for women bound to household duty, and Margaret made a contribution to the "simplified living movement": an electric automobile lunch buffet she designed herself. Resembling a "tiny electric runabout," the four-wheeled buffet featured electric cookers and warmers, a small refrigerator for cold dishes and drinks, a shelf for fruits and bonbons, space for dishes and silverware, and a serving tray. "When Mrs. Brown wishes to entertain her guests with a light, late lunch," the *Denver Times* reported, "the automobile buffet may be wheeled into the room and the guests served from it, a special arrangement being provided for quickly cooking eggs and lobster a la Newberg."[21]

Margaret and Alva had other things in common as well: they both were regularly mocked in the society pages. Colonel William d'Alton Mann, publisher of the scandal rag *Town Topics*—the newspaper upon which Polly Pry first patterned herself back in Denver—was society's self-appointed moral watchdog. His intention was to reform New York's Four Hundred by "making them too deeply disgusted with themselves to continue their silly, empty way of life."[22] But the colonel himself was not beyond reproach. He terrorized prominent families by publishing or threatening to publish lewd gossip to further a blackmail operation that kept his pockets nicely lined for nearly two decades. He held an unbelievable degree of power before being censured by the courts. "'Town Topics' stands for moral purity," he claimed when accused of writing maliciously. "It is written by gentle folk, for gentle folk, on topics of interest to gentle folk."[23] But each issue created a great sensation and was capable of ruining marriages and careers. When there was nothing concrete to say, the colonel still managed to make a point: "Mrs. Belmont dyes her hair. Though covered with diamond rings, her hands are wrinkled like a washerwoman's."[24]

FEMINISTS IN THE Newport and New York area generally fell into one of two camps: Alva Belmont's Political Equality League or Maud Howe Elliot's Newport County Suffrage League (also known as the Woman Suffrage Association of Newport County). The daughter of Julia Ward Howe, Maud Howe Elliott was a writer like her mother and believed that the extravagant New York Four Hundred—most of whom summered in Newport—were having a destructive impact on the quality of life and American ideology in general. The Political Equality League, of which Margaret was a prominent member and Alva Belmont a very vocal president, counted many wealthy New York and Newport women among its members but strove to identify with and support women from all walks of life.

Alva Belmont was one of the first to advocate Margaret's candidacy for political office. Like the suffragettes who had chained themselves to the high-railed fence outside Parliament in London in 1913, American feminists felt that true change would happen only when women held political office. Alva was a natural leader. As one of the organizers of the Women's Vote Parade, she led fifty thousand women and their supporters (including aging actress Lillian Russell) from Central Park down Fifth Avenue to Washington Square. Led by several brass bands and flanked by mounted police, she looked "serene and unselfconscious."[25] But she didn't care to run for office herself.

On February 23, 1914, the *Denver Post* announced that Margaret was "dropping a quiet word here and there" that she would like to succeed Helen Ring Robinson when Robinson gave up her seat as the first and only woman senator in the United States. In a statement perhaps intended to pacify some of the debate about whether or not a woman with domestic responsibilities could adequately hold public office, Margaret stated that since the marriage of her niece Florence, she finally had time to devote herself to more personal ambitions.[26] The next day the *New York City Mail* printed a photograph of Margaret next to a photograph of Helen Ring Robinson, who was lecturing in New York. Already there was speculation about the advisability of one prosuffrage woman vying against another.

But Margaret soon had an opportunity to show the world how she differed from some of her sisters in the fight for women's rights. Tensions between the United States and Mexico, combined with Mexico's internal political conflicts involving Pancho Villa and Emiliano Zapata, had been simmering for months. In 1912 Fort Logan, Colorado, became the headquarters for volunteer regiments destined for service in Mexico.[27] In response to the unending political unrest, a group of Mexican women soldiers organized in the province of Sonora. In Mexico City on April 21, 1914, a committee of women called on General Bianquet, the minister of war, and announced that a regiment of one thousand female soldiers was ready to engage in combat with the United States. They announced to the world that they realized the time had come for every Mexican woman as well as man to come to the defense of her country.

Margaret, who had already made a strong argument for women's rights and responsibilities at sea, agreed. If American women were to share equal rights with men during times of peace, she felt they should be willing to stand side by side with men on the battlefield. She immediately declared that the United States, and Colorado in particular, should send a regiment of "martially inclined" women soldiers to the front should war be declared with Mexico.

The idea was greeted with incredulity and ridicule. A reporter from the *Rocky Mountain News* immediately set out to find Denver women who would be willing to enlist. Dr. Jeanette Bolles said she certainly would. "Didn't the pioneer women of the West shoulder the musket with their menfolks and fight the Indians? Why shouldn't the women of today be able to do what they did?" Alma Lafferty, former legislator and president of the Women's Peace Association, said, "I wouldn't be afraid to go to the front. I have been in politics, remember. But Mrs. Brown can not count on me to enlist. It horrifies me to think that any woman should want to fight. There is never any necessity for war. It is uncivilized." Mary Lathrop, an attorney, said that although she was a strong woman, "I am beyond the age limit." And Mrs. E.P. Costigan, president of the Denver Press Woman's Club and a good friend of Margaret, hedged her bet: "I don't say I wouldn't enlist, but before I go to war I want my husband to go. I think he ought to go first. I am willing to go along and carry the bullets while he shoulders the musket."[28]

Reporters enjoyed the more colorful responses to Margaret's proposed regiment. Mrs. Harry Bellamy was willing but had certain reservations regarding dress. Noting that the "slit skirt would be exceedingly dangerous," she conceded that the new regiment would require a new kind of women's fashion.[29] Mrs. Martha Cranmer was perhaps most critical: "There are women who can shoot straight. However, mistakes will happen. I can conceive of the possibility of a member of Mrs. Brown's regiment shooting a comrade when she meant to aim at one of the enemy."[30]

Nevertheless, Margaret persevered and on April 23, 1914, sent a telegram to Senator Shafroth of Colorado to offer her personal services as a nurse and $1,000 a month to organize and equip a group of nurses to help in the conflict. Her message was read aloud in the Senate chamber. The next day Margaret received a telegram from Mildred Morris in Denver confirming that preparations had begun for a regiment of women soldiers to begin training: "Regiment of Colorado women being organized for service in Mexico. Want you to head it. Will you answer immediately? Regiment will do service in Red Cross if services as soldiers are rejected. Great opportunity to show that women with equal rights with men are willing to bear war burdens with men."[31] Margaret wired her acceptance.

The idea met with favor—in some circles—in New York. Colonel J. Hungerford Milbank had been one of the most active women fighting for suffrage and was a strong advocate of any type of reform that would help gender equality. Although she was married, she had long ago abandoned the title "Mrs." and inscribed her cards "J. Hungerford Milbank," believing that the custom of designating whether a woman was married or not was "absurd and unjust" considering the fact that no such designation was used by men. She organized a women's military company in New York, conducting drills in the Fourteenth Regiment Armory in Brooklyn. A New York newspaper mused, "What a strange freak of fate would it be if Uncle Sam accepted the services of the two regiments of women that have been offered him and that the Mexican and American Amazons would clash in combat."[32]

But Margaret's attention was diverted once again—and this time the conflict was closer to home. The United Garment Workers' Union of

Denver, based on Margaret's past assistance and her widely publicized offer of military aid, sent her an ominous telegram:

> Reading your generous and patriotic offer to our Government in the Mexican affair, we would call your attention to the terrible condition existing in the coal fields of Colorado, your fair state, where defenceless [sic] women and innocent babies are being murdered and burned alive by mine guards wearing our country's uniform. Knowing you spent your early life in the same environment, we appeal to your generous and sympathetic nature in behalf of our widowed sisters and orphaned babes in this State. We have volunteered the services of our organization, 400 members, to serve as Blue Cross nurses for our brothers fighting for their homes and loved ones against more heartless brutes than the Mexicans ever were.[33]

Margaret, well aware of the labor issues that had plagued Colorado mines for years, declared that she could not neglect an appeal from her own state. She canceled her plans to go to Mexico and took the next train to Denver instead.

At the Ludlow coal camp just north of Trinidad, and throughout southern Colorado, labor issues had been simmering for months, and the situation was critical. Trinidad was home not only to generations of Hispanic miners but also to a strong Italian and Greek community. Many of the benefits among the miners' demands were already supposedly guaranteed by Colorado law, but the laws had not been enforced. Miners and their families were forced to live in company-owned houses and buy their food and supplies at company-owned stores, and there were no schools available for children. Company scrip was issued as payment to the miners. The most volatile issues, however, centered on a guaranteed minimum wage and eight-hour day as well as recognition of the miners' union and the fact that hostile mine guards were reputedly hired from the local penitentiary. James Grant, previous governor of Colorado, spoke on behalf of the American Smelter and Refining Company (ASARCO) when he said, "The Western Federation of Miners now want eight hours. If we grant them that it will be only a question of time before they are asking for six."[34] Another significant lobbying point was the fact that owing to unsafe working conditions, Colorado had the highest coal mine fatality rate in the world. Hoping that the Colorado Fuel and Iron Company, the Rocky Mountain Fuel Company, and the Victor American

Fuel Company might agree to collective bargaining, union leader Frank J. Hayes twice held joint conferences, followed by a conference the miners themselves organized in Trinidad on September 15, 1913. But the mine operators refused to attend. On September 23, 1913, a strike was declared, and over eleven thousand men, or 95 percent of the total work force in southern Colorado, went on strike. The Ludlow miners were immediately evicted from their homes. With winter just ahead, the United Mine Workers (UMW) of America set up a colony of two hundred tents spread over forty acres and housing nearly a thousand people.

The conflict escalated when the Baldwin-Felts industrial detective organization appeared on the scene, followed by the Colorado National Guard under the command of Adjutant General John Chase along with Major Pat Hamrock and Lieutenant K.E. Linderfelt. Union organizers were taken hostage; many members of the new Colorado militia were company gunmen who had been quickly sworn in as soldiers. On April 20, 1914, members of the national guard demanded that Louis Tikas, leader of the Greeks, surrender two Italian men. Tikas refused to give up the men without a warrant for their arrest. A signal bomb was followed by a spray of bullets that killed five miners: Charles Costa; Frank Rubino; John Bartoloti; Louis Tikas, who was bludgeoned with the butt end of a rifle and then shot; and James Fyler, financial secretary of the Trinidad local union, an unarmed prisoner who was robbed as well as shot.[35] As evening settled, families fled to the surrounding hills. The soldiers—whom some accused of consuming liquor they had looted from the local saloon—set fire to the tent colony with oil-soaked torches and burned it to the ground. In a dugout under the largest tent were found the bodies of eleven children and two women—one apparently pregnant—who had been hiding in an underground cellar.

Mary Harris "Mother" Jones, a well-known labor organizer for the UMW, was present throughout the strike even though she was in her eighties. A petite woman capable of looking like someone's grandmother or swearing a blue streak, depending on what the situation required, she was called "the miners' angel" by the miners—although coal mine owners called her "the most dangerous woman in America."[36] Mother Jones wrote, "The smoke of armed battle rose from the arroyos and ravines of the Rocky Mountains. No one listened. No one cared. ... Then came Ludlow and the nation heard. Little children roasted alive make a front-page story. Dying by inches of starvation or exposure does not."[37] She claimed that the massacre had occurred by order of Lieutenant Linderfelt, "a savage, brutal executor of the will of the Colorado Fuel and Iron Company."

Margaret Brown arrived in Denver shortly after the massacre. "It makes no difference to me where I go," she declared. "I am ready to go anywhere that I am needed."[38] She immediately helped organize a corps of nurses to provide immediate relief as well as a committee to travel to Ludlow and review the situation while she remained temporarily in Denver to muster financial support. "I believe that the committee which has gone to the strike zone to investigate will do wonders," she said. "A large relief fund must be raised immediately so assistance can be offered as soon as the Peace League committee makes its report from Ludlow and Trinidad."[39] Margaret believed she could summon "scores of the nation's leading women" to help with the Ludlow situation. In a move similar to what she had done for Leadville miners in years past, she sent two hundred pairs of shoes and basic clothing for the miners' families.

Margaret met with representatives of the Denver United Garment Workers' Union, the Women's Peace Association, and the Young Women's Christian Association and arranged a benefit entertainment to be given on Friday of the second week of May, sponsored by the newly formed Women's Relief Committee. As chair of the committee she visited all the theaters in the city to convince stars of local shows to perform for free and paid for the rental of an auditorium herself. Proceeds from the event would buy clothing, shoes, and supplies for the miners' families.

"I am not taking sides," she said, "and am here to help all who need aid. I am interested in humanity and will do my duty impartially and conscientiously."[40] She declared that she refused to ally herself with either capital or labor but wanted to help the suffering families of both sides— militiamen had not been paid since January, and the strikers had been out of work since September.[41] However, as in the past, she felt that her most valuable role was as a publicist and educator. She organized lectures and granted newspaper interviews to raise awareness of the issue and gain public support. She described not only the conditions that led to the strike but the strenuous lives of the miners. Each morning at five A.M. the men climbed seven hundred feet to reach the mouth of the mine, and after they descended into the mine they rarely saw daylight, emerging again at or after nightfall. "Oilskin suits and caps have to be worn to shed the dampness in the mines, and in cold weather the hardships are doubled," she said. In the early aftermath of the Ludlow massacre, Margaret took a conciliatory approach. "Many of the deaths resulting from the firing and burning of the Ludlow camp were unintentional," she said. "The miners had dug trenches for their wives and children which saved them from the bullets, but were no protection against the smoke and flames. The people were also deceived by the military uniforms, which they took to mean was the symbol of the State's protection."[42]

But she began to abandon her moderate stance as detailed reports became available. On May 1, 1914, several people representing the miners' interests (including feminist Emma Goldman) were sent to visit John D. Rockefeller Sr. and demand arbitration in the Colorado mine strikes. Along with other women, Margaret picketed the CFI offices in Denver. Rockefeller refused, although his son, John D. Rockefeller Jr., came to Colorado to assess the situation. Rockefeller's biographer Ron Chernow wrote, "At CFI [Colorado Fuel and Iron] the Rockefellers found themselves in the indefensible position of being all-powerful yet passive amid a spiraling crisis."[43] The senior Rockefeller turned the problem over to his son, who "felt it his duty to engineer a turnaround situation, showing his father he could solve a difficult situation."[44] While admitting that the strike problem stemmed from the corrupt political influences and dominance of the Colorado Fuel and Iron Company, Margaret emphasized that John D. Rockefeller was not personally to blame except in the indirect way of being chief stockholder in the company's mining interests. "He knows nothing of the conditions there and is merely the target in the matter," she said.[45]

She then packed up her khaki dress and camping outfit—a detail duly noted by the press—and went to Ludlow herself. When she returned, she no longer defended Rockefeller. "There is but one solution to the present unrest," she said. "The solution is for the people of Colorado to rise in a body and demand that Rockefeller put into practice that which he has been teaching his Sunday school class. For years, this man has stood before his class and told them the answer to an ancient Biblical question. The question is, 'Am I my brother's keeper?' Now it is time that the entire state demand that he settle the strike."[46] John D. Rockefeller Jr. nevertheless maintained his position against the miners and claimed that the actions of the militia had been an act of self-defense.[47] "The Ludlow disaster," Chernow wrote, "threatened to undo all [Rockefeller Jr.'s] efforts to cleanse the family name."[48]

Margaret was critical of the more militant tactics of the union and stated that problems had been exacerbated by the fact that people from "thirty-two nations" were employed in the coal mines.

> The warring union miners have been augmented by a large number of
> aliens not unionized, but who share their grievances. Back of the fighting
> miners are all of the resources of the United Mine Workers of America,
> supplemented by the assistance of sympathetic labor organizations. But
> all of the revenue that can be mustered by the labor organizations is a
> mere bagatelle compared to the almost inexhaustible means of the oppos-
> ing capitalists. Mr. Rockefeller alone can almost treble the resources of
> the miners without any effort whatsoever.
>
> The inequality of the contest has driven the miners to their dependable
> ally—public sympathy. There is no question that the strong feeling of
> sympathy for the miner prevails. The stubborn unyielding attitude of the
> operators, the poor handling of the affair on the part of the Governor,
> the appalling catastrophes which have attended the clashes between the
> armed miners and the militia—all of these have prejudiced the public in
> favor of the "man from the depths."

Margaret went on to talk about her own family history with respect to working out labor difficulties. "In the mines of my family we had our troubles," she said, "but we met the just demands of our workmen and today we find them raising and educating intelligent and high types of families that will be a credit to any land. The recognition of the union is a mere thing for any capitalist. I have had the same thing brought forcibly home to me. I personally joined the union, got my card, and went back to the men. I told them that I was one of them and that we must pull together."[49]

Margaret accomplished her goal of garnering national and even international attention. For the next year she continued to lecture on the Ludlow massacre, as did Helen Ring Robinson, who was also in Trinidad shortly after the event. Six months after the killings, a slight problem occurred when Margaret received an itemized bill for $1,000 in expenses that had been charged by members of the committee sent to investigate the disaster. "I am a bit peeved, yes," she told a reporter. "It was my purpose to buy provisions and things for needy women and children, whereas I find that a goodly part of my money went for railroad and hotel bills for a lot of women who were more concerned about personal notoriety than they were about relieving the suffering at Ludlow." She accused Helen Ring Robinson and Alma Lafferty, both friends and fellow suffragists, of using her money to their own advantage. Robinson and Lafferty protested that they had used none of Mrs. Brown's personal money. Rather than play out the problem in the press, Margaret paid the bill and returned to New York with "a number of bitter memories, an equal number of bills marked 'paid in full,' and a determination to look well before she leaps in the future."[50]

John D. Rockefeller Jr. eventually softened his view toward the miners and their families and set in motion plans for a joint labor-management grievance committee as well as changes in health, sanitation, mine safety, recreation, and education policies.[51] But Ludlow would not be forgotten. The story became representative of the most explosive and divisive aspects of Eastern capitalists versus Western labor and entered the realm of American folklore with poems and songs, including "Struggle," penned by Woody Guthrie in 1946. Today a memorial—including the underground tunnel that entombed the women and children—stands in the middle of a lonely field a few hours south of Denver.

MARGARET RETURNED TO Newport in time to help Alva Belmont prepare for an international conference on July 25, 1914, celebrating women's rights and sponsored by the Political Equality League. "Newport is to be the centre of a vigorous movement among suffragists for new members not only in this city, but over the entire country," reported the *Newport Journal & Weekly News.*[52] Consuelo, Alva's daughter, wrote in a letter that her mother was "sacrificing her time, her wealth, even her personal feelings" to the women's rights movement.[53] But victory—winning the right to vote—seemed close. Much to the chagrin of her conservative Newport neighbors, Alva announced that she was reopening Marble House, closed since the death of her beloved husband, for a convention that would dwarf all of her earlier conferences. (Julia Ward Howe had attended a previous conference in 1909, remarking that there were about five hundred people "mostly very smartly dressed."[54]) The staunchest members of Newport society were appalled. Summer colonist Elizabeth Drexel Lehr exclaimed, "By all means walk in processions, or demonstrate your sympathies in any way

that appealed to you, but why let loose a horde of fanatics on the strong-
hold of your friends?"[55] Alva Belmont paid no attention to such protests,
and an enormous tent was erected on the grounds, a speaker's platform
built, and "Votes for Women" flags hung from two seventy-five-foot
flagpoles. Admission to the conference was $5, and the money went to
the cause of suffrage. Mrs. Lehr's fears became reality as women from
all walks of life "swarmed into the house that had earned the reputation
as being one of the most exclusive in Newport ... women in shirtwaists,
their jackets hanging over their arms, women carrying umbrellas and
paper bags. Man-hating college women with screwed-back hair and thin-
lipped, determined faces; old countrywomen red-cheeked and homely,
giggling shopgirls. ... What a contrast to the elegant garden parties of
former years, the splendid entertainments."[56]

The conference began with a reception to honor Alva's daughter,
Consuelo, the duchess of Marlborough, who had just arrived from
England. In her opening remarks Alva set off a flurry of reporters' pens
when she said, "The time is passing when a married woman might be
referred to as any man's wife. The women of tomorrow will be too
independent to tolerate any such expression." She then turned the stage
over to Consuelo, who began by describing her work in England with
Homes for Prisoners' Wives and Children and Hostels for Women.
Since 1904 she had worked to help families of prisoners find ways to
"tide over the time while bereft of the breadwinner without offering
them charity and the corresponding loss of self-respect." She had
opened a home and helped women obtain jobs, later adding another
building where the women could be self-employed as seamstresses and
laundresses. Her greater work, however, was an organization she had
formed that sought to secure respectable lodging houses or hostels for
working girls and women. Corporations in England and Scotland were
lobbied to provide "decent and respectable" hostels at the lowest possible price for working women, and Consuelo herself built a model hostel
accommodating fifty-six women. "For ten cents a woman can obtain a
full day's lodging, with a private bedroom and the use of kitchen, bath,
and sitting rooms. Food can be purchased at equally low rates, and they
can buy it cooked or cook it themselves," she said. The home, which
at that time had been open for just nine months, had been consistently
full. "The word home is essentially feminine," Consuelo declared, "and
if we destroy its meaning to a woman it is not only her loss, but a loss

to the whole structure of the State, which takes the home and family as its foundation. ... It is in order to obtain reforms such as these that we women are asking for the vote. Those of us who are engaged in any form of social service realize that without legislation individual and voluntary work can accomplish but little."[57]

Consuelo's comments were followed by addresses by Maude Ballington Booth of the Volunteers of America; Rose Schneiderman, known as "Rosie the garment worker," vice president of the Woman's Trade Union League; Mary M. Bartelme, assistant judge of the Chicago Juvenile Court; Katherine B. Davis, commissioner of correction of New York; Ella Flagg Young, superintendent of the Chicago public schools; Kate M. Gordon, president of the Southern States Women's Suffrage Association; and Florence Kelly, secretary of the National Consumers' League, among others. Colorado State Senator Helen Ring Robinson, who stayed at Margaret's home during the conference, stood on the stage and declared, "I want to tell you unpleasant things. The shame of Colorado is your shame, your problems just as truly as our problems. You speak of the infamy of the Colorado militia. What about the infamy of the West Virginia and Michigan militia?"[58]

This view was emphasized that very evening when Margaret Brown addressed an overflowing audience at the Woman's Suffrage headquarters. The New York newspapers quickly noted that although Margaret was the wife of a mine owner, she was in "complete sympathy and acquaintance with the workers." Margaret declared that the strike in Colorado was not merely the problem of an individual state but was of nationwide importance, as conditions were the same in mines throughout the country. After her lengthy speech there was a general discussion, and one audience member asked Margaret what the remedy might be for America's great "industrial evils." Her suggestion was for a "rights-for-all" movement that would bring a halt to industrial and political greed; universal suffrage, she claimed, was the key to larger reform.[59]

Suffrage events continued for the next two weeks. On July 19, 1914, Judge Ben Lindsey spoke with Alva Belmont in front of a large gathering at Margaret's cottage under the auspices of the Congressional Union for Woman Suffrage, founded and chaired by Alice Paul and considered one of the more militant suffrage organizations. His subject was "child welfare," and Lindsey defined the distinction between criminal behavior and mere mischief in children and traced the development of juvenile law in the United States and abroad. "Courts now deal with *persons* and not merely with what they do," he said. Over $1,000 was raised for Lindsey's juvenile work.

After the Marble House conference, many of the women formed a national speaking tour called the Hughes Alliance and toured twenty-eight states, giving lectures in seventy-six cities. But it would be another six years before women's suffrage became a reality. Alva Belmont was president of the National Woman's Party in 1919 when the constitutional amendment granting women the right to vote was drafted. After its passage in 1920 Alva took her show on the road and set out to enfranchise women in other countries. Whenever there was an international convention pertaining to law, Alva set up an office to ensure that "no international code of law would be projected on a basis of inequality for women."

The 1914 Marble House conference lingered in the minds of astonished Newporters, and some participants' remarks became legendary. One English suffragette told the gathering, "They say in London that I've got the brains of a man. Well, I should like to see the man whose brains I have!"

ENCOURAGED BY ALVA BELMONT and Judge Ben Lindsey, Margaret began to rally her supporters in a bid for political office. Her campaign was undertaken by the Congressional Union, fueled by the combined efforts of Alva Belmont and Alice Paul. Her candidacy for a seat in the Senate was endorsed by Mrs. Laidlaw, president of the National Women's Suffrage Association of New York, and on July 10, 1914, the Rhode Island Suffrage Association announced its support as well. Back in Colorado, partially due to her involvement in the aftermath of the Ludlow massacre, Margaret had the combined support of Progressives and Democrats in Denver, who selected her as their candidate for the House of Representatives on a fusion ticket,[60] and the full support of Colorado suffragists.[61] Some New York suffragists opposed Margaret's candidacy, as they accused her and other wealthy feminists such as Alva Belmont and Anne Morgan of taking a "voyeuristic interest in poverty and publicity" and pejoratively termed such women "the Mink Brigade."[62]

Margaret's candidacy was controversial for a number of other reasons as well. The most vocal opponent was Dr. Anna Shaw, president of the

National American Woman Suffrage Association (NAWSA), a rival organization of Alva Belmont's. Back in 1869 the American women's rights movement had split over disagreements regarding the Fourteenth and Fifteenth Amendments. More liberal feminists joined Elizabeth Cady Stanton and Susan B. Anthony to form the New York–based National Woman Suffrage Association (NWSA). Feminists who tended to be more conservative formed the Boston-based American Woman Suffrage Association (AWSA), organized by Lucy Stone, Henry Blackwell, and Julia Ward Howe. In 1890 the two organizations joined forces as the National American Woman Suffrage Association under Elizabeth Cady Stanton's leadership.

Anna Shaw, a physician and ordained minister, served as president of NAWSA from 1904 to 1915. Although an ardent advocate of suffrage, she was a controversial leader and was sometimes accused of holding a rather narrow view regarding women's political progress. Dr. Shaw said that in her opinion, it was treason for a woman to run against any other woman who had stood loyally for the cause of suffrage—in this case, Helen Ring Robinson. She accused followers of Margaret Brown and Alva Belmont of merely striving to get a woman from their camp into the legislature. Dr. Shaw also stated that she felt a strong male candidate in support of suffrage would be more effective in advancing the cause than a female candidate.

The issue was further complicated by the fact that despite Margaret's background and involvement in Colorado's political issues, many Westerners viewed her life in the East—and involvement with high-brow Eastern society—with suspicion. Some Easterners, on the other hand, considered Westerners uncultured and unsophisticated, and dismissed Margaret because of her humble Irish roots and years of living in a mining camp. The *Denver Post* reported that Margaret's candidacy "has started a lively tilt among the local suffragists and the national suffragettes that may result in a nationwide split of the feminist party."[63] A New York paper crowed, "Now it appears that the Army of Suffrage is divided against itself."[64]

Margaret told the newspapers she was staying out of the fray and "silently sawing wood," preparing her campaign and trying to determine beyond a doubt whether she would have enough support in Colorado to make a successful bid. In an interview with the *New York Times* she said, "If I go into this fight I am going to win. There will be no mincing matters—no pink tea policies. It will be a regular man's kind of campaign—stump speaking, spreadeagle and all. That I should be mentioned as a possible candidate for United States Representative from my home state—Colorado—is glory enough for any one woman. There is only one greater glory—to *be* that representative."[65]

The *Washington D.C. Pathfinder* supported Margaret's bid, calling her an "out-and-out, patriotic American."[66] At first, the fact that she was a wife, mother, and devoted aunt seemed to work in her favor. "A woman who has rocked so many cradles should be able to handle the United States Senate easily," one paper noted. But soon the debate regarding the suitability of a female representative—or whether male politicians would or should allow women in their midst—filled the newspapers. A New York paper noted,

Chances are that [Mrs. Brown] will be elected, as she has a strong following among both sexes. There is no constitutional disqualification of a woman member. But each house of congress is given the right to decide its own membership, having the power to reject any person as such. If the house should decide to declare Mrs. Brown ineligible, there is no power that could compel it to seat her. The Supreme Court would have no jurisdiction. So it is up to the congressmen themselves, and they are doing some tall thinking. To bar a woman might cause them to lose some votes in their own districts, or to let her in might cause them to lose some. They hardly know which, and that is where the proposition becomes very binding.

The antisuffrage and anti–women's rights movement had gathered steam. The *Newport Daily News* reported, "Cheering news comes from all the state associations opposed to woman suffrage," and numbers in antisuffrage organizations were rising.[67] Helen Ring Robinson, who was accustomed to personal criticism and was quick to speak up about it, had once said, "All those stories you read in the ladies' lingerie journals are false. Our feminine officeholders do not have faces like vinegar jugs. Neither do they drink cocktails and highballs and stuff ballot boxes as the 'antis' say they do." She recalled that when she first entered politics in 1889, people were astonished to learn that despite the fact that she was a politician, she still wore trailing gowns and took pains with her hair.[68]

Margaret was philosophical about her opposition. "Here I am," she said, "a woman who has traveled all over the world, who has eaten with chop sticks, sat tailor fashion, taught her son to dive and ride. I have even put on the [boxing] gloves with him. And I suppose there are some persons who would like me to sit down to devote the rest of my life to bridge. Times have changed, and there's no reason why I should, like my mother at forty, put on glasses and do little but read."[69]

Like Mother Jones, however, Margaret had learned to use the media to her advantage—and quickly earned the reputation of being a woman who could "show the iron hand beneath the glove of glistening silk."[70] She had been a winner in everything she undertook, she said, and if she was nominated, she was certain of election,[71] though her opponent would, indeed, have been the only other female senator in office. Helen Ring Robinson—although at first in favor of Margaret's candidacy— was uncertain about giving up her high-profile position, and NAWSA officials felt that it would be detrimental to the suffrage cause to have a woman run against another prosuffrage woman. Margaret consequently set her sights on Charles Thomas's Senate seat. Her belief in Colorado as a progressive and forward-thinking state was unshakable. "Our men out in Colorado do not question our right to vote," she said. "They have faith in our ability to maintain our mental and moral balance at the polls as well as at home. They realize our right to have a speaking part in the affairs of the country in which we, as well as they, must live. They have seen the results of such faith, and they are willing to give us a partnership in affairs of government. In other words, our men believe in us."[72] Helen Ring Robinson had earlier stated the situation in slightly different terms: "If the men ever tried to take the vote away from the women in Colorado, there would be things doing there that would make little old London look like Sleepy Hollow."[73]

Margaret continued to fight the Eastern perception that women in the West were uneducated and unsophisticated. "It is a mistake to think that Western women are crude and provincial," she protested. "There are hundreds, thousands, of wonderfully brilliant women in Colorado. They are largely the flower of womanhood from the East, the North, the South—women who have dared leave their native homes to come out where they might expand, found new homes, enlarge their horizon."[74]

As Margaret traveled around the country making speeches and granting interviews, she brought along young Helen Tobin, who had followed in the steps of her sister Florence and become famous for her dancing. At a dance exhibition on August 1, 1914, in Newport,

Helen impressed the crowd with her version of the Lulufado and the Argentine Serenade, the latest Parisian favorites. Both Helen and Margaret created a sensation on the campaign trail, and Margaret had a strong following. The *New York Times,* however, anticipated the mood of the nation when a reporter wrote,

> In proposing to nominate Mrs. James J. Brown of Denver and Newport for Congress her friends probably intend no more than to pay her a compliment and are aware of the kind that will please her. Mrs. Brown has displayed a good deal of activity and energy in a number of ways, and at the time of the Titanic disaster she showed courage and resource-fulness. ... If Hobson can run for office as "the hero of the Merrimac," why not Mrs. Brown as "the heroine of the Titanic"?
>
> But she probably will not. Women divide pretty much as men do in politics, and though they have the vote in ten States they have shown no disposition to make sex a determining consideration in electing candi-dates. Strange to say, they vote on party lines, and when party lines are broken they bolt in the same direction that men do—except in a few rare instances, as where they supported Judge Lindsey in a body when he was running independently. Colorado is the leading suffrage state, because it is the only large one where woman suffrage is more than an experiment, but in Colorado very few women have ever been elected to the Legislature, usually not more than one in any given election. The machines are not likely to nominate a woman for Congress, and an independent nomina-tion would probably give Mrs. Brown merely the pleasure of running.[75]

Once again, however, fate took an unexpected turn. On June 14, 1914, Austrian Crown Prince Franz Ferdinand and his wife, the Duchess of Hohenberg, were assassinated in their automobile by a Serbian nation-alist in the town of Sarajevo. A few weeks later Margaret received an urgent telegram from her sister, Helen, the Baroness Von Reitzenstein, in Germany stating that her husband had been called to the front to serve on the staff of Emperor William. Helen was forced to remain in Pottsdam, near Berlin. Her political advisers counseled her to postpone her bid. Margaret, who had already been contacted by the Vanderbilt family to help with establishing medical relief facilities in France, finally concurred. On August 11, 1914, she wired Helen Ring Robinson and stated that she would not attend the congressional primaries. "At the present time," she said, "I believe those in congress might be permitted to remain to finish the important business there, especially as war is on in several European countries."[76] However, she made it clear that she was merely postponing her political aspirations, and hoped two years thence to unseat U.S. Senator Charles S. Thomas, whose political career in Colorado had been characterized by scandal. Judge Ben Lindsey, and many others, considered Thomas an integral part of Denver's "machine politics," and Helen Ring Robinson herself (who had authored the book *Preparing Women for Suffrage*) stated repeatedly that she felt conditions were ripe for Margaret to begin her campaign for the nomination to succeed Thomas, whose term would expire in 1916. Margaret set her sights on the Senate bid, and the *New York Times* reported that "the women of Colorado are anxious to have [her] accept the nomination for United States Senator next fall."[77] Helen, however, did not share her aunt's political passions. "I don't see how Auntie expects to get any fun out of being a senator," she sniffed to a reporter at the Biltmore in New York City.

In the early fall of 1914, Margaret decided to follow William Jennings Bryan's example and "go on the lyceum platform" to familiarize the public with her goals and ideals. She developed a series of lectures on human rights, suffrage, the Ludlow incident, the life and writings of Mark Twain, and her travels and experiences in Europe and India. Her popular presentations included several hundred slides, and she gained reputation as a compelling and colorful speaker. She also began to prepare for her work overseas.

FAMILY ISSUES, HOWEVER, continued to occupy a large part of Margaret's life. Despite the fact that she and J.J. were separated and their relationship was sometimes acrimonious, J.J. continued to try to "keep her afloat" in her various financial endeavors, and she not only spoke of him with respect but worried about his continuing health problems. In January 1913 he underwent an operation in Los Angeles. Helen—who had been traveling frequently with Margaret—met him back in Tucson at his desert bungalow and spent the winter nursing him back to health.

Lawrence and Eileen, now with two small children (a son, Lawrence Jr., eventually known as "Pat," and a daughter, Elizabeth, known as "Betty" or "Bets," born July 30, 1913), struggled with their marriage and Lawrence's constantly changing employment situation. J.J. had promised both Lawrence and Helen that when the time was right, he would help them each build or buy a house. In the fall of 1914 he commissioned an architect to draw up plans for a home for Lawrence and Eileen. But the plans were loftier than J.J. expected. "The beauty of the structure on which you plan is good evidence of your broad ideas, as well, I might say, your extravagant inclinations," J.J. tactfully wrote the architect, who had consulted with Lawrence. "I would like to build such a house for my boy, but the cost of the building will far exceed anything which I had in mind."[78] Although J.J. and Lawrence were getting along better than they had in the past, J.J. nevertheless felt that Lawrence still hadn't settled into a solid career and, in light of a "lean salary," lived beyond his means.

Eileen might have agreed, although there were other problems as well. Years later she remarked that living with Lawrence was never dull. "He had a bad habit of chasing women," she noted. "He was extremely popular and could dance divinely. These two qualities were especially attractive to women. Laurie [her nickname for Lawrence] was very handsome, having had inherited his mother's full lips and soft eyes."[79] With very little fanfare, on July 5, 1915, Lawrence and Eileen Brown were granted a divorce in Jefferson County. Each parent was awarded custody of one child.

Margaret was shocked and dismayed. When she received the news she returned to Denver to try to effect a reconciliation between Lawrence and Eileen. She felt that their marital problems were a result of "temperament" and were not serious enough to warrant a complete separation, especially considering the ages of the children. "I know they will realize they cannot live apart," she said. She visited Lawrence in Golden, Colorado, where in the fall of 1915, still determined to make something of his life and perhaps in deference to his father's wishes, he had enrolled at Colorado School of Mines. On November 19, 1915, he was initiated into the Kappa Sigma Fraternity, one of the first fraternities at the college. Despite his recent divorce, these were happy days for Lawrence—his scrapbook is filled with photos, including one of a line of young men, the "class of 1918," trying to toss each other into Clear Creek in a rowdy tug of war. He managed to complete two full semesters before the war interfered.

Despite Margaret's good intentions, her attempt at saving her son's marriage was futile. What she wasn't able to accomplish, however, world politics did—the advent of World War I suddenly changed the couple's priorities. Just before Lawrence was sent to Europe, the couple remarried, much to the relief of both families. "Romance again has entered into the lives of Captain Lawrence P. Brown and Mrs. Eileen Horton Brown," the Denver papers reported—although Lawrence had successfully managed to keep his divorce out of the gossip pages. "When Laurie left for the war," Eileen recalled, "the whole family went down to New York to see him off." The marriage held steady for another eight years.

WHEN THE WAR first broke out, Margaret sent a wire to Admiral Austin M. Knight, commander of the second naval district, and offered her twenty-six-room Newport cottage, Mon Etui, as a hospital facility, which she was willing to equip herself.[80] Her telegram was forwarded to Senator Shafroth, a personal friend of Mrs. Brown, who referred the offer to the Secretary of War and the Senate. In late 1914 Margaret raised a service flag over her front porch for Lawrence and donated Mon Etui to the Newport Chapter of the American Red Cross. With a pair of trained nurses and several trunks of medical equipment, she then sailed to France to help establish a relief station. A New York reporter noted, "If I were requested to personify perpetual activity, I believe I'd name Mrs. James J. Brown, the Newport social figure, suffragette, patriot."[81]

By the time the United States under President Woodrow Wilson entered World War I in 1917, the most devastating years of the war had already passed. But many American volunteers joined the French cause early on, particularly in the field of medical assistance. Due to the high number of Americans living in Paris (including a large community of young American women living independently on the Left Bank), in 1910 the first American hospital was established in Paris on Rue Chauveau in Neuilly-sur-Seine.

During the first days of the war, Myron T. Herrick, an American ambassador, joined the director of the American Hospital to inquire about the possibility of building ambulances for the hospital. The response was more than favorable—the surgeon general of the French army suggested that the Americans undertake what the Red Cross alone could not accomplish: convert Neuilly's new, large school into a military hospital with a fleet of ten ambulances. Originally scheduled to open for students on October 1, 1914, the beautiful new school was instead transformed into an auxiliary military hospital run by American volunteers. For the first time in history, motorized ambulances were used. Mrs. William K. Vanderbilt donated the motor transport, and Harold White, manager of the Ford Motor Company's assembly plant in nearby Levallois-Perret, arranged for ten Model-T chassis. With the help of a local carriage builder, the ambulances were constructed by building a board floor on the body of the automobile, with room for two stretchers. A canvas roof supported by ribs stretched over the top. The driver sat on an open seat consisting of a plank over the gas tank. Once completed, the vehicles were each painted with a large red cross and the words "American Ambulance." On September 7, 1914, the first convoy of American ambulances headed for the front.

Eventually the Red Cross established more than 1,500 auxiliary hospitals in France, 300 in Paris alone. The violence that gripped Belgium in July and August 1914 gradually moved toward Paris, where for three years forces clashed along a front stretching from the Somme to the Vosges. The relief effort was immediately organized on both sides, and the numbers of wounded soldiers were nearly overwhelming.

Margaret Brown arrived in Paris to help with the American ambulance system, although she would earn her French Legion of Honor award primarily for the work she accomplished alongside Anne Morgan, daughter of J.P. Morgan. For Margaret, France was like her second home. Like many other Americans from wealthy or elite backgrounds, she had originally come to France to study culture. But her desire to help went beyond cultural and social motivations and her Christian-based humanism. The situation in France appealed to the tradition of charity among the ruling classes, "who were both Anglophiles and Francophiles and sensitive to the age-old watchword, noblesse oblige."[82]

American financiers and diplomats put their money and influence behind the war effort, and their wives, sisters, and daughters stepped in to organize and implement relief programs. The women enjoyed a great deal of freedom not only because of the necessity of humanitarian aid but because as foreigners they were allowed a certain amount of freedom of action. Representing the first generation of American women to truly benefit from higher education, they were able to put their intellectual and financial abilities to good use, with the full support of society on both sides of the Atlantic.

The Vanderbilt family made substantial contributions of time and money. Back in Newport Grace Vanderbilt and Cornelius Vanderbilt Jr., with the assistance of their mother, Mrs. Cornelius Vanderbilt, collected reading material to send to the troops. A dog show was held to raise money for surgical supplies for the French, and a black-and-white ball raised money for dependents of National Guardsmen.[83] But the most important relief efforts, of course, happened overseas. Mrs. William K. Vanderbilt presided over all the Red Cross Auxiliary hospitals, and Margaret first sailed to France to help in her efforts at Neuilly-sur-Seine. Mary Van Vorst, an American Red Cross volunteer, described her first encounter with Mrs. Vanderbilt. Driving up to the pink terraced building that had been converted from a boys' school to a Red Cross hospital, she noticed the row of famous khaki-colored motor ambulances before pushing open the door and going in search of Mrs. Vanderbilt. She wrote,

> I have always wanted to know Mrs. Vanderbilt. The first thing I heard
> about her was that she was doing good. It impressed me in a vague way.
> And then I heard again that she was doing more and greater good; until
> finally she grew to stand for me as someone constantly doing good every-
> where—a most enviable reputation. ... When I pushed open that door at
> the American Ambulance and went in and found myself actually standing
> before Mrs. Vanderbilt, without any introduction, I did not realize even
> then that a long-looked-for moment had come. Even in that moment, I
> forgot who she was in my desire to become sensibly part of that great
> machine, the American Ambulance, and I forgot that the quiet, dignified
> woman in her nurse's dress was the great and celebrated Mrs. Vanderbilt.[84]

After April 1917, when the United States finally entered the war, many of the American volunteer activities became militarized, but a new wave of American volunteers came to France. The American Committee for Devastated France (called CARD after its French acronym) was formed with the intention of helping to rebuild devastated areas behind the front line. The French high command believed that the reconstitution of civilian life would boost morale and remind French soldiers, mentally and physically exhausted, of the cause for which they were fighting.

Organized and led by Anne Tracy Morgan and Anne Murray Dike, CARD was established in June 1917 at the Chateau of Blerancourt outside Paris. Anne Morgan, daughter of the American financier J.P. Morgan and sister of the man whose bank was the intermediary between the Allies and their American suppliers, was well known in New York for her work in the women's rights movement. From her station at Blerancourt, a castle that had been damaged during the French Revolution, she adapted the principles of the American settlement house movement to one of the most devastated areas of rural France. Work undertaken by CARD was almost exclusively accomplished by women, including driving and repairing ambulances, providing medical assistance, and instructing young mothers. American volunteers— Margaret Brown, who was appointed a CARD director, among them— worked with government officials and local villagers to rebuild and refurnish houses and buildings and distribute food, clothing, household linen, and tools. They imported new livestock and seed for planting, established medical facilities and health education programs, and rebuilt schools and public libraries. They even provided cultural activities and exchanges, including dance and literary performances.

Even after the war ended, CARD continued to operate in the Aisne region until 1924. Anne Morgan and Anne Murray Dike founded the Museum of Franco-American Cooperation on the grounds where CARD once stood, the Chateau of Blerancourt, which now holds art and artifacts from the war that represent the cooperation between the two nations. Margaret Tobin Brown's name is engraved on a plaque commemorating the museum's most significant volunteers and benefactors.[85]

THERE WAS NEVER any question in the Brown family as to whether Lawrence would serve. Both Margaret and Lawrence agreed with Secretary of War Newton Baker's statement that there would be no favoritism: "Every man, whether he has had training in the regular army or not, whether he has had training in the guard or not, whether he be a member of the selective national army, is equal in dignity, in responsibility, and in opportunity a member of the army of the United States."[86]

Lawrence was sent to Fort Sheridan, where he "attracted attention for his competency in military manners and enthusiasm." Scrapbook photos of college friends were replaced with photos of men in trenches, boxing and sparring with bayonets, and a carefully scotch-taped ticket for the Military Ball at Fort Sheridan Gymnasium on October 5, 1917.

When Lawrence left for France to serve as an infantry captain with the American Expeditionary Forces, Eileen took the two children with her to live with relatives in New Mexico.

On June 14, 1917, when John Joseph Pershing, chief of the American Expeditionary Force, arrived in France, the U.S. Army had grown from 200,000 men in early 1917 to over four million. Lawrence Brown was part of the final wave of fresh troops brought in to attempt to bring the war to an end. He was on the fields of Ypres when Margaret cabled him a birthday greeting in August 1918. Lawrence responded with a letter dated August 28, 1918, a portion of which was reprinted in a Denver newspaper: "It's next to impossible to write here. You do it in the most impossible places and you are never in the humor. I am working harder than I ever did in my life, and at that I am enjoying it all more than I have ever enjoyed anything. However, I become intensely lonely at times. My mail never gets to me except its being months late. ... I have picked up a little French, but I have so little time to practice it I'm afraid I won't be so fluent when I get home."[87]

But a month later, Lawrence was lying in a hospital. At the Hindenburg line north of St. Quentin, where he was serving with other notable American and British officers, including the Prince of Wales, Lawrence was wounded by mustard gas on September 29, 1918. Official word did not reach his family until the following February, when Eileen received a letter from the War Department stating, "Captain Lawrence P. Brown, Infantry, was slightly gassed and under treatment, Nov. 15, 1918."[88] Lawrence's wallet, which was lost on the battlefield and later found, was also returned to her. It contained his identification, a crucifix, a copy of the Lord's Prayer, and—in honor of his Irish roots—a pressed four-leaf clover.

Lawrence was very ill until mid-December, after which he stayed with the Astor family in London to further recuperate before attempting a journey back to the United States. He received honors for being among those who helped smash the Hindenburg line and received an honorable discharge on January 23, 1919.[89]

When the Great War ended, tens of thousands of Americans had died, not only in battle but in the influenza-pneumonia epidemic that swept U.S. military camps in France. Lawrence saved a clipping from war critic Frank H. Simonds, who reported that "to say that the United States won the war, then, is accurate ... [but] one must recognize the fact that it is like saying that in a relay race, the man of the team who actually finished the race, wins it. It is idle to believe that our new troops could have won in 1916 or even 1917 as they did in 1918. Grimly as the German fought in the Meuse-Argonne, his machine was already worn, his men tired; toward the end things began to break down in an unexpected fashion."[90]

IN THE MONTHS FOLLOWING the end of the war, Margaret worked at Briar Cliff Lodge in New York teaching blind soldiers the necessary skills to allow them to make the transition back into civilian life. She also spearheaded an effort to have Mark Twain's work translated into braille. And she never lost her reputation for speaking her mind. In 1918 she stated that Mrs. Celine Villemin, who organized the Université Français for war relief work, did so merely for commercial purposes. Mrs. Villemin responded with a lawsuit—and Margaret retorted by accusing Mrs. Villemin of casting slurs on the bravery of American soldiers. The suit was dropped.

Lawrence and Eileen, now reunited, considered homesteading in North Park, Colorado, but instead moved to Fort Collins. Lawrence took a class in animal husbandry from Colorado State University, paid for by the army. George and Helen Benziger and their two young boys were frequent visitors. Most of the Benziger fortune was tied up in Europe because of the war, and for a time Helen and her two boys lived with Eileen and Lawrence in their spacious Fort Collins home. Lawrence became a member of the Disabled Emergency Officers Association and the Veterans of Foreign Wars. But he couldn't envision himself as a rancher or veterinarian, and despite his renewed commitment to Eileen, their relationship continued to be troubled.

NOW IN HIS SIXTIES, J.J. Brown—who had spent a good part of the last ten years of his life in hospitals and hotels—began to reflect upon his life. He pined for Leadville and in a letter wrote, "O, Leadville is very very quiet but I have wished a thousand times that I could withstand her winters. ... It will be a great camp again, and I feel just now as though I could do more than my share of redeeming the old camp, and bring it back to its own. ... O, if I could only stand the cold of old Leadville."[91] His children were always foremost in his mind; in a letter to Lawrence he wrote, "I note with pleasure your admiration and kind regard for Helen and hope and pray that you and Helen may forever and ever hold the respect and high esteem for one another [that you] give expression to ... I will be most delighted in hearing from time to time that you are both happy and content ... your welfare is my delight."[92] In December 1917 he wrote to Helen of his frustration with his health. "The doctors did me no good," he said. "I was just feeling rotten from the bottom of my feet up and into the top of my skull."[93] He was disturbed by his continuing conflicts with Lawrence, which Helen often tried to mediate, and had also heard that Margaret was considering selling the home on Pennsylvania Street, which had been occupied by tenants for years. "I thought away back in the past," he mused, "and of all the sacrifices made for others, and that at last, it should come to this. No family, home, or friends, all alone in a dingy old room ... no home, no house, no place at my own fireside, no place for you or the children." He tried to reconcile his deep love for his family with the fact that he couldn't control their feelings, lives, and destinies.

Even though J.J. deplored Margaret's public persona and her willingness to open her pocketbook—as well as her love of French culture—he seemed wistful that things hadn't worked out differently. He considered it a great pity that the family should be so rich in the world's goods and yet had lost its sense of home and connection. "You were young, your Brother was young, but your Mother carried you off and away among strangers," he wrote, "while I was in the Hills delving for some thing to make a home and a living. Now you are in New York and your mother in Hellknowswhere, spending her money." Yet even as he railed against what he perceived to be weaknesses in his children and estranged wife, he was even harsher on himself—and nearly every letter or telegram was accompanied by a check, sometimes large, sometimes small. The Brown fortune was gradually disappearing, and Margaret was having trouble making her rent payments in Newport. Nevertheless, J.J. continued to try to finance his family's hopes and dreams, including paying niece Anna Brown's tuition at the College of Mount St. Vincent in New York City.

Margaret and J.J. could match tempers, but they shared a kindred spirit as well. Years later Margaret would remark that there never was another man like James Joseph Brown. In an interview with Denver reporter Frances Wayne, she said, "Let me say here that I've been all over the world. I have known more or less intimately the greatest people in the world from the kings down, or up, as one cares to view them, and I've never met a finer, bigger, more worthwhile man than J.J. Brown. In spite of certain qualities of our natures which made companionship impossible between us, I salute his memory and claim him to have been without a peer." The reporter asked if Mrs. Brown would ever consider a second venture into the sea of matrimony. "My dear," Margaret exclaimed, "how can you ask such a question after what I have just said!" With a flourish of her ever-present ivory walking stick, she elegantly departed—looking, as she always did, like the "drum major of an imperial band."[94]

In the Spirit of
Sarah Bernhardt

1922–1932

J.J.'s HEALTH CONTINUED to worsen. In November 1921 he sent an urgent telegram to his daughter, Helen—to whom he was very close—in New York, asking her to come immediately to Los Angeles, where he was hospitalized. (Since his stroke years before, J.J.'s health had steadily declined.) Within hours she was on a train, leaving her husband and two young sons behind. For six weeks J.J. remained in the hospital with Helen by his side; when he was finally able to move to a hotel, he begged her to stay until the weather warmed up and he could travel back to New York with her. For Helen, the time began to seem interminable. When the weather improved they began the journey east, stopping in Denver and Leadville to visit old friends. Helen's sons, James and Peter, came to visit their "Uncle Larry" in Fort Collins, and see their grandfather in Leadville. James later recalled,

> As we were all walking down the main street of this celebrated mining town, my grandfather saw an old crony coming towards him. I shall never forget the encounter. At exactly the same moment they said to each other, "Why, you old cuss, I thought you had died years ago!" My mother would wish me to remark that the folksy lingo was only for the occasion. She always resented later myth-makers who presented her father as an oaf in order that my grandmother might shine more brightly by contrast. [Both Margaret and J.J.], with little schooling, had managed to speak standard English, whereas [Larry] with his expensive education often sounded as though he had spent all his life in an Army barracks.[1]

Because of his respiratory problems, combined with the altitude, J.J. spent one frightening night in Leadville gasping for breath, and Helen took a firm stand and said that they needed to leave immediately. She was anxious to get everyone back to her home in New York. She knew her father loved the West better than the East, but she felt that more than anything else he needed a loving home.

By the time they reached New York, J.J. had developed a racking cough. Colorado had long been a refuge for Easterners suffering from tuberculosis, and J.J. harbored a fear of developing the disease. Against Helen's wishes—she wanted him to stay home—he demanded to be taken to Nassau Hospital for tests to confirm that the cough was not tubercular. Two days later, while in the hospital, he had a heart attack, followed by a second. Helen wired Lawrence to come to New York and vowed to stay by J.J.'s bedside. But when J.J. died on the morning of September 5, 1922, he was alone—Helen, on her way from Hempstead, was twenty minutes too late. He was sixty-eight.

Margaret traveled all night from Newport to arrive one hour before the funeral. Everything went wrong—she couldn't find a hotel, was denied the use of a car, and found the situation unexpectedly tense. She was shocked to discover how ill J.J. had been and how heavily he had depended upon sedatives to ease his pain. The biggest surprise, however, was the fact that he had died without a legal will.

Condolences poured in from all over the country. J.J.'s old Leadville partner A.V. Hunter wrote to Helen that J.J.'s passing "was such a severe shock to me that I still can't realize it all has happened." Florence Tobin Harper, who was closer to J.J. than her sisters, wrote, "He really is much better off after such a long illness. ... I suppose you are very glad you stayed out West with him as long as you did, even if you did sacrifice a lot by being deprived of your home."[2]

Despite J.J.'s desire to be buried in the mountains of Colorado, he was laid to rest in the Holy Rood Cemetery (previously called St. Brigid's Cemetery) in Westbury Village, Long Island, New York. J.J. had wished to leave behind enough money to adequately care for his wife, children, and grandchildren. But complications related to distribution of the estate kept it in the courts for six years after his death, divided the family—for a time, at least—and filled the Denver newspapers.

Margaret requested, as J.J.'s legal wife, to be made administratrix of the estate. The request was denied. When Margaret's attorneys began to review J.J.'s holdings, it suddenly became apparent that a large transfer of assets to Lawrence and Helen had been made shortly before his death. One particularly large transfer to Helen caused the most suspicion.

Years before J.J. had promised his children that he would help them each build or buy a home. Lawrence now had a house in La Jolla, California, paid for by his father (although J.J. had rarely visited, as he disliked the fog that rolled in from the ocean every night). Despite the fact that Helen, George, and J.J. had spent countless hours with real estate agents combing the Hempstead area, they had been unable to find a suitable house. In the meantime, J.J. had generously paid their rent. Helen wrote to her attorney, "You see Father's idea was—Mother had a home—Brother had a home and all his dependent relatives had homes— naturally as I was nearest to him in every way it was only a combination of circumstances that I had no home until just before he died. ... It was most certainly not a gift in anticipation of death, but a fulfillment of a promise, and was really my wedding gift long deferred."[3] A house had been found weeks before J.J. died; the transfer, Helen stated, was made by J.J. so Helen and George could finally purchase their home.

J.J.'s mining, real estate, and stock holdings were extensive, compli- cated, and spread over many states. Margaret really had no idea how much money was involved in J.J.'s estate; on the other hand, her chil- dren and their lawyers had no idea how much money she had. Each was convinced the others had a substantial amount. Furthermore, the children were concerned that their mother spent her money a little too freely, particularly with respect to her charitable causes. Margaret grew distrustful; Lawrence and Helen closed ranks. Suits and countersuits were filed in rapid succession.

The battle over the estate brought up old tensions, even though the Browns had been separated for thirteen years. Both Helen and Lawrence were convinced at the time that their mother had become consumed by her pursuit for notoriety and a career. "She was not entirely to blame in the trouble with father, not originally," wrote Helen, "because he was difficult, hot-tempered in the extreme and hard to please. But whereas he tried and did mend his ways and controlled himself more and more as he grew older and through conscious efforts too, she succumbed more and more to what became not only a ruling passion in her life, but developed into a vice."[4]

Lawrence felt that his father's influence had somewhat hampered his own progress in the world and that all the years spent working in J.J.'s shadow entitled him to a portion of the estate. "I have always been sub- ject to my father's beck and call in the past and for this reason I have not been of a lot of use to anyone else that may have hired me. At least

I have always alibied myself to myself that this was the reason that I haven't been a howling success in the world," he wrote.[5]

Helen and Lawrence wanted to remain in control of the estate and put Margaret on a modest fixed income. Margaret, however, was convinced that her children were hiding almost $200,000 in property and bonds from her and wanted to put the entire estate in trust for all three of them or do nothing at all.

The case dragged on and on. Despite the tension in the courtroom, members of the press always duly noted Margaret's fashionable attire—on June 26, 1925, she appeared in court wearing a peach-colored crepe dress with matching straw hat and beads, mottled snakeskin slippers, and a white cane. Denver dressmakers took note, and Margaret once again was setting fashion trends. But the publicity wasn't always positive. On July 3, 1925, sensational headlines appeared when the *Denver Post* revealed that $207,686.38 had indeed been transferred to Helen and Lawrence before J.J.'s death—owing to a breach-of-promise suit that had been filed against J.J. by a woman named Sabra Simpson. The transfer allegedly was made to save the property from seizure if he should lose the case. J.J. had hired a detective agency to help in the investigation, and the case had eventually been settled out of court.

Surprisingly, most of the details of the Simpson case were kept out of the gossip pages, and on February 3, 1926, a settlement of the estate seemed imminent. On that particular day however, Margaret was not in the courtroom. Believing that the case was still nowhere near its conclusion, she had boarded a ship to head for a warmer climate. The note she sent to the judge in her absence made the front page of the newspapers. To a spellbound courtroom audience, Judge George A. Luxford read aloud:

> If, as habeas corpus, I appeared in court per schedule this morning it
> would be with two eyes like poached eggs, a nose all Roman, swollen
> to Jewish proportions, with breathing apparatus needing a pulmotor to
> pump breath into a congested head and lungs, suffocating with fine coal,
> soot, and tar. … Such is New York with a coal strike, in an atmosphere
> as foggy as London, of a pea-soup hue, and here I am taken by all but a
> litter or a stretcher to the high seas on an ocean-going greyhound. … I am
> booked on the court files to appear to press a claim for my wherewithal
> [but] must combat the microbes that grip the flu, that make a shroud for
> the corpse while the undertaker with his embalming fluid makes a putrid

decomposition until the hearse finds the grave in a cemetery. ... So here are greetings from the high seas, bound for the Bahamas.[6]

Despite the pleas of attorney J.J. Morrissey, who asked that the hearing be continued until April given the fact that Mrs. Brown had not been able to speak for herself in the courtroom, Judge Luxford declared that his court would no longer be made a mockery. He overruled all of Margaret's objections to the final settlement and approved the final report without her signature: $100,000 was placed in trust for Margaret, and $100,000 was placed in trust for Lawrence and Helen, with other property divided equally. Helen and Lawrence were permitted to keep all the assets that had been transferred prior to J.J.'s death.

Lawrence was convinced that his mother was mentally unstable. Helen, angry over the fact that Margaret had said her daughter's husband, George Benziger, "had no brains for business" and was the instigator of the alleged illegal transfer, claimed she never wanted to see her mother again. Margaret, believing she had been sorely wronged, rewrote her will and took Lawrence and Helen out completely. She told the *Denver Post* that she intended to convert the House of Lions as well as a smaller home at 700 Hemlock Street in Leadville into nursing utilities "where any person may obtain medical treatment or care as the guest and friend of this departed millionaire." She declared, "Our son and daughter are adequately provided for, so I shall devote my fortune, when I get it—and I'd like to know *when*—to bestowing what immortality I can on J.J. Brown."[7]

MARGARET RETURNED TO Denver in a better state of health and an improved state of mind, and was struck by an idea. She contacted Mrs. A.V. Hunter and Helen and Mary Phyllis Campion—the widow and daughters of J.J.'s old partners in Leadville—and asked them to join forces with her in demanding control of the directorship of the Ibex Mining Company in Leadville. The three women owned an overwhelming majority of the stock, and with Margaret's share they felt they should hold sway over the company. "There is no reason why the intelligent women folks of those undaunted mining pioneers should not step in, wrest control from the men, who through results of litigation have bored their way in, and manage our own mine," Margaret declared. She claimed J.J. had always said that a greater lode of ore would be discovered farther down in the depths of the earth; the women also wanted to develop 165 acres of adjacent mining land. In midsummer 1925, Margaret traveled to Boston and Newport to drum up financial support and set up a company to build a mill to treat the ore of the five-mile dump of the Little Jonny and work to develop the Omega Group in Evans Gulch. "Why should the fact that we are women preclude our activities as mine managers?" she demanded. "To the north of us a woman is a candidate for governor, and in Texas Mrs. Ferguson is running for the same office. Why shouldn't I rule over the domain created at Leadville by my husband and the Messrs. Hunter and Campion?" With a flourish of confidence that set the Ibex board of directors' teeth on edge, she stated that women probably made better managers than men anyway, declaring that "men of muscle and brawn would help bring [rich ore] into the sunlight under a woman's management."[8]

Not surprisingly, the idea was greeted with less than enthusiasm. The Leadville *Herald Democrat* reported that Mrs. Brown's efforts to promote a "feminist coalition" for the operation of the Little Jonny Mine had absolutely no chance of succeeding, as the stock of the original holders was in the hands of the trustees, executors, and other representatives of the estates of the pioneers. The affairs of the company were managed by a board of directors in Denver; the board dictated policy; and the board had no intention of relinquishing any control to Margaret or any other woman, regardless of whom they were related to.

If Margaret felt defeated, she kept it to herself. When asked if she might consider going into politics again, she was adamant: "Denver the beautiful is my home, but as for politics," she said, "nothing doing." She smiled, however, and added, "I'll wager there isn't a woman in this country who keeps posted on politics more closely than I do. When I am abroad, and mostly I am abroad, somewhere or other, I hire readers to read the daily papers to me. In Deauville instead of flirting or guzzling, or becoming a lounge lizard, what did I do? When the papers came from Paris and Berlin and London I went apart with my reader and when the hour was over I knew what was going on in the world. Shouldn't a passion for knowledge count for something in one's own development?"[9]

Her ongoing efforts in the political arena did not, however, go completely unrecognized. On November 22, 1922, Senators Lawrence C. Phipps and Samuel D. Nicholson announced their support for Margaret's secretaryship with the American Embassy to the Court of St. James in Great Britain. "The matter of achieving a position with the embassy was not of my own initiative," Margaret rather defensively explained to the *Denver Post*. "During my years of travel I have tried to justify my existence by hard, sincere study, not alone of languages, but of peoples. ... Now, many of my friends, especially among the English nobility and royalty, on my recent visit to England, broached the subject of the appointment of an American woman, since American women have attained enfranchisement, and thereby, political equality, to the ambassadorial staff."

"Women should be recognized in government," the senators agreed. "Where should women find themselves more adaptable than in diplomacy?"[10]

Margaret, however, did not receive the appointment.

WITH THE HOUSE OF LIONS rented to tenants and her Newport home increasingly difficult to afford, Margaret traveled. She visited her family in Hannibal at least once a year, at one point admitting to a Hannibal reporter that she still experienced nervous trouble owing to the *Titanic* disaster. Although America was ready to forget its *Titanic* victims, Margaret still told the story whenever she had the chance and paid personal tributes in her own way. On April 14, 1927, she spent the day at the Church of the Holy Ghost in religious meditation to commemorate the deaths of all those on the *Titanic*.[11]

For years, as chair of the *Titanic* Survivors' Committee, along with several others Margaret had tried to establish a memorial for those who had died on the *Titanic*. A committee of prominent women from Washington, D.C., headed by Mrs. Harry Payne Whitney, renewed efforts in 1927 to obtain a site for the erection of a memorial. The memorial figure had been created shortly after the disaster but had been in storage for fifteen years because a suitable site could not be obtained. Margaret was part of a small group of women that opposed the present site on the Potomac River, near the Lincoln Memorial, because they felt the ground was not firm enough. Despite the fact that $25,000 had been appropriated to complete a sea wall, she felt the plan was not sufficient to protect the statue. However, Mrs. Harry Payne Whitney, Mrs. William Howard Taft, and Mrs. Robert S. Chew renewed efforts to obtain the Potomac site, where the memorial was finally erected. The statue features a standing male figure with arms spread—an image that was picked up, perhaps not coincidentally, by director James Cameron in his film *Titanic*. Some feminists criticized the memorial, saying it was inappropriate to not only commemorate but perpetuate the notion of chivalry. Margaret responded that she thought it was very brave that some men had chosen to step aside and let women and children live—but the gesture should never have been required by law or custom.

In 1925 Helen was staying in Paris with her family, and Margaret sent a telegram with Christmas greetings. Tentatively they began to reestablish their relationship, and the family slowly began to mend. Margaret also began her efforts in historical restoration. In May 1926 she attended a Mark Twain celebration in Hannibal, where she was received with open arms by a host of friends.[12] The Tobins had never forgotten that Mark Twain's father had been a neighbor of John and Johanna Tobin, and through Margaret's efforts and those of her relatives, many of Twain's belongings were found and restored to the Mark Twain museum.

Margaret was interested in historical restoration in Denver as well. In 1881 a poet named Eugene Field had arrived in Denver as the new managing editor of the *Denver Tribune* and rented a small frame cottage at 315 West Colfax Avenue. He became known as a children's poet, author of "Wynken, Blynken, and Nod" and "Little Boy Blue," as well as a journalist, a would-be actor, a mimic and entertainer, and a very popular public figure. He satirized prominent citizens, especially the wealthy and pretentious—including Margaret Brown, and it is a testament to her character that she overlooked the fact that like Polly Pry he occasionally teased her mercilessly in newspaper editorials. After all, she was not alone. It was said that Eugene Field was adored in Denver, but it was love only that kept him from being lynched. Field eventually left Denver to accept an offer from the *Chicago Morning News* and died at a relatively early age, his best years having been spent in Denver. In 1927 Margaret discovered the Eugene Field house, cleaned and restored it, and opened it as the Eugene Field memorial home. The home contained Field's piano, desk, chair, and many other personal belongings. On November 2, 1927, one hundred people turned out for the dedication of the Eugene Field House. Margaret read two of Field's poems, "The Two Opinions" and "Our Lady of the Mines," while wearing a long cape with gold fringe. Two soloists from the Herrick Dramatic School and local dancers also entertained.[13]

In the spring of 1930 Margaret presented the house to the city of Denver, and it was relocated to Washington Park and used as a children's library and museum for forty years. The Eugene Field Foundation was organized to foster talent in children and in its first year sponsored four students, one a violinist who was sent to study in New York.

IN 1927 MARGARET returned to her beloved Egypt once more, this time returning with two sphinx-headed lionesses that "made news from Cairo to Colorado." She placed them prominently in front of the House of Lions (when the house was sold at her death, the famed sphinxes went to a Colorado Springs art dealer). She continued to present the city of Denver with gifts from her travels, including two paintings by French artist Rosa Bonheur and two mounted alligators from South America for the Natural History Museum.[14] That same year Judge Ben Lindsey got himself into trouble with the press again for advocating the development and legalization of the birth-control pill as well as a controversial idea called "companionate marriage," the notion that a childless couple might consider cohabiting without necessarily having to make a legally binding, lifelong commitment.[15] The traditional family, some social scientists believed, was an institution arranged for the purpose of regulating reproduction, educating children and conditioning them for society, and determining the inheritance of property. They felt that this institution was no longer considered adequate to meet the needs of modern society and had been profoundly affected by the industrial revolution, rapid urbanization, more widespread acceptance of divorce, and the growing knowledge about and acceptance of birth control. Advocates of companionate marriage proposed a new type of wedlock entered into solely for the purpose of companionship between a woman and man. Despite her strong Christian ethic and the fact that many of friends and family members disagreed with her viewpoints, Margaret was a strong proponent of social change.

The year 1927 was also when Margaret apparently finished her autobiography, titled *The Course of Human Events*. On April 6 she announced that the manuscript had been sent off to Doubleday, Page & Co.[16] The narrative, described as "thrilling," was a combination of fact and fantasy. "I'm preparing to explode a few myths centering on the Titanic," she said. "One or two halos will disappear. I am not using the hammer spitefully. But I am writing of my experiences and shall tell the truth. ... I've told it so well and thoroughly, so far, that my stenographer has gone into gales of laughter at certain chapters."[17] The first chapter, titled "All Roads Lead to Leadville," described Margaret as leaving Hannibal at age fifteen and told a tall tale of her caravan being waylaid and robbed by a band led by Jesse James. She declared that the book included descriptions of trips to Europe, life in prewar Germany, the glamour of foreign courts, romances of the Latin quarter of Paris, a trip around the world, a narrow escape from death in a typhoon on the Indian Ocean, and encounters with Indian princes.

But apparently the book has been lost to history. No record of it exists, with the exception of a few typed lines on old yellowed paper.[18]

During her earlier travels Margaret had made an indelible impression on a young Wyoming girl. Her friend Gertrude Vanderbilt Whitney had just completed a statue of Buffalo Bill, which was to be unveiled during the Fourth of July celebration in Cody, Wyoming. A special train bearing Mrs. Whitney's guests arrived in Denver from New York, and Mrs. Brown was invited to join them on the trip north. In Cody she stayed with the Ernest Shaws, owners of the *Cody Enterprise,* and had such a good time that she extended her stay from three days to a week. Margaret was quite taken with the Shaws' daughter, Peg, age five, and spoke of how much she loved children and how unfortunate it was that her own family had become estranged.

Peg's parents joked that they'd put a card with Peg's name and address around her neck and send her off on the train, but Peg never got to go. Nevertheless, Margaret and Peg exchanged letters over the years. When Margaret went to Paris and had gowns made, she asked the dressmaker to pack up all the scraps and send them to Peg for doll clothes. She also sent tiny handmade doll furniture, and once even sent Peg a tiny baby alligator, 2.5 inches long, packed in moss in a cigar box. The alligator didn't survive the trip, but the story survived for over fifty years.

At one point, much to the chagrin of Lawrence and Helen, Margaret declared that she was adopting a boy named George Seal, son of Josephine Cantrell Seal, an opera singer in Paris who was originally from Tennessee. Margaret claimed that she had placed the boy in a school in Paris, "where he will be given every advantage that wealth can bestow."[19] These claims have never been verified.

Little Peg's letters meant a great deal to Margaret. On March 18, 1925, she was staying at the Breakers Hotel in Palm Beach, Florida, when the second of two devastating fires (the first had occurred on June 9, 1903) broke out. Once again she never lost her wits and calmly led a group of hotel guests down a fire escape. "You should have seen me in this and that," she said, "with a stocking wrapped about my wrist and heaven knows what on my foot, joining the celebrities and millionaires on the plaza when we had been warned by the courageous telephone operator that the hotel was afire and preparing to fall upon us and cook us."[20]

Margaret lost everything—clothes, trinkets, books. She escaped wearing one black stocking and one white and carrying a bag containing the most recent letters from little Peg Shaw in Cody, Wyoming. After this escapade, Margaret's friends nicknamed her "the Salamander Lady," and one friend declared, "She *must* be a combination of fish and phoenix. She's been through fire and water before; she's hit the high spots of danger and come through unharmed. She must have a *charmed* existence. How does she do it?"[21]

ALTHOUGH A SETTLEMENT had been reached in J.J.'s estate, Margaret's lifestyle changed dramatically. In February 1922 she had been sent a notice to vacate Mon Etui in Newport for not paying rent. The *Denver Post*, knowing Margaret was still at sea on her way back from Europe, spitefully wrote, "The Unsinkable Mrs. Brown is about to have a new experience. In her meteoric rise from poverty to the realms of plutocracy she has had many abodes. Now her residence is to be moved to the sidewalk."[22]

When she returned to Denver later that year, a *Denver Post* reporter cornered her. "Of course I am being sued," she said cheerfully. "And of course I shall not give in to those spineless Yanks in those parts. I shall give battle, and what's more, I shall win out and get damages."[23]

But Margaret did not win her battle. She eventually had to give up her house in Newport and rented rooms there instead, dividing her time between the seacoast town and Palm Beach, where many of her friends stayed. Newport had changed dramatically, and Margaret had changed as well. Her best days in Newport had been when she was surrounded by her family and old friends, and now nearly everyone was gone. "It's been a long time since New York or Newport society had a real leader," she mused. "The death of the dowager Mrs. Astor and Mrs. Fish and others of that quality has left things at sort of loose ends, but a new day is dawning and, mark my words, the new leader is to be none other than Mrs. William Randolph Hearst. Unlimited money, unlimited power, graciousness, beauty, imagination, the drawing to her standard of scions of the most aristocratic families marks a social progress that will not be checked. ... The old social order is passing."[24]

MARGARET STILL HAD a few friends in high places. Princess Stephanie Dolgoruky was the widow of Prince Anatole Dolgoruky, an attaché of the Russian court under the previous three czars, and sister-in-law to the late Princess Yourievsky, the second wife of Czar Alexander II. Margaret had often visited Princess Stephanie in Russia and socialized with her in New York. However, three hundred years of uninterrupted rule by the Romanov family abruptly came to an end in 1918 when Vladimir Ilich Lenin personally ordered the assassination of Czar Nicholas II and his family (as well as the cook, maid, valet, and family physician). Stephanie barely escaped herself, and her husband's brother, Prince Paul Dolgoruky, was murdered. She told a dramatic story of her escape. "When the revolution came I had just entered the Kremlin palace at Moscow without the slightest warning of what was impending," she said. "A little boy asked me, 'Why are all the cars stopped?' and I looked from the window to see the streets filled with armed men. The royal guards and soldiers about the palace disappeared as if by magic and in a moment the throngs from the street flooded into the palace rooms searching savagely for every inmate."[25]

Stephanie and her husband slipped into a secret passage and changed clothes. He dressed as a peasant, and she put on the uniform of a nurse that she had worn during her volunteer service in Moscow during the war. "The Russian revolution was an earthquake lasting thirty minutes," she said, "in which the family of Czar Nicholas II and his royal household were being dragged through the streets of Petrograd by halters while a few escaped by secret passages to become fugitives from Russia."[26]

With help from friends, Stephanie and her husband traveled through the snows of west Russia to the coast of Finland, then sailed to France and spent several years in hiding. Through her connection with the Romanovs—of whom, she proudly noted, there were many living descendants—she was related to the British royal family and in London was received by King George and Queen Mary and gave a series of public lectures. A benefit ball in her honor was held by the Prince of Wales—"And he even danced with me!" she exclaimed. From London she was brought to the United States by her American friends, including Margaret Tobin Brown, who paid her passage and ensured safe travel. Margaret traveled to New York to meet her, and the two women were entertained in high style by the Cornelius Vanderbilts, the Astors, the Du Ponts, and others of the New York Four Hundred.

In the spring of 1927 the princess stayed with Margaret in her modest rooms in Newport, and then they traveled together to Denver and occupied a presidential suite at the Brown Palace Hotel. To Denverites, Stephanie didn't look like a princess. A stern-looking woman who spoke her mind just as freely as Margaret, Stephanie was slightly stout and dressed in a plain black gown, held together in various spots with white safety pins. She wore practical shoes and a plain hat, and her only jewelry consisted of a large double pendant of emeralds inherited from the wife of Czar Alexander II and a long necklace of carved betel nuts that had been a gift from an Indian prince. Almost like a politician herself, Princess Stephanie had just finished an account of her experiences in a book titled *Russia Before the Crash* and was eager to speak before audiences and spread the word of the atrocities she had witnessed. No flowing satin gowns and jeweled tiaras for this princess—she had a point to make. The Denver press, hoping for something a little more sensational, was bored. Many Denver citizens thought Princess Stephanie was a fake.[27]

Margaret, however, had a plan to help her friend spread the word of her horrifying experience and its political and cultural aftermath. She and a large group of her feminist friends from New York and Denver were in the midst of preparing to make an unprecedented visit to President Coolidge, summering with his wife in Rapid City, to make a personal plea for passage, or at least some recognition, of an Equal Rights Amendment for women. Princess Stephanie had never met the president, and Margaret said she couldn't think of a better audience for Stephanie's story.

Princess Stephanie agreed to go with Margaret in order to have the opportunity to meet the president, although she adamantly stated that women did not belong in politics. "I am not a woman politician," she declared to a newspaper reporter. "I once heard a lady declare she would like to be President of the United States, and I thought we ought to call a doctor and have her examined as to her sanity."[28] In a rare moment, in the accompanying newspaper photograph Margaret looked a little chagrined. It was likely that she was the one to whom Princess Stephanie referred.

Nevertheless, the two women made an extraordinary pair. With a large group of delegates from the National Woman's Party, they traveled to Rapid City, led by a Denver woman named Gail Laughlin. Laughlin, who had been the first woman to practice law in Maine, practiced law in Denver and was known for her work in trying to obtain the right for women to serve on juries.[29] On July 15, 1927, at 10 A.M., the suffragists arrived at the president's home in gaily decorated automobiles, a stream of reporters in their wake. They formed a long procession and moved down a hall to where the president waited. But the princess never got her chance. Treated by presidential guards with unexpected suspicion, she was asked to stay behind because her name was "not on the official list" and was forced to remain under police escort while the other women made their appeal. The appeal was in vain—President Coolidge's views against women's rights remained unchanged.

Margaret and Stephanie returned to Denver. The princess immediately set a limit—and a price—on the hordes of newspaper reporters that waited for her in the lobby of the Brown Palace Hotel. "The *Denver Post* is a great newspaper, paying well for its services," she said. "Why then should I give my views and tell of my experiences without compensation?"[30] Reporters left in a huff and wrote that the princess was obviously out of funds. Interviews were eventually accomplished, however, and the *Post* reported that despite Stephanie's decidedly dowdy appearance, there was something "unmistakably regal in the personality and manner of this royal Russian refuge." Princess Stephanie stayed in Denver to deliver a series of lectures on Russia. Helen Brown Benziger, in a brief visit to Denver to see her mother, met her, and they became friends.[31] Helen later visited Princess Stephanie in New York, where she was staying at the Plaza. "The reminiscent likeness of your dear Mother," Stephanie wrote, "brought my memories to such happy days in Paris, Denver, Colorado Springs, the Black Hills, and calling on the President."

DESPITE THE FACT that Margaret was getting older and was often bothered by health problems, she still longed for the stage and adored

Sarah Bernhardt, not only studying her roles but even buying her gowns. After the settlement of J.J.'s estate, and perhaps to avoid painful memories and associations in Denver and Newport, she spent a great deal of time abroad. In Paris she studied under a former instructor of Sarah Bernhardt and performed to appreciative audiences in *The Merchant of Venice* and *Cleopatra*. In January 1929 she began preparing for the lead role in *L'Aiglon*, the same part that the "Great Sarah" had played so many years before in Denver. After months of study she performed with a skeleton cast at a friend's home in Paris. In an interview in Paris with a United Press correspondent, she said that she hoped for the day when, as a graduation performance, she could pack her bags and go back to Denver to give a "real interpretation" for her fellow citizens. The reporter noted how "alive and witty" Mrs. Brown was and that she had "won by her own merits the position as uncrowned queen of smart Paris society. In all of the smart restaurants and theaters where society leaders gather, Mrs. Brown is a favorite. ... She has gone in for old world culture with the same strenuous manner she has aided American literature [and] pays regular, pious pilgrimage to the tomb of the Divine Sarah. She has studied opera and has no mean voice, and her Gallic wit has been bolstered by reading the French classics."[32] Several newspapers in Paris and the United States reported that Margaret had received international recognition for her success with Bernhardt's roles.

Margaret herself had a few words to add: "Some people find it strange that an American woman should aspire to play the roles of Bernhardt. I recall, too, that some people smirked when I brought home ancient statuary from Egypt and decorated up a few acres of the Rocky Mountains for my home, but I am sure that those who know the place will agree that culture knows no boundaries and that fine arts are international."[33]

In Denver they might have thought her eccentric and narcissistic, but in New York and Paris Margaret was a star. In May 1929 she was awarded the Palm of the Academy of France in recognition of her work in dramatic art for her interpretations of the work of Sarah Bernhardt. Denver was skeptical of her success — so she wrote a letter herself to the *Denver Post*. "As a mimic I can imitate Sarah Bernhardt's idiosyncrasies easily," she said. "Paris is known to be a garden of culture and it takes a lot of assurance, with ability, to be welcomed here. If their rising up and submerging me with cheers is any criterion, I have passed muster."[34]

But the most significant of Margaret's awards was still to come. In

April 1932 she received the French Legion of Honor award primarily in recognition of her work during the war. The exact language of the award commended her "overall good citizenship" and included more than just her efforts on behalf of blind French and American veterans. The committee noted that Margaret Brown was being recognized for a long list of humanitarian and philanthropic activities: helping organize the Alliance Française west of the Mississippi; promoting the Franco-American Art Association of New York; her ongoing work in raising funds for the *Titanic* victims and crew and continuing to serve as chairman of the *Titanic* Survivors' Committee; her work with Judge Ben B. Lindsey on the Juvenile Court of Denver; and even the restoration and donation of Eugene Field's house to the city of Denver. Anne Morgan, daughter of J.P. Morgan, was simultaneously awarded the Cross of Chevalier, as well as the noted French "poetess" Comtesse de Noailles, who had also assisted at Blerancourt and was a close friend of Margaret.

Margaret was recommended for the honor by the Maison Blerancourt in France and also by Captain Rostron of the *Carpathia,* who had received the same honor in a previous year. Margaret Tobin Brown had come a long way from an immigrant's cottage near the banks of the Mississippi River.

FOR THE NEXT three years Margaret traveled and performed scenes from *L'Aiglon,* often for charity benefits and fund-raisers, and continued to study and teach acting. Then, on October 26, 1932, she abruptly died in a room at the Barbizon Hotel in New York. She was sixty-five. The Barbizon Hotel had a long history of famous actress residents, including more recent guests such as Ingrid Bergman and Candice Bergen. It was said that Margaret enjoyed working with the talent and enthusiasm of young women who came to New York to try to make it on the stage.

There was some confusion regarding her death. On the death certificate her name was spelled "Marguerite," her mother listed incorrectly as "Laura Collins," and her occupation listed as "housewife." For the last few years of her life, Margaret had divided her time between the Hotels St. James and Albany in Paris and the Barbizon Hotel in New York, and her visits with family had grown fewer and fewer as her health declined. From 1930 to 1932 she began to complain of severe migraine headaches, often locking herself away in a hotel room for a few days until she could emerge, ring for tea, and resume her regular life.[35]

Although many newspapers reported that Margaret had died while belting out an opera aria or yodeling, her grandson James Benziger later recalled that his mother, Helen Brown Benziger, received a call late at night from the manager of the Barbizon Hotel. James Benziger said Margaret had apparently died in her sleep. After an autopsy, the family was told that there was a large tumor on her brain, which likely had been there for some time. On the death certificate, the cause of death was listed as a cerebral hemorrhage, with contributory arteriosclerosis.

Helen made the funeral arrangements, and Margaret was buried in Holy Rood Cemetery, next to J.J., the man she had continued to love despite all their differences. Eventually Helen and George Benziger were buried there as well.

A will was found in Margaret's room at the Barbizon that had been drawn up the year before by New York attorney L.J. Grannick. Petty differences had been forgotten: the primary beneficiaries of Margaret's estate were Lawrence and Helen. Other heirs were grandchildren George Jr. (Peter) and James Benziger; Lawrence Jr. (Pat) and Elizabeth (Bets) Brown; Margaret's three nieces Florence Tobin Harper of New York, Grace Tobin Carroll of Los Angeles, and Helen Tobin of St. Louis; Margaret's sister, Helen (now remarried and known as Helen Benet), in Seattle; and her brother William Tobin in San Diego. (Daniel Tobin had died.)

But there was very little left. Her real property was valued at $5,250; her physical belongings at $20,000, including the white polar bear rug and many boxes of books. The newspapers declared that the estate was valued at $50,000 or more; George Benziger, in a rare interview, said the fortune was "fata morgana." At the height of the Depression, even the House of Lions on Pennsylvania Street was worth only a fraction of what Margaret and J.J. had paid for it before the turn of the century.

One of the last letters Margaret ever wrote was on October 13, 1932, to her housekeeper, Edith Stiles, at the House of Lions, asking her to make sure that the house was readied for winter and all the dead leaves flushed out of the rain gutters.[36] She said she would be in Denver soon. She never made it. But the annual Christmas shipment of candy, clothing, and seven hundred pairs of socks for miners' children that arrived in Leadville a few weeks later was distributed by her faithful nephew, Ted Brown.

Condolences arrived from around the country. Margaret's rather beleaguered attorney, Morrison Shafroth, wired that she was "a woman of marvelous courage and personality." Helen Tobin wrote that she was shocked to hear of her aunt's death, "although she has been a stranger to all of us these past few years." Helen Benet, Margaret's sister, was "deeply grieved." Lawrence asked that the funeral be postponed until he could arrive from La Jolla, California. He, more than anyone, seemed haunted by the fact that he hadn't often seen his mother in recent years.

Princess Stephanie Dolgoruky sent a kind letter to Helen on stationery from the Plaza Hotel in New York, with an embossed gold crown at the top. "I had the privilege to be a close friend to your dear late mother," she wrote. "It was with a deep sorrow that I learned about her premature death and express to you all my feelings of sympathy."

Margaret, however, died in the manner in which she had hoped to go. "I am a daughter of adventure," she once wrote. "This means I never experience a dull moment and must be prepared for any eventuality. I never know when I may go up in an airplane and come down with a crash, or go motoring and climb a pole, or go off for a walk in the twilight and return all mussed up in an ambulance. That's my arc, as the astrologers would say. It's a good one, too, for a person who had rather make a snap-out than a fade-out of life."[37]

In an attempt to spice up a story that didn't need much spicing, in Margaret's obituary the *Rocky Mountain News* wrote that as a child with flaming red pigtails, Margaret Tobin had spent long afternoons on the banks of the Mississippi playing with none other than Mark Twain.[38] The myth was born.

REAL STORIES ABOUT Margaret Tobin Brown weren't hard to find for those who were willing to look. Denver residents had many tales to tell. Les Severn recalled that it was the year 1915 or 1916, when he was less than five years old, that Margaret Brown came to his rescue. At that time Denver closed off many of its downtown streets after a snowstorm so children could sled. Les was tobogganing with his brother when another child ran into him with a sled and knocked him out. He was taken to Margaret's house nearby and rested with his head in a woman's lap.

Once it was clear that he was all right, he left. He later learned that the woman who had held him was "the Unsinkable."[39]

Some Denverites took a less favorable attitude toward the opinionated Mrs. Brown. In 1924 Margaret—a proponent of Prohibition—raised the ire of every young debutante in Denver when she noted in a Paris interview that "the American girl can't hold her liquor; she shows it right away and grows mashy or wants to fight. When I was a girl we would have been ostracized forever had we appeared at a party with our breath even slightly tainted with alcohol. Yet today, society girls drink industrial alcohol to warm up on before they arrive at a party."[40]

A Denver reporter went in search of a real Denver debutante and found one named Cariata Russell who expressed a willingness to publicly disagree with Mrs. Brown. "I think Mrs. Brown has enough to do to paddle her own canoe without trying to paddle for the younger set also. ... As far as a woman's appearance is concerned, none looks her best after a few drinks. But there is no comparison between a younger woman and an older one. The younger one still looks fresh and pretty and seems to control herself better. But older women are disgusting, I think, and usually make themselves ridiculous."[41]

Some of the most infamous stories about Mrs. Brown had to do with her wonderful variety of hats. In her early years in Denver, Margaret often stopped at the Bon Marche Millinery Shop at 607 16th Street, considered the best millinery shop in Denver at the time. Proprietress Mary O'Shea, known as "Old Mary," had reputedly been Margaret's godmother, and an employee recalled how she would watch for the wonderful Mrs. Brown to make her appearance: "When Old Mary wasn't busy, she looked like a statue standing in the door at 16th Street, with her hair pulled back tight in a knot, and wearing a long black skirt to the floor and a black shirt."[42] When Mrs. Brown came in, "she just lit up the place," and always gave Mary a $100 tip. Employees remembered Margaret's striking hats, including a broad-brimmed hat to match a leopard skirt, a brown felt with a white seagull on the front, and an Easter hat of gossamer maline (French tulle) in shades of violet.

Vivian Daniels, an employee of the Plimpton Millinery Shop on Fifteenth Street, recalled a rather dowdy-looking Margaret Brown coming in for a visit in 1929. She chose five hats and paid for them without even trying them on. "She was wearing several dresses," Vivian recalled, "one on top of the other and the dresses were soiled even though they would have been expensive gowns at sometime in the past. The hats," she noted rather haughtily, "were of a style much too young for Mrs. Brown."[43]

Back in 1905 butchers and grocers made daily morning calls to the homes of the affluent. The story of Mrs. Brown's experience with "Lloyd the Butcher" was often told, thanks to his son and grandson. At most homes of Denver's elite, "a tradesman never got beyond the kitchen. With Mrs. Brown it was different," said Lloyd's son.

> She would see Papa in whatever room she happened to be in. She person-
> ally liked to discuss and decide on her meat order. Thick tender steaks,
> juicy pork crown roasts with each protruding rib-bone covered with
> a colored paper frill; larded rump roasts, a boned turkey stuffed with
> a boned chicken which was stuffed with a sausage dressing. J.J. loved
> corned beef and also lamb stew.
>
> My father always spoke of her in impersonal respectful tones. The
> thing that intrigued him most was the polar bear rug on her drawing
> room floor. He took great pride in providing the main entree for the
> dinner parties Molly gave. When she had leftover roast, she made sand-
> wiches for the neighborhood kids.

His father's favorite story about Margaret Brown involved an encounter when she was taking a bath. Lloyd called at the House of Lions and was told to go upstairs. As he reached the top, Mrs. Brown reportedly called, "Is that you, Lloyd? Come in, I'm taking a bath."

> Abashed, Papa stood still. He froze. He felt trapped. His impulse was to
> rush back down stairs. Finally, he turned the knob, pushed the bathroom
> door open and stepped to one side. "I can hear you from out here," he
> countered.
>
> Mrs. Brown's raucous laughter rang down the hallway. "Have it your
> way," she called. "I didn't think you would come in!" She then called
> out her dinner order. Papa felt that it was his turn to play the game.
> "What would you have done if I had come in?" he asked.
>
> "Why, I would have given you an order," she answered immediately.
> "What else?"[44]

MRS. BROWN ALWAYS stayed at the Brown Palace Hotel, and stories of her generosities and occasional eccentricities abounded. The Brown

Palace Hotel—which had nothing to do with the J.J. Brown family, despite the name—had been built by Henry Cordes Brown and opened August 12, 1892. It was famous for the fact that each of its four hundred rooms had a fireplace. However, Henry Cordes Brown, who had first come to Denver in 1860, was financially devastated a year after the opening of his famous hotel by the silver panic of 1893. He did his best to reestablish his fortune, however, and felt giddy enough at the age of seventy-four to marry a twenty-two-year-old woman who had worked as a cashier at a grocery store, his third wife. His second wife, whose name was Margaret, had often been dismayed to find herself confused with the "other" Mrs. Brown.

Peter O'Toole, a former manager of the hotel, had many stories to tell about Margaret. She "always had ambitions to be a person of the theater," he recalled. "She recited poetry, tried to learn acting under Sarah Bernhardt, and took singing lessons." He noted that whenever Mrs. Brown stayed at the hotel, her singing coach arrived daily at ten A.M., and her "vocal calisthenics" could be heard up and down the hall.[45]

Frank Dawson, a former employee of the First National Bank in Denver, recalled seeing Mrs. Brown at the Brown Palace Hotel in 1929. At a business dinner with a New York banker from the Bankers Trust, he noticed her dining alone at another table and sent his card over to ask her to join them. "We had a delightful evening together," he said, "discussing New York, Paris, and the *Titanic*." When asked to describe her appearance, he said, "She was a good conversationalist, a large woman, somewhat chunky, but you could see she had once been handsome."[46]

In late 1922 Morrison Shafroth, an attorney who was representing the administrators of J.J.'s estate, asked Margaret and Judge Ben Lindsey to dinner. He said,

> Mrs. Shafroth and I had a wager as to which one would out-talk the other. I was betting on Mrs. Brown to recount her story of the sinking of the *Titanic,* which she told us many times. Mrs. Shafroth was betting on Judge Lindsey, who was a dramatic storyteller. He and his wife Henrietta had just returned from a trip to New York where they viewed several of the Broadway plays. After dinner we sat around the fireplace. Mrs. Brown was knitting a tie for either George Vanderbilt or Thomas Lipton. I am not sure which one it was on that occasion, but she always carried her knitting and was always knitting for one or the other. Judge Lindsey was so enthusiastic about the plays he had seen that he not only told us about the plays

but acted them out. Mrs. Brown didn't get a word in edgewise, but seemed
to enjoy it just as much.[47]

In 1927 nephew Ted Brown and his wife came for a visit, and
Margaret made an indelible impression on Mrs. Ted Brown when she
gave her many pairs of brocaded satin slippers, size 5A to 5B, all made
to order. She added a red Morocco circular lounge and a few other
pieces of furniture. If someone remarked that they liked something
Margaret owned, it was said, she was apt to just give it to them.

Around 1928 Colorado writer Caroline Bancroft spotted Margaret
Tobin Brown in the lobby of the Brown Palace Hotel. Caroline was
twelve, standing next to her father, and it was the only time she ever
saw "the Unsinkable," although her father had told her many stories
from the newspapers. Mrs. Brown's dress made an impression on the
young girl—she was wearing a lavender suit and purple hat and carried
a shepherd's crook twined with real violets.

One fantastic story that seems to have a grain of truth is the infamous
tale of Mrs. Brown's engagement to a British gent. In March 1927 the
Denver Post announced that Margaret was engaged to the Duke of
Chatre, head of a prominent family. The following day it retracted the
announcement, stating that word had been received from Paris that the
title Duke of Chatre had long been extinct.[48]

Indeed, there was a gentleman who presented himself by such a title,
and Margaret had known him for about four years. His wife had recently
died—an English lady from whom he apparently inherited a substantial
fortune—but Margaret suspected his motives. "The duke's ardor for
Mrs. Brown has permitted him to engage in sacrificial measures," the
Post reported, as telegrams arrived daily at the Brown Palace Hotel.

However, in a letter to Margaret's housekeeper, Mrs. Grable, written
from the Barbizon Hotel in New York, Margaret seemed less than impressed: "The Duke looks bilious and grins like a Cheshire cat at what he
hopes to be his, but nay, nay, Pauline [an expression of the time], I would
be jailed for exposing him to a draft on charges of cruelty to animals. ...
Gee Whiz! his breath comes in short pants—he has asthma, spinal menin-
gitis, yellow jaundice and everything chronologically listed in the medical
journal. I would have to call the doctor while he takes his temperature."
In another conversation with a reporter, she noted that the duke was so
old he had "one foot in the grave and the other one on a banana peel."[49]

There is no doubt that Margaret Tobin Brown had only one love in her life. Despite the fact that J.J. had a reputation for "stepping out" and was a "tough Irishman, very belligerent when he drank too much,"[50] Margaret missed him terribly—in life, owing to the separation, and after his death. James Benziger, Margaret's grandson, recalled visiting J.J.'s grave with his brother, Peter, and his older cousin Florence Tobin Harper. "We stopped and walked towards the grave," he wrote. "Three persons were already standing by and reading the words on the stone. Florence and I recognized my grandmother. Out of mistaken loyalty to my mother, neither of us spoke. My mother later said we should have spoken to her in as natural a way as we could. It is possible that I had never before this encounter come across [understood] the phrase 'a ravaged face.'"[51]

Having endured the ups and downs of the Brown family fortune, Margaret was philosophical about her own life. "Money can't make man or woman. ... It isn't who you are, nor what you have, but what you are that counts," she said.[52] And what counted most in life, to her, was experience. "I was born under a lucky star, I suppose," she said. "They told me a long time ago that I was born under 'fire and water,' that is to say, in July, and that I need have no fear of either of those elements."[53] Once when a reporter asked her about her astrological sign, she answered in short order, "Fire and water! You can't sink me no matter how you try. Recently I was a guest on a ship bought by a firm from the government. We sailed away, a merry party. Before long, but when we were far away from shore, a fire was discovered and we had to wait to be taken off by another ship sent out by the same firm.

"The average person would have called that a day and a voyage," she continued. "Not I. We got aboard the relief ship and sailed across the briny. Nearing the shores of Norway, what happens? A floating mine gouges a hole in us and we go up to the edge of a wholesale sinking when rescue comes. I don't know what my destiny is, but it isn't to be sunk in the sea or blown into the air."[54]

Despite her experience on the *Titanic,* she never thought twice about traveling by sea. "Going to Europe today, of course, is merely commuting," she said. "One takes a taxi to the boat, the boat rushes across the seas; another taxi or bus awaits you, and today Paris and the Argonne can be done between luncheon and tea, so to speak. So shopping in Paris has lost some of its thrill."[55]

In a comment that no doubt raised the hackles of some of her friends as well as some of her descendants, she remarked that separating rich people from their money to help the poor had been the joy of her life.[56]

IN DECEMBER 1930, two years before Margaret's death, *Fortune* magazine printed an article about Margaret Tobin Brown claiming that she was as "legendary as Paul Bunyan but as real as Pikes Peak … a lambent flame in the Denver consciousness." A year after Margaret died, Gene Fowler published *Timberline,* which immediately became a regional bestseller. In 1944 an article titled "Leadville Molly Gets Mad" appeared in *True Magazine,* detailing the life of an aggressive, unnatural woman who "barked her shins against the gates of society heaven." *Reader's Digest* reprinted Fowler's chapter from *Timberline* about Mrs. Brown, and Fowler eventually sold the movie rights to Metro-Goldwyn-Mayer. A radio broadcast featuring Helen Hayes as "The Unsinkable Mrs. Brown" hit the airways. The Broadway musical *The Unsinkable Molly Brown* was a smash hit on Broadway, and the enormously popular film, also titled *The Unsinkable Molly Brown,* filled movie theaters in 1960. This hit was followed in 1963 by Caroline Bancroft's forty-four-page booklet, aimed at the tourist market, titled *The Unsinkable Mrs. Brown,* which stated that most of Margaret Brown's vaunted success had been nothing but fantasy.

None of these stories had anything to do with the real Margaret Tobin Brown. The rough-and-tough, rags-to-riches, social-climbing, tomboy-turned-seductress image of a "Western gal" was common in Western novels, movies, and media. Margaret's name was merely tacked on to a convenient stereotype. After all, turning lives into legends was what Western writers and entertainers did best. Upon Margaret's death, Henry C. Butler, owner and editor of the Leadville *Herald Democrat* and a long-time family friend of the Browns, noted philosophically, "The Leadville myth is growing. As the pioneers drop off they will be the subjects of obituaries that are tales of the marvels of the early days, and eventually these myths will be accepted as authentic history. And after all, the truth is wonderful enough."

The legend of Molly Brown entered the consciousness of mainstream America. In 1955 an advertisement for U.S. Savings Bonds portrayed Mrs. Brown in a *Titanic* lifeboat with a Colt .45 strapped to her bloomers. In

March 1965 the *Gemini 3* spacecraft was unofficially named the "Molly Brown." (The flight was mostly uneventful and was considered a success although it became notorious for the fact that one astronaut smuggled on board a partly eaten corned-beef sandwich from Wolfie's on North Atlantic Avenue in Cocoa Beach.) In 1967 the Marion County Historical Society restored Margaret's birthplace and childhood home, just a few blocks from Mark Twain's childhood home. In 1998 the home was re-opened as a museum after a remarkable restoration by Hannibal residents Vicki and Terrell Dempsey.

The House of Lions also experienced a revival in the public consciousness. Margaret had rented the house to a family from 1911 to 1920. In 1926 she had to take legal action to evict a tenant who was subletting rooms, and then decided to convert the place into a boardinghouse with her stalwart housekeeper, Ella Grable, in charge of renting rooms. In February 1927, however, Margaret was an active member of the Society Arts Club, an art organization with branches throughout the country. Against her children's wishes, she hoped to turn her home over to the club to use as a studio where renowned singers, painters, and actors could practice and perform.[57] In 1930 she again attempted to convert the house on Pennsylvania Street into a beaux-arts museum for the city of Denver, to hold art from around the world.[58] She set about collecting the original manuscripts and autographed first editions of the poetry of the Comtesse de Noailles of France, which she claimed would be one of the museum's most significant holdings. The family protested, however, and the house never became a museum.

After Margaret's death the neighborhood declined and the house fell into disrepair. In the 1960s, in an ironic twist of fate that was likely lost on the current occupants, the home was turned into a halfway house for teenaged Denver girls and renamed, briefly, the Jane Addams House, managed by none other than the Denver Juvenile Court.

In 1970 Historic Denver, Inc., one of the first organizations of its kind in the country, bought the House of Lions, restored it to its original 1890s splendor, and opened it as a museum to an enthusiastic Denver. The house was popular for years, but after the release of James Cameron's movie *Titanic*, it was filled with throngs of tourists eager to learn about Margaret's extraordinary life.

❧

AFTER HER DEATH, Margaret's family struggled with her legacy. Both Helen and Lawrence, as well as their descendants, felt concerned and even angry about the depiction of their mother in the media. In a letter dated July 21, 1953, Helen Brown Benziger wrote that a Denver publicist had come to Westbury when Helen was gone and interviewed her neighbors. Helen was furious. "Since this high-handed procedure came to my knowledge, I have talked it over with an attorney," she wrote.[59] Helen felt close to both her mother and father, and recalled with great affection her Tobin grandparents and all the stories they had told her and Lawrence about life in Hannibal. She felt inclined to publish her own version of events. She held the family treasure trove of letters and scrapbooks, in addition to her own letters, and felt that she had enough material to pull something into shape "for quick publication, should I be driven this far by any more activities on this front."[60]

Lawrence and his wife in California at first tolerated the media, believing such cooperation would help stem the flow of inaccurate facts. Through time Helen remained adamant. "You can't seriously have believed that I would consent to, or encourage, further public annals about Mother," Helen wrote. "I will never, never place information in the hands of anyone out in Colorado, conditioned as they are so obviously by the string of myths dreamed up by the local press."[61]

She also mentioned that someone had gone into the old files at the *Denver Post* and "rifled" them for stories on the Browns.[62] "Since such files are open to the public, someone went to quite a lot of trouble unnecessarily," she said. "Certainly nothing like a veridical story of Margaret Tobin could be compiled from such files. It would have to be padded three ways and then some."[63] She emphasized that except for the last two years of her life, when Margaret was performing abroad and hardly wrote at all, Helen had been in close contact with her mother.

Will Tobin, Margaret's brother, threatened to sue Gene Fowler over *Timberline*. In 1947 Lawrence visited the librarian at the Denver Public Library to discuss a way to stop the "preposterous stories" about his mother. Helen Hayes was set to do the radio broadcast, which Lawrence considered particularly outrageous, and Lawrence called the head of NBC to complain bitterly. He was told that the network had "fixed it" in such a way that there was nothing he could object to. The librarian suggested that if the real facts and records were on file, there would be little reason for these "so-called writers" to dream up fantastic tales. Lawrence made a special trip to Hannibal to interview family members and see what he could find. However, in Hannibal Lawrence discovered there were no birth records prior to 1910, and he found few records regarding the Tobins.[64]

Family members in Hannibal were equally vehement about how the family story had been distorted over the years. Albert Frier, grandson of Margaret's half-sister Catherine, said, "In my day, the *Denver Post* was the worst paper in the country. What they printed about Mag Brown was ridiculous. *Denver Post* articles would be reprinted in the *Hannibal Courier Post,* and my grandmother [Catherine Tobin Becker] didn't like it."[65]

THIRTY YEARS AFTER the death of Margaret Tobin Brown, Clara M. Van Schaack, described as one of Denver's best-known women of society, was interviewed by the *Denver Post.* She remembered Margaret well. "She was a most cordial person and was very sweet to all the younger people in Denver. Her son, Lawrence—we called him Lawrie—and her daughter, Helen, were our friends," she said.

"A great deal has been said about how unkind the Denver society leaders were," she continued. "I don't remember them as being really unkind. They were kind of tongue-in-cheek about Mrs. Brown. She always dressed in elaborate, striking ways. She wore feather boas, large hats, and heavily beaded gowns. I feel that she sought attention, and naturally won it. ... You must remember that people were not as lenient then as they are now. They didn't judge you as much on your worth and ability as they did on your family and background. That simply was the way it was. All of our families were pretty smug."[66]

Father Johnson, a retired Catholic priest, knew Margaret in the '20s when he was young and had been a priest only two or three years. He remarked that she had frequently attended services and other events in the church and that she was very well read. "The Sacred Thirty-six was only a group of self-elected socialites, never involved in notable charity work but banding together to control Denver. Socially, their 'organization' harmed the growth of Denver and its reputation as a new state desiring new blood and new enthusiasm. They were self-elected and closed to anyone who didn't conform."

Nevertheless, the world loved the legend of "the Unsinkable Molly

Brown" and didn't care much for the real facts. When Lawrence Brown died, he donated his scrapbooks to the Colorado Historical Society, demanding that they remain sealed for twenty-five years. Helen Brown Benziger packed up all her letters and scrapbooks and kept them hidden in a basement. The three nieces, Grace, Florence, and Helen, did the same.

WHAT HAPPENED TO all the people who had filled Margaret's life? Her half-sister Catherine Bridget Tobin Becker died in 1931 in Hannibal, where she had raised a family and lived her entire life. Her other half-sister, Mary Ann Landrigan, spent her remaining days in Monticello, Nevada, with her large family.

Dan Tobin died on July 9, 1926, in Lowell, Massachusetts, and was buried in New York. He was fifty-nine years old at the time of his death. William Tobin lived in California and then Gunnison, often struggling to make ends meet. Margaret's sister, Helen Tobin, who spent a good part of her life in Berlin, had four husbands. Helen Brown Benziger noted that a movie should have been made of Helen's life, not Margaret's. One husband was a doctor, "one a millionaire who went broke with a bang, [and] one a Prussian nobleman in the Kaiser's elite guard … [Helen] had more madly amorous gents in her train than you could count. Yet she escaped publicity with the greatest of ease."[67] Helen's last husband was Sam Benet, whom Lawrence had known in Beverly Hills.

Lawrence and Eileen divorced again in 1925—Eileen remarking that Lawrence still liked to "drink, spend money, and drive fast cars."[68] This time Eileen retained custody of both children. Their daughter, Bets, who was twelve at the time of the divorce, eventually went to school at the Dominican Convent in San Rafael, California, and became a nun at age seventeen, against the wishes of both her parents. Pat married and had two children, Lance and Muffet Laurie Brown, named after her grandfather. Eileen remarried a man in San Francisco named Edmund Lyons, whose family built a substantial business as suppliers to restaurants and food services. (The Lyons name carries on in a chain of restaurants.)

After his divorce Lawrence eventually became involved in films and worked with John Gorman Pictures. He was general manager during the production of *Home Sweet Home,* a silent film produced just before the "talkies," and five other pictures. In 1926 he married Mildred Gregory, a twenty-two-year-old actress from Grand Rapids, Michigan.

She had left home at eighteen and, with no stage experience, tried to make it in Hollywood. "She asked for a chance. It was given her—and in time—she made good."[69] They honeymooned in Ensenada, Mexico, then moved to La Jolla, California, where J.J. helped them purchase a home. They led a high-society life, spending each Christmas in Paris where Mildred's parents lived. Mildred got along very well with the children from Lawrence's first marriage as well as the Benziger clan.

Lawrence eventually abandoned filmmaking and sold insurance and real estate before becoming active in mining again. In 1935 he moved to Leadville with Mildred and their three dogs and became a board member of the Leadville Historical Association, eventually serving as director of the Colorado Mining Association. Lawrence died of pneumonia in St. Vincent's Hospital in Leadville at the age of sixty-one on April 3, 1949. After Lawrence died, Mildred—who in her younger days had starred in over fourteen motion pictures—moved back to Denver.

As Lawrence grew older, he became almost obsessed with trying to discover the type of person his mother had really been in her youth and wrote to many people who had known her. He was never able to completely reconcile the real Margaret Tobin Brown and the Fowler/ Bancroft myth. In January 1978, twenty-five years after Lawrence's death, the seven boxes of documents and photographs he had left behind were opened to the public. Two volunteers from Historic Denver, Inc., Lyn Spenst and Elaine Witherwax, spent eighteen months sorting through them. Nonetheless, the myth persisted.

Helen Brown Benziger, never as much of a social person as Margaret had been, spent a great deal of time with the Benziger family in Salzburg at the family's Schloss Walchen and enjoyed society in London, Prague, and New York. George Joseph Benziger died on January 10, 1948, at the age of seventy-one in Nassau Hospital after a fall in his home. He was buried at Holy Rood Cemetery, next to J.J. and Margaret. Helen, who was only fifty-five when he died, lived another twenty-two years and died in 1970. Their son James, an exceptional scholar, went to Princeton and eventually became an English professor at the University of Illinois, Carbondale. He married a woman who had studied under Carl Jung, and they eventually had three children: Brad, Katherine, and Vincent. James Benziger counted Buckminster Fuller among his many notable friends. Helen's son Peter married in 1942, eventually having four daughters (Lynne, Pam, Helen, and Heidi), and was president of

248   *Molly Brown*

Ridder-Johns, Inc. He became a publisher like his father, managing the Community Newspapers, a number of regional newspapers on Long Island. Peter also became a glider pilot and was a pilot in World War II in the invasion of southern France.

Nieces Grace, Florence, and Helen led interesting lives influenced by Margaret's work on the stage. Helen Tobin changed her name to Helene and starred in the show *The Cradle Snatcher* in the late '20s. She met her husband, King Kosure, while playing in St. Louis, and they were married there, where he was manager of the Coronado Hotel. They later moved to Kansas City, where he managed the Hotel Bellerive and Helene worked in radio. She was also a member of the Red Cross Motor Corps and a volunteer nurses' aid. In 1943, while King was manager of the Park Plaza Hotel in St. Louis, the *St. Louis Post Dispatch* reported that Helene had been killed in a fall from the tenth floor of the Hotel Pierre in New York. She was forty-two. She had been staying at the hotel, which was owned by a friend of her husband, for the previous month. A hotel employee said that the window was raised about twenty inches, and it was possible that Mrs. Kosure had been leaning out to observe the lights on Fifth Avenue, as the wartime dimout had been lifted three days earlier. Kosure said that his wife's death was "probably accidental." The Great Depression significantly impacted all the Brown family members.

Florence Tobin Harper also died at a young age, at forty-six after a long illness. She and William—who had a reputation just as notorious as Lawrence's—had no children. William Harper became an engineer with the Canadian Car and Foundry Company. Grace Tobin Carroll had two daughters: Dorothy Louise Carroll, who eventually married Charles William Vollrath, had been a child actress in the silent *Our Gang* shows. Florence Helen Carroll married William Hasket and had two children. Their descendants inherited the scrapbooks the three nieces had so lovingly put together about the exciting life they had shared with their aunt.

By the late 1920s, Margaret's old nemesis and friend Polly Pry (then in her seventies) had retired from active reporting and begun an autobiography titled *My Life as a Reporter*. When she was in her sixties, she had volunteered for foreign duty with the Red Cross and served in Albania and Greece. Her articles were syndicated throughout the world. She was a popular speaker for young college women interested in careers in journalism, and told them, "You can get what you want out of life if you make up your mind what it is, and at the same time are willing to hustle for it!" She never completed her book. A heart attack at the age of eighty-one sent her to St. Joseph's Hospital, where she reportedly raised herself up on one elbow and exclaimed to the nurse, "I must be up ..." before death abruptly overtook her. Leonel Ross O'Bryan is buried in Colorado's Fairmount Cemetery—an untold legend, but a story just as colorful, significant, and representative of women in the West as Margaret Brown's.[70]

The Comtesse de Noailles, a good friend of Margaret's as well as a recipient of the Cross of Chevalier, died in 1933. A well-known French poet, Anna Elisabeth Mathieu de Noailles had presided over a literary salon in Paris that had included Marcel Proust, Colette, and Jean Cocteau.

Alva Erskine Smith Vanderbilt Belmont—Margaret's closest friend in Newport—died in February 1933 and was eulogized by the *New York Times* as "one of the most colorful female figures in American life."[71] Her funeral at St. Thomas Episcopal church on Fifth Avenue at Fifty-third Street was attended by thousands, and the casket was surrounded by an honor guard of volunteers from the National Woman's Party. A purple-white-and-gold banner lay across the casket, inscribed, "In Tribute to Our Comrade." She had composed her own funeral hymn, which was sung by a choir of women. Doris Stevens, Woman's Party advisory counsel, speaking from the Alva Belmont House in Washington, D.C., said, "There is not a woman living today who is not nearer the benefits and beauties of freedom because of Mrs. Belmont."[72] Alva was living in France at the time of her death; on September 10, 1932, Marble House was sold for $100,000, or less than a penny on every 1892 dollar it had taken to build and furnish it. Alva died four months later.

IT TOOK A powerful myth to obscure the significance of Margaret Tobin Brown's own life. A reporter for the *Denver Post* wrote Margaret a fitting eulogy: "Not being a man, she determined to be a successful woman, to see this world, to meet its best and be one of them. ... She had a definite, fearless personality. She knew what she wanted and went after it, and seldom failed her goal." Her greatest quality, he noted, was her courage to always be herself. *Fortune* magazine christened her "Denver's Own Particular Goddess."

Envoi

April 18, 1912

ON A COLD, rainy night four days after the *Titanic* first set sail, Margaret Tobin Brown stood on the deck of the *Carpathia*, still wearing the black velvet suit she had put on the evening of April 14.[1] The shoreline of New York Harbor was barely visible in the driving rain. Margaret reached into her pocket and curled her fingers around the tiny turquoise statue from Cairo—her good-luck charm, all she had left from the trunks of clothing, art, and souvenirs from her trip across Europe that now lay at the bottom of the sea. Looking toward the shore, she saw a moving blanket of lights, blurred in the black mist, slowly advancing toward them as if pulled by a magnet. "Ah," gasped the young woman standing next to her, but whether in awe or terror Margaret couldn't tell. She was one of three Irish girls whom Margaret, along with the others who had combed the ship for extra blankets and clothing, had found hiding in a steerage corridor. Now wrapped in makeshift clothes and blankets, the three girls stood next to her in the driving rain. The last few days had seemed eternal. Of the 866 *Titanic* survivors the *Carpathia* had plucked from the icy waters off the coast of Newfoundland, 161 had died in the hours and days following their rescue. Hypothermia, shock, broken limbs, and frostbitten feet and hands were common afflictions. Some people had bouts of hysteria; others withdrew into silent shells. Only 705 of the *Titanic*'s estimated 2,227 passengers lived to see the black skies and freezing rain of New York Harbor.

Suddenly from the dark mist the boats emerged: a flotilla of tugs, pleasure boats, skiffs, and ragboats. The lights split the darkness, and the deck of the *Carpathia*, somber and resolute in its steady progression toward shore, broke into chaos.

A voice bellowed from the water's surface. *"Titanic!"* barked a man through a megaphone, standing on the prow of a skiff. *"Titanic* survivors!"

Rushing to the edge of the deck, an officer leaned out over the rail. "Get out of the way!" he shouted. "We can't make our way!"

A beam of light reached up to the deck from a boat where a figure stood with a huge placard. Margaret could barely read the hand-lettered names: Astor. Guggenheim. Strauss.

"Mrs. Astor!" a man shouted from below. "Is Mrs. Astor on board?"

"Fifty dollars for the first survivor's story!" a voice roared through a megaphone.

"Get back!" cried the officer. "Let us through!" He waved his arms broadly in the air.

"One hundred! One hundred dollars for a story!" The skiff drew alongside. "Survivors, come aboard!" the megaphone shouted. Popping lights splintered the darkness as photographers' flashbulbs snapped like firecrackers. Margaret drew the women closer to her, and they pulled back, away from the lights. A commotion arose on the other side of the ship; a reporter had scrambled up through an open cargo door in the side of the ship. He sprinted across the wet wooden planks toward the group of survivors, now grown to almost two hundred, who had gathered on the deck.

"Get him!" shouted an officer, and several men sprinted toward the man, tackling him and knocking him to the ground. Captain Rostron appeared. "Put him under close arrest immediately," he barked. "Lock him in my cabin." He positioned crew members along the rail and ordered everyone back inside.

Margaret, who like many others had barely slept in the past four days, felt the thin crust of self-control that had served her so well begin to crack slightly. No one could have anticipated the fracas that welled around the ship. Who would meet her at the shore? Did her family know she was alive? Her eyes met those of Emma Bucknell, who had worked side by side with Margaret over the past three days. A different kind of terror now shone in Emma's eyes as the ship slowly parted the swarming flotilla. Margaret's face felt windburned and beaten; her arms and legs were sore; she longed for a bath and a change of clothing. This part of their journey could be no worse than what they had already endured—shock and exhaustion had turned into a ribbon of adrenaline that had pulled her through the past four days, and she couldn't stop now. "Come now." She turned and spoke to her Irish companions. "Who is to meet you on shore? Do you have family or friends here? We have to ready ourselves." She bustled them back inside.

TENS OF THOUSANDS of people crowded the long Cunard pier awaiting the first glimpse of the *Carpathia*, the high whine of ambulance sirens and the occasional blast of an auto horn rising above the noise of the crowd. A glistening wet canopy had been drawn up over the pier, and a group of several hundred—most of whom had relatives or friends on the *Titanic*—pressed up against each other as if poised to spill right over into the harbor. Police had arranged the pier into alphabetically designated sections, with family and friends of known survivors allowed to stand nearest, but few paid attention to the rules. For more than three hours people had waited and cried and fainted and argued and commiserated with one another. And then waited some more. A line of customs officials stood shoulder to shoulder, forming a human line of defense against the pushing throng. Their faces were wooden and exhausted.

A short, stocky man with a puffy, florid face stood next to a Denver reporter, nervously chewing his cigar. "I have five on board," he said. "I don't know if they're all alive—I can't tell. They've taken their names off the lists and put them on again—"

The chugging of a tugboat sounded from out in the North River. The man's ruddy face went white. "My God!" he said. The crowd suddenly fell silent. The sound of the tug's lusty churning filled the air. People strained to see beyond the canopy; a long wooden spar appeared, followed by a mast gliding silently past. Then the white bow of the *Carpathia* appeared.

"They're smoking!" shrieked a woman, her voice startling everyone. The incongruity of the remark fit the peculiar sight of a solid row of faces streaming past as the *Carpathia* slid into view. Like tiny bright stars, lighted cigars glowed in the mass of humanity standing on the deck. No single face emerged from the dark apparition, only dark bodies pressed together.

"Guess there are lots of them able to smoke," the florid man quipped, and then stopped. "My sister was drowned," he added after a moment, as though in apology. The reporter nodded and steadied his camera. He still felt a little awkward with the magnesium flash.

The crew of the *Carpathia*, unresponsive to the shouts of reporters and the whistles of police officers in their wake, solemnly let down *Titanic*'s thirteen lifeboats at the White Star pier. The lifeboats, now all that remained of the ship that had been as large as a stadium, knocked against each other with each slap of a wave and hardly looked capable of

saving the lives of eight hundred people. *Carpathia* completed its duty
and allowed itself to be pulled up to Pier 54, the Cunard pier, where
tens of thousands turned their faces to the glistening bow. The ship was
warped into the berth and stood steaming at the dock. For a long, tense
moment the two throngs of people looked upon one another, searching,
and then the dock exploded into pandemonium. The gangplank was
swung aboard. Hundreds of cameras stood poised to capture the first
Titanic survivor to walk down the plank.

There must have been some consideration regarding who would
take this place in history, for the crowd grew restless. At last a figure
appeared. Dr. Henry W. Frauenthal, a distinguished surgeon from
New York, emerged in fine form. His wife, young enough to be his
daughter, balanced herself with his elbow and matched him stride for
stride. Dr. Frauenthal's red beard was neatly combed, and his shoes and
hat "bespoke careful attention." His wife was equally well coifed. He
smiled tightly, nodding left and right to the burst of photographers'
magnesium bulbs, and with measured gait the couple strolled toward
the exit. The Denver reporter noted that Dr. Frauenthal might have
been "alighting from a ferry boat after a day in Jersey City."

The next passenger was not as composed. A young woman emerged
alone, her hair wild and loose about her face, her cheeks flushed and
eyes red and swollen. She wore odds and ends of unmatched clothing
and didn't seem to notice the fact that thousands of eyes were trained
upon her. She walked straight toward the crowd, now beginning to
break free from the customs officials. Abruptly halting, she thrust her
hands out into the air, the fingers clutching at nothing, the cords in her
thin wrists "standing out like strings on a violin." Not a single word or
sob escaped her throat, but at last her eyes found what they sought, and
she staggered headlong into the arms of an elderly woman and wilted
into a quiet heap on the ground.

The procession was halted while a tidy group of white-coated
physicians, dutifully followed by white-capped nurses bearing "great
packages of surgical bandages and cases of evil-looking little knives and
saws," entered the ship. Ten minutes later the first physician emerged
to calm the mounting tension outside. "Thank heaven," he announced,
mopping his brow. "There was nothing for me to do."

A nurse carried out a chubby baby boy who began wailing at the
top of his lungs. Four small children were brought out on miniature

stretchers. Two burly men made a chair of their arms and shoulders and brought out a man whose feet were so frozen he couldn't walk—despite his disability, the man deftly smoked a cigar as he made his exit.

Suddenly it seemed as if a dam had broken, and the passengers streamed out in groups of five and ten. Nearly all of them wore clothing that was ill sized, ill matched, torn, and dilapidated. One after another they fell into the arms of frantic relatives and friends. Customs officers, some of them overcome with as much emotion as those who had been reunited, allowed people to break rank and fall forward into the surging path of survivors. They made way for couples and families with arms locked about each others' necks, sobbing in grief and joy, and the anxious ones who still waited hopefully.

Madeleine Astor, despite rumors that she was critically ill, walked steadily on her own down the gangplank and into the arms of her father. Wearing a heavy white sweater that had been given to her, she declared to reporters that she held faith that John Jacob had not perished. "I hope he is alive somewhere," she said. "I cannot think of anything else, but I am sure he will be saved." Her husband's last words to her, she said, had been "I will meet you in New York, dear." The Astor family quickly bundled her into an automobile and took her to the Astor home on Fifth Avenue. For a full hour and a half, *Titanic* survivors straggled down the gangplank and were met by family and friends as well as a sea of newspaper reporters "pouring queries faster than tongues could answer."

After the first wave of survivors had emerged, Margaret darted out, frantically searching the crowd for her family. Her brother Daniel Tobin and friend Genevieve Spinner quickly materialized. "Margaret!" Genevieve cried, and broke into hysterical sobs. Margaret held her tightly. "I'm fine, dear, fine," she said, and turned to her brother. "What about Pat?" she asked. "Is the baby all right?"

"The baby's fine," he said, trying to keep the tears from his eyes. "Healthy as can be. It was the milk—something about the milk disagreed with him."

"And Helen, and Lawrence, and the girls?"

"Grace, Florence, and Helen are still at the house in Denver, and they know that you're okay. We'll wire them again tonight. Helen is waiting in Paris and knows you're safe. Lawrence is on his way to meet you in Denver."

"Thank God!" Margaret cried, and hugged them both.

"Let's get you to the hotel," Genevieve cried. "You look completely worn. Look at your dress!"

"No, no, I can't," Margaret said, and pulled back. "All these women and children, and some men too—they have no place to go. They can't speak English, and we can't just turn them out on the street. Emma and I are standing there at the door with a list and marking off names, only allowing people off the ship if they have someone to meet them. Otherwise we are making arrangements for them."

"But you must be so exhausted yourself," Daniel said. "Your health will be ruined." The rain still pounded steadily; the night air had grown so cold they could see their breath.

"Listen," Margaret said, ignoring his remark. "You must go to the Ritz-Carlton and get my room. I will be coming with some people— there's a Russian woman in particular who has lost everything, and is so terrified she won't leave the ship. I'm bringing her with me. And there are so many others who need help. From the room we can begin to make arrangements with embassies and the like. And they all need clothes. And money. We've got to—"

"I know," Daniel interrupted gently. He knew his sister well. "Go back inside. We'll go and get the room. But don't be too long, or we'll send the Ritz-Carlton cab after you."

BY FIVE A.M. on the morning of April 19, 1912, the last *Titanic* survivor had disembarked. The crowd was gone and the dock deserted. The rain beat down steadily in the cold gray dawn, and the crew and passengers of *Carpathia* slept. Just hours before, Captain Rostron had met with the officials of the Cunard Line and agreed to have his ship ready to sail again at four that afternoon, despite the fact that his crew was exhausted. U.S. government officials had issued orders that no one was to be allowed on *Carpathia*'s pier, but now nearly twenty drays stood at the docks, ready for cargo to be transferred. Soon the city began to rouse itself, but the ship was still silent. In an act of kindness, Cunard Line officials had relented—despite their obvious desire to get the *Carpathia* on its way back to Gibraltar as soon as possible, the crew was allowed to sleep in.

Margaret Tobin Brown was asleep in her room at the Ritz-Carlton, her new Russian friend slumbering nearby. By the time the sun rose above the horizon she would be up with Genevieve and Daniel, another list in hand, organizing a buying party to replace the wardrobes of passengers and crew who had lost or given away their clothing. She slept fitfully, already haunted by the faces of those she had watched go to their deaths—particularly Ida and Isidor Straus. But the dawn would bring a whole new wave of troubles to solve for people whose languages she could speak and whose problems she could understand.

In hospitals and hotel rooms and shelters and boardinghouses, the 705 people who had survived the sinking of the *Titanic* awoke, gathered their belongings and the remnants of their lives, and slowly filtered out of the city. Despite the flurry of media that surrounded them at the time, America would eventually forget them in the unfathomable tragedy to come: the first World War. Death would assume a new face.

Decades later Americans would begin to question why the *Titanic* still obsessively occupies our imaginations and fuels our greatest fears. But in late April 1912, as New York City was just beginning to feel the spring, most *Titanic* survivors left little trace of who they were or where they were going. Or how they would carry the grief of 1,500 souls lost one frigid night in the icy waters of the north Atlantic.

Afterword: Unraveling the Myth

Muffet Laurie Brown

WHEN I WAS a little girl, I was amazed to learn that my father's grandmother had been very wealthy and had survived the sinking of the greatest ocean liner in the world. Although tremendously proud of my ancestor's courage and generosity, I was possessed with fourth-generation survivor's guilt (if such a thing exists). My imagination's only comfort, amidst the horror of those people trapped aboard the sinking ship, was that my great-grandmother, one of the lucky few to escape safely, did so to the benefit of so many other survivors.

The *Titanic* story was brought even closer to home when I learned that she had booked that fateful voyage primarily so she could get home to see my father, Lawrence Palmer Brown Jr., who was a very sick little baby in early 1912. In my many public appearances, each time I retell this family episode, which ends with "Molly's" heroics and Daddy's recovery, I find myself saying, "… and the rest is history."

I suppose I should laugh at myself for using such a cliché! The popular history about Margaret Brown's life before, during, and after the sinking of the *Titanic* is anything but historical and universally understood. One thing I have learned from working with Dr. Kristen Iversen this year is that where Mrs. Brown was concerned, one cannot trust much of what was written about her, even in her own lifetime. This year, with interest in the *Titanic* at an all-time high because of the success of the smash-hit film *Titanic*, I'm sure the publishers of this book join me in thankfulness that no one has rushed out to print the last thing the world needs—another poorly researched volume on Molly Brown.

Strangely enough, the revelation that contemporaneous writing cannot be trusted came as a huge relief to me. With almost all who knew her gone, like many Molly Brown enthusiasts I have been dependent on the written and photographic record. Some articles and tales were so unflattering or ridiculous that I didn't know what to believe. It was illogical to believe it all. Over time this process left me with mixed feelings, feelings only as good as the last thing I had read. Now, with the publication of Dr.

Iversen's book, we have a critical evaluation of those sources (not to mention years' worth of research distilled into a single, convenient reference!).

But wait—the theatrical Molly is such fun—how much light can one shine on Margaret's life without losing the heart of the story we have all grown to love? Surely her house would not be standing today if not for Hollywood's spunky caricature. Fortunately for us all, Dr. Iversen takes us on a journey that will satisfy and inspire Molly fans, historians, feminists, and family. Take heart, Molly fans, because for every myth she buries Kristen unearths a little-known, real accomplishment that will doubly impress you.

When I first heard Dr. Iversen speak in the Arts and Entertainment *Biography* episode "Molly Brown: An American Original," in which I also appeared, I was skeptical of the overwhelmingly positive spin she put on Margaret Brown. I have been a challenging critic of Kristen's work, asking her many hard questions. She's answered each one to my satisfaction.

It was after the *Titanic* wreck was discovered, when I was in my midtwenties, that I started to research my family history. Apparently Caroline Bancroft had the nerve to send our family an autographed copy of her insulting biography, "The Unsinkable Mrs. Brown." When I read that pamphlet, along with some old news clippings, I pictured Molly as a sadly quixotic character who couldn't keep her mouth shut after her *Titanic* glory had faded. When I traveled to Colorado and met Lyn Spenst, director of the Molly Brown House Museum, the dedicated staff and volunteers, and Stan Oliner of the Colorado Historical Society, my faith was temporarily bolstered. My great-grandmother's spirit had inspired these people to unbelievable loyalty to her memory and home! Nevertheless, I would read news clippings and think, "She said what?" I could just imagine the press annoying my great-grandfather at work all the next day to get his reaction to one of Margaret's bold, controversial public statements!

Future generations of our family will owe a great debt to Dr. Iversen. None of my generation knew their great-grandmother. Only one or two grandchildren spent much time with their globe-trotting "old Grandmama," as she called herself. Much of what they knew was influenced by the attitudes of their parents, each of whom had their own issues with their unusual family and the complications in settling their father's estate. My grandfather, Margaret's son, Lawrence, passed on before my parents even met. My father and his sister both died in the

'70s, before Lawrence's family documents were unsealed at the Colorado Historical Society (he had asked that they remain sealed for twenty-five years for the protection of his sister and her boys). At that time I was not old enough to ask penetrating questions about the family. My father seemed to take a laissez-faire attitude to the popular legend. So, like many children of the '60s I was raised loving *The Unsinkable Molly Brown* musical, but I knew little more than highlights of her *Titanic* story and tales of the House of Lions in Denver.

In fact, we Brown and Benziger families have to accept some of the blame for the prevalence of misconceptions. In their aversion to publicity, Margaret's children were silent. This silence posed no opposition to the media hogwash. I was amused to read a letter Lawrence wrote to his sister's husband about how he really wanted to deliver a good thrashing to the author of one particularly wacky account of his mother's life, but he figured that assaults or lawsuits would draw even more publicity. So, for lack of a better idea, they decided to do nothing. Ironically, later in life, when my grandfather was giving his nephew a view into the nitty-gritty world of mining, he recommended *Timberline,* the very book that was the basis for the theatrical Molly Brown! To his sister, Helen Brown Benziger, who did not agree with her mother's liberal politics and who married into a family of the utmost dignity and sophistication, the folklore brought nothing but embarrassment and pain. The fact that Dr. Iversen is the first biographer to gain the confidence of the family is a great credit to her.

Although the myth about Molly's desperate bid for acceptance in Denver society is endearing and humanizing, it had always been hard for me to imagine an ancestor who was as vulgar as legend portrayed her. I was raised in a modest home with high standards and a sense of class independent of wealth. In fact, much of my upbringing might have steered me away from association with a woman like folklore's Molly Brown. Though I can imagine that Margaret never conformed entirely, Dr. Iversen finally proves that Margaret Brown was indeed well respected in mainstream Denver society. Kristen helped me see that the progressive causes for which Margaret fought required her to ruffle a few feathers, and that J.J.'s mining business was a competitive, litigious one in which he was both respected and feared. Each drew fire from poisoned pens. The important thing is not that everyone loved Margaret but that she was true to herself and her causes.

Myth or no myth, as a child I'd have been terribly intimidated by the outspoken Mrs. Brown. It is only with the maturity and wisdom of a thirtysomething woman who has watched obvious paths disappoint while diverse friendships ripened that I believe now that I could embrace the old gal, taking the best and leaving the rest. And now, thanks to Dr. Iversen's excellent research "the rest" has been reduced to practically nothing!

It's been a watershed year, filled with serendipity. My friendship with Kristen and the television exposure have brought me together with other great grandchildren, a great-grandniece and -nephew, and a treasure trove of family letters and photos that had been hidden away for over fifty years. I traveled in Margaret's footsteps to research places where she was born, lived, and died. The satisfaction of fitting together the puzzle pieces that each part of the family holds into something useful has been tremendous. The Tobin, Brown, and Benziger descendants, as well as the old-timers from Hannibal, Missouri, and Leadville, Colorado, have been a joy to meet. I thank all my hosts around the country this year for helping me help Kristen make this book what it is. So much has fallen into place that I know this is the right book to publish, for the public and for our family.

IT MUST HAVE been the wanderlust of my "unsinkable" ancestor that drew me to travel by myself to one of her favorite places in the spring of 1997. For years I had breathlessly watched documentaries and read travelogues about Egypt, but it took me a long time to resolve to visit such an exotic land without the security of a big, strong (read "husband") travel mate. Once I arrived there, my eyes drank in all the ancient art, and my ears were tuned intently to my tour guide. By the second day, however, it was clear that our guide was embellishing his subjects with colorful stories that did not jibe with what I had read, and in my enthusiasm for more information, I asked many follow-on questions. My curiosity translated into an unwelcome challenge to his Muslim male ego, and he became increasingly annoyed with me, to the point that I realized I would have to surrender my need for truth in order to keep peace in the group.

I decided to laugh at the whole situation. Adding perspective, I reasoned that neither he nor I had been there 3,500 years ago to witness the pharaonic politics, and even if we had, we would probably still argue about who was so-and-so's father, and how so-and-so met his demise.

The adventure in Egypt taught me three things that have helped me come to terms with the legacy of my "unsinkable" great-grandmother: that you can have the most exciting experiences when you travel alone; that the male-dominated Old World in which Margaret Brown lived had to have been an extremely frustrating place for a woman with brains; and that there are many other ways to come to terms with the world when absolute truth is simply not available.

Not every event or letter belongs in a biography. I also believe Margaret was "a bit of a confabulator." I know very few men who don't overstate their capability or tell fish stories here and there. Margaret just played by men's rules. When people ask me for my family stories, I warn them that I suspect they lie somewhere between the legend and the truth.

In a passionate letter saved with my family papers, Margaret's daughter, Helen, vowed to squelch any attempt by Hollywood to adapt her mother's life story. Helen threatened to publish her own immaculately documented biography, one sure to flatten the proverbial balloon with its account of a life not nearly as romantic as people believed. There's a part of me that is glad my great-aunt never played her trump card, as I believe Margaret's life was significant on many different levels, and even more so because she could not rely on beauty to open doors for her. As many stories as Helen may have added to our knowledge of Margaret Brown, I think Dr. Iversen has a better appreciation for what she was trying to accomplish, so I am glad Dr. Iversen is this book's author.

So the legend persisted; Hollywood eventually had its way with the story, injecting heavy doses of both romance and flamboyance; and Mrs. Brown's name lived on beyond the names of most of her contemporaries. Wherever she is, Molly is smiling and laughing robustly. She's laughing because the journalists, historians, and opponents who tried to snuff out her feminist legacy with outlandish stories concocted to marginalize her succeeded in doing just the opposite by portraying a character so colorful her legend would never die. And she's smiling because, with the help of Dr. Iversen, her descendants have begun to come together and regain their heritage, in their own terms, in their own time.

Notes

A Bump in the Night

This chapter is based on the written records of survivors' interviews, recollections, and testimonies, including those of Margaret Tobin Brown and others in Lifeboat Six.

1. Notes made by Caroline Bancroft, author of the booklet *The Unsinkable Mrs. Brown*, based on oral interviews conducted with Brown relatives and friends in the late 1950s, Molly Brown House Museum, Denver. I have relied upon Bancroft's material only insofar as it relates to primary documented statements made by interviewees.

2. Ibid.

3. Margaret Tobin Brown, "The Sailing of the Ill-Fated Steamship *Titanic*," *Newport Herald*, May 28, 29, and 30, 1912. Margaret's own story of her experience on the *Titanic* was picked up by numerous other newspapers throughout the country.

4. "Palmist Warned Mrs. Brown of *Titanic* Disaster: Egyptian Pictured Ship Sinking; Hundreds Dead," ca. April 1912, scrapbook of Helen Tobin Kosure, Vollrath collection.

5. *Denver Post*, April 27, 1912, p. 5.

6. Geoffrey Marcus, *The Maiden Voyage* (New York: The Viking Press, 1969), p. 49.

7. The dialogue in this chapter is based on actual testimony and written recollections of survivors.

8. Brown, "Sailing of the Ill-Fated Steamship *Titanic*."

9. Marcus, *Maiden Voyage*, p. 89.

10. Brown, "Sailing of the Ill-Fated Steamship *Titanic*."

11. Ibid. Margaret reported that nearly half the first-class passengers were in attendance.

12. Marcus, *Maiden Voyage*, p. 47

13. Bancroft notes.

14. Marcus, *Maiden Voyage*, p. 82

15. *Encyclopedia Titanica* website, http://www.rmplc.co.uk/eduweb/sites/phind/.

16. Marcus, *Maiden Voyage*, p. 82.

17. Bancroft notes.

18. Marcus, *Maiden Voyage*, p. 114.

19. Ibid., p. 98.

20. Ibid., p. 93.

21. Ibid., p. 126.

22. Ibid., p. 119.

23. *Encyclopedia Titanica* website.

24. Bancroft notes.

25. Marcus, *Maiden Voyage*, p. 121.

26. Walter Lord, *A Night to Remember* (New York: Ameroen House, 1987), p. 14.

27. Brown, "Sailing of the Ill-Fated Steamship *Titanic.*"

28. Ibid. and Lord, *Night to Remember*, p. 17.

29. Lord, *Night to Remember*, p. 46.

30. Ancient Egyptian figurine, Shawabti or Ushabti, ca. 700 B.C., described as faience with turquoise glaze, Stanley Lehrer collection.

31. *Encyclopedia Titanica* website. Of the sixty-six members of the staff of the À la Carte Restaurant, only three survived: Miss Ruth Bowker, cashier; Miss Margaret "Mabel" E. Martin, second cashier, and Paul Mauge (or Manga), chef's assistant.

32. Lord, *Night to Remember*, p. 44.

33. Brown, "Sailing of the Ill-Fated Steamship *Titanic.*"

34. Lord, *Night to Remember*, p. 61.

35. Mrs. Candee's miniature of her mother was recovered from Edward Kent's body and returned to her.

36. Lord, *Night to Remember*, p. 45.

37. Col. Archibald Gracie, in *The Truth About the Titanic* (New York: Mitchell Kennerley, 1913), wrote that Helen Candee caught her foot in the oars as she stepped into the lifeboat and broke her ankle (p. 176). Later accounts claimed that she broke one or both legs.

38. There is conflicting information about whether this boy was actually dropped into Lifeboat Six and inadequate confirmation that he was in the lifeboat at all. The women in Lifeboat Six were not allowed to testify at the Senate hearing; consequently, scholars must rely on newspaper and historical accounts that are sometimes uneven.

39. Brown, "Sailing of the Ill-Fated Steamship *Titanic.*"

40. Ibid. and Jack Winocour, ed., *The Story of the Titanic as Told by Its Survivors* (New York: Dover, 1960), p. 179.

41. *Encyclopedia Titanica* website.

42. Lord, *Night to Remember*, p. 19.

43. Brown, "Sailing of the Ill-Fated Steamship *Titanic.*"

44. The dialogue in this section is based primarily on Major Peuchen's court testimony. See Tom Kuntz, ed., *The Titanic Disaster Hearings: The Official Transcripts of the 1912 Senate Investigation* (New York: Pocket Books, 1998), pp. 197–208.

45. Margaret Brown and others estimated that they had rowed nearly a mile; Major Peuchen estimated five-eighths of a mile.

46. Compiled from several sources, including the *American Legion Magazine,* March 1972, p. 53.

47. Brown, "Sailing of the Ill-Fated Steamship *Titanic.*"

48. Several sources indicate that passengers in the lifeboats may have set articles of clothing afire as distress signals.

49. Brown, "Sailing of the Ill-Fated Steamship *Titanic.*"

50. Logan Marshall, *The Sinking of the Titanic,* ed. Bruce Caplan (Seattle: Hara Publishing, 1998 [1912]), p. 112.

51. Two women are said to have died during the night, though this statement is unconfirmed. The identity of the adolescent boy is unknown.

52. Brown, "Sailing of the Ill-Fated Steamship *Titanic.*"

53. Ibid.

54. Ibid.

55. Julia Cavendish, quoted in Gracie, *Truth About the Titanic.*

56. Ibid.

57. Brown, "Sailing of the Ill-Fated Steamship *Titanic.*"

A Legend Born

1. Jack Winocour, ed., *The Story of the Titanic as Told by Its Survivors* (New York: Dover, 1960), p. 319.

2. Ibid., p. 53.

3. Margaret Tobin Brown, "The Sailing of the Ill-Fated Steamship *Titanic,*" *Newport Herald,* May 28, 29, and 30, 1912.

4. Winocour, *Story of the Titanic,* p. 183.

5. James George Benziger, "Memories of a Grandson," unpublished manuscript.

6. Brown, "Sailing of the Ill-Fated Steamship *Titanic.*"

7. Marshall Everett, ed., *Story of the Wreck of the Titanic, The Ocean's Greatest Disaster* (Chicago: L. H. Walter, 1912), p. 86.

8. Walter Lord, *The Night Lives On* (New York: William Morrow and Co., Inc., 1986), p. 160.

9. Article ca. 1917, scrapbook of Helen Tobin Kosure, Vollrath collection.

10. Ibid.

11. Walter Lord, *A Night to Remember* (New York: Ameroen House, 1987), p. 167.

12. Article ca. 1917, scrapbook of Helen Tobin Kosure, Vollrath collection.

13. Logan Marshall, *The Sinking of the Titanic*, ed. Bruce Caplan (Seattle: Hara Publishing, 1998 [1912]), p. 133.

14. Brown, "Sailing of the Ill-Fated Steamship *Titanic*."

15. Marshall, *Sinking of the Titanic*, p. 134.

16. Lord, *The Night Lives On,* p. 162.

17. *Denver Times,* April 19, 1912.

18. Brown, "Sailing of the Ill-Fated Steamship *Titanic*."

19. Everett, *Story of the Wreck of the Titanic*, p. 56.

20. *Denver Times,* April 21, 1912, p. 2.

21. "Carpathia Heroes Blush Like Schoolboys When They Receive Medals: Captain Rostron Hears Praises Sung and Declares All Credit Goes to Loyal Men," scrapbook of Helen Tobin Kosure, Vollrath collection.

22. Everett, *Story of the Wreck of the Titanic*, p. 141.

23. Ibid., p. 187.

24. Ibid., p. 141.

25. Ibid., p. 47.

26. Quoted in Steven Biel, *Down with the Old Canoe: A Cultural History of the Titanic Disaster* (New York: W. W. Norton, 1996), p. 57.

27. *Denver Post* article, scrapbook of Helen Tobin Kosure, Vollrath collection.

28. *Denver Times,* April 21, 1912.

29. Geoffrey Marcus, *The Maiden Voyage* (New York: The Viking Press, 1969), p. 197.

30. Ibid., p. 198.

31. Brown, "Sailing of the Ill-Fated Steamship *Titanic*."

32. Everett, *Story of the Wreck of the Titanic*, p. 67.

33. Marcus, *Maiden Voyage,* p. 198.

34. Brown, "Sailing of the Ill-Fated Steamship *Titanic*."

35. *Denver Post,* April 21, 1912.

36. *Denver Post,* April 23, 1912.

37. *Denver Post,* April 30, 1912.

38. Everett, *Story of the Wreck of the Titanic*, p. 67.

39. Ibid., p. 186.

40. Ibid., p. 17.

41. George Bernard Shaw's opinion was echoed by other writers and journalists at the time.

42. Everett, *Story of the Wreck of the Titanic*, p. 104.

43. Brown, "Sailing of the Ill-Fated Steamship *Titanic*."

44. *Daily News* article, scrapbook of Helen Tobin Kosure, Vollrath collection.

45. Brown, "Sailing of the Ill-Fated Steamship *Titanic*."

46. Winocour, *Story of the Titanic*, p. 236.

47. Benziger, "Memories of a Grandson."

48. Ibid.

49. Ibid.

50. Ibid.

51. Brown, "Sailing of the Ill-Fated Steamship *Titanic*."

52. Everett, *Story of the Wreck of the Titanic*, p. 174.

53. *Denver Times*, April 19, 1912.

54. *Colorado Heritage*, April 1987.

55. Winocour, *Story of the Titanic*, p. 300.

56. At press time for this book, it was rumored that a forthcoming "director's cut" of *Titanic* would include some of these edited scenes.

Raised on the Milk of a Nanny Goat

1. The date of birth, 1868, on Margaret Tobin Brown's tombstone in Holy Rood Cemetery in New York is incorrect.

2. Hannibal historian Roberta Hagood provided much of the source material for this chapter through letters and photocopies of portions of her books about Hannibal (now out of print; see the Bibliography for titles).

3. James George Benziger, "Memories of a Grandson," unpublished manuscript.

4. *Denver Times*, April 21, 1899.

5. Benziger, "Memories of a Grandson." Numerous newspaper articles confirm this information.

6. Scrapbook of Helen Tobin Kosure, Vollrath collection.

7. Christine Whitacre, *Molly Brown: Denver's Unsinkable Lady* (Denver, Colo: Historic Denver, Inc., 1984), p. 10.

8. Benziger, "Memories of a Grandson."

9. Roberta Hagood, letter to Kristen Iversen dated November 14, 1997.

10. Benziger, "Memories of a Grandson."

11. Ibid.

12. Roberta Hagood, letter to Kristen Iversen dated June 1, 1998.

13. Ibid.

14. *Hannibal Daily Courier*, February 13, 1879.

15. Kristen Iversen, interview with Albert Frier, Hannibal, Missouri, July 17, 1998.

16. Ibid.

17. Rose Drescher Weatherly of Kansas City, Missouri, unpublished essay, 1954, provided by Roberta Hagood, Iversen collection.

18. Ibid.

19. Frier interview.

20. Ibid.

21. Mary Lou Montgomery, *Local Legacies,* manuscript collection and clippings file, Molly Brown House Museum, Denver.

22. Frier interview.

23. Scrapbook of Helen Tobin Kosure, Vollrath collection.

24. Leadville city directory, 1886.

25. Benziger, "Memories of a Grandson."

26. *Denver Post,* April 19, 1912.

27. Gene Fowler, *Timberline* (Garden City, N.Y.: Garden City Publishing Co., 1933), p. 329.

28. Ibid.

29. Ibid.

30. Ibid.

31. Ibid.

32. Ibid., p. 330.

33. Ibid.

34. "Leadville Molly Gets Mad," *True* Magazine, 1944.

35. Ibid.

36. *Hannibal Courier Post,* March 20, 1957, p. 3.

37. "Mrs. Matabelle Kettering: Who Visited in Denver Last Summer as the Guest of Mrs. J.J. Brown" (accompanied by photograph), Hannibal newspaper, 1904, scrapbook of Helen Tobin Kosure, Vollrath collection.

Better Off with a Poor Man

1. James E. Fell Jr., "The Carbonate Camp: A Brief History and Selected Bibliography of Leadville," *Colorado History* 1 (1997), p. 72.

2. Edward Blair, *Leadville: Colorado's Magic City* (Boulder, Colo.: Pruett Publishing Company, 1980), p. 61.

3. Marcia Goldstein, "The Backbone of Leadville and the Great Strike of 1880," *Mountain Diggings* 12 (1982), p. 12.

4. Fell, "Carbonate Camp," p. 72.

5. Goldstein, "Backbone of Leadville," p. 11.

6. Ibid., p. 12.

7. Ibid., p. 15.

8. Fell, "Carbonate Camp," p. 73.

9. Leadville *Herald Democrat,* July 2, 1880.

10. "Boiled Down Figurative Facts About Leadville" (reprinted from the *Daily Chronicle,* 1879), *Mountain Diggings* 14 (1984).

11. Mrs. Herman Simons, "A Girl's First Trip to Early Leadville" (reprinted from the *Carbonate Chronicle,* December 31, 1917), *Mountain Diggings* 12 (1982), p. 28.

12. Fell, "Carbonate Camp," p. 75.

13. Blair, *Leadville,* p. 123.

14. William Heldman, "Bedcomforts and Calico: The Nun's Story," *Mountain Diggings* 10, 1 (1980), pp. 36–37.

15. "After Two Years a Chronicle Reporter Talks with the First Settler of Leadville" (reprinted from the *Daily Chronicle,* May 9, 1879), *Mountain Diggings* 11 (1981), p. 4.

16. Michael F. Donovan, "The Leadville Irish," *Mountain Diggings* 3, 1 (April 1973), p. 12.

17. Ibid.

18. Goldstein, "Backbone of Leadville," p. 31.

19. A sketch of the original Daniels, Fisher, & Smith building at 301–303 Harrison Avenue appears in *Mountain Diggings* 9, 1 (1979), p. 30.

20. Blair, *Leadville,* p. 89.

21. Thomas Cahill, letter to Lawrence Brown dated January 20, 1947, family papers.

22. Goldstein, "Backbone of Leadville," p. 16.

23. Bernard Pacheco, "James Joseph Brown," *Mountain Diggings* 10, 1 (1980), p. 25.

24. Quoted in Byron Bronstein, untitled article in manuscript collection and clippings file, Molly Brown House Museum, Denver, no date.

25. Jay F. Manning, *Leadville, Lake County, and the Gold Belt* (Denver, Colo.: Manning, O'Keefe, and De Lasamutt Publishers, 1895), p. 96.

26. Bronstein article.

27. J.J. Brown, letter to H.D. Lemon dated December 9, 191?, family papers

28. Annie Schenk, journal. 1871. Stephen Hart Library, Colorado Historical Society.

29. Thomas Tonge, "Obituary," *Mining Journal* (September 1922), p. 23.

30. Blair, *Leadville,* p. 177.

31. Cahill letter.

32. Newspaper clipping, manuscript collection and clippings file, Molly Brown House Museum, Denver.

33. Christine Whitacre, *Molly Brown: Denver's Unsinkable Lady* (Denver, Colo.: Historic Denver, Inc., 1984), p. 17.

34. Leadville *Herald Democrat,* September 1, 1886.

35. Cahill letter.

36. Ibid.

37. Donovan, *Mountain Diggings,* p. 12.

38. Mary Hren, "Here Lies Stumpftown 1880–1920s," *Mountain Diggings* 8, 1 (1978), p. 1.

39. Ibid.

40. Notes made by Caroline Bancroft, author of the booklet *The Unsinkable Mrs. Brown,* based on interview conducted with Leadville resident (no name), ca. 1952, Molly Brown House Museum, Denver.

41. Manuscript collection and clippings file, Molly Brown House Museum, Denver.

42. Harvey Green, "The Light of the Home," photocopy of old article, Iversen collection.

43. The drawing appeared as an illustration in Mary Ebuna, "The History of a Leadville Home," *Mountain Diggings* 15 (1985), p. 5. Before the Browns rented it, the house was owned by Jack McCombe, a prominent Leadville citizen.

44. Blair, *Leadville,* p. 131.

45. Whitacre, *Molly Brown,* p. 19.

46. *Denver Post,* January 31, 1997.

47. Blair, *Leadville,* p. 118.

48. Frank Lewis Nason, *Colorado Heritage* 1 (1982), p. 56.

49. James George Benziger, "Memories of a Grandson," unpublished manuscript.

50. Billie Barnes Jensen, "Let the Women Vote," *The Colorado Magazine* (1964), p. 19.

51. *Denver Times,* December 14, 1902.

52. Kristen Iversen, interview with Lyn Spenst, Denver, October 14, 1998 (based on Spenst's recollection of her own interview of Lorraine Schuck).

53. *Rocky Mountain News* (anniversary article), November 8, 1993.

54. Cahill letter.

55. Blair, *Leadville,* p. 176.

56. Evalyn Walsh McLean, *Father Struck It Rich* (Fort Collins, Colo.: First-Light Publishing, 1996).

57. Blair, *Leadville,* p. 177.

58. Leadville *Herald Democrat,* January 15, 1971.

59. Georgina Brown, "Sport of the Carbonate Kings," *Mountain Diggings* 3 (April 1973).

60. Louise Day, "Memories of Miss Louise Day," manuscript collection and clippings file, Molly Brown House Museum, Denver, 1974.

61. Benziger, "Memories of a Grandson."

62. Brown, "Sport of the Carbonate Kings."

63. Blair, *Leadville,* p. 79.

64. Ibid., p. 174.

65. Whitacre, *Molly Brown,* p. 9.

66. Blair, *Leadville,* p. 175.

67. "Little Jonny Strike to Revive Leadville," 1895 clipping, scrapbook of Lawrence Brown.

68. Scrapbook of Helen Tobin Kosure, Vollrath collection.

69. Blair, *Leadville,* p. 175.

70. Ibid.

71. Notes made by Caroline Bancroft, author of the booklet *The Unsinkable Mrs. Brown,* based on oral interviews conducted with Brown descendants and friends in the late 1950s, Molly Brown House Museum, Denver.

72. Tonge, "Obituary."

73. Cahill letter.

An Unfortunate Disposition

1. Agnes Leonard Hill, *Social Questions No. 2: What Makes Social Leadership?* (Denver, Colo.: Chain and Hardy, 1893). Western History Room, Denver Public Library.

2. *Denver Times,* 1906, scrapbook of Helen Tobin Kosure, Vollrath collection.

3. *Denver Times,* August 12, 1898, p. 11.

4. Ibid.

5. Leadville 1900 census.

6. James George Benziger, "Memories of a Grandson," unpublished manuscript. Benziger also wrote that the child was known by the name "Leonard."

7. Muriel Sibell Wolle, *Stampede to Timberline* (Athens: Ohio University Press, 1974 [1949]).

8. Michael C. Barber, "Avoca Lodge: A Short History of 2690 South Wadsworth Blvd., Denver, Colorado," unpublished manuscript, manuscript collection and clippings file, Molly Brown House Museum, Denver, December 1, 1989, p. 8.

9. Ibid.

10. *Rocky Mountain News,* December 25, 1904.

11. Notes made by Caroline Bancroft, author of the booklet *The Unsinkable Mrs. Brown,* based on oral interviews conducted with Brown descendants and friends in the late 1950s, Molly Brown House Museum, Denver.

12. *Rocky Mountain News,* July 4, 1896.

13. Ibid.

14. *Who's Who in Denver Society: 1909,* Western History Room, Denver Public Library.

15. Stephen J. Leonard and Thomas J. Noel, *Denver: Mining Camp to Metropolis* (Niwot, Colo.: University Press of Colorado, 1990), p. 103.

16. Edward Blair, *Leadville: Colorado's Magic City* (Boulder, Colo.: Pruett Publishing Company, 1980), p. 178.

17. Interview notes, manuscript collection and clippings file, undated, Molly Brown House Museum, Denver.

18. *Rocky Mountain News,* May 3, 1895.

19. *Rocky Mountain News,* April 15, 1894.

20. Minutes of meetings and related material, Denver Woman's Club, manuscript collection, Colorado Historical Society.

21. Ibid.

22. All yearbook citations ibid.

23. *Denver Times,* January 13, 1905.

24. Scrapbook of Helen Tobin Kosure, Vollrath collection, and scrapbook of Lawrence Brown, Colorado Historical Society. Margaret Tobin Brown published numerous essays and commentaries in Denver, Newport, New York, and possibly Paris. These essays currently exist in clippings in scrapbooks and manuscript files; further research is needed to determine the exact dates and places of their publication. Margaret's autobiography, though submitted at least in part to a New York publisher, was never published, and the manuscript apparently has been lost.

25. Polly Pry, "Town Topics," *A Journal of Comment and Criticism,* January 30, 1904.

26. *Denver Times,* August 5, 1898, p. 10.

27. *Denver Times,* April 18, 1899, p. 6.

28. *Denver Times,* August 5, 1898, p. 10.

29. Article dated December 10, 1898, scrapbook of Helen Tobin Kosure, Vollrath collection.

30. Bernard Pacheco, "James Joseph Brown," *Mountain Diggings* 10, 1 (1980), p. 28.

31. Benziger, "Memories of a Grandson."

32. Scrapbook of Helen Tobin Kosure, Vollrath collection.

33. *Denver Times,* April 9, 1899, p. 3.

34. *Denver Times,* May 12, 1899.

35. Benziger, "Memories of a Grandson."

36. *Denver Republic,* May 11, 1899.

37. *Denver Times,* May 12, 1899.

38. *Denver Times,* May 28, 1899.

39. Scrapbook of Helen Tobin Kosure, Vollrath collection.

40. *Rocky Mountain News,* July 28, 1899, p. 1.

41. *Rocky Mountain News,* August 18, 1900.

42. *Denver Times,* October 11, 1900, p. 9.

43. Denver 1900 census.

44. *Denver Times,* November 15, 1900, p. 7.

45. *Denver Times,* December 6, 1900, p. C7.

46. *Denver Times,* October 1, 1900, p. 5.

47. *Denver Times,* October 29, 1900.

48. *Denver Times,* November 8, 1900, p. 8.

49. *Denver Times,* November 30, 1900, p. 5.

50. *Denver Times,* November 25, 1900, p. 8.

51. *Denver Times,* November 2, 1900.

52. *Denver Times,* November 9, 1900.

53. *Denver Times,* December 23, 1900.

54. Benziger, "Memories of a Grandson."

55. Carnegie Institute website, http://www.cmu.edu/home/about/about_history.html.

56. *Hannibal Morning Journal,* May 15, 1901.

57. Benziger, "Memories of a Grandson."

58. *Denver Republic,* February 22, 1903.

59. Polly Pry, "Town Topics," *A Journal of Comment and Criticism,* September 5, 1903.

60. Quoted in Western Writers of America, *The Women Who Made the West* (New York: Doubleday and Co., Inc., 1980), p. 113.

61. Charles Larsen, *The Good Fight: The Remarkable Life and Times of Judge Ben Lindsey, the Colorful American Reformer Who Helped to Start the Juvenile Court System, Advocated a Sexual Revolution, and Battled the Establishment in the Early 20th Century* (Chicago: Quadrangle Books, 1972), p. 7.

62. Ibid., p. 16.

63. Ibid., p. 17.

64. Ibid., p. 18.

65. Polly Pry, "Town Topics," *A Journal of Comment and Criticism,* May 7, 1904.

66. Ibid.

67. Western Writers of America, *Women Who Made the West.*

68. Ibid., p. 113.

69. Polly Pry, "Town Topics," *A Journal of Comment and Criticism,* September 5, 1903.

70. Western Writers of America, *Women Who Made the West,* p. 113.

71. *Hannibal Courier Post,* September 14, 1904; *Denver Times,* September 15, 1904.

72. *Denver Times,* April 29, 1904.

73. Scrapbook of Helen Tobin Kosure, Vollrath collection.

74. Polly Pry, "Town Topics," *A Journal of Comment and Criticism,* May 21, 1904.

75. Ibid., February 13, 1904.

76. Ibid., January 28, 1905.

77. *Denver Times,* April 20, 1904.

78. Polly Pry, "Town Topics," *A Journal of Comment and Criticism,* December 3, 1904.

79. Stephen J. Leonard and Thomas J. Noel, *Denver: Mining Camp to Metropolis* (Niwot, Colo.: University Press of Colorado, 1990), p. 164.

80. Ibid., p. 79.

81. Polly Pry, "Town Topics," *A Journal of Comment and Criticism,* November 26, 1904.

82. "War on Society," March 7, 1906, scrapbook of Helen Tobin Kosure, Vollrath collection.

83. Benziger, "Memories of a Grandson."

84. *Hannibal Courier Post,* April 10, 1905.

85. Benziger, "Memories of a Grandson."

86. *Denver Times,* September 16, 1903, p. 5.

87. "Would Anyone Like to Buy a Country Place?" scrapbook of Helen Tobin Kosure, Vollrath collection.

88. *Denver Times,* December 9, 1900.

Why Be Mildewed at Forty?

1. Stephen J. Leonard and Thomas J. Noel, *Denver: Mining Camp to Metropolis* (Niwot, Colo.: University Press of Colorado, 1990), p. 316.

2. "Cathedral Fair Arrangements: Preliminary Reports Predicate a Great Financial and Social Success," scrapbook of Helen Tobin Kosure, Vollrath collection.

3. "Colored Catholics Very Much Alive," scrapbook of Helen Tobin Kosure, Vollrath collection.

4. *Denver Times,* July 16, 1906.

5. Scrapbook of Helen Tobin Kosure, Vollrath collection.

6. Scrapbook of Helen Tobin Kosure, Vollrath collection.

7. Leonard and Noel, *Denver,* p. 65.

8. Quoted in ibid., p. 316.

9. *Denver Post,* August 28, 1906.

10. Scrapbook of Helen Tobin Kosure, Vollrath collection.

11. Scrapbook of Helen Tobin Kosure, Vollrath collection.

12. "Society Woman Runs a Gold Mine to Help Street Waifs out of Trouble," scrapbook of Helen Tobin Kosure, Vollrath collection.

13. William Jottesan, letter to Helen Brown dated November 13, 1911, family papers.

14. James Montes (a friend of Helen Brown), letter to Helen Brown dated April 5, 1911, family papers.

15. Scrapbook of Helen Tobin Kosure, Vollrath collection.

16. Lawrence Brown, letter to Helen Brown dated January 24, 1912, family papers.

17. Scrapbook of Helen Tobin Kosure, Vollrath collection.

18. James Benziger, "Memories of a Grandson," unpublished manuscript.

19. Kristen Iversen, interviews with Katherine Benziger and Heidi Benziger Rautio, 1997 and 1998.

20. Scrapbook of Helen Tobin Kosure, Vollrath collection.

21. Scrapbook of Helen Tobin Kosure, Vollrath collection.

22. Ibid.

23. "Friend Says Word for Young Brown," scrapbook of Helen Tobin Kosure, Vollrath collection.

24. *Denver Republican,* September 21, 1909.

25. Manuscript of interview with Eileen Horton Brown, no date, manuscript collection and clippings file, Molly Brown House Museum, Denver.

26. *New York Times,* April 19, 1911.

27. "Rich Man's Son Toils in Mine to Feed Wife and Baby," January 4, 191?, scrapbook of Helen Tobin Kosure, Vollrath collection.

28. Eileen Brown, letter to Margaret Brown, April 3, 191?, family papers.

29. *Denver Post,* June 28, 1910, p. 8; July 3, 1910, p. 2.

30. *New York Times,* April 19, 1911.

31. Benziger, "Memories of a Grandson."

32. *Denver Republican,* November 3, 1907.

33. "Mrs. Brown Is Only American Woman Who Has Mastered Art of Yodeling," scrapbook of Helen Tobin Kosure, Vollrath collection.

34. *New York Herald Tribune* clipping, scrapbook of Helen Tobin Kosure, Vollrath collection.

35. Lawrence Brown's army placement questionnaire, April 12, 1943, scrapbook of Lawrence Brown, Colorado Historical Society.

36. *Denver Post,* September 6, 1904, p. 1.

37. *Denver Post,* March 26, 1943.

38. *Denver Post,* March 30, 1972, p. 39.

39. "Society Crowded the Broadway to Make Juvenile Court Benefit a Grand Success," *Denver Times,* scrapbook of Helen Tobin Kosure, Vollrath collection.

40. "Patron's Night at the Art Exhibit at the Brown Attracts a Brilliant Assembly," *Denver Times,* March 19, 1909, scrapbook of Helen Tobin Kosure, Vollrath collection.

41. *Denver Post,* November 1909.

42. Files of the Molly Brown House Museum, Denver.

43. Separation agreement, and Joan Thill, interview with Morrison Shafroth (Margaret Brown's attorney), March 14, 1973, Molly Brown House Museum, Denver.

44. J.J. Brown, letter dated February 28, 1910, Molly Brown House Museum, Denver.

45. *Daily News,* May 15, 1911.

46. *Denver Times,* April 23, 1912.

47. William H. Morris, letter to Helen Brown dated March 23, 1912, family papers.

48. *Denver Post,* May 8, 1912.

49. Ibid. (Helen's letter was published in the newspaper article).

50. Lawrence Brown, telegram dated April 18, 1912, family papers.

51. Lawrence Brown, letter to Helen Brown dated April 29, 1912, family papers.

52. Lawrence Brown, letter to Margaret Brown dated April 1912, Muffet Laurie Brown collection.

53. *Hannibal Courier Post,* April 16, 1912.

54. Margaret Brown, letter to Helen Brown dated May 8, 1912, family papers.

55. *Denver Times,* April 24, 1912.

56. "Miss Tobin Awaiting Word to Join Mrs. Brown on Trip," scrapbook of Helen Tobin Kosure, Vollrath collection.

57. *Denver Post,* April 27, 1912, p. 5.

58. Scrapbook of Helen Tobin Kosure, Vollrath collection.

59. *Denver Post,* April 30, 1912, p. 5.

60. "Life One Long Rush to Mrs. Brown," scrapbook of Helen Tobin Kosure, Vollrath collection.

61. *Denver Post,* April 27, 1912, p. 5.

62. *Denver Post,* April 30, 1912, p. 5.

63. "A Story Shockingly Brutal ... ," scrapbook of Helen Tobin Kosure, Vollrath collection.

64. Tom Kuntz, ed., *The Titanic Disaster Hearings: The Official Transcripts of the 1912 Senate Investigation* (New York: Pocket Books, 1998), p. 533.

65. *Denver Post,* April 22, 1912, p. 1.

66. *Encyclopedia Titanica* website, http://www.rmplc.co.uk/eduweb/sites/phind/.

67. Scrapbook of Helen Tobin Kosure, Vollrath collection.

68. *Denver Post,* April 21, 1912.

69. Meryl Alberta Eaves Stewart (a Colorado resident interviewed for an oral history project), audiotape, Colorado Reflections, Media Tape F, 776, C66, no. 190 (a series of audiotapes held at the Auraria Library, University of Colorado, Denver).

70. *Denver Post,* April 21, 1912.

71. Ibid.

72. *Rocky Mountain News,* April 12, 1912.

73. *Denver Times,* May 2, 1912.

74. Ibid.

75. *Newport Herald* article, 1914, scrapbook of Helen Tobin Kosure, Vollrath collection.

76. *New York Times,* April 20, 1912.

77. Scrapbook of Helen Tobin Kosure, Vollrath collection.

Drum Major of an Imperial Band

1. "Newport's Best Gowns at End of Horse Show," September 5, 1912, scrapbook of Helen Tobin Kosure, Vollrath collection.

2. Henry James, *The American Scene* (Bloomington and London: Indiana University Press, 1968 [1907]).

3. Scrapbook of Helen Tobin Kosure, Vollrath collection.

4. *Newport Daily News* collection.

5. Program for Newport Hospital benefit, "Songs of Old France," scrapbook of Helen Tobin Kosure, Vollrath collection.

6. Howard Chandler Christy, *The American Girl as Seen and Portrayed by Howard Chandler Christy* (New York: Moffat, Yard and Co., 1906), p. 53.

7. "Just 18 years old; engaged to be married twice … ," scrapbook of Helen Tobin Kosure, Vollrath collection.

8. "Prince Caracciolo Says Newport Would Charm Worst Misogynist," November 9, 1912, scrapbook of Helen Tobin Kosure, Vollrath collection.

9. *Rocky Mountain News,* September 28, 1912.

10. "Mr. Benziger to Wed Daughter of Mrs. J.J. Brown," November 9, 1912, scrapbook of Helen Tobin Kosure, Vollrath collection.

11. J.J. Brown, letter to Helen Brown dated June 11, 1913, family papers.

12. Helen Brown, letter to George Benziger, family papers.

13. Ibid.

14. "Newport's Most Beautiful Girl of This Season," scrapbook of Helen Tobin Kosure, Vollrath collection.

15. Scrapbook of Helen Tobin Kosure, Vollrath collection.

16. Manuscript collection and clippings file, Molly Brown House Museum, Denver.

17. Quoted in John Foreman, *The Vanderbilts and the Gilded Age: Architectural Aspirations 1879–1901* (New York: St. Martin's Press, 1991), p. 220.

18. Quoted in Richard O'Connor, *The Golden Summers: An Antic History of Newport* (New York: G. P. Putnam's Sons, 1974), p. 292.

19. Foreman, *Vanderbilts and the Gilded Age,* p. 223.

20. *Denver Times,* January 7, 1912.

21. "With the Summer Visitors: Mrs. Brown Is an Inventor," scrapbook of Helen Tobin Kosure, Vollrath collection.

22. Quoted in O'Connor, *Golden Summers,* p. 109.

23. Quoted in ibid., p. 119.

24. Quoted in ibid., p. 116.

25. Ibid., p. 295.

26. *Denver Post,* February 23, 1914.

27. *Denver Times,* April 24, 1912.

28. *Rocky Mountain News,* April 21, 1914, scrapbook of Helen Tobin Kosure, Vollrath collection.

29. Ibid.

30. "Mrs. J.J. Brown on Her Way to Denver to Organize Force of Soldiers," scrapbook of Helen Tobin Kosure, Vollrath collection.

31. "Regiment of Women Drilling to Nurse if They Can't Fight," Newport, April 24, 1914, scrapbook of Helen Tobin Kosure, Vollrath collection.

32. "The Hand That Rocks the Cradle May Even Carry a Gun," scrapbook of Helen Tobin Kosure, Vollrath collection.

33. "Mrs. J.J. Brown Leaves to Command Regiment," April 27, 1914, scrapbook of Helen Tobin Kosure, Vollrath collection.

34. Quoted in Stephen J. Leonard and Thomas J. Noel, *Denver: Mining Camp to Metropolis* (Niwot, Colo.: University Press of Colorado, 1990), p. 171.

35. George Gershon Korson, *Coal Dust on the Fiddle: Songs and Stories of the Bituminous Industry* (Philadelphia: University of Pennsylvania Press, 1943), pp. 390–391.

36. *Rocky Mountain News,* November 8, 1993.

37. Quoted in Korson, *Coal Dust on the Fiddle.*

38. *Rocky Mountain News,* May 1, 1914.

39. "Strike Victims Promised Help," May 4, 1914, scrapbook of Helen Tobin Kosure, Vollrath collection.

40. Ibid.

41. *Denver Express,* May 1, 1914.

42. "Colorado Strike Subject of Talk: Mrs. James J. Brown of Denver Addresses Large Audience," scrapbook of Helen Tobin Kosure, Vollrath collection.

43. Ron Chernow, *Titan: The Life of John D. Rockefeller, Sr.* (New York: Random House, 1998), p. 572.

44. Ibid.

45. "Colorado Strike Subject of Talk."

46. *Rocky Mountain News,* May 1, 1914; *Denver Post,* May 1, 1914.

47. Chernow, *Titan,* p. 578.

48. Ibid., p. 481.

49. *Denver Post,* July 9, 1914.

50. "Mrs. J.J. Brown, heroine of the *Titanic* disaster, godmother to the destitute in the Trinidad strike district ... ," scrapbook of Helen Tobin Kosure, Vollrath collection.

51. Chernow, *Titan,* p. 589.

52. *Newport Journal & Weekly News,* July 24, 1914.

53. Quoted in O'Connor, *Golden Summers,* p. 292.

54. Julia Ward Howe, letter to Maud Howe Elliot dated August 28, 1909.

55. Quoted in O'Connor, *Golden Summers,* p. 295.

56. Quoted in ibid., p. 297.

57. *New York Times,* July 8, 1914.

58. Ibid.

59. "Colorado Strike Subject of Talk."

60. *Newport Herald,* June 22, 1914.

61. *New York Times,* June 4, 1914, p. 3.

62. Michelle Perrot, "Stepping Out," in *A History of Women: Emerging Feminism from Revolution to World War,* ed. Geneviéve Fraisse and Michelle Perrot (Cambridge, Mass., and London: The Belknap Press of Harvard University Press, 1993), p. 462.

63. *Denver Post,* July 29, 1914.

64. "Man's Fight, No Pink Tea, if Woman Runs for Congress," scrapbook of Helen Tobin Kosure, Vollrath collection.

65. *New York Times,* July 1914.

66. *Washington D.C. Pathfinder,* June 13, 1914.

67. *Newport Daily News,* July 22, 1914.

68. *Rocky Mountain News,* January 8, 1889.

69. *New York City Mail,* July 23, 1914.

70. "Man's Fight, No Pink Tea."

71. *New York City Mail,* July 23, 1914.

72. "Man's Fight, No Pink Tea."

73. *Rocky Mountain News,* January 8, 1889.

74. "Man's Fight, No Pink Tea."

75. *New York Times,* June 6, 1914, p. 8.

76. *Rocky Mountain News,* August 12, 1914.

77. *New York Times,* July 19, 1914, p. 5.

78. J.J. Brown, letter to E. G. Groves, family papers.

79. Joan Thill, interview with Eileen Horton Brown Lyons, November 1975, Molly Brown House Museum, Denver.

80. *New York Times,* April 23, 1914.

81. Scrapbook of Helen Tobin Kosure, Vollrath collection.

82. "Notable American Volunteers of the Great War," *1853–1947: The Americans of the Legion of Honor,* catalog, 1993 summer exhibition, French National Museum of Franco-American cooperation at Blerancourt (Aisne), curated by Veronique Weisinger, Réunion des Musées Nationaux.

83. "Mrs. Cornelius Vanderbilt Assists Her Children in War Relief Work," scrapbook of Helen Tobin Kosure, Vollrath collection.

84. Mary Van Vorst, *War Letters of an American Woman* (New York: John Lane, 1916).

85. *Paris Herald,* April 20, 1932.

86. Scrapbook of Lawrence Brown, July 22, 1917, Colorado Historical Society.

87. Lawrence Brown, letter to Margaret Brown dated August 28, 1918, scrapbook of Lawrence Brown, Colorado Historical Society.

88. Telegram dated February 6, 1919, family papers.

89. Lawrence P. Brown papers, box 5, Colorado Historical Society.

90. Frank H. Simonds, McClure Newspaper Syndicate, 1919, scrapbook of Lawrence P. Brown, Colorado Historical Society.

91. J.J. Brown, letter to Lawrence Brown dated September 4, 1920, Lawrence P. Brown papers, box 84, Colorado Historical Society.

92. J.J. Brown, letter to Lawrence Brown dated May 8, 1913, family papers.

93. J.J. Brown, letter to Helen Brown dated December 1917, family papers.

94. *Denver Post,* November 12, 1922.

In the Spirit of Sarah Bernhardt

1. James George Benziger, "Memories of a Grandson," unpublished manuscript.

2. Florence Tobin Harper, telegram to Helen Brown Benziger dated September 24, 1922, family papers.

3. Helen Brown Benziger, letter to attorney James J. Sullivan dated December 11, 1922, Colorado Historical Society, Molly Brown House Museum.

4. Ibid.

5. Lawrence Brown, letter to James J. Sullivan dated October 2, 1923, Colorado Historical Society, Molly Brown House Museum.

6. "Mrs. J.J. Brown Loses Fight to Block Estate Settlement," *Denver Post,* February 3, 1926, p. 1.

7. *Denver Post,* August 9, 1923.

8. Reprinted in Leadville *Herald Democrat,* January 29, 1971.

9. *Denver Post,* November 12, 1922.

10. *Denver Post,* November 31, 1922.

11. *Rocky Mountain News,* April 14, 1927.

12. *Denver Post,* May 31, 1926.

13. *Rocky Mountain News,* November 2, 1927.

14. Manuscript collection, Molly Brown House Museum, Denver.

15. Charles Larsen, *The Good Fight: The Remarkable Life and Times of Judge Ben Lindsey, the Colorful American Reformer Who Helped to Start the Juvenile Court System, Advocated a Sexual Revolution, and Battled the Establishment in the Early 20th Century* (Chicago: Quadrangle Books, 1972).

16. *Denver Post,* May 31, 1926.

17. *Denver Post,* June 5, 1925.

18. Christine Whitacre, *Molly Brown: Denver's Unsinkable Lady* (Denver, Colo.: Historic Denver, Inc., 1984), p. 10.

19. *Denver Post,* January 8, 1927.

20. *Denver Post,* June 5, 1925.

21. *Salt Lake Tribune,* May 3, 1925.

22. *Denver Post,* February 22, 1922.

23. *Denver Post,* November 12, 1922.

24. *Denver Post,* June 5, 1925.

25. "Romanoff Princess Visits Denver," *Denver Post,* July 10, 1927, p. 10.

26. Ibid.

27. Information compiled from articles in scrapbook of Helen Tobin Kosure, Vollrath collection, and Molly Brown House Museum files.

28. "Romanoff Princess Visits Denver."

29. *Rocky Mountain News,* November 8, 1993.

30. *Denver Post,* May 2, 1927.

31. "Romanoff Princess Visits Denver."

32. Paris clipping, January 20, 1929, scrapbook of Helen Tobin Kosure, Vollrath collection.

33. Ibid.

34. *Denver Post,* June 2, 1929.

35. Benziger, "Memories of a Grandson."

36. Margaret Tobin Brown, letter to Edith Stiles dated October 13, 1932, Molly Brown House Museum, Denver.

37. *Denver Post,* August 9, 1923.

38. *Rocky Mountain News,* October 28, 1932.

39. Stephen Friesen, telephone interview with Les Severn, September 23, 1994. Molly Brown House Museum, Denver.

40. "Hip Flasks Ruin U.S. Debs, Says Mrs. J.J. Brown," Paris, May 5, 1930, scrapbook of Helen Tobin Kosure, Vollrath collection.

41. *Denver Post,* May 6, 1930.

42. Manuscript collection and clippings file, Molly Brown House Museum, Denver.

43. Murla Ralston, interview with Vivian Daniels, November 20, 1973, Molly Brown House Museum, Denver.

44. Manuscript collection and clippings file, Molly Brown House Museum, Denver.

45. Corinne Hunt, *History of the Brown Palace Hotel* (Denver, Colo.: Rocky Mountain Writers Guild, 1982), p. 49.

46. Gail Evans, interview with Frank Dawson, September 28, 1973, Molly Brown House Museum, Denver.

47. Morrison Shafroth, personal narrative, Molly Brown House Museum, Denver.

48. *Denver Post*, May 4, 1927.

49. "Hip Flasks Ruin U.S. Debs."

50. Notes made by Caroline Bancroft, author of the booklet *The Unsinkable Mrs. Brown*, based on interview with Frank McLister, April 25, 1952, Molly Brown House Museum, Denver.

51. Benziger, "Memories of a Grandson."

52. *Denver Post*, April 27, 1912, p. 5.

53. *Denver Post*, April 30, 1912.

54. "Rugged Men of West Superior to Sweet Scented Europeans," *Denver Post*, November 12, 1922, p. 15, scrapbook of Helen Tobin Kosure, Vollrath collection.

55. *Denver Post*, December 14, 1926.

56. "Life One Long Rush for Mrs. Brown," scrapbook of Helen Tobin Kosure, Vollrath collection.

57. *Denver Post*, December 12, 1927.

58. *Rocky Mountain News*, July 13, 1930.

59. Helen Brown Benziger, letter to Mildred Gregory Brown dated July 21, 1953, Muffet Laurie Brown collection.

60. Ibid.

61. Ibid.

62. Brown family papers, photographs, and newspaper clippings at both the Colorado Historical Society and the Western History Room at the Denver Public Library have been tampered with and in some cases stolen or destroyed. Much of this damage appears to have occurred during the 1950s.

63. Helen Brown Benziger, letter to Mildred Gregory Brown dated July 21, 1953.

64. Mildred Gregory Brown, letter to Helen Brown Benziger dated June 18, 1947, family papers.

65. Kristen Iversen, interview with Albert Frier, Hannibal, Missouri, July 17, 1998.

66. *Denver Post*, October 15, 1961.

67. Helen Brown Benziger, letter to Mildred Gregory Brown dated July 21, 1953.

68. Scrapbook of Lawrence Brown, Colorado Historical Society, Denver.

69. Scrapbook of Lawrence Brown, Colorado Historical Society, Denver.

70. Western Writers of America, *The Women Who Made the West* (New York: Doubleday and Co., Inc., 1980), p. 117.

71. Richard O'Connor, *The Golden Summers: An Antic History of Newport* (New York: G. P. Putnam's Sons, 1974), p. 219.

72. Quoted in John Foreman, *The Vanderbilts and the Gilded Age: Architectural Aspirations 1879–1901* (New York: St. Martin's Press, 1991), p. 220.

Envoi

1. The events and dialogue for this chapter are culled from various accounts in Denver and New York newspapers regarding exactly what occurred as the *Carpathia* entered New York Harbor, particularly the *Denver Times*, April 19, 1912.

Bibliography

Newspapers and Journals

Colorado Heritage News
Colorado Prospector
Daily Democrat
Denver Express
Denver Post
Denver Republican
Denver Times
Hannibal Courier Post
Hannibal Morning Journal
Leadville *Herald Democrat*
Mountain Diggings (Official Publication of the Lake County Civic Center Association)
Newport Daily News
New York City Mail
New York Daily News
New York Times
Paris Herald
Rocky Mountain News
Salt Lake Tribune
Washington D.C. Pathfinder

Books

Arps, Louisa Ward. *Denver in Slices: A Historical Guide to the City.* Athens, Oh.: Ohio University Press, 1998 [1959].

Bancroft, Caroline. *The Unsinkable Mrs. Brown.* Boulder, Colo.: Johnson Publishing Company, 1963.

Bancroft, Caroline, and May Bennett Wills. *The Unsinkable Molly Brown Cookbook.* Denver, Colo: Cleworth Associates, 1989 [1966].

Biel, Steven. *Down with the Old Canoe: A Cultural History of the Titanic Disaster.* New York: W. W. Norton and Co., 1996.

Blair, Edward. *Leadville: Colorado's Magic City.* Boulder, Colo.: Pruett Publishing Company, 1980.

———. *Palace of Ice.* Denver, Colo.: Timberline Books, Ltd., 1974.

Chernow, Ron. *Titan: The Life of John D. Rockefeller, Sr.* New York: Random House, 1998.

Christy, Howard Chandler. *The American Girl as Seen and Portrayed by Howard Chandler Christy.* New York: Moffat, Yard and Co., 1906.

Cullen-Dupont, Kathryn, ed. *The Encyclopedia of Women's History in America.* New York: Facts on File, 1996.

Dary, David. *Red Blood and Black Ink: Journalism in the Old West.* New York: Alfred A. Knopf, 1998.

Eaton, John P., and Charles A. Hass. *Titanic: Destination Disaster—The Legends and the Reality.* London and New York: W. W. Norton, 1996.

Elliot, Maud Howe. *This Was My Newport.* Cambridge, Mass: A. Marshall Jones, 1944.

Everett, Marshall, ed. *Story of the Wreck of the Titanic, The Ocean's Greatest Disaster.* Chicago: L.H. Walter, 1912.

Foreman, John. *The Vanderbilts and the Gilded Age: Architectural Aspirations 1879–1901.* New York: St. Martin's Press, 1991.

Foster, John Wilson. *The Titanic Complex.* Vancouver. B.C., Canada: Belcouver Press, 1997.

Fowler, Gene. *Timberline.* Garden City, N.Y.: Garden City Publishing Co., 1933.

Gracie, Col. Archibald. *The Truth About the Titanic.* New York: Mitchell Kennerley, 1913.

Hagood, J. Hurly and Roberta (Roland). *Hannibal, Too.* Marceline, Mo.: Walsworth Publishing Company, 1986.

———. *Hannibal Yesterdays.* Marceline, Mo.: Jostens Publishing Company, 1992.

———. *Story of Hannibal.* Hannibal, Mo.: Hannibal Bicentennial Commission, 1976.

Hill, Agnes Leonard. *Social Questions No. 2: What Makes Social Leadership?* Denver, Colo.: Chain and Hardy, 1893. Western History Room, Denver Public Library.

Hine, Al. *The Unsinkable Molly Brown.* [A novel based upon the stageplay, book by Richard Morris, music and lyrics by Meredith Wilson, original screenplay by Helen Deutsch.] Greenwich, Conn.: Gold Medal Books, Fawcett Publications, 1964.

Hunt, Corinne. *History of the Brown Palace Hotel.* Denver, Colo.: Rocky Mountain Writers Guild, 1982.

James, Henry. *The American Scene.* Bloomington and London: Indiana University Press, 1968 [1907].

Korson, George Gershon. *Coal Dust on the Fiddle: Songs and Stories of the Bituminous Industry* (Philadelphia: University of Pennsylvania Press, 1943).

Kuntz, Tom, ed. *The Titanic Disaster Hearings: The Official Transcripts of the 1912 Senate Investigation.* New York: Pocket Books, 1998.

Larsen, Charles. *The Good Fight: The Remarkable Life and Times of Judge Ben Lindsey, the Colorful American Reformer Who Helped to Start the Juvenile Court System, Advocated a Sexual Revolution, and Battled the Establishment in the Early 20th Century.* Chicago: Quadrangle Books, 1972.

Leonard, Stephen J., and Thomas J. Noel. *Denver: Mining Camp to Metropolis.* Niwot, Colo.: University Press of Colorado, 1990.

Lockwood, Charles. *The Breakers: A Century of Grand Traditions.* Palm Beach, Fla.: The Breakers Palm Beach, Inc., 1996.

Lord, Walter. *A Night to Remember.* New York: Ameroen House, 1987.

———. *The Night Lives On.* New York: William Morrow and Co., Inc., 1986.

Manning, Jay F. *Leadville, Lake County, and the Gold Belt.* Denver: Manning, O'Keefe, and De Lasamutt Publishers, 1895.

Marcus, Geoffrey. *The Maiden Voyage.* New York: The Viking Press, 1969.

Marshall, Logan. *The Sinking of the Titanic,* ed. Bruce Caplan. Seattle: Hara Publishing, 1998 [1912].

McLean, Evalyn Walsh. *Father Struck It Rich.* Fort Collins, Colo.: FirstLight Publishing, 1996.

Noel, Thomas J. *Catholic Catholicism and the Archdiocese of Denver 1857–1989.* Denver, Colo., 1989.

"Notable American Volunteers of the Great War." *1853–1947: The Americans of the Legion of Honor.* Catalog, 1993 summer exhibition, French National Museum of Franco-American cooperation at Blerancourt (Aisne). Curated by Veronique Weisinger. Réunion des Musées Nationaux.

O'Connor, Richard. *The Golden Summers: An Antic History of Newport.* New York: G.P. Putnam's Sons, 1974.

Rector, Margaret. *Alva, That Vanderbilt-Belmont Woman.* Wickford, R.I.: Dutch Island Press, 1992.

Robertson, Morgan. *Futility, or The Wreck of the Titan.* Buccaneer Books, 1991 [1898].

Suggs, George G., Jr. *Colorado's War on Militant Unionism.* Oklahoma City: University of Oklahoma Press, 1988.

Thomas, Sewell. *Silhouettes of Charles S. Thomas.* The Caxton Printers, Ltd., 1959.

Ubbelohde, Carl, Maxine Benson, and Duane A. Smith. *A Colorado History.* Boulder, Colo.: Pruett Publishing Co., 1972.

Van Vorst, Mary. *War Letters of an American Woman.* New York: John Lane, 1916.

Western Writers of America. *The Women Who Made the West.* New York: Doubleday and Co., Inc., 1980.

Whitacre, Christine. *Molly Brown: Denver's Unsinkable Lady.* Denver, Colo.: Historic Denver, Inc., 1984.

Who's Who in Denver Society. Denver, Colo.: W.H. Kistler, 1908.

Winocour, Jack, ed. *The Story of the Titanic as Told by Its Survivors.* New York: Dover, 1960.

Wolle, Muriel Sibell. *Stampede to Timberline.* Athens, Oh.: Ohio University Press, 1974 [1949].

Articles

"After Two Years a Chronicle Reporter Talks with the First Settler of Leadville." Reprinted from the *Daily Chronicle,* May 9, 1879. *Mountain Diggings* 11 (1981), pp. 1–4.

"Boiled Down Figurative Facts About Leadville." Reprinted from the *Daily Chronicle,* 1879. *Mountain Diggings* 14 (1984).

Brown, Georgina. "Sport of the Carbonate Kings." *Mountain Diggings* 3 (April 1973).

Carter, Matthew. "History of Annunciation Church." *Mountain Diggings* 10, 1 (1980), pp. 30–34.

Donovan, Michael F. "The Leadville Irish." *Mountain Diggings* 3, 1 (April 1973).

Ebuna, Mary. "The History of a Leadville Home." *Mountain Diggings* 15 (1985).

Fell, James E., Jr. "The Carbonate Camp: A Brief History and Selected Bibliography of Leadville." *Colorado History* 1 (1997).

"The Financing of the Cathedral." Diamond Jubilee of the Cathedral Parish. Compiled and published by Rt. Rev. Monsignor and Hugh L. McMenanin, LL.D. Rector of the Cathedral.

"Fruits and Fusion: A Review of the Thomas Administration. Facts and Figures from the Official Records." Western History Department, Denver Public Library.

Goldstein, Marcia. "The Backbone of Leadville and the Great Strike of 1880." *Mountain Diggings* 12 (1982).

Griswold, Don and Jean. "The Twin Lakes in 1871." Extracted from the *Twin Lakes Monthly Mirror,* May 1894. *Mountain Diggings* 14 (1984).

Heldman, William. "Bedcomforts and Calico: The Nun's Story." *Mountain Diggings* 10, 1 (1980), pp. 36–40.

"History of Alliance Française de Denver and General French History in Colorado." Pamphlet. Alliance Française de Denver.

Hren, Mary. "Here Lies Stumpftown 1880–1920s." *Mountain Diggings* 8, 1 (1978), pp. 1–9.

Jensen, Billie Barnes. "Let the Women Vote." *The Colorado Magazine* (1964).

Pacheco, Bernard. "James Joseph Brown." *Mountain Diggings* 10, 1 (1980), pp. 25–29.

Perrot, Michelle. "Stepping Out." In *A History of Women: Emerging Feminism from Revolution to World War*, ed. Geneviéve Fraisse and Michelle Perrot. Cambridge, Mass., and London: The Belknap Press of Harvard University Press, 1993.

Simons, Mrs. Herman. "A Girl's First Trip to Early Leadville." Reprinted from the *Carbonate Chronicle*, December 31, 1917. *Mountain Diggings* 12 (1982), pp. 23–30.

Tonge, Thomas. "Obituary." *Mining Journal* (September 1922), p. 23

Unpublished Manuscripts

Barber, Michael C. "Avoca Lodge: A Short History of 2690 South Wadsworth Blvd., Denver, Colorado." December 1, 1989, Molly Brown House Museum, Denver.

Benziger, James George. "Memories of a Grandson." Iversen collection.

Brown, Lawrence P. Scrapbook. Stephen Hart Library, Colorado Historical Society, Denver.

The Denver Woman's Club minutes and notes. Colorado Historical Society, Denver.

Johnson, Karen. "The Peripatetic Mrs. Brown." Manuscript collection and clippings file, Molly Brown House Museum, Denver.

Kosure, Helen Tobin. Scrapbook. Vollrath family collection.

Weatherly, Rose Drescher. Unpublished essay, 1954, provided by Roberta Hagood. Iversen collection. Weatherly grew up in Hannibal and remembered the Tobin and Becker families.

Margaret Tobin Brown's Own Works

Most of Margaret's writings currently exist as clippings in scrapbooks and manuscript files; further research is needed to determine the exact dates and places of their publication. Margaret's autobiography, though submitted at least in part to a New York publisher, was never published, and the manuscript apparently has been lost. Following is a rough list of titles and what is known about these pieces.

The Course of Human Events (autobiography). Unpublished.

"Crossing the Alps in Modern Times: An Interesting Account of a Motor Journey in Europe by a Prominent Denver Society Woman." Published December 1908.

"The French Women Seen with American Eyes." Published.

"Mark Twain's Boyhood Home." *Denver Times*, June 9, 1905; St. Louis *Daily Globe-Democrat*, July 1, 1900; possibly other places as well.

"The Sailing of the Ill-Fated Steamship *Titanic*." Published May 28, 29, and 30, 1912, *Newport Herald* and other newspapers.

"Shadows of Hindu Life." Published.

"The Veil of Fancy Stripped from the French." Published.

Interviews

Various Brown descendants and friends interviewed by Caroline Bancroft, author of the booklet *The Unsinkable Mrs. Brown*, in the late 1950s, Molly Brown House Museum, Denver.

Brown, Edward L., nephew of J.J. Brown, August 13, 1952 (Molly Brown House Museum, Denver).

Bennett, Mrs. Horace (Julie), knew Margaret Tobin Brown when both were young brides and recalled Margaret's yodeling, October 17, 1952 (Molly Brown House Museum, Denver).

Benziger, Katherine, great-granddaughter of Margaret Tobin Brown, granddaughter of Helen Brown Benziger, daughter of James and Patricia Benziger. Interviewed by Kristen Iversen December 11, 1997, and numerous other occasions spring and summer 1998, Denver.

Benziger, Patricia Rey, wife of James Benziger, Helen Brown Benziger's son and Margaret Tobin Brown's grandson. Interviewed by Kristen Iversen by telephone, April 1998.

Brown, Muffet Laurie, great-granddaughter of Margaret Tobin Brown, granddaughter of Lawrence Brown, daughter of Lawrence Palmer "Pat" and Margery Sunkel Brown. Interviewed by Kristen Iversen on several occasions, spring and summer 1998, Denver and Hannibal.

Cady, Claude L., briefly knew the Tobin girls, April 14, 1952 (Molly Brown House Museum, Denver).

Coe, Margaret Shaw, befriended as a child by Margaret Tobin Brown. Interviewed by Kristen Iversen by telephone, spring 1998.

Darby, Edwin, knew Margaret Tobin Brown and remembered dancing with her, May 1, 1952 (Molly Brown House Museum, Denver).

Frier, Albert, and his wife, Margaret, great-nephew of Margaret Tobin Brown, grandson of Catherine Tobin Becker. Interviewed by Kristen Iversen July 17, 1998, Hannibal.

Gregory, John, a Leadville friend who remembered the picnic where J.J. first met Margaret, August 14, 1952 (Molly Brown House Museum, Denver).

Grinstead, Leigh, director Molly Brown House Museum, Denver. Interviewed by Kristen Iversen on several occasions, winter and spring 1998, Denver.

Lyons, Eileen Horton Brown, daughter-in-law of Margaret Tobin Brown, first wife of Lawrence Brown. Interviewed by Joan Thill in November 1975 (Molly Brown House Museum, Denver).

Marsh, Laury, friend of Margaret Tobin Brown who recalled her singing Irish songs, August 13, 1952 (Molly Brown House Museum, Denver).

McKinney, Helen Benziger, great-granddaughter of Margaret Tobin Brown, granddaughter of Helen Brown Benziger, daughter of Peter Benziger. Interviewed by Kristen Iversen July 11, 1998, Hannibal.

McLister, Frank, a family friend of the Browns and Tobins, April 25, 1952 (Molly Brown House Museum, Denver).

Rautio, Heidi Benziger, great-granddaughter of Margaret Tobin Brown, granddaughter of Helen Brown Benziger, daughter of Peter Benziger. Interviewed by Kristen Iversen June 4 and July 16, 1998, Casper, Wyoming.

Spenst, Lyn, previous director Molly Brown House Museum, Denver. Interviewed by Kristen Iversen October 14, 1998, Denver.

Walker, Elizabeth, curator, Molly Brown House Museum, Denver. Interviewed by Kristen Iversen on several occasions, spring and summer 1998, Denver.

Index

291

A Conversation with Kristen Iversen

What led you to write a book about Margaret Brown?
I've been fascinated with the story of Molly Brown for as long as I can remember. When I was a little girl, my mother took me and my sisters to see the 1964 movie *The Unsinkable Molly Brown*, starring Debbie Reynolds. My mother loved the music, and no doubt she thought it would be an inspirational story for her impressionable young daughters. It certainly did make an impression — and I memorized the lyrics to all the songs! But it wasn't until I started graduate school at the University of Denver and began to think about issues like narrative, feminism, and women's stories in the West that I began to wonder about the real life story of this woman who, at the time, seemed little more than a silly myth. At that point I turned into a sleuth and began looking for clues about her real life story.

How much research went into the book?
I spent eight years researching this book. In fact, I could write another book about researching the life of Margaret Tobin Brown and how it led me down many unexpected paths, including the fascinating people I met along the way. Fortunately Margaret Brown led a very public life and there was a strong trail to follow. I began with the photographs and scrapbooks that she put together herself. I combed early newspaper articles, where I discovered a great deal of information about Margaret and her husband J.J. There were family letters and reminiscences. It was a huge turning point for the book when the family allowed me access to primary documents and materials that had been stored away in boxes for decades. A wealth of material on Margaret, her family, and others like Judge Ben Lindsay was available at the Colorado Historical Society. I spent time tracking down leads and materials in Leadville and Newport. And Margaret wrote a great deal herself. She was a lively writer, and although only a few of her essays and articles remain, I was able to get a sense of her voice and personality. For every fact in the book, I tried to have at least two independent sources that confirmed the information.

When I first began this project, people told me there was very little information available about the life of Margaret Tobin Brown. By the time I had finished, I was shocked that the historical record had been so skewed and so much information had been almost willfully overlooked. Part of this is due to Hollywood and the power of myth, and part of it is due to the fact that until recently, many women's lives were absent from the historical record, including those who were pretty famous in their own lifetime.

Why are there conflicting accounts in some of the newspaper articles and early books about Margaret's life?
Politics played a huge role in the early newspapers of the West, and it was very common to see "yellow journalism"; that is, newspaper articles that exploit, distort, or exaggerate the news in such a way as to attract readers, sway political opinion, or turn the public taste for or against a particular person or family. Margaret's husband, J.J., was a prominent man in Denver and Leadville. The Brown family was deeply involved in politics, and Margaret in particular was very progressive in her ideas and actions. Some people liked it, and some people didn't. Margaret did not confine herself to the proper role of a Victorian-era woman, and often she paid a price for that in the newspapers. The two major newspapers in Denver at the time, *The Rocky Mountain News* and the *Denver Times* (one conservative and one more progressive), sometimes supported J.J. Brown's political and business endeavors and sometimes they didn't. The colorful and often ironic, tongue-in-cheek newspaper articles and editorials of the time are a good barometer of the Browns' social, political, and business standing, but they aren't always accurate or even meant to be. An important part of my research was to distinguish fact from fiction or hyperbole.

One early biographer of Molly Brown, Caroline Bancroft, did a great deal to intentionally distort the story. Her motives are complicated and may have been profit-driven. She sold a lot of booklets. I guess we can be grateful to her for helping to keep the story alive for all these years.

In what ways does the mythology that surrounds Margaret Brown's story reflect her actual personality?
I believe the myth is, in many ways, a reflection of Margaret's spirit. She was optimistic, enthusiastic, idealistic, and certainly energetic. She was undaunted by challenges and refused to feel constrained by traditional ideas of gender and class. She loved to travel, she loved to dance, she

enjoyed being around other people. She lived her life as fully as possible. Margaret felt that through hard work, persistence, and vision, she could make the world a better place. You see all of these characteristics in the myth of Molly Brown, although the story itself is inaccurate.

How is the mythology of Margaret Brown similar to the stories of other legendary western women such as Baby Doe Tabor or Annie Oakley? What do their legends tell us about the American West or about how the West was perceived?
When I first began researching the story of Molly Brown, it was interesting to me that people often confused the Brown story with the tale of Baby Doe Tabor, even though the stories are completely different. (Baby Doe Tabor and Margaret Tobin Brown did, in fact, meet in person at least once, but there was a significant age difference and their lives were dissimilar in many ways.) Women's stories in the West, including that of Annie Oakley and others, tend to fall into certain predictable stereotypes. The saloon girl, the prostitute with a heart of gold, the angel of the prairie—these are familiar stories and images. The problem with such stereotypes is that they marginalize and obscure the real stories of women who made significant and lasting historical and cultural contributions to the American West.

Could Margaret Brown have been who she was without J.J. Brown? What impact did he have on her life? Could she have accomplished some of the same things if she had been a single woman or divorced?
J.J. Brown was an extraordinary man and is deserving of a more prominent place in Colorado history. When Margaret and J.J. first met, it must have been a remarkable encounter. They were both smart, largely self-educated, and very ambitious. They each believed in social and political change—and, above all, hard work. They made a great team, and their marriage was rather exceptional for the time. I have no doubt that Margaret would have accomplished many of the things she did regardless of whom she married—or if she married at all—but particularly in the early years, her marriage to J.J. helped her to find and define her goals. The money they made in Leadville helped provide the seed money for some of her projects (she was a great fundraiser, too), and allowed Margaret to move in social and political circles far beyond Leadville and Denver. But Margaret had a very clear sense of who she was and what she wanted to accomplish. In later years, she and J.J. did not always agree on things, but they remained respectful of each other.

How did Margaret feel about her children? Did she fulfill the conventional role of wife and mother?
Margaret raised five children. She was very close to her own two children, Helen and Lawrence, and she also raised the three daughters of her brother, Grace, Helen, and Florence Tobin, after their mother died. One of the ways in which her story continues to be relevant is that she was doing what many and perhaps most women do now: balancing family life and a career.

Margaret felt that women should have the same opportunities as men in education, business, politics, and the social world. She was a gracious hostess in Denver, New York, and Paris (the myth of Molly Brown greatly exaggerates her social struggles with Denver society). She decorated her home in Denver with taste and style (although it was not ostentatious), and she always enjoyed the latest dress fashions. In many ways she was very typical of other women at that time who were wives and mothers. But she never felt limited to the domestic sphere.

Did Margaret Tobin Brown do much writing herself? Did she ever write a memoir?
Margaret wrote and published a number of travel articles and essays, some of which have survived. She wrote and lectured about Mark Twain, and she wrote a number of speeches, particularly about women's rights. The newspapers refer to some of these speeches by name and date, but little in its entirety has survived. We know from the essays that do survive that Margaret wrote with a lively voice and style and could be very witty. There are several historical references to a memoir she wrote or intended to write, probably in the late 1920s or early 1930s, but no actual manuscript has ever been found. Perhaps some day it will turn up.